ACCA

S T U D Y   T E X T

PAPER F4

CORPORATE AND BUSINESS LAW (ENGLISH)

In this edition approved by ACCA

- We **discuss** the **best strategies** for studying for ACCA exams
- We **highlight** the **most important elements** in the syllabus and the **key skills** you will need
- We **signpost** how each chapter links to the syllabus and the study guide
- We **provide** lots of **exam focus points** demonstrating what the examiner will want you to do
- We **emphasise** key points in regular **fast forward summaries**
- We **test your knowledge** of what you've studied in **quick quizzes**
- We **examine your understanding** in our **exam question bank**
- We reference all the important topics in our **full index**

BPP's **i-Learn** and **i-Pass** products also support this paper.

FOR EXAMS IN DECEMBER 2008 AND JUNE 2009

LEARNING MEDIA

First edition 2007

Third edition July 2008

ISBN 9870 7517 4724 9
(Previous ISBN 9870 7517 4615 0)

British Library Cataloguing-in-Publication Data
A catalogue record for this book
is available from the British Library

Published by

BPP Learning Media Ltd
BPP House, Aldine Place
London W12 8AA

www.bpp.com/learningmedia

Printed in the UK by CPI William Clowes Beccles NR34 7TL

We are grateful to the Association of Chartered Certified
Accountants for permission to reproduce past
examination questions. The suggested solutions in the
exam answer bank have been prepared by BPP Learning
Media Ltd, unless where otherwise stated.

Your learning materials, published by BPP Learning
Media Ltd, are printed on paper sourced from
sustainable, managed forests.

Contents

How the BPP ACCA-approved Study Text can help you pass

Tackling studying

Studying can be a daunting prospect, particularly when you have lots of other commitments. The **different features** of the text, the **purposes** of which are explained fully on the **Chapter features** page, will help you whilst studying and improve your chances of **exam success**.

Developing exam awareness

Our Texts are completely **focused** on helping you pass your exam.

Our advice on **Studying F4** outlines the **content** of the paper and the **necessary skills** the examiner expects you to demonstrate.

Exam focus points are included within the chapters to highlight when and how specific topics were examined, or how they might be examined in the future.

Using the Syllabus and Study Guide

You can find the syllabus, Study Guide and other useful resources for F4 on the ACCA web site:

www.accaglobal.com/students/study_exams/qualifications/acca_choose/acca/fundamentals/CL/

The Study Text covers **all aspects** of the syllabus to ensure you are as fully prepared for the exam as possible.

Testing what you can do

Testing yourself helps you develop the skills you need to pass the exam and also confirms that you can recall what you have learnt.

We include **Questions** – lots of them - both within chapters and in the **Exam Question Bank**, as well as **Quick Quizzes** at the end of each chapter to test your knowledge of the chapter content.

Chapter features

Each chapter contains a number of helpful features to guide you through each topic.

Topic list

Topic list	Syllabus reference

Tells you what you will be studying in this chapter and the relevant section numbers, together the ACCA syllabus references.

Introduction

Puts the chapter content in the context of the syllabus as a whole.

Study Guide

Links the chapter content with ACCA guidance.

Exam Guide

Highlights how examinable the chapter content is likely to be and the ways in which it could be examined.

> Knowledge brought forward from earlier studies

What you are assumed to know from previous studies/exams.

> FAST FORWARD

Summarises the content of main chapter headings, allowing you to preview and review each section easily.

Examples

Demonstrate how to apply key knowledge and techniques.

Key terms

Definitions of important concepts that can often earn you easy marks in exams.

Exam focus points

Tell you when and how specific topics were examined, or how they may be examined in the future.

Formula to learn

Formulae that are not given in the exam but which have to be learnt.

 Question

Give you essential practice of techniques covered in the chapter.

 Case Study

Provide real world examples of theories and techniques.

Chapter Roundup

A full list of the Fast Forwards included in the chapter, providing an easy source of review.

Quick Quiz

A quick test of your knowledge of the main topics in the chapter.

Exam Question Bank

Found at the back of the Study Text with more comprehensive chapter questions. Cross referenced for easy navigation.

Studying F4

In approaching the F4 exam you should bear in mind what the paper is about, the skills you are expected to demonstrate in the exam and how you can improve your chances of passing the exam. We shall look at each of these points in turn.

1 What F4 is about

The main aims of the F4 exam are:

- To develop knowledge and skills in the understanding of the general legal framework and of specific legal areas relating to business, but

- To recognise the need to seek further specialist legal advice where necessary

The exam is not designed to turn you into a legal expert. Instead you will be a well-informed professional accountant who appreciates the legal issues of doing business but who recognises the boundaries of their legal knowledge and therefore the point at which professional legal expertise must be sought.

The sequence of the syllabus and study guide takes you through the main areas of what you need to know.

Essential elements of the legal system

In this part of the syllabus you are covering areas that underlie all the other areas, namely: what is law and how the UK legal system creates and administers it. The distinctions between criminal law and civil law, between common law and civil law and between public law and private law, are very important. Most of the paper is concerned with civil law, namely the law that sets out the rights and duties of persons in relation to each other. There are elements of criminal law in relation to companies, insolvency, insider dealing and money laundering, in addition to the topical area of human rights legislation.

Law of obligations

The syllabus clearly distinguishes two important types of obligation that individuals and businesses have.

Contract

When individuals or businesses make agreements, a legally binding contract may be formed. This paper focuses on the requirements that must be met for a contract to be binding on the parties, what valid contracts must contain, under which circumstances the contractual terms are breached and what remedies are available for the affected party.

Tort

All members of society have a duty not to harm others and this principle forms the basis of tort. The tort of negligence is highly topical and has an impact on individuals, businesses and professionals (such as accountants). It is important for you to understand how such a duty is formed, the circumstances that will cause a breach of that duty and if there are any defences to a breach that the perpetrator can call on. The syllabus also covers a range of other torts such as assault, battery, false imprisonment, libel and defamation.

Employment law

Employees and employers are bound to each other by an employment contact. It is important that you have a good understanding of the contents of such a contract. Both employers and their employees owe duties to each other and breach of these duties can result in legal action being taken.

Termination of employment can be fraught with danger for employers if it is not handled correctly. The terms of 'wrongful' and 'unfair' dismissal are used commonly in the media, but the causes and remedies are distinct and it is important for you to understand the difference.

Formation and constitution of business organisations

The syllabus is very concerned with the various legal forms through which business transactions may be conducted. It is important to distinguish initially between natural persons (human beings) and legal persons (including natural persons, but extending to some forms of partnership and, most significantly, companies). The law of agency underlies a substantial part of our study of business forms, since partners and directors can and sometimes do act as agents.

Capital and financing of companies

Most trading companies are financed by a mix of share capital (provided by their owners) and loan capital (provided by third party lenders). Share capital in turn may take a variety of forms, with each class of share having different rights within the company. However, the primary responsibility of the shareholder is to contribute funds to the company in accordance with the terms of the company's constitution and the shares which they own. The return of these funds to shareholders is restricted since they are seen as the 'creditors' buffer', that is the funds which are available to settle creditors' outstanding debts in preference to amounts due to shareholders. Hence there are detailed laws on 'capital maintenance'. These extend to how far companies may distribute accumulated retained earnings to their shareholders in the form of dividends or buyback of shares.

Loan capital is usually provided by lenders only if they can be assured of its repayment to them. If lenders supply funds in return for debentures in the company, they usually require security for their loan: the debenture is secured by means of a registered charge on particular or general assets of the company, which can (within limitations) be realised so that the loan is repaid.

Management, administration and regulation of companies

As an artificial legal person a company cannot manage itself. This is the role primarily of the company's directors, who owe duties to the company to manage it for the benefit of the company and thereby for the benefit of its owners, the shareholders. There are a great many legal rules which regulate the appointment, remuneration, disqualification, powers and duties of directors. These have grown up largely because of problems that frequently occur. Most of these can be said to arise from conflicts between directors' personal interests and their duties to act in the company's interest. Directors are termed officers of the company along with the company secretary. Many companies also have to have an auditor.

Directors come into immediate contact with shareholders via company meetings, and the resolutions that are passed at these meetings. There are therefore a plethora of legal rules on meetings and resolutions, designed to ensure that the company is taking decisions properly and in accordance with the legitimate interests of shareholders as a body.

Legal implications of companies in difficulty or in crisis

Not everything goes according to plan and frequently companies will encounter financial or other difficulties, or will even reach crisis point and find themselves insolvent. At this point all parties – shareholders, directors, lenders, customers, suppliers and employees – are in danger of losing out. There are procedures designed to protect struggling companies to give them a 'breathing space' while they resolve their issues. There are also rules for how a company which cannot be saved should be 'wound up', depending on whether or not the company has any funds left.

Corporate governance

Corporate governance means trying to ensure that companies are well-managed and controlled. While there are plenty of legal rules designed to ensure good corporate governance, there are also (semi-)voluntary codes of practice which apply to some but not all companies. The Combined Code on Corporate Governance applies to all companies listed on the London Stock Exchange, but is also recommended to other companies. It seeks to protect shareholders and addresses the problems of conflicts of interest in part by implementing the principle of separation of duties between executive and non-executive directors. It also covers directors' remuneration, external audit, nominations to the board of directors and other issues.

Fraudulent behaviour

Finally the syllabus covers the situations where activities of directors and others have strayed into criminal behaviour. This often arises in the context of companies running out of money, but the law is also concerned with company insiders with superior knowledge benefiting from insider dealing, and crime in the form of money laundering.

2 What skills are required?

To pass the F4 exam you will need to bring a number of different professional attributes to bear.

First you need **technical knowledge**. There is a huge amount of technical content in the syllabus: case law, conventions, codes of practice, and legislation. You need to learn this and be able to identify which parts of the knowledge you have are being called for in a particular question.

Secondly you need to be able to **apply knowledge** to the scenarios that are presented in the last three questions on the paper. You are aiming to solve practical problems here. Generally in scenario questions there will be marks available for stating the law, identifying the issues in the scenario in relation to the law, applying the law and reaching a conclusion.

Thirdly you need **written skills** in order to be able to explain, and advise on the basis of, your technical knowledge. Explaining means providing simple definitions and covering why and how these approaches have been developed. You'll gain higher marks if your explanations are clearly focused on the question and you can supplement your explanations with examples.

3 How to improve your chances of passing

To pass the exam you need to **cover the syllabus thoroughly**. The exam requires you to answer all TEN questions on the paper. Each topic that you fail to cover represents 10% fewer marks in the exam.

You should **practise answering questions** as much as possible, making sure that your answers are focused, specific and completely relevant to the question.

Ten questions is a lot to answer in three hours so your **exam technique** is very important, especially:

- Strict **time management**: only 18 minutes per answer

- Deciding on **the order in which you attempt questions** carefully: use your 15 minutes reading and planning time carefully to make sure that you attempt your best topics first when you start to write. This will bolster your confidence and help to ensure that you manage your time properly, so long as you don't overrun your time allocation on the early, 'better' questions

- **Reading the question** carefully: make sure you identify precisely the key issues requiring your attention

Only **answering the question set**: do not stray into irrelevant areas of, say, contract law. You will gain no marks and you will lose time.

The exam paper

Format of the paper

The examination is a three hour paper consisting of seven, ten-mark questions testing knowledge and three, ten-mark application (scenario) questions.

Guidance

As all questions are compulsory it is vital to attempt all of them. Even if you are not confident about an area of law, it is often easier to earn marks by starting a question and putting something down, than by adding material to an already developed answer.

When answering scenario questions follow the **ISAC** approach

Identify the legal issues
State the relevant law
Apply the law
Conclude

This structure will maximise your marks as you identify what the problem is, state what the law says about the problem, apply the law and come to a reasonable conclusion – exactly what the examiner wants.

You are expected to quote case names and section numbers in your answers. Do your best to learn as many as you can (at least a handful in each topic area), but don't worry if in the exam you forget the case name or section number – as long as you correctly state the principle of law you will earn most of the marks.

The December 2007 exam

The December 2007 exam saw the first **tort** question under the new syllabus. It required candidates to explain the concept of '**remoteness of damage**'. According to examiner's report on the sitting, the vast majority of candidates ignored the reference to tort and answered the question on the basis of **contract law**. They consequently scored very low marks. When studying please remember that 'remoteness of damage' under tort and contract are completely unrelated concepts. **Do not mix them up in an exam question**.

Analysis of past papers – F4 Corporate and Business Law (English)

The table below provides details of when each element of the syllabus has been examined and the question number and section in which each element appeared. Further details can be found in the Exam Focus Points in the relevant chapters.

Covered in Text chapter		Dec 2007	Pilot Paper
	ESSENTIAL ELEMENTS OF THE LEGAL SYSTEM		
1	The English legal system	1	
2	Sources of English law		1
3	Human rights		
	THE LAW OF OBLIGATIONS		
4, 5	Formation of contracts	2, 8	8
6	Terms of contract		2
7	Breach of contract		
8	Torts	3	3
9	Professional negligence		
	EMPLOYMENT LAW		
10	Employment contract		
11	Dismissal and redundancy	6	7
	THE FORMATION AND CONSTITUTION OF BUSINESS ORGANISATIONS		
12	Agency law		
13	Organisations and legal personality		
14	Company formation		4
15	Constitution of a company	4	
	CAPITAL AND THE FINANCING OF COMPANIES		
16	Share capital		9
17	Borrowing and loan capital		
18	Capital maintenance and dividend law	5	
	MANAGEMENT, ADMINISTRATION AND REGULATION OF COMPANIES		
19	Company directors and other company officers	7, 10	
20	Company meetings and resolutions		5
	LEGAL IMPLICATIONS OF COMPANIES IN DIFFICULTY OR IN CRISIS		
21	Insolvency and administration	9	
	GOVERNANCE AND ETHICAL ISSUES RELATING TO BUSINESS		
22	Corporate governance		6
23	Fraudulent behaviour		10

Essential elements of the legal system

1

The English legal system

Topic list	Syllabus reference
1 What is law?	A1(a)
2 Types of law	A1(a)
3 The system of courts	A1(b)
4 Tribunals	A1(b)

Introduction

Welcome to your study of **Corporate and Business law**. In this chapter we set the scene and framework of the English Legal System.

We start by **defining** what law is and why it is important to society. Our study continues by considering the **different types of law** that we have in the UK and how they have developed over time.

The chapter concludes with an analysis of the **Criminal and Civil court systems**. Tribunals are also discussed as an alternative method of dispute resolution.

Study guide

		Intellectual level
(A)	**Essential elements of the legal system**	
1	Court structure	
(a)	Define law and distinguish types of law	1
(b)	Explain the structure and operation of the courts and tribunals system	1

Exam guide

The nature of law and the operation of the legal system form a basis for your later studies but could also be examined as a topic all by itself.

1 What is law?

FAST FORWARD

> **'Law is a formal mechanism of social control'**, *Business Law 5th Edition*, David Kelly, Ann Holmes and Ruth Hayward

Human society has developed over thousands of years from a primitive culture where the very survival of the species was at stake to the complex, diverse and dominating species that humans are today.

Much of the success of this development can be attributable to **rules** and **regulations** laid down by society. With a little further study the need for such rules becomes clear. In the early days of human existence, **survival** was achieved by working as a group. There was a fine line between **life** and **death**, for example the **stealing** of food from another group member could eventually result in starvation or death of the victim.

Social order, created by rules is at the foundation of the society that we see today. The framework that was created influences how **individuals interact** and how **businesses** operate. In other words, it provides social control.

The framework of social control can be viewed as having two aspects:

- **Formal** control mechanisms
- **Informal** control mechanisms

Law is a formal control mechanism. It provides a **structure** for dealing with and resolving disputes that may arise, as well as providing some **deterrent** to those wishing to disrupt social order.

Informal mechanisms include **ethical** and **moral guidance**. These are 'norms' or behavioural expectations that society has developed over time through its culture. Such mechanisms have **little formal structure** to organise, control or to punish – such matters are dealt with informally by pressure from other individuals or groups.

2 Types of law

The English legal system distinguishes several different types of law.

- **Common** law and **equity**
- **Statute** law
- **Private** law and **public** law
- **Criminal** law and **civil** law

2.1 Common law and equity

The earliest element of the English legal system is **common law**, a system of rigid rules laid down by **royal courts** following the Norman conquest. Application of law was by **judges** who travelled around the country to keep the King's peace and judgements often resulted in harsh **consequences**.

The judges actually made the law by **amalgamating** local customary laws into one 'law of the land'. **Remedies** under common law are **monetary**, and are known as **damages**.

However, there are times when money is not a **suitable remedy**. For example, you have agreed to buy a unique painting from an art dealer. Should the dealer at the last minute sell the painting to someone else, damages are unlikely to be acceptable, after all you wanted *that* painting.

Equity was developed two or three hundred years after common law as a system to resolve disputes where damages are not a suitable remedy and to introduce **fairness** into the legal system. We shall be studying common law and equity further in the next chapter.

2.2 Statute law

Whilst the judiciary is responsible for the creation of common law, **Parliament** is responsible for **statute law**. Statute law is usually made in areas so **complicated** or **unique** that suitable common law alternatives are unlikely, or would take an unacceptable length of time, to develop – company law is one example of this. We shall be studying statute law as a source of law in the next chapter.

2.3 Private law and public law

Most of the law that you will be studying is **private law**. That is law which deals with **relationships** and **interactions** between businesses, customers, employees and other **private individuals**, **groups** or **organisations**.

The **state** provides a **framework** for dealing with **disputes** and for **enforcing decisions**, but it is for individuals to handle matters between themselves. For example, the Sale of Goods Act 1979 regulates the sale of goods. It provides **rules** that must be adhered to when making a sale. Should any dispute arise that is covered by the act, it is up to **the parties** to resolve the matter **themselves** using rules laid down by the legislation, the **state** does not get involved.

Public law is mainly concerned with **government** and the **operation** and **functions** of **public organisations** such as councils and local authorities. It will not be of great interest to you in your studies of corporate law, however examples of public law can be found in **planning rules** that must be adhered to when building or expanding offices.

A key **distinction** between **public** and **private** law is who takes up the case when a wrong is committed. The **state** prosecutes the alleged perpetrator under **public** law, whereas we have already seen, under **private** law it is for the **individual** concerned to take action.

Criminal law is a part of **public** law. We shall see in the next section that it deals with behaviour that the **state** considers unwelcome and wishes to prevent. Criminal law also decides how those guilty of committing unlawful behaviour should be **punished**. You will notice the names of criminal cases are reported as *R v Jones* or *Regina v Jones*. This indicates that the state takes action on behalf of the crown (*Regina* is Latin for Queen).

2.4 Criminal and civil law

FAST FORWARD

The distinction between **criminal liability** and **civil liability** is central to the English legal system.

It is often the **criminal law** about which the general public has a clearer perception and keener interest. Some of the high profile criminal cases at **London's Old Bailey** are deemed extremely newsworthy. **Civil law**, on the other hand, receives less overt media coverage. However, every time you buy or sell goods, or start or finish an employment contract, your actions, and those of the other party, are governed by civil law.

The **distinction** between criminal and civil liability is central to the English legal system and to the way the court system is structured.

2.4.1 Criminal law

In criminal cases, the **state** prosecutes the wrongdoer.

Key term

A **crime** is conduct prohibited by the law.

In a criminal case the State is the prosecutor because it is the community as a whole which suffers as a result of the law being broken. Persons guilty of crime may be punished by **fines** payable to the State, **imprisonment**, or a community-based punishment.

Generally, the **police** take the initial decision to prosecute, but this is then reviewed by the Crown Prosecution Service. Some prosecutions are started by the Director of Public Prosecutions, who is the head of the Crown Prosecution Service.

In a criminal trial, the **burden of proof** to convict the **accused** rests with the **prosecution**, which must prove its case **beyond reasonable doubt**.

2.4.2 Civil Law

Civil law exists to regulate disputes over the rights and obligations of persons dealing with each other and seeks to compensate injured parties.

Civil law is a form of **private law**. In civil proceedings, the case must be proved on the **balance of probability**. The claimant must convince the court that it is more probable than not that their assertions are true.

There is no concept of **punishment**, and **compensation** is paid to the wronged person. Both parties may choose to **settle** the dispute **out of court** should they wish.

Terminology in civil cases is different to that of criminal cases. A **claimant** sues a **defendant**. A civil case would therefore be referred to as, for example, *Smith v Megacorp plc*.

One of the most important areas of civil liability for business, and accountants in particular, is the law of **contract**. The law of contract is looked at in detail in Part B of this text.

2.4.3 Distinction between criminal and civil cases

It is not an act or event which creates the distinction, but the legal consequences. A single event might give rise to criminal and civil proceedings.

 Illustration

A broken leg caused to a pedestrian by a drunken driver is a single event which may give rise to:

- **Criminal case** (prosecution by the State for the offence of driving with excess alcohol), and
- **Civil case** (the pedestrian sues for compensation for pain and suffering).

The two types of proceedings can be easily distinguished because three vital factors are different:

- The **courts** where the case is heard
- The **procedures**
- The **terminology**

Illustration

In criminal cases the rules of evidence are very strict. For example, a confession will be carefully examined to see if any pressure was brought to bear upon the accused, but an admission in a civil case will not be subjected to such scrutiny.

Question Criminal and civil law

While on a sales trip, one of your employees is involved in a car accident. The other vehicle involved is damaged and it is alleged that your employee is to blame. What legal proceedings may arise as a result of this incident?

Answer

Your employee may be guilty of a driving offence such as careless driving. The police, to whom the incident should be reported, will investigate, and if the facts indicate a driving offence, they will prosecute him. The owner of the damaged vehicle (or his insurers) may sue the driver at fault in civil proceedings to recover damages.

3 The system of courts

The **courts** have to be organised to facilitate the working of the legal system. There are four main functional aspects of the court system which underlie its structure.

(a) **Civil and criminal law** differ so much in substance and procedure that they are best administered in separate courts.

(b) **Local courts** allow the vast bulk of small legal proceedings to be decentralised. But important civil cases begin in the High Court in London.

(c) Although the courts form a single system and many courts have a general civil jurisdiction, there is some **specialisation** both within the High Court and in other courts with separate functions.

(d) There is a system of review by **appeals** to higher courts.

3.1 The civil court structure

FAST FORWARD

The **civil court structure** comprises the following.

- **Magistrates' courts** mostly deal with small domestic matters.
- **County courts** hear claims in contract and tort, equitable matters and land and probate disputes among others.
- The **Crown Court** hears appeals from magistrates' courts.
- The **High Court** is divided into three specialist divisions; Queen's Bench, Family and Chancery
- The **Court of Appeal** hears appeals from the County Court, the High Court, the Restrictive Practices Court, and from the Employment Appeal Tribunal.
- The **House of Lords** hears appeals from the Court of Appeal and the High Court.

The diagram below sets out the English **civil** court structure.

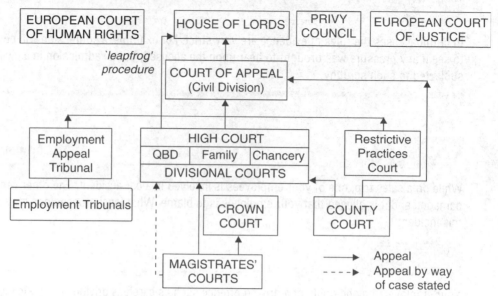

In appropriate cases it is possible to refer a case to either the **European Court of Human Rights** or the **European Court of Justice**, although they are not strictly within the English court structure.

3.2 The criminal court structure

FAST FORWARD

The **criminal court structure** comprises the following.

- **Magistrates' courts** hear summary offences and committal proceedings for indictable offences.
- The **Crown Court** tries serious criminal (indictable) offences and hears appeals from magistrates' courts.
- The **Divisional Court of QBD** hears appeals by way of case stated from magistrates' courts and the Crown Court.
- The **Court of Appeal** hears appeals from the Crown Court.
- The **House of Lords** hears appeals from the Court of Appeal or a Divisional Court of QBD.

The diagram below sets out the English **criminal** court structure.

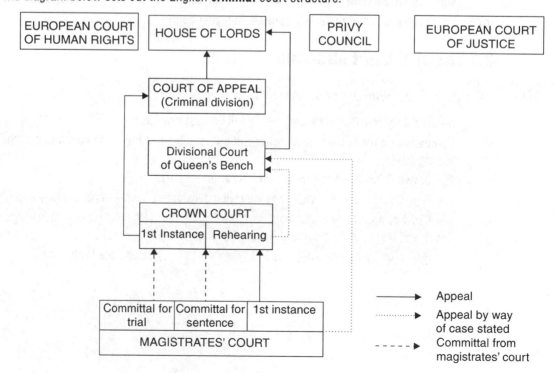

A limited number of Commonwealth countries allow appeal to the Privy Council in London, which is mostly staffed by House of Lords judges.

3.3 Magistrates' courts

Magistrates' courts are the **lowest ranked criminal courts**.

- They try **summarily** (without a jury) all minor offences.
- They conduct **committal proceedings**, which are preliminary investigations of the prosecution case, when the offence is **triable** only on indictment (by a Crown Court).

Key terms

> **Indictable offences** are more serious offences that can only be heard in a Crown Court.
>
> **Summary offences** are minor crimes, only triable summarily in magistrates' courts.
>
> Some offences are **'triable either way'**, meaning the accused has the choice of court that is used.

Magistrates also have **some civil jurisdiction** which includes the following:

- **Family proceedings** (financial provision for parties to a marriage and children, the custody or supervision of children and guardianship, and adoption orders).
- Various types of **licensing**
- Enforcement of **local authority** charges and rates

3.4 Appeals

A defendant convicted on a criminal charge in a magistrates' court has a general right to a rehearing by a Crown Court. A **'case stated' appeal** is based on the idea that magistrates or the Crown Court have **wrongly interpreted the law**. If not, then the case may be sent back to the lower court with instructions as to how it should be decided.

On **family matters**, appeals are to the Crown Court with a further (or alternative) appeal on a point of law to a divisional court of the **Family Division of the High Court**.

3.5 Personnel

The key personnel in the magistrates court are the **magistrates** who hear the cases. These fall into two categories:

- Magistrates, who are lay persons selected by the Lord Chancellor (Justices of the Peace)
- District Judges (professional paid magistrates)

The magistrates' courts are also staffed by **clerks**, who can provide legal advice for lay magistrates.

3.6 The County Court

County courts have **civil jurisdiction only** but deal with almost every kind of civil case. The practical importance of the county courts is that they deal with **the majority of the UK's civil litigation**.

The county court is involved in the following matters.

- **Contract and tort** (except defamation of character) claims.
- **Equitable matters** concerning trusts, mortgages and partnership dissolution.
- Disputes concerning **land**.
- **Undefended matrimonial** cases.
- **Probate matters**.
- **Miscellaneous matters** conferred by various statutes, for example the Consumer Credit Act 1974.
- Some **bankruptcy**, company winding-up and admiralty cases.

The county court deals with the following:

- All small claims track cases, and
- All fast track cases.

Multi-track cases are allocated either to the county court or to the High Court if they are complex.

3.6.1 Appeals

From the county court there is a right of appeal direct to the **Civil Division of the Court of Appeal** for multi-track cases. In most other cases an appeal goes to the relevant Division of the **High Court**.

3.6.2 Personnel

The personnel in the county court consists of:

- Circuit judges, assisted by
- District judges

3.7 Civil Procedure Rules

Civil procedures encourage parties to consider **alternative methods** of dispute resolution and to avoid **expensive litigation**, resolving cases **quickly and without unnecessary confrontation.** Early settlement of disputes is encouraged during proceedings.

The court has the power to control every aspect of the litigation process, shifting responsibility away from the litigants and their advisers. The court is intended to be a place of **last, rather than first, resort**.

There are two principal areas in which the civil procedure rules are relevant:

(a)   Tracking
(b)   Case management

3.7.1 Tracking

After a defence has been filed, the case will be allocated to one of three tracks.

(a)   In the **small claims track**, claims of no more than £5,000 will be heard. These are cases that are to be dealt with quickly and informally, often without the need for legal representation or for a full hearing.

(b)   The **fast track** is for claims of between £5,000 and £15,000 where the trial is to last no longer than one day. These are subject to a simplified court procedure and a fixed timetable designed to enable the claim to be determined within 30 weeks.

(c)   Under the **multi-track**, claims of over £15,000 which are to be managed by the courts will be heard.

3.7.2 Case management

After allocation, the court will give directions setting out the procedures to be followed in bringing multi-track cases to trial. These will be an initial 'case management conference' to encourage parties to settle the dispute or to consider alternative dispute resolutions (such as mediation or arbitration). Features of the procedures include the following.

(a)   A **pre-action protocol**, which entails setting out the claim to the defendant in an attempt to negotiate a settlement. The emphasis is placed on co-operation to identify the main issues. Failure to co-operate may lead to cost penalties, regardless of the eventual outcome of the case.

(b)   A strict **timetable** for exchange of evidence is set by the court, including witness statements and relevant documents.

(c)   A three week **trial window** is allocated once the defence has been received. This does not change and the trial can fall anytime within this period.

(d)   There are cost **penalties** for failing to meet any deadline or date set by the court.

There is a senior judge with overall responsibility for civil justice, known as the **Head of Civil Justice**. His appointment is designed to raise the status of civil justice, which had long been in the shadow of the criminal justice system.

3.8 The Crown Court

The Crown Court is a single court forming part of the **Supreme Court**, but it sits in 90 different towns and cities and also at the **Central Criminal Court** (the Old Bailey) in London.

It deals with the following matters:

- **Indictable offences** with a jury.
- **Appeals** from magistrates' courts.
- **Committals for sentencing** from magistrates' courts.

The Crown Court deals with a few types of **civil case**, for example **appeals** from the magistrates' court on matters of affiliation, betting, gaming and licensing.

3.8.1 Appeals

From the Crown Court there is a right of appeal on criminal matters to the **Criminal Division of the Court of Appeal**. An appeal by way of 'case stated' on a point of law may also be made to a **Divisional Court of the Queen's Bench Division**, in the High Court.

3.8.2 Personnel

The Crown Court has the following personnel:

- High Court judges (for serious offences)
- Circuit judges
- Recorders

3.9 The High Court

The High Court is organised into three divisions:

- Queen's Bench Division
- Chancery Division
- Family Division

3.9.1 Queen's Bench Division

The Queen's Bench Division (QBD) deals mainly with common law matters, such as:

- Actions based on contract or tort.
- Some appeals from the county court
- Appeals by way of case stated from magistrates' courts.
- Some appeals from the Crown Court.

It also has a **supervisory role** over inferior courts. It is the largest of the three divisions, having 73 judges of which the Principal Judge is the Lord Chief Justice. It includes a separate Admiralty Court to deal with shipping matters, and a Commercial Court which specialises in commercial cases. The QBD sits in London and a small number of large cities in England and Wales.

It may issue a writ of *habeas corpus*, which is an order for the release of a person wrongfully detained, and also prerogative orders against inferior courts, tribunals and other bodies such as local authorities.

There are three types of **prerogative order.**

- A **mandatory order** requiring the court or other body to carry out a public duty.
- A **prohibitory order** preventing a court or tribunal from exceeding its jurisdiction (before it has done so).
- A **quashing order** ordering a court or tribunal which has taken action to submit the record of its proceedings to the High Court for review.

3.9.2 Chancery Division

This division headed by the Lord Chancellor, deals with traditional equity matters.

- **Trusts** and **mortgages**
- **Revenue** matters
- **Bankruptcy** (though outside London this is a county court subject)
- Disputed **wills** and administration of estates of deceased persons
- **Partnership** and company **matters**

There is a separate **Companies Court** within the division which deals with liquidations and other company proceedings, and a Patents Court established under the Patents Act 1977.

3.9.3 Family Division

This division deals with:

- **Matrimonial** cases
- **Family property** cases
- **Proceedings relating to children** (wardship, guardianship, adoption, legitimacy)
- **Appeals** from magistrates' courts on family matters.
- **Appeals** from county courts on family matters

3.9.4 Appeals

Civil appeals from the High Court may be made to the **Court of Appeal (Civil Division)** or to the **House of Lords**, under what is known as the **'leapfrog'** procedure. This procedure is rarely used.

Criminal appeals are made direct to the House of Lords where the case has reached the High Court on appeal from a magistrates' court or from the Crown Court.

3.9.5 Personnel

The High Court is staffed by **High Court (puisne) judges**. The chief judges in each division are as follows:

- Queen's Bench Division: Lord Chief Justice
- Family Division: President
- Chancery Division: Lord Chancellor (nominally), in practice the Vice Chancellor

3.10 The Court of Appeal

Key terms

> A **court of first instance** is the court where the case is originally heard in full. The **appeal court** is the court to which an appeal is made against the ruling or the sentence.

If the appeal court finds in favour of the appellant the original decision is **reversed** ie the result is changed, but the law is not. This is different from **overruling** which happens when a higher court finds a lower court's decision to be wrong in law and in future the law is changed.

3.10.1 Civil Division

The Civil Division of the Court of Appeal can hear appeals from the **High Court, county courts**, and from certain **other courts** and **special tribunals**. It may uphold or reverse the earlier decision or order a new trial.

3.10.2 Criminal Division

The Criminal Division of the Court of Appeal hears appeals from the **Crown Court**. It may also be invited to review a criminal case by the **government** or to consider a point of law at the request of the **Attorney General**.

3.10.3 Appeals

Appeals lie to the House of Lords.

3.10.4 Personnel

The Court of Appeal is staffed by the Lord Justices of Appeal. The chief judges in each division are as follows:

- Civil division: Master of the Rolls
- Criminal division: Lord Chief Justice

3.11 The House of Lords

The House of Lords is staffed by **Lords of Appeal in Ordinary** (also called **Law Lords**). It has a **judicial role**, as the highest appeal court of the legal system. Judges in the House of Lords are also made life peers so they may choose to attend sittings of the House of Lords when it is exercising its legislative. function (ie as part of Parliament) but they rarely do so.

3.11.1 The Constitutional Reform Act 2005

The **Constitutional Reform Act 2005** which received Royal Assent on 24th March 2005 and that is expected to come into effect in 2008, will sever the link between the **legislative** and **judicial** functions of the House of Lords.

A **Supreme Court** of the United Kingdom will be established consisting of **12 judges** known as *'Justices of the Supreme Court'* and its members will include a **President** and a **Deputy President**. The initial members will be the Lords of Appeal in Ordinary who are in tenure at the time.

Its **role** will be the same as the existing House of Lords' judicial function, however it will extend into other matters outside the scope of your syllabus.

The House of Lords will continue with its current **legislative role** once the Supreme Court has been established.

3.12 The European Court of Human Rights

The European Court of Human Rights is the **supreme court** of those European states who have signed up to the **European Convention of Human Rights**. Any individual who alleges that their human rights have been violated can bring an action against those responsible.

Since the **Human Rights Act 1998** (see Chapter 3), the UK has incorporated the European Convention of Human Rights into UK law, enabling enforcement to be exercised by UK courts.

3.13 The European Court of Justice

The **European Court of Justice** has the role of **interpreting** European Treaty law and ensuring it is **observed**. European laws are enacted in the UK and are therefore directly applicable to **individuals** and **businesses** within the UK. Cases are usually between nation states or European institutions, however, individuals **can appeal** to the ECJ if they are affected personally.

3.14 The Privy Council

The **Judicial Committee of the Privy Council** is the final Court of Appeal for certain Commonwealth countries. Their decisions are also important to cases heard in the UK as they have **persuasive influence** over hearings concerning points of law applicable under the UK's jurisdiction.

Question

List the court (or courts) to which an appeal may be made from each of the following:

(a)   The County court

(b)   The High Court (civil cases)

(Refer to the court structure diagram in Section 3.1)

Answer

(a)   The civil division of the Court of Appeal or the High Court.

(b)   The civil division of the Court of Appeal or the House of Lords.

4 Tribunals

FAST FORWARD

The court system is not the only way to settle disputes. There is also the alternative system of **tribunals**.

There are a number of **other courts** and **tribunals** which feature prominently in the English legal system, either because they have a relatively important status or because they have a heavy caseload. For example **tribunals** deal with over 250,000 cases each year on issues ranging from employment and social security matters, to land disputes. They are supervised by the **Council on Tribunals**.

Tribunals usually consist of **three members**, including one who is legally qualified (normally made chairman). The other two are **lay members** who may have **specialist knowledge** of the matters to be considered by the tribunal.

There are also a number of statutory tribunals, however you need only concern yourself with Employment tribunals.

4.1 Employment tribunals

Employment tribunals (formerly known as industrial tribunals) are governed by the Employment Tribunals Act 1996 as amended by the Employment Tribunals (Constitution and Rules of Procedure) Regulations 2004.

4.1.1 Composition

Each tribunal is staffed by a legally qualified **chairman** and two other persons selected from a panel. One person represents the interests of employers and one represents the interests of employees. However, in some circumstances, and with the consent of the parties, a tribunal may be convened with a chairman and one other person.

4.1.2 Jurisdiction

Tribunals have a wide jurisdiction over most disputes between UK **employees and employers** such as:

*   Disputes about **redundancy** pay
*   Complaints of **unfair dismissal**
*   Questions as to **terms of contracts** of employment
*   **Equal pay** claims or disputes over issues such as **maternity pay**
*   Appeals against **health and safety** notices
*   Complaints about sex, race and disability **discrimination**
*   Disputes over **trade union** membership

4.1.3 Procedure

The following procedure is to be followed when taking a dispute to a tribunal:

Stage 1 The claim is made in writing, setting out the claimant's case. It is presented to the Employment Tribunal Office on a prescribed claim form (ET1).

Stage 2 On receipt of the claim, the tribunal secretary will consider whether or not to accept it. Claims will be rejected at this stage if they are incomplete or if the matter is outside the jurisdiction of a tribunal.

Stage 3 Copies of accepted claims are sent to all relevant parties and the respondent has 28 days to file a reply to the claim made against them (on form ET3). Not presenting a reply can lead to a default judgement being made.

Stage 4 The tribunal secretary considers the reply and accepts it providing it is complete, received in time and meets other acceptance criteria. Copies of the reply are sent to all parties. At this stage the respondent may make a counterclaim against the claimant.

Stage 5 The claim, reply and any counterclaims are reviewed by a chairman and where appropriate an order may be made without a hearing.

Stage 6 Where a case goes to a hearing, the chairman has full powers to manage the case including pre-hearing reviews and interim hearings (case management discussions) where appropriate.

Stage 7 The parties are encouraged to seek conciliation to resolve the dispute and at any stage either party may withdraw.

Stage 8 A date, time and place is set for the final hearing which proceeds with parties giving evidence and calling witnesses. The tribunal considers the evidence and makes an order or a final judgement.

Stage 9 Parties may apply to have certain judgements and decisions reviewed.

4.1.4 Appeal

There is a right of appeal to the **Employment Appeal Tribunal (EAT)**. This is a court of equal status with the High Court. It hears appeals from tribunals mainly on employment matters. A **High Court judge** and two **lay assessors** from a panel appointed on the Lord Chancellor's recommendation sit. From the EAT there is a right of appeal to the Court of Appeal. It will only hear appeals on points of law, it will not re-examine facts.

4.1.5 Advantages and disadvantages of tribunals

Advantages include: speed of proceedings, cheaper costs, informality in comparison to courts, flexibility (not bound by rules of precedent) accessibility to individuals and lack of publicity.

Disadvantages include: no unified, formal appeals procedure, lack of legal aid for most parties, presentation of arguments by people who are not qualified lawyers.

Exam focus point

> The process of tribunals and its advantages and is an area of quite topical interest. Make sure you keep up to date on events in this area.

Chapter Roundup

- **'Law is a formal mechanism of social control'**, *Business Law 5th Edition*, David Kelly, Ann Holmes and Ruth Hayward

- The distinction between **criminal liability** and **civil liability** is central to the English legal system.

- In criminal cases, the **state** prosecutes the wrongdoer.

- **Civil law** exists to regulate disputes over the rights and obligations of persons dealing with each other and seeks to compensate injured parties.

- The **civil court structure** comprises the following.

    - **Magistrates' courts** mostly deal with small domestic matters.

    - **County courts** hear claims in contract and tort, equitable matters and land and probate disputes among others.

    - The **Crown Court** hears appeals from magistrates' courts.

    - The **High Court** is divided into three specialist divisions; Queen's Bench, Family and Chancery.

    - The **Court of Appeal** hears appeals from the County Court, the High Court, the Restrictive Practices Court, and from the Employment Appeal Tribunal.

    - The **House of Lords** hears appeals from the Court of Appeal and the High Court.

- The **criminal court structure** comprises the following.

    - **Magistrates' courts** hear summary offences and committal proceedings for indictable offences.

    - The **Crown Court** tries serious criminal (indictable) offences and hears appeals from magistrates' courts.

    - The **Divisional Court of QBD** hears appeals by way of case stated from magistrates' courts and the Crown Court.

    - The **Court of Appeal** hears appeals from the Crown Court.

    - The **House of Lords** hears appeals from the Court of Appeal or a Divisional Court of QBD.

- The court system is not the only way to settle disputes. There is also the alternative system of **tribunals**.

Quick Quiz

1   **Fill in the blanks** in the statements below.

The distinction between (1) .... and (2) .... liability is central to the English legal system.

2   What is the standard of proof in civil proceedings?

3   What kind of judge sits in the House of Lords?

4   The Employment Appeal Tribunal is a court of equal status with the High Court.

True ☐

False ☐

5   All the following statements relate to criminal and civil law. Which one of the statements is correct?

A   A criminal case may subsequently give rise to a civil case, but a civil case cannot subsequently give rise to a criminal case

B   The main purpose of civil law is to compensate the injured party and to punish the injuring party

C   A custodial sentence can be passed on the defendant in a civil case, providing the defendant is a natural person and not an incorporated body

D   The main purpose of civil law is to enforce the claimant's rights rather than to punish the defendant.

6   What are the three tracks in the tracking system that allocates civil court cases?

7   Which court or courts might hear an appeal from the High Court in a civil case?

8   What is the monetary limit for civil claims allocated to the track?

Answers to Quick Quiz

1   (1) criminal (2) civil

2   The case must be proved on the balance of probability

3   Lords of Appeal in Ordinary, or Law Lords

4   True. See diagram in Section 3.1.

5   D. Punishment is not an objective of Civil law. A Civil case may subsequently give rise to a criminal case.

6   (1) Small claims track (2) fast track (3) multi-track

7   (1) The Court of Appeal (Civil Division) (2) The House of Lords (under the leapfrog procedure)

8   £5,000

Now try the question below from the Exam Question Bank

Number	Level	Marks	Time
Q1	Examination	10	18 mins

Sources of English law

2

Topic list	Syllabus reference
1 Case law and precedent	A2(a)
2 Legislation	A2(b)
3 Statutory interpretation	A2(c)

Introduction

Continuing with our study of the English Legal system, we now look at **sources of law** and how law is **interpreted** by the courts.

You will discover that the main law making bodies are the **Courts** (who develop the 'common law') and **Parliament** which produces statutes and delegated legislation.

EU law is another source of law for the UK, however it is outside the scope of your syllabus.

The rules on **statutory interpretation** are used by Judges when deciding cases that involve statutes which are open to several different meanings.

Study guide

		Intellectual level
(A)	**Essential elements of the legal system**	
2	Sources of law	
(a)	Explain what is meant by case law and precedent within the context of the hierarchy of the courts	2
(b)	Explain legislation and evaluate delegated legislation	2
(c)	Illustrate the rules and presumptions used by the courts in interpreting statutes	1

Exam guide

You could be asked to describe the operation of case law and precedent or how legislation is passed by government and interpreted by the courts. The pilot paper demonstrates how you could be asked to evaluate delegated legislation.

1 Case law and precedent

FAST FORWARD

The first legal source of law, consisting of decisions made in the courts, is **case law,** which is judge-made law based on the underlying principle of consistency. Once a legal principle is decided by an appropriate court it is a **judicial precedent**.

1.1 Common law and equity

As we saw in Chapter 1, the earliest element of the legal system to develop was the **common law**, a system incorporating rigid rules applied by royal courts, often with harsh consequences. **Equity** was developed, two or three hundred years later, as a system of law applied by the Lord Chancellor in situations where justice did not appear to be done under common law principles.

Key terms

> **Common law** is the body of legal rules common to the whole country which is embodied in judicial decisions.
>
> **Equity** is a term which applies to a specific set of legal principles which were developed by the Court of Chancery to supplement (but not replace) the common law. It is based on fair dealings between the parties. It added to and improved on the common law by introducing the concept of fairness.

The interaction of equity and common law produced three major changes.

(a) **New rights**. Equity recognised and protected rights for which the common law gave no safeguards.

(b) **Better procedure**. Equity could be more effective than common law in bringing a disputed matter to a decision.

(c) **Better remedies**. The standard common law remedy for the successful claimant was the award of damages for his loss. The Chancellor developed remedies not available in other courts. Equity was able to make the following orders.

    (i) That the defendant must do what he had agreed to do (**specific performance**)

    (ii) That the defendant must abstain from wrongdoing (**injunction**)

    (iii) Alteration of a document to reflect the parties' true intentions (**rectification**)

    (iv) Restoration of the pre-contract status quo (**rescission**)

Where equitable rules **conflict** with common law rules then **equitable rules** will **prevail**. *Earl of Oxford's case 1615*

Case law incorporates decisions made by judges under both historic legal systems and the expression 'common law' is often used to describe all case law whatever its historic origin. **A court's decision** is expected to be **consistent with previous decisions** and to provide an opinion which can be used to direct future relationships. This is the basis of the system of **judicial precedent**.

1.2 Doctrine of judicial precedent

The system of judicial precedent is based on a fundamental feature of English law which is that **principles of English law do not become inoperative through the lapse of time**.

> The doctrine of consistency, following precedent, is expressed in the maxim **stare decisis** which means 'to stand by a decision'. In any later case to which a legal principle is relevant the same principle should (subject to certain exceptions) be applied.
>
> A **precedent** is a previous court decision which another court is bound to follow by deciding a subsequent case in the same way.

The doctrine of **judicial precedent** means that a judge is bound to apply a decision from an earlier case to the facts of the case before him, provided, among other conditions, that there is no material difference between the cases and the previous case created a 'binding' precedent.

Judicial precedent is based on three elements.

- **Reports.** There must be adequate and reliable reports of earlier decisions.
- **Rules.** There must be rules for extracting a legal principle from a previous set of facts and applying it to current facts.
- **Classification.** Precedents must be classified into those that are **binding** and those which are merely **persuasive.**

1.3 Law reports

There are several major series of law reports bound as annual volumes. In addition, there are several electronic databases which include cases reported in the paper reports and other cases.

Every case has a title, usually (in a civil case) in the form *Carlill v Carbolic Smoke Ball Co.* This denotes Carlill (claimant) versus Carbolic Smoke Ball Co (defendant). In the event of an appeal, the **claimant's** name is still shown first, whether he is the **appellant** or the **respondent**. All judgements of the superior courts are given a 'uniform citation' to facilitate publication on the Internet. A House of Lords judgement will be referenced [year] UKHL [unique number].

Some cases are cited by reference to the **subject matter**. Thus case names have included *Re Barrow Haematite Steel Co* (a company case), *Re Adams and Kensington Vestry* (a trust case) and in shipping cases the name of the ship, for example, *The Wagon Mound*.

Some older cases may be referred to by a **single name**, for example *Pinnel's case.* In a full citation the title of the case is followed by abbreviated particulars of the volume of the law reports in which the case is reported, for example, *Best v Samuel Fox & Co Ltd 1952* 2 All ER 394 (the report is at p 394 of Vol. 2 of the All England Reports for 1952).

As regards content a **full law report** includes details of the following.

• Names of the parties	• Facts
• Court in which the case was decided	• Names of counsel and their arguments
• Judge or judges	• Verbatim text of the judgement
• Date of the hearing	• Order of the court
• Points of law established	• Whether leave to appeal was granted
• Earlier cases cited	• Solicitors
• Previous history of the litigation	• Reporting barrister

It is only decisions of the **higher courts** in important cases (the High Court, the Court of Appeal and the Judicial Committee of the House of Lords) which are included in the general law reports.

Students are often perplexed as to how much they are expected to memorise of cases referred to in textbooks. By far the most important aspect of a case for examination purposes is what it was about; that is, **the point of law which it illustrates or establishes**. This is the knowledge that you must apply when answering exam questions.

It is not generally necessary to recite the exact details of the events behind a case. However, knowing the facts of cases is helpful, not least because exam questions may well include scenarios in which the facts are based on a well-known case.

The doctrine of judicial precedent is designed to provide **consistency** in the law. Four things must be considered when examining a precedent before it can be applied to a case.

(a)   A decision must be based on a **proposition of law** before it can be considered as a precedent. It may **not** be a decision on a **question of fact**.

(b)   It must form part of the **ratio decidendi** of the case.

(c)   The **material facts** of each case must be comparable.

(d)   The preceding court must have had a **superior (or in some cases, equal) status** to the later court, such that its decisions are binding on the later court.

1.4 Ratio decidendi

FAST FORWARD

Statements made by judges can be classified as **ratio decidendi** or **obiter dicta**.

A judgement will start with a description of the facts of the case and probably a review of earlier precedents. The judge will then make **statements of law applicable to the legal problems** raised by the material facts which, **if used as the basis for the decision**, are **known as the ratio decidendi** of the case. This is the **vital element that binds future judges**.

Key term

'The **ratio decidendi** of a case is any rule of law expressly or impliedly treated by the judge as a necessary step in reaching his conclusion, having regard to the line of reasoning adopted by him, or a necessary part of his direction to the jury.'

(Cross: *Precedent in English Law*.)

Statements made by a judge are either classed as **ratio decidendi** or **obiter dicta**. There are two types of obiter dicta, (which means something said 'by the way').

- A judge's statements of **legal principle** that do not form the basis of the decision.
- A judge's statements that are not based on the material facts, but on **hypothetical facts**.

Key term

Obiter dicta are words in a judgement which are said 'by the way'.
They **do not** form part of the **ratio decidendi** and are not binding on future cases but merely persuasive.

It is not always easy to identify the **ratio decidendi**. In decisions of appeal courts, where there are three or even five separate judgements, the members of the court may reach the same conclusion but give different reasons. Many judges indicate in their speeches which comments are 'ratio' and which are 'obiter'.

1.5 Distinguishing the facts

Although there may arguably be a finite number of **legal principles** to consider when deciding a case, there is an infinite variety of facts which may be presented.

It is necessary to consider how far the facts of the previous and the latest case are similar. If the differences appear significant the court may **distinguish the earlier case on the facts** and thereby **avoid following it as a precedent**.

1.6 Status of the court

Not every decision made in every court is binding as a judicial precedent. The **court's status** has a significant effect on whether its decisions are binding, persuasive or disregarded. You may want to refer back to the court structure diagrams in Chapter 1 while you read the following table.

Court	Bound by	Decisions binding
Magistrates' Court	<ul><li>High Court</li><li>The Court of Appeal</li><li>House of Lords</li><li>European Court of Justice</li></ul>	<ul><li>No one</li><li>Not even itself</li></ul>
County Court	<ul><li>High Court</li><li>The Court of Appeal</li><li>House of Lords</li><li>European Court of Justice</li></ul>	<ul><li>No one</li><li>Not even itself</li></ul>
Crown Court	<ul><li>High Court (QBD)</li><li>The Court of Appeal</li><li>House of Lords</li><li>European Court of Justice</li></ul>	<ul><li>No one</li><li>However, its decisions are reported more widely and are more authoritative</li></ul>
The High Court consists of divisions: • **Queen's bench** • **Chancery** • **Family**	<ul><li>Judge sitting alone<ul><li>– The Divisional Court</li><li>– The Court of Appeal</li><li>– House of Lords</li><li>– European Court of Justice</li></ul></li></ul>	<ul><li>Judge sitting alone<ul><li>– Magistrates' court</li><li>– County Court</li><li>– Crown Court</li></ul></li></ul>
	<ul><li>Judges sitting together<ul><li>– Any Divisional Court</li><li>– The Court of Appeal</li><li>– House of Lords</li><li>– European Court of Justice</li></ul></li></ul>	<ul><li>Judges sitting together<ul><li>– Magistrates' Court</li><li>– County Court</li><li>– Crown Court</li><li>– Divisional Courts</li></ul></li></ul>
The Court of Appeal	<ul><li>Own decisions</li><li>House of Lords (subject to an exception below)</li><li>European Court of Justice</li></ul>	<ul><li>All inferior English courts</li><li>Itself (subject to the exception)</li></ul>
The House of Lords	<ul><li>Itself (except in exceptional cases)</li><li>European Court of Justice</li></ul>	<ul><li>All English Courts</li><li>Itself (except in exceptional cases)</li></ul>
The European Court of Justice	<ul><li>No one</li><li>Not even itself</li></ul>	<ul><li>All English Courts</li></ul>

1.7 Court of Appeal exception

In *Young v Bristol Aeroplane Co 1944,* it was decided that the **civil division** of the Court of Appeal is usually bound by its own decisions and those of the House of Lords, unless:

- Two of its previous decisions conflict, when it must decide which to follow
- The previous decision conflicts with a subsequent House of Lords decision
- The previous decision was made with a lack of care (*per incuriam*)

Exam focus point

It is particularly important that you know the position of the Court of Appeal and the House of Lords in this hierarchy.

Question

What do you think are the advantages of case law as a source of law?

Answer

The law is decided fairly and **predictably**, so that businessmen and individuals can regulate their conduct by reference to the law. The **risk** of mistakes in individual cases is reduced by the use of **precedents**. Case law can **adapt** to changing circumstances in society, since it arises directly out of the actions of society. Case law, having been developed in **practical** situations, is suitable for use in other practical situations.

1.8 Persuasive precedents

Apart from binding precedents, reported decisions of any court may be treated as **persuasive precedents**. Persuasive precedents may be, but need not be, followed in a later case.

A court of higher status is not only free to disregard the decision of a court of lower status, it may also deprive it of authority and expressly **overrule** it. Remember that this **does not reverse** the previous decision. Overruling a decision does not affect its outcome.

Point to note

> Where an earlier decision was made by a lower court, the judges can **overrule** that earlier decision if they disagree with the lower court's statement of the law. **The outcome of the earlier decision remains the same, but will not be followed in future**.
>
> If the decision of a lower court is appealed to a higher one, the higher court may **reverse** the decision if they feel the lower court has wrongly interpreted the law. **When a decision is reversed, the higher court is usually also overruling the lower court's statement of the law**.

Question

Decisions

The following definitions are types of court decision.

Match each of them to the correct term below.

(a)   A court higher up in the hierarchy overturns the decision of a lower court in the same case.
(b)   A principle laid down by a lower court is overturned by a higher court in a different, later case.
(c)   A judge states that the material facts of the case before him are sufficiently different from those of an earlier case as to enable the application of a different rule of law.
    (1)   Distinguishing
    (2)   Overruling
    (3)   Reversing

Answer

(a)   (3)   (b)   (2)   (c)   (1)

Reversing decisions occur when a case is appealed. Overruling occurs when a previous legal precedent is overturned.

If, in a case before the House of Lords, there is a **dispute about a point of European Union law** it must be referred to the European Court for a ruling. The European court does not create or follow precedents as such, and the provisions of EU directives should not be used to interpret UK legislation.

1.9 Avoidance of a binding precedent

Even if a precedent appears to be binding, there are **a number of grounds on which a court may decline to follow it**.

(a)   It may be able to distinguish the facts.

(b)   It may declare the ratio decidendi obscure, particularly when a Court of Appeal decision by three or five judges gives as many rationes.

(c)   It may declare the previous decision made per incuriam: without taking account of some essential point of law, such as an important precedent.

(d)   It may declare it to be in conflict with a fundamental principle of law; for example where a court has failed to apply the doctrine of privity of contract: *Beswick v Beswick 1968*.

(e)   It may declare an earlier precedent to be too wide. For example, the duty of care to third parties, created by *Donoghue v Stevenson 1932,* has since been considerably refined.

| Question | Binding precedent |

Fill in the following table, then check your answer to the table in Section 1.6.

Name of court	Binds	Bound by
Magistrates' court		
County Court		
Crown Court		
High Court (single judge)		
High Court (Divisional court)		
Court of Appeal		
House of Lords		
European Court of Justice		

1.10 The advantages and disadvantages of precedent

Many of the strengths of judicial precedent as the cornerstone of English law also indicate some of its weaknesses.

Factor	Advantage	Disadvantage
Certainty	The law is decided fairly and predictably Guidance given to judges and risk of mistake reduced.	Judges may sometimes be forced to make illogical distinctions to avoid an unfair result.
Clarity	Following the reasoning of ratio decidendi should lead to statements of general legal principles	Sometimes, judgements may appear to be inconsistent with each other or legal principles followed.
Flexibility	The system is able to change with changing circumstances	The system can limit judges' discretion.

Factor	Advantage	Disadvantage
Detail	Precedent states how the law applies to facts and should be flexible enough to allow for details to be different.	The detail produces a vast body of reports to take into account. Judges often distinguish on the facts to avoid a precedent.
Practicality	Case law is based on experience of actual cases brought before the courts. This is an advantage over legislation which can be found wanting when tested.	Unfair precedents may be created that allow wrongdoing to be perpetrated.

2 Legislation

FAST FORWARD

The second major source of law is **legislation**. This is also known as statute law and may take the form of **Acts of Parliament** or **delegated legislation** under the Acts.

Statute law is made by **Parliament** (or in exercise of law-making powers delegated by Parliament). Until the United Kingdom entered the European Community (now the EU) in 1973 the UK Parliament was completely **sovereign**.

In recent years however, UK membership of the European Union has restricted the previously unfettered power of Parliament. There is an **obligation**, imposed by the Treaty of Rome, **to bring UK law into line with the Treaty itself and with directives**. Regulations, having the force of law in every member state, may be made under provisions of the Treaty of Rome.

2.1 Parliamentary sovereignty

Parliamentary sovereignty gives rise to a number of consequences. Parliament may

- **Repeal** earlier statutes
- **Overrule** or modify case law developed in the courts, or
- **Make new law** on subjects which have not been regulated by law before.

In practice, Parliament usually follows certain **conventions** which limit its freedom.

- No Parliament can legislate so as to **prevent** a future Parliament changing the law.

- Judges have to **interpret** statute law and they may find a meaning in it which those who promoted the statute did not intend.

- The **validity** of an Act of Parliament cannot be questioned. However, judges may declare an Act to be **'incompatible'** with the European Convention on Human Rights (see Chapter 3).

Cheney v Conn 1968

The facts: The claimant objected to his tax assessment under the Finance Act 1964 because some of the tax collected was used to fund the manufacture of nuclear weapons. He alleged that this was contrary to the Geneva Conventions Act 1957 and in conflict with international law.

Decision: The 1964 Act gave clear authority to collect the taxes.

2.2 Types of legislation

In addition to making new law and altering existing law, Parliament may make the law clearer by passing a **codifying** statute putting case law on a statutory basis (such as the Sale of Goods Act 1979). It may also pass **consolidating** statutes that incorporate an original statute and its successive amendments into a single piece of legislation (such as the Employment Rights Act 1996 or the Companies Act 2006).

Legislation can also be **categorised** in the following ways:

- **Public Acts**; legislation that affects the **general public**
- **Private Acts**; legislation that affects **specific individuals and groups**
- **Enabling legislation that empowers a specific individual or body** to produce the detail required by a parent Act. See delegated legislation in Section 2.5.

2.3 Parliamentary procedure

A proposal for legislation can be brought by the government, a backbench MP, or a peer. A government bill may be aired in public in a **Government Green** or **White Paper**. A government bill may be introduced into either the House of Commons or the House of Lords. When it has passed through one House it must then go through the same stages in the other House.

In each House the successive stages of dealing with the Bill are as follows.

Stage 1   *First reading.* Publication and introduction into the agenda. No debate.

Stage 2   *Second reading.* Debate on the general merits of the Bill. No amendments at this stage.

Stage 3   *Committee stage.* The Bill is examined by a Standing Committee of about 20 members, representing the main parties and including some members at least who specialise in the relevant subject. If the Bill is very important all or part of the Committee Stage may be taken by the House as a whole sitting as a committee.

Stage 4   *Report stage.* The Bill as amended in committee is reported to the full House for approval.

Stage 5   *Third reading.* This is the final approval stage.

When it has passed through both Houses it is submitted for the **Royal Assent** which is given on the Queen's behalf by a committee of the Lord Chancellor and two other peers. It then becomes an Act of Parliament (statute) but it does not come into operation until a commencement date is notified by statutory instrument.

2.4 Advantages and disadvantages of statute law

Statute law has the following advantages and disadvantages:

(a) **Advantages**
   (i) The House of Commons is elected at intervals of not more than five years. Hence the law making process is theoretically **responsive** to public opinion.
   (ii) Statute law can in theory deal with **any** problem.
   (iii) Statutes are **carefully constructed** codes of law.
   (iv) A **new problem** in society or some **unwelcome development** in case law can be dealt with by passing an Act of Parliament.

(b) **Disadvantages**
   (i) Statutes are **bulky**.
   (ii) **Parliament** often **lacks time** to consider draft legislation in **sufficient detail**.
   (iii) A substantial statute can take up a lot of **Parliamentary time**.
   (iv) Statute law is a statement of general rules. **Those who draft it cannot anticipate every individual case** which may arise.

2.5 Delegated legislation

To save time in Parliament, Acts usually contain a section by which power is given to a minister, or public body such as a local authority, to make **subordinate or delegated legislation**.

> **Delegated legislation** means rules of law, often of a detailed nature, made by subordinate bodies to whom the power to do so has been given by statute.

Delegated legislation appears in various forms.

- Ministerial powers are exercised by **statutory instruments.** Statutory instruments are the most common form of delegated legislation.
- **Local authorities** are given statutory powers to make **bye-laws**.
- **Rules of Court** may be made by the judiciary to control court procedure.
- **Professional Regulations** concerning certain occupations (such as law) can be delegated to authorised bodies (such as the Law Society).
- **Orders in council** in certain circumstances, the government may resort to introducing legislation through the Privy Council as it circumvents the need to go through the full Parliamentary process. However this may reduce the popularity of the government and is likely to be used only in instances of national emergency.

2.5.1 Control over delegated legislation

Parliament exercises some **control** over delegated legislation by keeping the production of new delegated legislation under review.

- Some statutory instruments do not take effect until approved by **affirmative resolution** of Parliament.
- Most other statutory instruments must be **laid** before Parliament for 40 days before they take effect.

There are standing **Scrutiny Committees** of both Houses whose duty it is to examine statutory instruments from a technical point of view and may raise objections if necessary. However they have no authority to object to an instrument's nature or content.

A statutory instrument may be **challenged** in the courts on the grounds that Parliament exceeded its authority to delegate and has acted *ultra vires* or that the legislation has been made without due compliance with the correct procedure.

The **Human Rights Act (HRA)** does not give courts power to strike out primary legislation which is contrary to the HRA. However, as **secondary legislation**, delegated legislation is not affected and courts **are permitted** to **strike out** any delegated legislation that runs contrary to the HRA.

Both statutes and delegated legislation made under it are expressed in **general terms**. It is not possible to provide in the Act for each eventuality which falls within its remit. It therefore often falls to judges to interpret Acts.

2.5.2 Advantages and disadvantages

Delegated legislation has the following **advantages**:

- It **saves time** as Parliament does not have to examine matters of detail.
- Much of the content of delegated legislation is **technical** and is better worked out in consultation with professional, commercial or industrial groups outside Parliament.
- If new or altered regulations are required later, they can be **issued without referring** back to Parliament.
- The system allows the law to be enacted **quickly**.

The **disadvantages** of the system are as follows.

- There are concerns over the **accountability** of Parliament. Individual MPs and their civil service staff effectively become the source of law rather than Parliament whose actions are open to questioning and public scrutiny.
- The system is **unrepresentative** in that some power is given to civil servants who are not democratically elected.
- Because delegated legislation can be produced in large **volumes**, ordinary MPs and the public find it difficult to keep up to date with developments.
- The different sorts of delegated legislation which may be produced by virtue of one statute can greatly **confuse** users.

3 Statutory interpretation

FAST FORWARD

Legislation must be **interpreted correctly** before judges can **apply it fairly**. The **literal, golden** and **mischief rules** of interpretation developed over time. Nowadays a **purposive approach** is taken.

Judges are faced with task of **applying** legislation to the particular case heard before them. To apply the legislation they must first **interpret** and **understand** it. Problems occur when the judge has difficulty interpreting the statute.

There are a number of situations which might lead to a need for statutory interpretation.

(a) **Ambiguity** might be caused by an error in drafting or words may have a dual meaning.

(b) **Uncertainty** may arise where the words of a statute are intended to apply to a range of factual situations and the courts must decide whether the case before them falls into any of these situations.

(c) There may be **unforeseeable developments**.

(d) The draft may use a **broad term**. Thus, the word 'vehicle' may need to be considered in relation to the use of skateboards or bicycles.

There are a number of different sources of assistance for a judge in his task of statutory interpretation.

- Rules
- Presumptions
- Other aids (intrinsic or extrinsic)

3.1 Rules of statutory interpretation

In interpreting the words of a statute, courts have developed a number of well-established general rules.

3.1.1 The literal rule and golden rule

Key terms

> The **literal rule** means that words in the Act should be given their literal and grammatical meaning rather than what the judge thinks they mean. It is extended by the **golden rule** which states that word should be given their plain, ordinary or literal meaning unless this would give rise to manifest absurdity or inconsistency with the rest of the statute.

Normally a word should be construed in the **same literal sense** wherever it appears throughout the statute.

Illustration

In *Whitely v Chapell 1868* a statute aimed at preventing electoral malpractice made it an offence to impersonate 'any person entitled to vote' at an election. The accused was acquitted because he impersonated a dead person, who was clearly not entitled to vote.

3.1.2 The mischief rule

Key term

Under the **mischief rule** a judge considers what mischief the Act was intended to prevent. Where a statute is designed to remedy a weakness in the law, the correct interpretation is the one that which achieves it.

The 'golden' and 'mischief' rules were used until relatively recently. The **Law Commissioners** recommended that judges interpret statute using the *general purposes* behind it and the intentions of Parliament. This is known as **Purposive interpretation**.

3.1.3 The purposive approach

Key term

Under the **purposive approach** to statutory interpretation, the words of a statute are interpreted not only in their **ordinary**, **literal** and **grammatical** sense, but also with reference to the **context** and **purpose** of the legislation, ie what is the legislation trying to achieve?

This case shows how the court took account of the mischief or weakness which the statute was explicitly intended to remedy.

Gardiner v Sevenoaks RDC 1950

The facts: The purpose of an Act was to provide for the safe storage of film wherever it might be stored on 'premises'. The claimant argued that 'premises' did not include a cave and so the Act had no application to his case.

Decision: The purpose of the Act was to protect the safety of persons working in all places where film was stored. If film was stored in a cave, the word 'premises' included the cave.

The key to the purposive approach is that the judge construes the statute in such a way as to **be consistent with the purpose of the statute** as he understands it, even if the wording of the statute could be applied literally without leading to manifest absurdity.

Exam focus point

Human Rights Act 1998

UK courts are now required to interpret UK legislation in a way compatible with the human rights convention so far as it is possible to do so (see Chapter 3). This is an example of **purposive interpretation**.

3.1.4 The contextual rule

Key term

The **contextual rule** means that a word should be construed in its context: it is permissible to look at the statute as a whole to discover the meaning of a word in it.

A more purposive approach is also being taken because so many international and EU regulations come to be interpreted by the courts.

3.2 General rules of interpretation

The following general rules of interpretation have also been developed by the courts.

3.2.1 The eiusdem generis rule

Statutes often list a number of **specific things** and end the list with more general words. In that case the general words are to be limited in their meaning to other things of the same kind as the specific items which precede them.

> *Evans v Cross 1938*
>
> *The facts:* E was charged with driving his car in such a way as to 'ignore a traffic sign', having crossed to the wrong side of a white line. 'Traffic sign' was defined in the Act as 'all signals, warning signposts, direction posts, signs or other devices'.
>
> *Decision:* 'Other device' must be limited in its meaning to a category of such signs. A painted line was quite different from that category.

3.2.2 Expressio unius est exclusio alterius

To express one thing is by implication to **exclude anything else**.

3.2.3 Noscitur a socis

It is presumed that words draw meaning from the **other words around them**. If a statute mentioned 'children's books, children's toys and clothes', it would be reasonable to assume that 'clothes' meant children's clothes.

3.2.4 In pari materia

If the statute forms part of a series which deals with **similar** subject matter, the court may look to the interpretation of previous statutes on the assumption that Parliament intended the same thing.

3.3 Presumptions of statutory interpretation

Unless the statute contains express words to the contrary it is assumed that the following **presumptions** of statutory interpretation apply, each of which may be rebutted by contrary evidence.

- **A statute does not alter the existing common law**. If a statute is capable of two interpretations, one involving alteration of the common law and the other one not, the latter interpretation is to be preferred.
- **If a statute deprives a person of his property**, say by nationalisation, he is to be compensated for its value.
- **A statute is not intended to deprive a person of his liberty**. If it does so, clear words must be used. This is relevant in legislation covering, for example, mental health and immigration.
- **A statute does not have retrospective effect** to a date earlier than its becoming law.
- **A statute does not bind the Crown**. In certain areas, the Crown's potential liability is great and this is therefore an extremely important presumption.
- **A statute generally has effect only in the UK**. However a statute does not run counter to international law and should be interpreted so as to give effect to international obligations.
- **A statute cannot impose criminal liability** without proof of guilty intention. Many modern statutes rebut this presumption by imposing strict liability, say for dangerous driving under the Road Traffic Act.
- **A statute does not repeal other statutes**. Any point on which the statute leaves a gap or omission is outside the scope of the statute.

3.4 Other assistance in interpretation

Key terms

> **Intrinsic aids** are those words contained in the Queen's Printer's copy of the statute. **Extrinsic aids** are those found elsewhere.

3.4.1 The Interpretation Act 1987

The **Interpretation Act 1987** defines certain terms frequently found in legislation. The Act also states that, unless a specific intention to the contrary exists, the use in a statute of masculine gender terminology also includes the feminine, and vice versa. Similarly, words in the singular include plurals, and vice versa.

3.4.2 Intrinsic aids

Intrinsic aids to statutory interpretation consist of the following.

- The **long title** of an Act, which may give guidance as to the Act's general objective.
- The **preamble** of an Act often directs the judge as to its intentions and objects.
- **Interpretation sections** to Acts. Particularly long, complicated and wide-ranging Acts often contain self-explanations.
- **Side notes**. Statutes often have summary notes in the margin.

3.4.3 Extrinsic aids

Extrinsic aids include the following.

(a) Reports of the Law Commission, Royal Commissions, the Law Reform Committee and other official committees.

(b) Hansard, the official journal of UK Parliamentary debates. This follows a decision of the House of Lords in *Pepper v Hart 1992* where the House of Lords decided that it is acceptable to look at the original speech which first introduced a bill to ascertain its meaning, but only if the statute is ambiguous or obscure or its literal meaning would lead to absurdity.

Chapter Roundup

- The first legal source of law, consisting of decisions made in the courts, is **case law,** which is judge-made law based on the underlying principle of consistency. Once a legal principle is decided by an appropriate court it is a **judicial precedent**.

- Statements made by judges can be classified as **ratio decidendi** or **obiter dicta**.

- The second major source of law is **legislation**. This is also known as statute law and may take the form of **Acts of Parliament** or **delegated legislation** under the Acts.

- Legislation must be **interpreted correctly** before judges can **apply it fairly**. The **literal**, **golden** and **mischief rules** of interpretation developed over time. Nowadays a **purposive approach** is taken.

Quick Quiz

1   **Fill in the blanks** in the statements below, using the words in the box.

In order that (1) .... provides (2) .... in the law, a precedent must be carefully examined before it can be applied to a particular (3) .... It must be a statement of (4) .... The (5) .... must be identified. The (6) .... must be the same.

The (7) .... of the court which set the precedent must be such as to (8) .... the present court.

• bind	• judicial precedent
• case	• status
• ratio decidendi	• law
• material facts	• consistency

2   What is the final step in the life of a Bill?

3   Obiter dicta form part of the ratio decidendi.

True ☐

False ☐

4   Which of these decisions bind the Crown Court?

Decisions of the County Court ☐

Decisions of the High Court ☐

Decisions of the Court of Appeal ☐

Decisions of the House of Lords ☐

5   In 2008, Mr Justice Jeffries, a High Court judge sitting alone, is deciding a case which has similar material facts to one decided by the Court of Appeal in 1908. He can decline to be bound by this decision by showing that
   A   The status of the previous court cannot bind him
   B   The decision was taken too long ago to be of any relevance
   C   The decision does not accord with the rules of a statute passed in 1975
   D   The obiter dicta are obscure

6   Overruling a decision of a lower court affects the outcome of that earlier decision.

True ☐

False ☐

7   **Fill in the blank** in the statement below.

The rule that a statute should be construed to give effect to the intended outcome of the legislation is known as the .... rule.

Answers to Quick Quiz

1   (1) judicial precedent (2) consistency (3) case (4) law (5) ratio decidendi (6) material facts (7) status (8) bind

2   The third reading (the final approval stage).

3   False. Obiter dicta do not form part of the ratio decidendi.

4   Decisions of the High Court, Court of Appeal and House of Lords.

5   C. A High Court judge is bound by decisions of the Court of Appeal. However, he can decline to be bound if it conflicts with a principle of law. In this case the 1975 statute has effectively overruled the previous decision.

6   False. The decision in that case will stand.

7   Purposive rule.

Now try the questions below from the Exam Question Bank

Number	Level	Marks	Time
Q2	Examination	10	18 mins

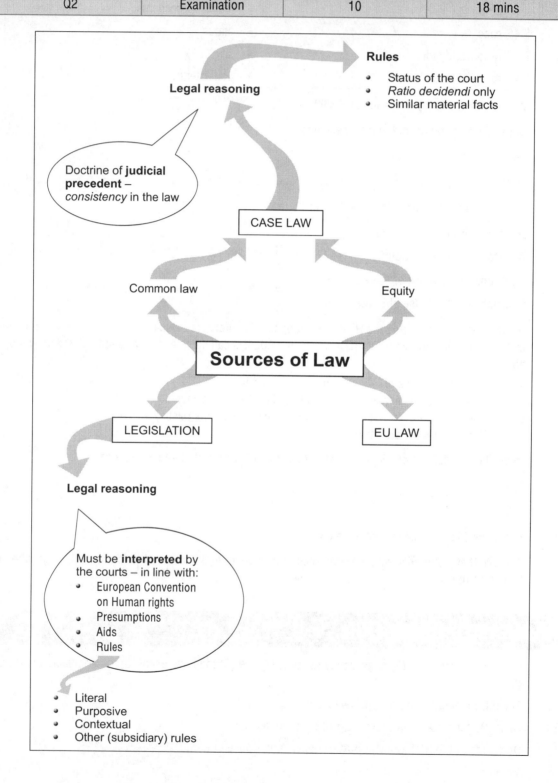

Rules

- Status of the court
- *Ratio decidendi* only
- Similar material facts

Legal reasoning

Doctrine of **judicial precedent** – *consistency* in the law

CASE LAW

Common law

Equity

Sources of Law

LEGISLATION

EU LAW

Legal reasoning

Must be **interpreted** by the courts – in line with:
- European Convention on Human rights
- Presumptions
- Aids
- Rules

- Literal
- Purposive
- Contextual
- Other (subsidiary) rules

Human rights

Topic list	Syllabus reference
1 The European Convention on Human Rights	A3(a)
2 The Human Rights Act 1998	A3(a)
3 Convention rights	A3(a)
4 The impact of the Act	A3(b), A3(c)

Introduction

Human Rights is a highly **topical** subject at the moment.

The Human Rights Act 1998 was effective from October 2000. Case law is still in its relatively **early days**, so you must read the press and keep up to date with developments in this area of law.

We start the chapter by introducing the **European Convention of Human Rights** and discuss the objectives of the Human Rights Act. The Convention sets out certain Human Rights that all nations who have agreed to be **bound** by the convention must respect. Individuals have the right to take a case to the **European Court of Human Rights** should they allege their rights have been violated.

Study guide

		Intellectual level
(A)	**Essential elements of the legal system**	
3	Human rights	
(a)	Identify the concept of human rights as expressed in the Human Rights Act 1998.	2
(b)	Explain the impact of human rights law on statutory interpretation	2
(c)	Explain the impact of human rights law on the common law	2

Exam guide

This is a topical and important area of your studies. You must be able to explain the rights given to individuals and the impact the act has on statutory interpretation and the common law.

The examiner has yet to set questions on the case law in this area, but read all of them incase they are examined in future.

1 The European Convention on Human Rights

FAST FORWARD

The **Human Rights Act 1998** came into effect on 2 October 2000 and is a key example of the influence of International law in the United Kingdom.

The Act incorporates the **'European Convention for the Protection of Human Rights and Fundamental Freedoms'** (more commonly referred to as the 'European Convention on Human Rights') into UK domestic law.

The **European Convention on Human Rights** is an agreement on basic human rights, put together by major powers in the wake of the human rights abuses that occurred during World War Two and signed by those powers, including the United Kingdom, in 1951.

During the second half of the **twentieth century**, the European Convention on Human Rights was used as a **guideline** in the English courts. It was widely believed that UK political and legal institutions were well suited to the protection of **fundamental human rights** and that incorporation of the Convention into English law was not necessary. However, any individual who felt his rights had been violated could take a case to the **European Court of Human Rights** in Strasbourg.

Towards the end of the 1990s, it became clear that the **British government** was of the opinion that it was **not sufficient** to rely on existing law to ensure protection of human rights. The **Human Rights Act** was developed as a means of ensuring that these fundamental rights were enshrined in the English legal system. English courts now have a statutory duty to ensure that English laws are interpreted 'as far as possible' in a manner which is compatible with the **convention rights** incorporated by the Human Rights Act.

Thus an individual can ask the UK courts to consider his **convention rights**, instead of taking their case to Strasbourg. However the ECHR remains the final **appeal court** for human rights issues.

2 The Human Rights Act 1998

FAST FORWARD

The **Human Rights Act 1998** incorporates the European Convention on Human Rights (ECHR) into UK domestic law.

The impact of the legislation is **pervasive** in many areas of UK law.

The HRA has the **potential** to affect many different areas of law. You should be aware of its provisions so that you can see the potential impacts throughout the Corporate and Business law syllabus.

This text will highlight some of the **early cases** and some areas which might be affected by the HRA. You should ensure that your knowledge of the **Convention** is sufficient that you can understand the **impacts** which are pointed out, and identify further impacts if required.

The Act binds **public authorities** (defined as bodies undertaking functions of a public nature). These include government departments, local authorities, courts and schools. These public authorities must not breach (or derogate) an **individual's rights**. In the case of proceedings against a public authority, there is a limitation period of one year from the date on which the act complained of is alleged to have occurred.

The **rights** outlined below can be relied upon by any **individual** or **non-government organisation** including **companies**. However, where rights have been derogated, the public authority can mitigate its actions by demonstrating a **legitimate** need to derogate and that the derogation was **proportionate** to the need.

3 Convention rights

FAST FORWARD

The Human Rights Act protects a number of **Convention rights**.

3.1 Articles

We set out the gist of the most relevant articles.

THE ARTICLES

Article 2 Right to life

1   Everyone's right to life shall be protected by law. No one shall be deprived of his life intentionally, unless by the carrying out of the death penalty in a country where this is allowed by law.

Article 5 Right to liberty and security

1   Everyone has the right to liberty and security of person. No one shall be deprived of his liberty save in the following cases and in accordance with a procedure prescribed by law:

(a)   The lawful detention of a person after conviction by a competent court;

(b)   The lawful arrest or detention of a person for non-compliance with the lawful order of a court or in order to secure the fulfilment of any obligation prescribed by law;

(c)   The lawful arrest or detention of a person reasonably suspected of having committed an offence or being liable to do so.

(d)   The detention of a minor by lawful order for the purpose of educational supervision or for the purpose of bringing him before the competent legal authority;

(e)   The lawful detention of persons for the prevention of the spreading of infectious diseases, of persons of unsound mind, alcoholics or drug addicts or vagrants;

(f)   The lawful arrest or detention of a person to prevent his effecting an unauthorised entry into the country or of a person against whom action is being taken with a view to deportation or extradition.

2   Everyone who is arrested shall be informed promptly, in a language which he understands, of the reasons for his arrest and of any charge against him.

3   Everyone arrested or detained shall be promptly brought before a judge and is entitled to a trial within a reasonable time.

Article 6 Right to a fair trial

1   Everyone is entitled to fair and public hearing within a reasonable time by an independent and impartial tribunal established by law. Any judgement should be publicly pronounced unless that constitutes a security risk.

2   Everyone charged with a criminal offence should be presumed innocent until proven guilty according to law.

3   Everyone charged with a criminal offence has the following minimum rights:

   (a)   To be informed promptly, in a language which he understands and in detail, of the nature and cause of the accusation against him;

   (b)   To have adequate time and facilities for the preparation of his defence;

   (c)   To defend himself in person or through legal assistance;

   (d)   To examine or have examined witnesses against him;

   (e)   To have the free assistance of an interpreter if he cannot understand or speak the language used in court.

Article 7 No punishment without law

No one can be found guilty of an act which was not a crime at the time it was committed.

Article 8 Right to respect for private and family life

Everyone has a right to respect for his private and family life, his home and his correspondence.

Article 9 Freedom of thought, conscience and religion

Everyone has the right to freedom of thought, conscience and religion; this right includes freedom to change his religion or belief and freedom, either alone or in community with others and in public or private, to manifest his religion or belief, in worship, teaching, practice and observance.

Article 10 Freedom of expression

Everyone has the right to freedom of expression, including the freedom to hold opinions and to receive and impart information and ideas without interference by public authority and regardless of frontiers.

Article 11 Freedom of assembly and association

Everyone has the right to freedom and peaceful assembly and to freedom of association with others including the right to form and to join trade unions for the protection of his interests.

Article 12 Right to marry

Men and women of marriageable age have the right to marry and to found a family, according to the national laws governing the exercise of this right.

Article 14 Prohibition of discrimination

There should be no discrimination on any ground such as sex, race, colour, language, religion, political or other opinion, national or social origin, association with a national minority, property, birth or other status.

The rights under the Act fall into three categories.

(a)   **Absolute rights** cannot be restricted in any circumstances, even in times of war or public emergency. They are **inalienable**.

(b)   **Derogable rights** may be derogated by the government. This means that the government may opt out of particular rights (although not simply for reasons of public interest).

(c)   **Qualified rights** are those which are subject to restriction in order to take the public interest into account (for example in areas of public safety or the prevention of disorder and crime).

3.2 Protocols

The Convention also contains a number of **protocols**, which supplement the Convention.

PROTOCOLS

Part II – The First Protocol

Article 1 Protection of property

Every natural or legal person is entitled to the peaceful enjoyment of his possessions. No one shall be deprived of his possessions except in the public interest and subject to the conditions provided for by law and by the general principles of international law.

Article 2 Right to education

No person shall be denied the right to education. The State shall respect the right of parents to ensure such education and teaching in conformity with their own religious and philosophical convictions.

Article 3 Right to free elections

The High Contracting Parties undertake to hold free elections at reasonable intervals by secret ballot.

Part III – The Sixth Protocol

Article 1 Abolition of the death penalty

The death penalty shall be abolished. No one shall be condemned to such a penalty or executed.

---

4 The impact of the Act

FAST FORWARD The Act has had an impact on **new legislation**, **statutory interpretation** and the **common law**.

This Study Text highlights areas of **potential impact** in relevant later chapters. Some ideas of where the legislation could impact on the rest of UK law are summarised here.

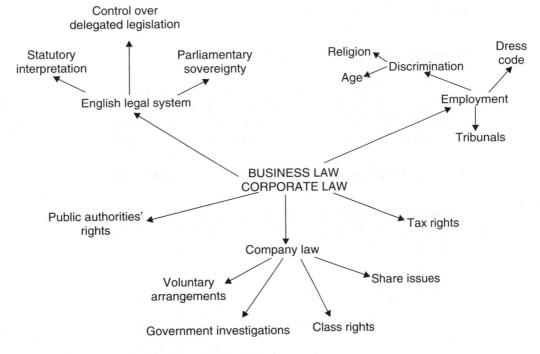

The impact of the Act can be considered in the following areas:

- Impact on **new legislation**
- Impact on **statutory interpretation**
- Impact on the **common law**

4.1 Impact on new legislation

Section 19 of the HRA requires the person **responsible** for a Bill to make a **statement of compatibility** with the Convention before the Bill's second reading. Where a Bill is **incompatible** with the convention, a statement to that effect can be made should the government wish to continue with the Bill anyway.

We saw in Chapter 2 how the Act may affect primary and secondary legislation through the courts and how courts can **strike out secondary legislation** that is contrary to the act. However, courts **do not** have this power where primary legislation is concerned, but they can issue a declaration of incompatibility should they desire *(Bellinger V Bellinger 2003)*.

4.2 Impact on statutory interpretation

Under section 3 of the HRA **UK courts are required to interpret UK law in a way compatible with the Convention** so far as it is possible to do so.

Existing legislation must therefore be **interpreted** in a way which is **compatible** with **convention rights**. This means that courts must take into account **decisions** and **judgements** of the European Court of Human Rights when hearing a case.

Where legislation can be interpreted in two ways, one **compatible** with the Convention and one that is **incompatible**, courts must follow the interpretation that is compatible. However, if a court feels that legislation is incompatible with the Convention and that it cannot interpret it in such a way to make it compatible, it may make a **declaration of incompatibility**. You should note that such a declaration **does not** make the legislation invalid, however it is up to the legislator to **remedy** the situation which can be **fast-tracked** by a procedure provided for in section 10 of the act.

> *Bellinger v Bellinger 2003*
>
> *The facts:* The House of Lords had to consider whether or not a male to female transsexual could be treated as a female under the Matrimonial Causes Act 1973.
>
> *Decision:* The court was unable to interpret the act to allow the transsexual to be considered female. It did however issue a declaration of incompatibility.

4.3 Impact on the common law

We have seen above that **UK courts** must take into account the **judgements** and **decisions** of the ECHR when interpreting UK law, however section 2 of the HRA goes further and requires UK courts to take into account the **case law** of the European Court of Justice when making judgements. This greatly impacts the **doctrine of precedent** as it permits the **overruling** of English law where it **conflicts** with the ECHR.

4.4 Recent cases decided under the Human Rights Act

Exam focus point

> There has been limited case law to date in this area of law, therefore you should focus on high profile cases relating to the Act and you should watch for new cases in the press.

4.4.1 Proportionality case

We saw in Section 2 that the government can **derogate** rights under the HRA if they have a **legitimate** reason, and that the action is **proportionate**.

Brown v Stott 2001

The facts: Police were called to a shop where B was suspected of having stolen a bottle of gin. They believed her to be drunk and asked her how she had got to the shop. B said she had driven there. She was breathalysed and the test proved to be positive. B was charged with the offence of driving a car after consuming excessive alcohol. The prosecution intended to rely on B's admission at the trial. B contended that the use of this admission would infringe her right to a fair hearing under the Human Rights Act.

Decision: The use of this admission did not infringe the defendant's right to free trial. It is in the public interest that road traffic laws be upheld, and this means that it is reasonable to identify who was driving and therefore who committed the offence.

4.4.2 Interpretation case

In Section 4.2 we noted that UK courts have a **duty** to interpret legislation in line with the ECHR.

Ghaidan v Godin-Mendozat 2004

The facts: Under the Rent Act 1977, statutory tenancies could only be inherited by either the husband or wife of the deceased. As same-sex partners were not considered to be husband or wife , they were prevented from inheriting such a tenancy. This was the position held by a previous case *Fitzpatrick v Sterling Housing Association Ltd 1999.*

Decision: The House of Lords considered the Act incompatible with article 14 of the convention (prohibition of discrimination). The problem was rectified by reasoning that the Act could be interpreted including those 'as if they were his or her husband' therefore including same-sex partners within the scope of the Act.

4.4.3 Dignity of life cases

In recent years the debate over **dignity of life** and **assisted suicide** have gained much popular and media support, however the courts in the UK have not yet fully supported the argument.

Pretty v DPP 2001

The facts: The terminally ill applicant wished her husband to assist her to commit suicide at a time and in a manner of her choosing. The husband would be liable to prosecution under s2(1) Suicide Act 1961, which makes it an offence to aid, abet, counsel or procure the suicide of another. The applicant sought an undertaking from the DPP that her husband would not be prosecuted, since the offence was inconsistent with her right to life under the Convention. The DPP gave no such undertaking and the applicant contended that her rights under various Articles of the Convention, including articles 2 and 3, were being infringed.

Decision: The right to the dignity of life was not a right to die with dignity but the right to live with as much dignity as possible until that life reached its natural end. The 1961 Act was not incompatible with the claimant's convention rights.

The **impact** of the Act will not be **fully known** until it has been further tested in the courts. For example, it is not clear exactly what is meant by the right of **'respect for private and family life'** or the **'right to a fair trial'**. In addition, the question of conflict between the right to respect for private and family life and the right of **'freedom of expression'** has been pointed out by many commentators.

NHS Trust A v M 2001

The facts: A hospital trust wanted to withdraw artificial nutrition and hydration from a patient in a permanent vegetative state. The court was asked to consider whether stopping such treatment would contravene the right to life under the Human Rights Act 1998. The main questions at issue were:

(a)   Does stopping treatment constitute a deliberate deprivation of life?

(b)   If not, does that article of the Convention impose a positive obligation to provide life sustaining treatment?

(c)   If treatment can be withdrawn, would the prohibition on inhumane and degrading treatment be breached during the period between the withdrawal of treatment and the patient's death? Alternatively could that article be invoked to ensure protection of the right of a patient in a permanent vegetative state to die with dignity?

Decision:

(a)   The phrase 'deprivation of life' implies a deliberate act, as opposed to an omission, by someone acting on behalf of the state which resulted in death. A decision to discontinue treatment which is no longer in the best interests of the patient and would therefore be a violation of his autonomy, is not deprivation of life. This is the case even though that discontinuance would have the effect of shortening his life.

(b)   The article does not impose an obligation to provide life sustaining treatment.

(c)   The article on the prohibition on inhumane and degrading treatment requires the victim to be aware of the treatment, which in this case he wasn't.

It was in the best interests of the patient to withdraw treatment and therefore lawful for the trust to do so.

Question

The European Convention on Human Rights sets out a number of rights available to individuals.

Think about how the above cases and those currently in the media relate to those rights and the reasoning behind the judgements.

Chapter Roundup

- The **Human Rights Act 1998** came into effect on 2 October 2000 and is a key example of the influence of International law in the United Kingdom

- The **Human Rights Act 1998** incorporates the European Convention on Human Rights (ECHR) into UK domestic law.

- The impact of the legislation is **pervasive** in many areas of UK law.

- The Human Rights Act protects a number of **Convention rights**.

- The Act has an impact **on new legislation**, **statutory interpretation** and the **common law**.

Quick Quiz

1   What is the right of appeal from the European Court of Human Rights?

2   Give an example of a dignity of life case.

3   List the three categories of right protected by the HRA.

   (1)   ....
   (2)   ....
   (3)   ....

4   **Fill in the blanks** in the statement below.

   Those responsible for introducing new legislation into the UK must make a .... of .... with the European Convention on Human Rights.

5   UK Courts must interpret legislation in a way that is compatible with the ECHR.

   True   ☐
   False ☐

Answers to Quick Quiz

1   There is no right of further appeal

2   *Pretty v DPP 2001*

3   (1)   Absolute
    (2)   Derogable
    (3)   Qualified

4   **Statement** of **compatibility**. Those introducing new legislation must make a statement that it is compatible with the ECHR.

5   True. UK courts must interpret legislation in a way that is compatible with the ECHR and where there are two possible interpretations, and one is incompatible, they must choose the one that is compatible with the convention.

Now try the question below from the Exam Question Bank

Number	Level	Marks	Time
Q3	Introductory	10	18 mins

The law of obligations

Formation of contracts I

Topic list	Syllabus reference
1 Definition of contract	B1(a)
2 Factors affecting the modern contract	B1(a)
3 The essentials of a contract	B1(a)
4 Form of a contract	B1(a)
5 Offer	B1(b)
6 Termination of offer	B1(b)
7 Acceptance	B1(c)
8 Communication of acceptance	B1(c)
9 Agreement without offer or acceptance	B1(b), B1(c)

Introduction

We begin our study of **the Law of Obligations** by considering Contract Law.

Individuals and businesses form contracts all the time. Despite what many people believe, contracts **do not** all need to be written and signed documents, indeed many valid contracts involve no written or spoken communication at all – for example where a person buys something from a shop.

This chapter **describes** what a contract is, **the essential elements** that make up a contract and the various forms contracts may take.

It continues by analysing the first requirement for a valid contract – **agreement**, which consists of an **offer** and **acceptance** of the offer.

You must be able to **distinguish offers** from **invitations to treat** and to explain what the consequences of acceptance are. The rules concerning when offers can be **terminated** and how acceptance should be communicated are vital knowledge since exam questions may require you to use them to determine whether or not a valid contract exits.

Study guide

		Intellectual level
(B)	**The law of obligations**	
1	Formation of contract	
(a)	Analyse the nature of a simple contract	2
(b)	Explain the meaning of offer and distinguish it from invitations to treat	2
(c)	Explain the meaning and consequence of acceptance	2

Exam guide

Questions may require you to identify whether a valid contract exists, so it is important to understand the circumstances where valid offers are made and where acceptance is communicated acceptably.

1 Definition of contract

FAST FORWARD

> A **valid contract is a legally binding agreement**, formed by the mutual consent of two parties.

Key term

> A **contract** may be defined as an **agreement which legally binds the parties.** The underlying theory is that a contract is the outcome of 'consenting minds'. However, parties are judged by what they have said, written or done, rather then by what they were actually thinking.

2 Factors affecting the modern contract

FAST FORWARD

> The law seeks to protect the idea of 'freedom of contract', although **contractual terms** may be regulated by **statute**, particularly where the parties are of unequal bargaining strength.

2.1 Inequality of bargaining power

Where two parties make an agreement, they invariably have differing levels of **bargaining power**. Many contracts are made between experts and ordinary consumers. The law will intervene **only** where the former takes unfair advantage of his position and not simply because one party was in an inferior bargaining position. **Freedom of contract** is a term sometimes used and can be defined as follows.

> 'The principle that parties are completely unrestricted in deciding whether or not to enter into an agreement and, if they do so, upon the terms governing that relationship. In practice, this is not always the case because one may be in a much stronger economic position, and legislation has been introduced in order to redress the balance.'

2.2 The standard form contract

Mass production and nationalisation have led to the **standard form contract**.

Key term

> The **standard form contract** is a document prepared by many large organisations setting out the terms on which they contract with their customers. The individual must usually take it or leave it. For example, a customer has to accept his supply of electricity on the electricity board's terms – he is not likely to succeed in negotiating special terms, unless he represents a large consumer such as a factory.

2.3 Consumer protection

In the second half of the twentieth century, there was a surge of interest in consumer matters. The development of a mass market for complex goods meant that the consumer can no longer rely on his own judgement when buying sophisticated goods or services. Consumer interests are now served by two main areas.

(a)   **Consumer protection agencies**, which include government departments (the Office of Fair Trading) and independent bodies (the Consumers' Association).

(b)   **Legislation**.

Public policy sometimes requires that the freedom of contract should be modified. For example, the **Consumer Credit Act 1974** and the **Unfair Contract Terms Act 1977** both regulate the extent to which contracts can contain certain terms.

Exam focus point

Contract law questions commonly take the form of scenarios that require you to advise one or all of the parties of the legal position in a dispute.

2.4 The electronic contract

English law has been concerned with formulating the rules for oral and written contracts for centuries, and cases decided in the 1800s continue to be valid today. As you will see, there are a number of **important rules** which deal with the timing of the sending and receipt of letters by post. With the advent of **telex** and **fax machines**, the law has had to be applied to new situations. Now the development of the internet for commercial purposes has brought new challenges as new ways of doing business come into being. We look at electronic contracts further in the next chapter.

3 The essentials of a contract

FAST FORWARD

The **three essential elements** of a contract are **offer and acceptance**, **consideration** and **intention to enter into legal relations**.

The courts will usually look for evidence of **three essential elements** in any contract.

- There must be an **agreement** usually made by **offer and acceptance**.
- There must be a bargain by which the obligations assumed by one party are supported by **consideration** (value) given by the other.
- The parties must have an **intention to create legal relations** between themselves.

In this chapter we will consider the first element – offer and acceptance. Consideration and intention will be explored in the next chapter.

3.1 Validity factors

Even if these essential elements can be shown, a contract may not necessarily be valid or may only be partially valid. The validity of a contract may also be affected by any of the following factors.

- **Capacity**. Some persons have restricted capacity to enter into contracts.

  Minors cannot enter into contracts for goods other than necessities, nor do they have the capacity to contract for loans.

  Those who lack **mental capacity** or who were **intoxicated** can avoid contracts if they can show they did not understand the nature of their actions and the other party ought to have known about their disability. They still must pay a reasonable price for the goods received.

- **Form**. Some contracts must be made in a particular form.

- **Content**. In general the parties may enter into a contract on whatever terms they choose. Some terms which the parties do not express may be **implied**, and some terms which the parties do express are **overridden** by statutory rules.

- **Genuine consent**. A mistake or misrepresentation made by one party may affect the validity of a contract. Parties may be induced to enter into a contract by **undue influence** or **duress**.

- **Legality**. The courts will not enforce a contract which is deemed to be illegal or contrary to public policy.

Question	Essentials of a binding contract

What are the essential elements of a binding contract?

Answer

There must be an intention to create legal relations. There must be an agreement made by offer and acceptance. There must be consideration.

A contract which does not satisfy the relevant tests may be either **void, voidable** or **unenforceable**.

Key terms

> A **void contract** is not a contract at all. The parties are not bound by it and if they transfer property under it they can sometimes recover their goods even from a third party.
>
> A **voidable contract** is a contract which one party may set aside. Property transferred before avoidance is usually irrecoverable from a third party.
>
> An **unenforceable contract** is a valid contract and property transferred under it cannot be recovered even from the other party to the contract. But if either party refuses to perform or to complete their part of the performance of the contract, the other party cannot compel them to do so. A contract is usually unenforceable when the required evidence of its terms, for example, written evidence of a contract relating to land, is not available.

4 Form of a contract

FAST FORWARD

> As a general rule, **a contract may be made in any form**. It may be **written**, or **oral**, or **inferred** from the conduct of the parties

As a general rule, **a contract may be made in any form**. It may be **written**, or **oral**, or **inferred** from the conduct of the parties. For example, a customer in a self-service shop may take his selected goods to the cash desk, pay for them and walk out without saying a word.

Writing is not usually necessary except in the following circumstances.

- Some contracts must be by **deed.**
- Some contracts must be in **writing.**
- Some contracts must be **evidenced in writing.**

4.1 Contracts by deed

A contract by deed must be in **writing** and it must be **signed**. Delivery must take place. Delivery is conduct indicating that the person executing the deed intends to be bound by it.

These contracts must be by deed.

- **Leases** for three years or more

- A **conveyance** or transfer of a legal estate in land (including a mortgage)
- A promise **not** supported by **consideration** (such as a **covenant** for example a promise to pay a regular sum to a charity)

4.2 Contracts which must be in writing

Some types of contract are required to be in the form of a written document, usually signed by at least one of the parties.

These contracts must be in writing.

- A **transfer of shares** in a limited company
- The sale or disposition of an **interest in land**
- **Bills of exchange** and **cheques**
- **Consumer credit** contracts

A contract for the sale or disposition of land promises to transfer title at a future date and must be in writing. The conveyance or transfer must be by deed and will therefore also be in writing.

In the case of consumer credit transactions, the effect of failure to make the agreement in the prescribed form is to make the agreement unenforceable against the debtor unless the creditor obtains a court order.

4.3 Contracts which must be evidenced in writing

Certain contracts may be made orally, but are not enforceable in a court of law unless there is written evidence of their terms. The most important contract of this type is the contract of **guarantee**.

5 Offer

FAST FORWARD

The first essential element in the formation of a binding contract is **agreement**. This is usually evidenced by **offer and acceptance**. An offer is a definite promise to be bound on specific terms, and must be distinguished from the mere **supply of information** and from an **invitation to treat**.

Key term

An **offer** is a **definite promise to be bound on specific terms** and may be defined as follows.

'An express or implied statement of the terms on which the maker is prepared to be contractually bound if it is accepted unconditionally. The offer may be made to one person, to a class of persons or to the world at large, and only the person or one of the persons to whom it is made may accept it.'

A definite offer does not have to be made to a particular person. It may be made to a class of persons or to the world at large.

Exam focus point

The case below is very important in the law of contract. Learn it before you learn any others.

Carlill v Carbolic Smoke Ball Co 1893

The facts: The manufacturers of a patent medicine published an advertisement by which they undertook to pay '£100 reward .... to any person who contracts .... influenza .... after having used the smoke ball three times daily for two weeks'. The advertisement added that £1,000 had been deposited at a bank 'showing our sincerity in this matter'. The claimant read the advertisement, purchased the smoke ball and used it as directed. She contracted influenza and claimed her £100 reward. In their defence the manufacturers argued against this.

(a) The offer was so vague that it could not form the basis of a contract, as no time limit was specified.

(b) It was not an offer which could be accepted since it was offered to the whole world.

Decision: The court disagreed.

(a) The smoke ball must protect the user during the period of use – the offer was not vague.

(b) Such an offer was possible, as it could be compared to reward cases.

You should note that Carlill is an unusual case in that advertisements are not usually regarded as offers, as you will see shortly.

A statement which is vague cannot be an offer but an apparently vague offer can be made certain by reference to previous dealing or customs.

Gunthing v Lynn 1831

The facts: The offeror offered to pay a further sum for a horse if it was 'lucky'.

Decision: The offer was too vague and no contract could be formed.

Hillas & Co Ltd v Arcos Ltd 1932

The facts: The claimants agreed to purchase from the defendants '22,000 standards of softwood goods of fair specification over the season 1930'. The agreement contained an option to buy a further 100,000 standards in 1931, without terms as to the kind or size of timber being specified. The 1930 transaction took place, but the sellers refused to supply any wood in 1931, saying that the agreement was too vague.

Decision: The missing terms of the agreement could be ascertained by reference to the previous transactions.

An offer must be distinguished from a statement which supplies of information, from a statement of intention and from an invitation to treat.

5.1 Supply of information

Only an offer in the proper sense may be accepted so as to form a binding contract. A statement which sets out possible terms of a contract is not an offer unless this is clearly indicated.

Harvey v Facey 1893

The facts: The claimant telegraphed to the defendant 'Will you sell us Bumper Hall Pen? Telegraph lowest cash price'. The defendant telegraphed in reply 'Lowest price for Bumper Hall Pen, £900'. The claimant telegraphed to accept what he regarded as an offer; the defendant made no further reply.

Decision: The defendant's telegram was merely a statement of his minimum price if a sale were to be agreed. It was not an offer which the claimant could accept.

If in the course of negotiations for a sale, the vendor states the price at which he will sell, that statement may be an offer which can be accepted.

Bigg v Boyd Gibbons 1971

The facts: In the course of correspondence the defendant rejected an offer of £20,000 by the claimant and added 'for a quick sale I would accept £26,000 .... if you are not interested in this price would you please let me know immediately'. The claimant accepted this price of £26,000 and the defendant acknowledged his acceptance.

Decision: In this context the defendant must be treated as making an offer which the claimant had accepted.

Reference to a more detailed document will not necessarily prevent a statement from being an offer.

> *Bowerman and Another v Association of British Travel Agents Ltd 1996*
>
> *The facts*: The case arose out of the insolvency in 1991 of a tour operator through whom a school party had booked a holiday. The party claimed a full refund under the ABTA scheme of protection. The ABTA scheme did not extend to one item, namely the holiday insurance premium and this was explained in ABTA's detailed handbook. The claimant argued that the 'ABTA promise' (to refund holiday expenses, widely advertised in the press) constituted an offer to the public at large, and that offer was accepted when the holiday was booked with the relevant tour operator.
>
> *Decision*: The public had been encouraged by ABTA to read the written 'ABTA promise' as creating a legally binding obligation to reimburse all the expenses of the holiday.

5.2 A statement of intention

Advertising that an event such as an auction will take place is not an offer to sell. Potential buyers may not sue the auctioneer if the auction does not take place: *Harris v Nickerson 1873*. This is an example of a statement of intention which is not actionable.

5.3 An invitation to treat

Where a party is initiating negotiations he is said to have made an invitation to treat. An **invitation to treat** cannot be accepted to form a binding contract. Examples of invitations to treat include.

- **Auction** sales
- **Advertisements** (for example, price lists or newspaper advertisements)
- **Exhibition** of goods for sale
- An **invitation** for tenders

Key term

> An **invitation to treat** can be defined as follows.
>
> 'An indication that a person is prepared to receive offers with a view to entering into a binding contract, for example, an advertisement of goods for sale or a company prospectus inviting offers for shares. It must be distinguished from an offer which requires only acceptance to conclude the contract.'
>
> (Note that on the facts of a particular case, advertisements etc may be construed as an offer: the Carlill case is an example. However, in most exam questions, advertisements are invitations to treat: read the facts of the question carefully.)

5.3.1 Auction sales

The bid itself is the offer, which the auctioneer is free to accept or reject: *Payne v Cave 1789*. An auction is defined as a contract for the sale of property under which offers are made by bidders stating the price at which they are prepared to buy and acceptance takes place by the fall of the auctioneer's hammer. Where an auction is stated to be 'without reserve' the auctioneer is offering goods for sale and the bid is the acceptance *Barry v Davies 2000*. A reserve is a specified minimum price.

5.3.2 Advertisements

An advertisement of goods for sale is usually an attempt to induce offers.

> *Partridge v Crittenden 1968*
>
> *The facts:* Mr Partridge placed an advertisement for 'Bramblefinch cocks, bramblefinch hens, 25s each'. The RSPCA brought a prosecution against him for offering for sale a brambling in contravention of the Protection of Birds Act 1954. The justices convicted Partridge and he appealed.

Decision: The conviction was quashed. Although there had been a sale in contravention of the Act, the prosecution could not rely on the offence of 'offering for sale', as the advertisement only constituted an invitation to treat.

The circulation of a price list is also an invitation to treat: *Grainger v Gough 1896,* where it was noted:

'The transmission of such a price-list does not amount to an offer.... If it were so, the merchant might find himself involved in any number of contractual obligations to supply wine of a particular description which he would be quite unable to carry out, his stock of wine of that description being necessarily limited'.

5.3.3 Exhibition of goods for sale

Displaying goods in a shop window or on the open shelves of a self-service shop or advertising goods for sale, is normally an invitation to treat.

Fisher v Bell 1961

The facts: A shopkeeper was prosecuted for offering for sale an offensive weapon by exhibiting a flick knife in his shop window.

Decision: The display of an article with a price on it in a shop window is merely an invitation to treat.

Pharmaceutical Society of Great Britain v Boots Cash Chemists (Southern) 1952

The facts: Certain drugs could only be sold under the supervision of a registered pharmacist. The claimant claimed this rule had been broken by Boots who displayed these drugs in a self-service shop. Boots contended that there was no sale until a customer brought the goods to the cash desk and offered to buy them. A registered pharmacist was stationed at this point.

Decision: The court found for Boots and commented that if it were true that a customer accepted an offer to sell by removing goods from the shelf, he could not then change his mind and put them back as this would constitute breach of contract.

5.3.4 Invitation for tenders

A **tender** is an estimate submitted in response to a prior request. When a person tenders for a contract he is making an offer to the person who has advertised a contract as being available. An invitation for tenders does not generally amount to an offer to contract with the person quoting the lowest price, except where the person inviting tenders actually makes it clear that he is making an offer.

Question

Offer

Bianca goes into a shop and sees a price label on a CD for £5. She takes the CD to the checkout, but the checkout operator tells her that the label is misprinted and should read £15. Bianca maintains that she only has to pay £5. How would you describe the price on the price label in terms of contract law?

Answer

Display of goods for sale with a price label is an invitation to treat (*Fisher v Bell 1961*), that is an invitation to the customer to make an offer which the shop can either accept or reject. But note that it can be a criminal offence to mislabel goods in this way.

6 Termination of offer

An offer may only be accepted while it is still open. In the absence of an acceptance, an offer may be **terminated** in any of the following ways.

- Rejection
- Counter-offer
- Lapse of time
- Revocation by the offeror
- Failure of a condition to which the offer was subject
- Death of one of the parties

6.1 Rejection

As noted earlier, outright rejection terminates an offer. A counter-offer, when the person to whom the offer was made proposes new or amended terms, also terminates the original offer.

Hyde v Wrench 1840

The facts: The defendant offered to sell property to the claimant for £1,000 on 6 June. Two days later, the claimant made a counter-offer of £950 which the defendant rejected on 27 June. The claimant then informed the defendant on 29 June that he accepted the original offer of £1,000.

Decision: The original offer of £1,000 had been terminated by the counter-offer of £950.

6.2 Counter-offer

Acceptance must be **unqualified agreement to the terms of the offer**. A purported acceptance which introduces any new terms is a counter-offer, which has the effect of terminating the original offer.

Key term

A **counter-offer** is a final rejection of the original offer. If a counter-offer is made, the original offeror may accept it, but if he rejects it his original offer is no longer available for acceptance.

A counter-offer may of course be accepted by the original offeror.

Butler Machine Tool Co v Ex-cell-O Corp (England) 1979

The facts: The claimant offered to sell tools to the defendant. Their quotation included details of their standard terms. The defendant 'accepted' the offer, enclosing their own standard terms. The claimant acknowledged acceptance by returning a tear-off slip from the order form.

Decision: The defendant's order was really a counter-offer. The claimant had accepted this by returning the tear-off slip.

6.2.1 Request for information

It is possible to respond to an offer by making a **request for information**. Such a request may be a request as to whether or not other terms would be acceptable – it is not a counter-offer.

Stevenson v McLean 1880

The facts: The defendant offered to sell iron at '40s net cash per ton, open till Monday'. The claimant enquired whether he would agree to delivery spread over two months. The defendant did not reply and (within the stated time limit), the claimant accepted the original offer. Meanwhile the defendant had sold the iron to a third party.

Decision: There was a contract since the claimant had merely enquired as to a variation of terms.

6.3 Lapse of time

An offer may be expressed to last for a **specified time**. If, however, there is no express time limit set, it expires after a **reasonable time**.

Ramsgate Victoria Hotel Co v Montefiore 1866

The facts: The defendant applied to the company in June for shares and paid a deposit. At the end of November the company sent him an acceptance by issue of a letter of allotment and requested payment of the balance due. The defendant contended that his offer had expired and could no longer be accepted.

Decision: The offer was for a reasonable time only and five months was much more than that. The offer had lapsed.

6.4 Revocation of an offer

The offeror may **revoke** his offer at any time before acceptance: *Payne v Cave 1789*. If he undertakes that his offer shall remain open for acceptance for a specified time he may nonetheless revoke it within that time, unless by a separate contract he has bound himself to keep it open.

Routledge v Grant 1828

The facts: The defendant offered to buy the claimant's house for a fixed sum, requiring acceptance within six weeks. Within the six weeks specified, he withdrew his offer.

Decision: The defendant could revoke his offer at any time before acceptance, even though the time limit had not expired.

Revocation may be an **express statement** or may be an **act** of the offeror. His revocation does not take effect until the revocation is communicated to the offeree. This raises two important points.

(a)   The first point is that **posting** a letter of revocation is not a sufficient act of revocation.

Byrne v Van Tienhoven 1880

The facts: The defendants were in Cardiff; the claimants in New York. The sequence of events was as follows.

1 October	Letter posted in Cardiff, offering to sell 1,000 boxes of tinplates.
8 October	Letter of revocation of offer posted in Cardiff.
11 October	Letter of offer received in New York and telegram of acceptance sent.
15 October	Letter confirming acceptance posted in New York.
20 October	Letter of revocation received in New York. The offeree had meanwhile resold the contract goods.

Decision: The letter of revocation could not take effect until received (20 October); it could not revoke the contract made by the telegram acceptance of the offer on 11 October.

(b)   The second point is that **revocation of offer may be communicated by any third party who is a sufficiently reliable informant**.

Dickinson v Dodds 1876

The facts: The defendant, on 10 June, wrote to the claimant to offer property for sale at £800, adding 'this offer to be left open until Friday 12 June, 9.00 am.' On 11 June the defendant sold the property to another buyer. A. B, who had been an intermediary between Dickinson and Dodds, informed Dickinson that the defendant had sold to someone else. On Friday 12 June, before 9.00 am, the claimant handed to the defendant a formal letter of acceptance.

Decision: The defendant was free to revoke his offer and had done so by sale to a third party; the claimant could not accept the offer after he had learnt from a reliable informant of the revocation of the offer to him.

However, this case should be treated with caution and it may be that only an agent can revoke an offer.

6.5 Failure of a condition

An offer may be conditional in that it is dependent on some event occurring or there being a change of circumstances. If the condition is not satisfied, the offer is not capable of acceptance.

Financings Ltd v Stimson 1962

The facts: The defendant wished to purchase a car, and on 16 March signed a hire-purchase form. The form, issued by the claimants, stated that the agreement would be binding only upon signature by them. On 20 March the defendant, not satisfied with the car, returned it. On 24 March the car was stolen from the premises of the dealer, and was recovered badly damaged. On 25 March the claimants signed the form. They sued the defendant for breach of contract.

Decision: The defendant was not bound to take the car. His signing of the agreement was actually an offer to contract with the claimant. There was an implied condition in this offer that the car would be in a reasonable condition.

6.6 Termination by death

The **death** of the offeree terminates the offer. The offeror's death terminates the offer, unless the offeree accepts the offer in ignorance of the death, and the offer is not of a personal nature.

Bradbury v Morgan 1862

The facts: X offered to guarantee payment by Y in respect of goods to be supplied by the claimant. X died and the claimant, in ignorance of his death, continued to supply goods to Y. The claimant then sued X's executors on the guarantee.

Decision: X's offer was a continuing commercial offer which the claimant had accepted by supply of goods after X's death. The guarantee stood.

7 Acceptance

FAST FORWARD

Acceptance must be an unqualified agreement to all the terms of the offer. **Acceptance** is generally not effective until **communicated** to the offeror, except where the **'postal rule'** applies. In which case acceptance is complete and effective as soon as it is posted.

Key term

Acceptance may be defined as follows.

'A positive act by a person to whom an offer has been made which, if unconditional, brings a binding contract into effect.'

The contract comes into **effect** once the offeree has **accepted** the terms presented to them. This is the point of no return; after acceptance, the offeror **cannot withdraw** their offer and both parties will be **bound** by the terms that they have agreed.

Acceptance may be by **express words**, by **action** or **inferred from conduct**.

> **Brogden v Metropolitan Railway Co 1877**
>
> *The facts:* For many years the claimant supplied coal to the defendant. He suggested that they should enter into a written agreement and the defendant's agent sent a draft to him for consideration. The parties applied to their dealings the terms of the draft agreement, but they never signed a final version. The claimant later denied that there was any agreement between him and the defendant.
>
> *Decision:* The conduct of the parties was only explicable on the assumption that they both agreed to the terms of the draft.

7.1 Silence

There must be some **act** on the part of the offeree to indicate his acceptance.

> **Felthouse v Bindley 1862**
>
> *The facts:* The claimant wrote to his nephew offering to buy the nephew's horse, adding 'If I hear no more about him, I consider the horse mine'. The nephew intended to accept his uncle's offer but did not reply. He instructed the defendant, an auctioneer, not to sell the horse. Owing to a misunderstanding the horse was sold to someone else. The uncle sued the auctioneer.
>
> *Decision:* The action failed. The claimant had no title to the horse.

Goods which are sent or services which are rendered to a person who did not request them are not 'accepted' merely because he does not return them to the sender: **Unsolicited Goods and Services Act 1971**. The recipient may treat them as an unsolicited gift.

7.2 Acceptance 'subject to contract'

Acceptance **'subject to contract'** means that the offeree is agreeable to the terms of the offer but proposes that the parties should negotiate a formal contract. Neither party is bound until the formal contract is signed. Agreements for the sale of land in England are usually made 'subject to contract'.

Acceptance 'subject to contract' must be distinguished from outright acceptance made on the understanding that the parties wish to replace the preliminary contract with another at a later stage. Even if the immediate contract is described as 'provisional', it takes effect at once.

> **Branca v Cobarro 1947**
>
> *The facts:* A vendor agreed to sell a mushroom farm under a contract which was declared to be 'a provisional agreement until a fully legalised agreement is signed'.
>
> *Decision:* By the use of the word 'provisional', the parties had intended their agreement to be binding until, by mutual agreement, they made another to replace it.

7.3 Letters of intent

Key term

> A **letter of intent** is a means by which one party gives a strong indication to another that he is likely to place a contract with him.

Thus a building contractor tendering for a large construction contract may need to sub-contract certain (specialist) aspects of the work. The sub-contractor will be asked to provide an estimate so that the main contractor can finalise his own tender.

Usually, a letter of intent is worded so as not to create any legal obligation. However, in some cases it may be phrased so that it includes an invitation to commence preliminary work. In such circumstances, it creates an obligation to pay for that work.

> *British Steel Corpn v Cleveland Bridge and Engineering Co Ltd 1984*
>
> *The facts:* The defendants asked the claimants to supply nodes for a complex steel lattice-work frame, and sent the claimants a letter of intent, stating their intention to place an order on their standard terms. The claimants stated that they were unwilling to contract on such terms, but started work, and eventually completed and delivered all the nodes. They sued for the value of the nodes and the defendants counter-claimed for damages for late delivery.
>
> *Decision:* Since the parties had not reached agreement over such matters as late delivery, there was no contract, and so there could be no question of damages for late delivery. However, since the claimants had undertaken work at the request of the defendants and the defendants had accepted this work, the claimants were entitled to a reasonable remuneration for services rendered.

7.4 Acceptance of a tender

As we saw earlier, an invitation for tenders is an invitation to treat. There are two distinct types of tender.

(a)   A tender to perform one task, such as building a new hospital, is an offer which can be accepted.

(b)   A tender to supply or perform a series of things, such as the supply of vegetables daily to a restaurant, is not accepted until an order is placed. It is a standing offer. Each order placed by the offeree is an individual act of acceptance creating a separate contract. Until orders are placed there is no contract and the tenderer can terminate his standing offer.

> *Great Northern Railways v Witham 1873*
>
> *The facts:* The defendant tendered successfully for the supply of stores to the claimant over a period of one year. In his tender he undertook 'to supply ... such quantities as the company may order from time to time'. After making some deliveries he refused to fulfil an order which the claimant had given.
>
> *Decision:* He was in breach of contract in refusing to fulfil the order given but might revoke his tender and need not then fulfil any future orders within the remainder of the 12 month period.

7.5 Counter-offers and requests for information

As we saw in Section 6, a counter-offer does not constitute acceptance; it is the making of a new offer which may in turn be accepted or rejected. Nor is a request for further information an acceptance.

Question   Offer and acceptance

In January Elle offered to buy Jane's boat for £3,000. Jane immediately wrote a letter to Elle saying 'For a quick sale I would accept £3,500. If you are not interested please let me know as soon as possible.' Elle did not see the letter until March when she returned from a business trip but then replied. 'I accept your offer. I trust that if I pay £3,000 now, you can wait until June for the remaining £500.' On receiving the letter, Jane attached a 'sold' sign to the boat but forgot to reply to Elle. Is there a contract between Elle and Jane? If so, what are its terms?

Answer

Elle's offer of £3,000 is an **offer**. Many offers are in fact made by prospective purchasers rather than by vendors. Jane's letter forms a **counter-offer**, which has the effect of terminating Elle's offer: *Hyde v Wrench 1840*. Elle may now accept or reject this counter-offer.

There is nothing to indicate that Jane's (counter) offer is not still open in March. An offer may be expressed to last for a **specified time**. It then expires at the end of that time. If, however, there is no express time limit set, it expires after a **reasonable time**.

Elle's reply, using the words 'I accept your offer' **appear conclusive. However they are not**. The enquiry as to variation of terms does not constitute acceptance or rejection: *Stevenson v McLean 1880*. The effect of Elle's reply is probably best analysed as being a **new counter-offer** including terms as to deferred payment, which **Jane purports to accept by affixing a 'sold' sign**. The court would need to decide whether, in all the circumstances, acceptance can be deemed to have been communicated.

Following *Butler Machine Tool Co v Ex-Cell-O Corp (England) 1979*, the **counter-offer introduces new terms**, that is, price. The price is therefore £3,500. As to **date of payment**, it would appear that the attachment of a 'sold' sign to the boat is confirmation that the revised terms proposed by Jane are acceptable.

8 Communication of acceptance

The general rule is that acceptance **must be communicated** to the offeror and that it is not effective (and hence there is no contract) until this has been done. However this rule does not apply in all cases.

8.1 Waiver of communication

The offeror may **dispense** with the need for communication of acceptance. Such a waiver may be express or may be inferred from the circumstances. In *Carlill v Carbolic Smoke Ball Co 1893*, it was held that it was sufficient for the claimant to act on the offer without notifying her acceptance of it. This was an example of a **unilateral contract**, where the offer takes the form of a promise to pay money in return for an act.

8.2 Prescribed mode of communication

The offeror may call for communication of acceptance by **specified means**. Communication of acceptance by some other means **equally expeditious** generally constitutes a valid acceptance unless specified otherwise: *Tinn v Hoffmann 1873*. This would probably apply also to acceptance by fax machine or e-mail. The offeror would have to use very precise wording if a specified means of communication is to be treated as mandatory.

> *Yates Building Co v R J Pulleyn & Sons (York) 1975*
>
> *The facts:* The offer called for acceptance by registered or recorded delivery letter. The offeree sent an ordinary letter which arrived without delay.
>
> *Decision:* The offeror had suffered no disadvantage and had not stipulated that acceptance must be made in this way only. The acceptance was valid.

8.3 No mode of communication prescribed

The offeree can use any method but must ensure that his **acceptance is understood** if he chooses an **instantaneous method of communication**.

> *Entores v Miles Far Eastern Corporation 1955*
>
> *The facts:* The claimants sent an offer by telex to the defendants' agent in Amsterdam and the latter sent an acceptance by telex. The claimants alleged breach of contract and wished to serve a writ.
>
> *Decision:* The acceptance took effect (and the contract was made) when the telex message was printed out on the claimants' terminal in London. A writ could therefore be issued.

8.4 The postal rule

The offeror may **expressly** or by **implication** indicate that he expects acceptance by means of a letter sent through the post.

Key term

The **postal rule** states that, where the use of the post is within the contemplation of both the parties, the acceptance is complete and effective as soon as a letter is posted, even though it may be delayed or even lost altogether in the post.

Adams v Lindsell 1818

The facts: The defendants made an offer by letter to the claimant on 2 September 1817 requiring an answer 'in course of post'. It reached the claimants on 5 September; they immediately posted a letter of acceptance, which reached the defendants on 9 September. The defendants could have expected a reply by 7 September, and they assumed that the absence of a reply within the expected period indicated non-acceptance and sold the goods to another buyer on 8 September.

Decision: The acceptance was made 'in course of post' (no time limit was imposed) and was effective when posted on 5 September.

The **intention** to use the post for communication of acceptance may be deduced from the **circumstances**.

Household Fire and Carriage Accident Insurance Co v Grant 1879

The facts: The defendant handed a letter of application for shares to the claimant company's agent in Swansea for posting to the company in London. The company posted an acceptance which never arrived. The defendant was called upon to pay the amount outstanding on his shares.

Decision: The defendant had to pay. The contract had been formed when the acceptance was posted, regardless of the fact that it was lost.

Under the postal rule, the offeror may be unaware that a contract has been made. If that possibility is clearly inconsistent with the nature of the transaction the letter of acceptance takes effect only when received. In particular, if the offer stipulates a particular mode of communication, the postal rule may not apply.

Holwell Securities v Hughes 1974
The facts: Hughes granted to the claimant an option to purchase land to be exercised 'by notice in writing'. A letter giving notice of the exercise of the option was lost in the post.

Decision: The words 'notice in writing' must mean notice actually received by the vendor; hence notice had not been given to accept the offer.

Acceptance of an offer may **only** be made **by a person authorised** to do so. This will usually be the offeree or his authorised agents.

Powell v Lee 1908

The facts: The claimant was appointed to a post as a headmaster. Without authorisation, he was informed of the appointment by one of the managers. Later, it was decided to give the post to someone else. The claimant sued for breach of contract.

Decision: Since communication of acceptance was unauthorised, there was no valid agreement and hence no contract.

Exam focus point

Offer and acceptance are key areas of contract law. You must be able to both identify and explain any relevant legal rules and principles, these will allow you to present a reasoned answer.

Frank writes to Xiao-Xiao on 1 July offering to sell him his sailing dinghy for £1,200. On 8 July, having received no reply, he decides to withdraw this offer and sends a second letter. On 10 July, Xiao-Xiao receives the original offer letter and immediately telephones his acceptance to Frank's wife. He follows this up with a letter posted the same day. Frank's second letter arrives on 14 July and Xiao-Xiao learns that Mel has bought the boat the previous day. What is the legal situation?

Answer

The revocation takes effect when received on 14 July (*Byrne v Van Tienhoven 1850*). The acceptance by Xiao-Xiao takes effect when posted on 10 July (*Adams v Lindsell 1818*). Therefore a contract is formed on 10 July and Frank's sale of the dinghy to Mel is in breach of his contract with Xiao-Xiao.

8.5 Cross-offers

If two offers, identical in terms, cross in the post, there is no contract: *Tinn v Hoffmann 1873*.

Illustration

If A offers to sell his car to B for £1,000 and B offers to buy A's car for £1,000, there is no contract, as there is no acceptance.

8.6 Unilateral contracts

The question arises as to whether contractual obligations arise if a party, in ignorance of an offer, performs an act which fulfils the terms of the offer. If A offers a **reward** to anyone who finds and returns his lost property and B, in ignorance of the offer, does in fact return it to him, is B entitled to the promised reward? There is agreement by conduct, but B is not accepting A's offer since he is unaware of it.

> *R v Clarke 1927*
>
> *The facts:* A reward was offered for information leading to the arrest and conviction of a murderer. If the information was provided by an accomplice, he would receive a free pardon. C claimed the reward, admitting that he had acted to save his own skin and that all thought of the reward had passed out his mind.
>
> *Decision:* There could not be acceptance without knowledge of the offer.

However, acceptance may still be **valid** even if the offer was not the sole reason for the action.

> *Williams v Carwardine 1833*
>
> *The facts:* A reward was offered to bring criminals to book. The claimant, an accomplice in the crime, supplied the information, with knowledge of the reward.
>
> *Decision:* As the information was given with knowledge, the acceptance was related to the offer.

John offers to sell his car to Ahmed for £2,000 on 1 July saying that the offer will stay open for a week. Ahmed tells his brother that he would like to accept the offer. Unknown to Ahmed, his brother informs John of this on 4 July. On 5 July John, with his girlfriend present, sells the car to Gina. John's girlfriend tells Ahmed about this later that day. The next day, Ahmed delivers a letter of acceptance to John. Is John in breach of contract?

Communication of acceptance may only be made by a person authorised to do so (*Powell v Lee 1908*), therefore Ahmed's brother's purported acceptance is not valid. Revocation of an offer may be communicated by a reliable informant (*Dickinson v Dodds 1876*), so Ahmed is made aware of the revocation on 5 July. His attempted acceptance on 6 July is therefore not valid.

As there was no consideration to support any separate agreement to keep the offer open for a week, John is free to sell the car to Gina.

As we saw above, *Carlill v Carbolic Smoke Ball Company 1893* is one example of a unilateral contract. Here the defendants advertised that they would pay £100 to anyone who caught influenza while using their product. This was held to be an offer to the world at large capable of being accepted by anyone fulfilling the necessary conditions. However, it was not necessary that anyone fulfilled the conditions, but as soon as Carlill began to **use** the product, the defendants were bound by their offer.

An ordinary offer can be revoked at any time before complete acceptance and, once revoked, can no longer be accepted (*Routledge v Grant 1828*). However, in the case of a unilateral contract, the courts have held that an offer cannot be revoked once the offeree has begun to perform whatever act is necessary (*Errington v Errington 1953*).

9 Agreement without offer and acceptance

FAST FORWARD

Agreement may exist without strict offer and acceptance if the **actions** of the parties can infer a contract.

Because the courts cannot ascertain the intentions of the parties, they must rely on what the parties **say or do**. In certain cases they may go beyond what can be inferred from the words and actions of the parties and **construct** a contract.

Clarke v Dunraven 1897

The facts: The owners of two yachts entered them for a regatta. Each undertook in a letter to the Club Secretary to obey the Club's rules, which included an obligation to pay all damages caused by fouling. The defendant's yacht fouled the claimant's yacht, which sank. The claimant sued for damages. The defendant argued that his only liability was under the Merchant Shipping Act 1862 and was therefore set at £8 per ton.

Decision: A contract had been created between the parties when they entered their yachts for the regatta, at which point they had accepted the club's rules. The claimant was entitled to recover full damages.

9.1 Collateral contracts

FAST FORWARD

In certain circumstances, the courts may infer the existence of a contract without the formalities of offer and acceptance. This type of contract is a **collateral contract**.

Key term

A **collateral contract** is a contract where consideration is provided by the making of another contract. For example, if there are two separate contracts, one between A and B and one between A and C, on terms which involve some concerted action between B and C, there may be a contract between B and C.

There is a contract between B and C despite the absence of direct communication between them.

Shanklin Pier Ltd v Detel Products Ltd 1951

The facts: The defendants gave assurances to the claimants that their paint would be satisfactory and durable if used to repaint the claimant's pier. The claimants in their contract with X for the repainting of the pier specified that X should use this paint. The paint proved very unsatisfactory. The claimants sued the defendants for breach of undertaking. The defendants argued that there was no contract between the claimants and themselves.

Decision: The contract between the claimants and X requiring the use of the defendant's paint was the consideration for a contract between the claimants and the defendant.

Chapter Roundup

- A **valid contract is a legally binding agreement**, formed by the mutual consent of two parties.

- The law seeks to protect the idea of 'freedom of contract', although **contractual terms** may be regulated by **statute**, particularly where the parties are of unequal bargaining strength.

- The **three essential elements** of a contract are **offer and acceptance**, **consideration** and **intention to enter into legal relations**.

- As a general rule, **a contract may be made in any form**. It may be **written**, or **oral**, or **inferred** from the conduct of the parties

- The first essential element of a binding contract is **agreement**. This is usually evidenced by **offer and acceptance**. An offer is a definite promise to be bound on specific terms, and must be distinguished from the mere **supply of information** and from an **invitation to treat**.

- An offer may only be accepted while it is still open. In the absence of an acceptance, an offer may be **terminated** in any of the following ways.

    - Rejection
    - Counter-offer
    - Lapse of time
    - Revocation by the offeror
    - Failure of a condition to which the offer was subject
    - Death of one of the parties

- **Acceptance** must be an unqualified agreement to all the terms of the offer. **Acceptance** is generally not effective until **communicated** to the offeror, except where the **'postal rule'** applies. In which case acceptance is complete and effective as soon as it is posted.

- The general rule is that acceptance **must be communicated** to the offeror and that it is not effective (and hence there is no contract) until this has been done. However this rule does not apply in all cases.

- **Agreement** may exist without strict offer and acceptance if the **actions** of the parties can infer a contract.

- In certain circumstances, the courts may infer the existence of a contract without the formalities of offer and acceptance. This type of contract is a **collateral contract**.

Quick Quiz

1 Give the name of a case in which an offer was made to the world at large.

2 How is the circulation of a price list categorised in the law of contract?

offer	tender
invitation to treat	auction

3 **Fill in the blanks** in the statements below, using the words in the box.

As a general rule, acceptance must be (1) .... to the (2) .... and is not effective until this has been done.

An (3) .... is a definite promise to be bound on specific terms, and must be distinguished from a supply of (4) .... and from an (5) ....

A counter-offer counts as (6) .... of the original offer

• information	• offer	• invitation to treat
• rejection	• communicated	• offeror

4 Advertising an auction is an offer to sell

True ☐

False ☐

5 As a general rule, silence cannot constitute acceptance.

True ☐

False ☐

6 Define the postal rule.

7 Give four instances when an offer is terminated.

8 **Fill in the blanks** in the statement below

A valid contract is a legally binding agreement. The three essential elements of a contract are (1) ...., (2) .... and (3) ....

9 A voidable contract is not a contract at all.

True ☐

False ☐

Answers to Quick Quiz

1   *Carlill v Carbolic Smoke Ball Co 1893*

2   Invitation to treat. *Grainger v Gough (1896)*

3   (1) communicated (2) offeror (3) offer (4) information (5) invitation to treat (6) rejection

4   False. Advertisements for auctions are not offers to sell.

5   True. Generally, silence cannot constitute acceptance.

6   The postal rule states that, where the use of the post is within the contemplation of both the parties, the acceptance is complete and effective as soon as a letter is posted, even though it may be delayed or even lost altogether in the post.

7   Any four of the following:

    Rejection
    Counter-offer
    Lapse of time
    Revocation by the offeror
    Failure of a condition to which the offer was subject
    Death of one of the parties

8   (1) Offer and acceptance (agreement) (2) consideration (3) intention to create legal relations

9   False. Voidable contracts may be cancelled by one party if they choose to. They may continue as a valid contract if the affected party chooses to.

Now try the questions below from the Exam Question Bank

Number	Level	Marks	Time
Q4	Introductory	10	18 mins
Q5	Examination	10	18 mins

Formation of contracts II

Topic list	Syllabus reference
1 Consideration	B1(d)
2 Adequacy and sufficiency of consideration	B1(d)
3 Promissory estoppel	B1(d)
4 Intention to create legal relations	B1(f)
5 Privity of contract	B1(e)
6 Contract formation checklist	B1(a to f)
7 The electronic contract	B1(a)

Introduction

In this chapter we complete our study of the essential requirements for a valid contract by looking at **consideration** and **intention.**

Consideration is what both parties bring to a contract and the key principle to remember is that it has to be **sufficient** but not necessarily **adequate.**

Agreements between family members are presumed not to have the **intention** of being legally binding, but those between strangers or businesses do have that intention.

Promissory estoppel and **privity of contract** are important concepts that could be easily used in an exam question to confuse the situation. Make sure you can explain both concepts.

Finally we consider the impact of technology on contracts by examining **electronic contracts**. There is not much case law in this area so keep an eye on the press for developments.

Study guide

		Intellectual level
(B)	**The law of obligations**	
1	Formation of contract	
(d)	Explain the need for consideration	2
(e)	Analyse the doctrine of privity	2
(f)	Distinguish the presumptions relating to intention to create legal obligations	2

Exam guide

Questions may require you to identify whether a valid contract exists. They may also test your ability to spot whether acceptable consideration has passed between the parties and whether they can be legally held to have intended to be bound by the contract. You may be required to give advice as to whether a third party can sue on a contract as well.

1 Consideration

FAST FORWARD

Consideration is an **essential** part of most contracts. It is what each party brings to the contract.

Key term

> **Consideration** has been defined as:
>
> 'A valuable consideration in the sense of the law may consist either in some right, interest, profit or benefit accruing to one party, or some forbearance, detriment, loss or responsibility given, suffered or undertaken by the other.' *From Currie v Misa 1875*

Using the language of purchase and sale, it could be said that one party must know that he has bought the other party's **promises** either by performing some act of his own or by offering a promise of his own.

Illustration

An example of giving consideration by suffering **detriment** is in *Carlill v Carbolic Smoke Ball Co*. Mrs Carlill gave consideration by using the smoke ball as she was instructed.

1.1 Valid consideration

FAST FORWARD

Consideration may be **executed** (an act in return for a promise) or **executory** (a promise in return for a promise). It may not be **past**, unless one of three recognised exceptions applies.

There are two broad types of valid consideration – **executed** and **executory**. If consideration is **past** then it is not enforceable.

Executed consideration **is an act in return for a promise**. The consideration for the promise is a performed, or executed, act.

Illustration

A offers a reward for the return of lost property, his promise becomes binding when B performs the act of returning A's property to him. A is not bound to pay anything to anyone until the prescribed act is done. Therefore in Carlill's case, the claimant's act, in response to the smoke ball company's promise of reward, was executed consideration.

Key term

> **Executed consideration** can be defined as follows.
>
> 'That which takes place at the present time. Thus in a contract for the sale of goods, the consideration is executed if the price is paid at the same time that the goods are delivered.'

Executory consideration is a promise given for a promise. The consideration in support of each promise is the other promise, not a performed act.

Illustration

If a customer orders goods which a shopkeeper undertakes to obtain from the manufacturer, the shopkeeper promises to supply the goods and the customer promises to accept and pay for them. Neither has yet done anything but each has given a promise to obtain the promise of the other. It would be breach of contract if either withdrew without the consent of the other.

Key term

> **Executory consideration** can be defined as follows.
>
> 'That which is to take place at some future time. The consideration for the delivery of goods would be executory if it is a promise to pay at a future date.'

1.1.1 Additional rules for valid consideration

As well as being either executed or executory, there are **additional** rules that must be met for consideration to be valid:

- **Performance must be legal**, the courts will not enforce payment for illegal acts
- **Performance must be possible,** agreeing to perform the impossible is not a basis for a binding contract
- **Consideration must pass from the promisee**, (see privity of contract later in this chapter)
- **Consideration must be sufficient but necessarily adequate**, (see Section 2 in this chapter)

1.2 Past consideration

Key term

> **Past consideration** can be defined as follows.
>
> '… something which has already been done at the time the promise is made. An example would be a promise to pay for work already carried out, unless there was an implied promise to pay a reasonable sum before the work began.'

Anything which has already been done before a promise in return is given is past consideration which, as a general rule, is not sufficient to make the promise binding. The following is the key case in this area:

> **Re McArdle 1951**
>
> *The facts:* Under a will the testator's children were entitled to a house after their mother's death. In the mother's lifetime one of the children and his wife lived in the house with the mother. The wife made improvements to the house. The children later agreed in writing to repay the wife 'in consideration of your carrying out certain alterations and improvements'. But at the mother's death they refused to do so.
>
> *Decision:* The work on the house had all been completed before the documents were signed. At the time of the promise the improvements were past consideration and so the promise was not binding.

If there is an **existing contract** and one party makes a further promise, no contract will arise. Even if the promise is directly related to the **previous bargain**, it will be held to have been made upon past consideration.

> **Roscorla v Thomas 1842**
>
> *The facts:* The claimant agreed to buy a horse from the defendant at a given price. When negotiations were over and the contract was formed, the defendant told the claimant that the horse was 'sound and free from vice'. The horse turned out to be vicious and the claimant brought an action on the warranty.
>
> *Decision:* The express promise was made after the sale was over and was unsupported by fresh consideration.

In three instances past consideration for a promise is sufficient to make the promise binding.

(a)   Past consideration is sufficient to create liability on a **bill of exchange** (such as a cheque) under s 27 Bills of Exchange Act 1882. Most cheques are issued to pay existing debts.

Key term

> **A bill of exchange** can be defined as:
>
> 'A negotiable instrument, drawn by one party on another, for example by a supplier of goods on a customer, who by accepting (signing) the bill, acknowledges the debt, which may be payable immediately (a sight draft) or at some future date (a time draft). The holder of the bill can thereafter use an accepted time draft to pay a debt to a third party or discount it to raise cash.'

(b)   After six (or in some cases twelve) years the right to sue for recovery of a debt becomes **statute barred** by the Limitation Act 1980. If, after that period, the debtor makes written acknowledgement of the creditor's claim, the claim is again enforceable at law.

(c)   When a request is made for a **service** this request may imply a promise to pay for it. If, after the service has been rendered, the person who made the request promises a specific reward, this is treated as fixing the amount to be paid.

> **Lampleigh v Braithwaite 1615**
>
> *The facts:* The defendant had killed a man and had asked the claimant to obtain for him a royal pardon. The claimant did so at his own expense. The defendant then promised to pay him £100. He failed to pay it and was sued.
>
> *Decision:* The defendant's request was regarded as containing an implied promise to pay, and the subsequent promise merely fixed the amount.

Both parties must have assumed during their negotiations that the services were ultimately to be paid for.

> **Re Casey's Patents 1892**
>
> *The facts:* A and B, joint owners of patent rights, asked their employee, C, as an extra task to find licensees to work the patents. After C had done so, A and B agreed to reward him for his past services with one third of the patent rights. A died and his executors denied that the promise was binding.
>
> *Decision:* The promise to C was binding since it merely fixed the 'reasonable remuneration' which A and B by implication promised to pay before the service was given.

Question

Emma, a law student, is in her car, waiting for the traffic lights to change at a busy intersection. Roger steps off the pavement with a bucket and cloth and proceeds to clean the windscreen of her car. Afterwards, Emma tells him that she will pay him £5. She then drives away. Advise Roger.

Answer

Emma is not bound to pay the £5, because at the time the promise was made, Roger's actions were past consideration.

2 Adequacy and sufficiency of consideration

The long-established rule is that consideration need **not be adequate** but it **must be sufficient**.

The court will also seek to ensure that a particular act or promise can actually be deemed to be consideration. Learn these rules:

(a) **Consideration need not be adequate** (that is, equal in value to the consideration received in return). There is no remedy at law for someone who simply makes a poor bargain.

(b) **Consideration must be sufficient**. It must be capable in law of being regarded as consideration by the courts.

2.1 Adequacy

It is presumed that each party is capable of serving his own interests, and the courts will not seek to weigh up the comparative value of the promises or acts exchanged.

Thomas v Thomas 1842

The facts: By his will the claimant's husband expressed the wish that his widow should have the use of his house during her life. The defendants, his executors, allowed the widow to occupy the house (a) in accordance with her husband's wishes and (b) in return for her undertaking to pay a rent of £1 per annum. They later said that their promise to let her occupy the house was not supported by consideration.

Decision: Compliance with the husband's wishes was not valuable consideration (no economic value attached to it), but the nominal rent was sufficient consideration.

2.2 Sufficiency

Consideration is sufficient if it has some identifiable value. The law only requires an element of bargain, not necessarily that it should be a good bargain.

Chappell & Co v Nestle Co 1960

The facts: As a sales promotion scheme, the defendant offered to supply a record to anyone who sent in a postal order for 1s.6d and three wrappers from 6d bars of chocolate made by them. The claimants owned the copyright of the tune. They sued for infringement of copyright. In the ensuing dispute over royalties the issue was whether the wrappers, which were thrown away when received, were part of the consideration for the promise to supply the record. The defendants offered to pay a royalty based on the price of 1s.6d per record, but the claimants rejected this, claiming that the wrappers also represented part of the consideration.

Decision: The wrappers were part of the consideration as they had commercial value to the defendants.

As stated earlier, forbearance or the promise of it may be **sufficient** consideration if it has some value, or amounts to giving up something of value.

Horton v Horton 1961

The facts: Under a separation agreement, the defendant agreed to pay his wife (the claimant) £30 per month. Under the deed this amount was a net payment after deduction of income tax; for nine months the husband paid it without any deduction so that the wife had to make the deductions herself. He then signed a document agreeing to pay such amount as 'after the deduction of income tax should amount to the clear sum of £30'. He paid this for three years, then stopped, pleading that the later agreement was not supported by consideration.

Decision: The later agreement was supported by consideration: the wife could have sued to have the original agreement rectified, but did not.

2.2.1 Performance of existing contractual duties

Performance of an **existing obligation imposed by statute** is no consideration for a promise of reward.

Collins v Godefroy 1831

The facts: The claimant had been subpoenaed to give evidence on behalf of the defendant in another case. He alleged that the defendant had promised to pay him six guineas for appearing.

Decision: There was no consideration for this promise.

But if some **extra service** is given that is sufficient consideration.

Glasbrook Bros v Glamorgan CC 1925

The facts: At a time of industrial unrest, colliery owners, rejecting the view of the police that a mobile force was enough, agreed to pay for a special guard on the mine. Later they repudiated liability saying that the police had done no more than perform their public duty of maintaining order, and that no consideration was given.

Decision: The police had done more than perform their general duties. The extra services given, beyond what the police in their discretion deemed necessary, were consideration for the promise to pay.

In the *Glasbrook* case the threat to law and order was not caused by either of the parties. Where one party's actions lead to the need for heightened police presence, and the police deem this presence necessary, they may also be entitled to payment.

Harris v Sheffield United F.C. Ltd 1988

The facts: The defendants argued that they did not have to pay for a large police presence at their home matches.

Decision: They had voluntarily decided to hold matches on Saturday afternoons when large attendances were likely, increasing the risk of disorder.

2.2.2 Promise of additional reward

If there is already a contract between A and B, and B promises **additional reward** to A if he (A) will perform his existing duties, there is no consideration from A to make that promise binding.

Stilk v Myrick 1809

The facts: Two members of the crew of a ship deserted in a foreign port. The master was unable to recruit substitutes and promised the rest of the crew that they would share the wages of the deserters if they would complete the voyage home short-handed. The shipowners however repudiated the promise.

Decision: In performing their existing contractual duties the crew gave no consideration for the promise of extra pay and the promise was not binding.

If a claimant does **more than perform an existing contractual duty**, this may amount to consideration.

Hartley v Ponsonby 1857

The facts: 17 men out of a crew of 36 deserted. The remainder were promised an extra £40 each to work the ship to Bombay. The claimant, one of the remaining crew-members, sued to recover this amount.

Decision: The large number of desertions made the voyage exceptionally hazardous, and this had the effect of discharging the original contract. The claimant's promise to complete the voyage formed consideration for the promise to pay an additional £40.

The courts now appear to be taking a slightly different line on the payment of **additional consideration**. It may be that where the party promising the additional reward has received a 'practical' benefit that will be treated as consideration even if, in law, he has received no more that he was already entitled to under the contract.

Williams v Roffey Bros & Nicholls (Contractors) Ltd 1990

The facts: The claimants agreed to do carpentry work for the defendants, who were engaged as contractors to refurbish a block of flats, at a fixed price of £20,000. The work ran late and so the defendants, concerned that the job might not be finished on time and that they would have to pay money under a penalty clause, agreed to pay the claimants an extra £10,300 to ensure the work was completed on time. They later refused to pay the extra amount.

Decision: The fact that there was no apparent consideration for the promise to pay the extra was not held to be important, as in the court's view both parties derived a practical benefit from the promise. The telling point was that the defendants' promise had not been extracted by duress or fraud: it was therefore binding. The defendant had avoided the possible penalty.

Exam focus point

Williams v Roffey Bros is important because it is a newer case than the bulk of contract cases, most of which were decided in the nineteenth century.

Re Selectmove 1994

The facts: A company which was the subject of a winding up order offered to settle its outstanding debts by instalment. An Inland Revenue inspector agreed to the proposal. The company tried to enforce it.

Decision: Despite the verdict in *Williams v Roffey Brothers* the court followed *Foakes v Beer* (see Section 2.2.4) in holding that an agreement to pay in instalments in unenforceable. Even though the creditor may obtain some practical benefit this is not adequate consideration to render the agreement legally binding in respect of part payment of debts.

2.2.3 Performance of existing contractual duty to a third party

If A promises B a reward if B will perform his **existing contract** with C, there is consideration for A's promise since he obtains a benefit to which he previously had no right, and B assumes new obligations.

> *Shadwell v Shadwell 1860*
>
> *The facts:* The claimant, a barrister, was engaged to marry E. His uncle promised the claimant that if he (the nephew) married E (as he did), the uncle would during their joint lives pay to his nephew £150 pa until such time as the nephew was earning 600 guineas pa at the bar (which never transpired). The uncle died after eighteen years owing six annual payments. The claimant claimed the arrears from his uncle's executors, who denied that there was consideration for the promise.
>
> *Decision:* There was sufficient consideration for the reasons given above.

2.2.4 Waiver of existing rights

 Illustration

If X owes Y £100 but Y agrees to accept a lesser sum, say £80, in full settlement of Y's claim, there is a promise by Y to waive his entitlement to the balance of £20. The promise, like any other, should be supported by consideration.

The case below is important.

> *Foakes v Beer 1884*
>
> *The facts:* The defendant had obtained judgement against the claimant. Judgement debts bear interest from the date of the judgement. By a written agreement the defendant agreed to accept payment by instalments, no mention being made of the interest. Once the claimant had paid the amount of the debt in full, the defendant claimed interest, claiming that the agreement was not supported by consideration.
>
> *Decision:* She was entitled to the debt with interest. No consideration had been given by the claimant for waiver of any part of her rights against him.

There are, however, exceptions to the rule that the debtor (denoted by 'X' in the following paragraphs) must give consideration if the waiver is to be binding.

	Exceptions
Alternative consideration *Anon 1495* *Pinnel's Case 1602*	If X offers and Y accepts anything to which Y is not already entitled, the extra thing is sufficient consideration for the waiver. • Goods instead of cash • Early payment
Bargain between the creditors *Woods v Robarts 1818*	If X arranges with creditors that they will each accept part payment in full entitlement, that is bargain between the creditors X has given no consideration but he can hold the creditors individually to the agreed terms
Third party part payment *Welby v Drake 1825*	If a third party (Z) offers part payment and Y agrees to release X from Y's claim to the balance, Y has received consideration from Z against whom he had no previous claim
Promissory estoppel	The principle of promissory estoppel may prevent Y from retracting his promise with retrospective effect.

3 Promissory estoppel

FAST FORWARD

> The principle of **promissory estoppel** was developed in *Central London Property Trust v High Trees House 1947*. It means that in some cases where someone has made a promise they can be prevented from denying it.

Key term

> The doctrine of **promissory estoppel** works as follows.
>
> If a creditor (Y) makes a promise (unsupported by consideration) to the debtor (X) that Y will not insist on the full discharge of the debt, and the promise is made with the intention that X should act on it and he does so, Y is **estopped** from retracting his promise, unless X can be restored to his original position.

> *Central London Property Trust v High Trees House 1947*
>
> *The facts:* In September 1939, the claimants let a block of flats to the defendants at an annual rent of £2,500 pa. It was difficult to let the individual flats in wartime, so in January 1940 the claimants agreed in writing to accept a reduced rent of £1,250 pa. Note, no consideration passed from the defendants in return for the reduced rent. There was no time limit set on the arrangement but it was clearly related to wartime conditions. The reduced rent was paid from 1940 to 1945 and the defendants sublet flats during the period on the basis of their expected liability to pay rent under the head lease at £1,250 only. In 1945 the flats were fully let. The claimants demanded a full rent of £2,500 pa, both retrospectively and for the future.
>
> *Decision:* The agreement of January 1940 ceased to operate early in 1945. The claim for full rent after the war was upheld. However, the 1940 agreement had estopped any claim for the period 1940 to 1945.

If the **defendants** in the *High Trees* case had sued on the promise, they would have **failed** as they provided no consideration to the 1940 agreement. Therefore, the principle of promissory estoppel is **'a shield not a sword'** and cannot become a cause of action in its own right.

> *Combe v Combe 1951*
>
> *The facts:* A wife obtained a divorce decree *nisi* against her husband. He then promised her that he would make maintenance payments of £100 per annum. The wife did not apply to the court for an order for maintenance but this forbearance was not at the husband's request. The decree was made absolute; the husband paid no maintenance; the wife sued him on his promise. In the High Court the wife obtained judgement on the basis of the principle of promissory estoppel.
>
> *Decision:* Promissory estoppel 'does not create new causes of action where none existed before. It only prevents a party from insisting on his strict legal rights when it would be unjust to allow him to enforce them'. The wife's claim failed.

Promissory estoppel only applies to a promise of waiver which is **entirely voluntary**.

> *D and C Builders v Rees 1966*
>
> *The facts:* The defendants owed £482 to the claimants who were in acute financial difficulties. The claimants reluctantly agreed to accept £300 in full settlement. They later claimed the balance.
>
> *Decision:* The debt must be paid in full. Promissory estoppel only applies to a promise voluntarily given. The defendants had been aware of and had exploited the claimants' difficulties.

Question

Ahmed agrees to paint Emma's dining room for £400. When the job is completed, Emma tells him she will only pay £300. He accepts reluctantly, because he needs some money quickly. Is he entitled to claim the full amount the following week?

Answer

A promise to waive an existing right is not binding unless separate consideration is given, so Ahmed is not bound to accept less. He would be bound if he had made the waiver with the intention that Emma should place reliance on it and she had actually done so. The fact that the waiver was not entirely voluntary (*D&C Builders v Rees 1966*) is not relevant, as promissory estoppel is not being claimed. Ahmed may claim the balance.

4 Intention to create legal relations

FAST FORWARD

Various cases give us a set of rules to apply when determining whether the **parties** to a contract intended to be **legally bound** by it.

Where there is no express statement as to whether or not legal relations are intended, the courts apply one of two **rebuttable presumptions** to a case.

- **Social, domestic and family arrangements** are not usually intended to be binding.
- **Commercial agreements** are usually intended by the parties involved to be legally binding.

The word 'presumption' means that it is assumed that something is the case, for example it is presumed that social arrangements are not deemed to be legally binding. 'Rebuttable' means that the presumption can in some cases be refuted, as, for example, in some of the cases described below.

Key term

Intention to create legal relations can be defined as follows.

'An agreement will only become a legally binding contract if the parties intend this to be so. This will be strongly presumed in the case of business agreements but not presumed if the agreement is of a friendly, social or domestic nature.'

4.1 Domestic arrangements

4.1.1 Husband and wife

The fact that the parties are husband and wife does not mean that they cannot enter into a **binding contract** with one another. Contrast the following two cases.

Balfour v Balfour 1919

The facts: The defendant was employed in Ceylon. He and his wife returned to the UK on leave but it was agreed that for health reasons she would not return to Ceylon with him. He promised to pay her £30 a month as maintenance. Later the marriage ended in divorce and the wife sued for the monthly allowance which the husband no longer paid.

Decision: An informal agreement of indefinite duration made between husband and wife whose marriage had not at the time broken up was not intended to be legally binding.

> **Merritt v Merritt 1970**
>
> *The facts:* The husband had left the matrimonial home, which was owned in the joint names of husband and wife, to live with another woman. The spouses met and held a discussion, in the course of which he agreed to pay her £40 a month out of which she agreed to keep up the mortgage payments. The wife made the husband sign a note of these terms and an undertaking to transfer the house into her name when the mortgage had been paid off. The wife paid off the mortgage but the husband refused to transfer the house to her.
>
> *Decision:* In the circumstances, an intention to create legal relations was to be inferred and the wife could sue for breach of contract.

Where agreements between husband and wife or other relatives relate to **property matters** the courts are very ready to impute an intention to create legal relations.

4.1.2 Relatives

Agreements between other family members may also be examined by the courts.

> **Jones v Padavatton 1969**
>
> *The facts:* The claimant wanted her daughter to move to England to train as a barrister, and offered to pay her a monthly allowance. The daughter did so in 1962. In 1964 the claimant bought a house in London; part of the house was occupied by the daughter and the other part let to tenants whose rent was collected by the daughter for herself. In 1967 the claimant and her daughter quarrelled and the claimant issued a summons claiming possession of the house. The daughter sued for her allowance.
>
> *Decision:* There were two agreements to consider: the daughter's agreement to read for the bar in exchange for a monthly allowance, and the agreement by which the daughter lived in her mother's house and collected the rent from tenants. Neither agreement was intended to create legal relations.

4.1.3 Other domestic arrangements

Domestic arrangements extend to those between people who are not related but who have a **close relationship** of some form. The nature of the agreement itself may lead to the conclusion that legal relations were intended.

> **Simpkins v Pays 1955**
>
> *The facts:* The defendant, her granddaughter and the claimant, a paying boarder, took part together each week in a competition organised by a Sunday newspaper. The arrangements over postage and other expenses were informal and the entries were made in the grandmother's name. One week they won £750; the paying boarder claimed a third share, but the defendant refused to pay on the grounds that there was no intention to create legal relations.
>
> *Decision:* There was a 'mutuality in the arrangements between the parties', amounting to a contract.

Exam focus point

> This is the sort of question which could be argued either way. The examiner will give you credit for valid arguments. Intention is an integral part of the formation of a contract and so should not be ignored.

4.2 Commercial agreements

When business people enter into commercial agreements it is presumed that there is an intention to enter into legal relations unless this is **expressly disclaimed** or the **circumstances indicates otherwise**.

Rose and Frank v Crompton 1923

The facts: A commercial agreement by which the defendants appointed the claimant to be its distributor in the USA contained a clause described as 'the Honourable Pledge Clause' which expressly stated that the arrangement was 'not subject to legal jurisdiction' in either country. The defendants terminated the agreement without giving notice as required, and refused to deliver goods ordered by the claimants although they had accepted these orders when placed.

Decision: The general agreement was not legally binding as there was no obligation to stand by any clause in it. However the orders for goods were separate and binding contracts. The claim for damages for breach of the agreement failed, but the claim for damages for non-delivery of goods ordered succeeded.

The words relied on by a party to a commercial agreement to show that legal relations are not intended are not always clear. In such cases, the **burden of proof** is **on the party seeking to escape liability**.

Edwards v Skyways Ltd 1964

The facts: In negotiations over the terms for making the claimant redundant, the defendants gave him the choice either of withdrawing his total contributions from their contributory pension fund or of receiving a paid-up pension. It was agreed that if he chose the first option, the defendants would make an ex gratia payment to him. He chose the first option; his contributions were refunded but the ex gratia payment was not made. He sued for breach of contract.

Decision: Although the defendants argued that the use of the phrase ex gratia showed no intention to create legal relations, this was a commercial arrangement and the burden of rebutting the presumption of legal relations had not been discharged by the defendants.

4.3 Statutory provisions

Procedural agreements between **employers and trade** unions for the settlement of disputes are not intended to give rise to legal relations in spite of their elaborate content: s 179 **Trade Union and Labour Relations (Consolidation) Act 1992**.

4.4 Letters of comfort

For many years, holding companies have given **'letters of comfort'** to creditors of subsidiaries which purport to give some comfort as to the ability of the subsidiary to pay its debts. Such letters have always been presumed in the past not to be legally binding.

Kleinwort Benson Ltd v Malaysia Mining Corpn Bhd 1989

The facts: The claimants lent money to the defendant's subsidiary, having received a letter from the defendant stating 'it is our policy to ensure that the business is at all times in a position to meet its liabilities to you.' The subsidiary went into liquidation, and the bank claimed against the holding company for the outstanding indebtedness.

Decision: The letter of comfort was a statement of existing policy and not a promise that the policy would continue in the future. Because both parties were well aware that in business a 'letter of comfort' imposed moral and not legal responsibilities, it was held not to have been given with the intention of creating legal relations.

4.5 Transactions binding in honour only

If the parties state that an agreement is **'binding in honour only'**, this amounts to an express denial of intention to create legal relations.

> *Jones v Vernons Pools 1938*
>
> *The facts:* The claimant argued that he had sent to the defendant a football pools coupon on which his predictions entitled him to a dividend. The defendants denied having received the coupon. A clause on the coupon stated that the transaction should not 'give rise to any legal relationship ... but ... be binding in honour only'.
>
> *Decision:* This clause was a bar to an action in court.

5 Privity of contract

FAST FORWARD

As a general rule, only a person who is a party to a contract has enforceable rights or obligations under it. This is the doctrine of **privity of contract**. The Contracts (Rights of Third Parties) Act 1999 has had a fundamental effect on the doctrine.

There is a maxim in contract law which states that **consideration must move from the promisee**. As consideration is the price of a promise, the price must be paid by the person who seeks to enforce the promise.

Illustration

A promises B that (for a consideration provided by B) A will confer a benefit on C. Therefore, C cannot as a general rule enforce A's promise since C has given no consideration for it.

> *Tweddle v Atkinson 1861*
>
> *The facts:* The claimant married the daughter of G. On the occasion of the marriage, the claimant's father and G exchanged promises that they would each pay a sum of money to the claimant. G died without making the promised payment and the claimant sued G's executor for the specified amount.
>
> *Decision:* The claimant had provided no consideration for G's promise.

In *Tweddle's* case each father could have sued the other but the claimant could not sue. The rule that consideration must move from the promisee overlaps with the rule that **only a party to a contract can enforce it**. No-one may be entitled to or bound by the terms of a contract to which he is not an original party: *Price v Easton 1833*.

Key term

> **Privity of contract** can be defined as follows.
>
> As a general rule, only a person who is a party to a contract has enforceable rights or obligations under it. Third parties have no right of action save in certain exceptional instances.

The following is the leading case on privity of contract.

> *Dunlop v Selfridge 1915*
>
> *The facts:* The claimant supplied tyres to Dew & Co, a distributor, on terms that they would not re-sell the tyres at less than the prescribed retail price. If Dew & Co sold the tyres wholesale to trade customers, they must impose a similar condition on those buyers to observe minimum retail prices. Dew & Co resold tyres on these conditions to the defendant. Under the terms of the contract between Dew & Co and Selfridge, Selfridge was to pay to the claimant a sum of £5 per tyre if it sold tyres to customers below the minimum retail price. They sold tyres to two customers at less than the minimum price. The claimant sued to recover £5 per tyre as liquidated damages.
>
> *Decision:* The claimant could not recover damages under a contract (between Dew & Co and Selfridge) to which it was not a party.

The party to the contract who imposes the condition or obtains a promise of a benefit for a third party can usually enforce it, but damages cannot be recovered on the third party's behalf, since a claimant can only recover damages for a loss he has suffered. Other remedies may be sought however.

Where the contract is one which provides something for the enjoyment of both the contracting party and third parties – such as a family holiday – the contracting party may be entitled to recover damages for his loss of the benefit: *Jackson v Horizon Holidays Ltd 1975*.

5.1 Exceptions

There are a number of exceptions to the rule of privity of contract.

	Exceptions
The third party can sue in another capacity	*Beswick v Beswick 1968* The facts: X transferred his business to the defendant, his nephew, in consideration for a pension of £6.10s per week and, after his death, a weekly annuity to X's widow. Only one such annuity payment was made. The widow brought an action against the nephew, asking for an order of specific performance. She sued both as administratrix of her husband's estate and in her personal capacity as recipient. *Decision:* As her husband's representative, the widow was successful in enforcing the contract for a third party's (her own) benefit. In her personal capacity she had no right of action.
Collateral contracts	*Shanklin Pier Ltd v Detel Products Ltd 1951* *The facts*: Shanklin Pier contracted with painters to have the pier repainted using products from Detel. Detel had already communicated their paint's suitability to the claimants. The paint was not suitable and Shanklin took action against Detel Products even though their contract was with the painters. *Decision:* It was held that a collateral contract (see Chapter 4) existed between Shanklin and Detel. Detel had confirmed the paint's suitability in return for Shanklin requiring the painters to use it.
Valid assignment	Benefit from a contract can be re-assigned from the original beneficiary to a third party if it is in writing, it transfers the same or no more benefits to the new beneficiary and has the consent of the other party.
Foreseeable loss to the third party	*Linden Gardens Trust Ltd v Lenesta Sludge Disposals Ltd 1994* The facts: Linden Gardens contracted with the defendants for work to be done on their property. The defendants knew there was the likelihood that the property would be transferred to a third party soon after. After the transfer it became apparent that the workmanship amounted to breach of contract. As the third party had no action against the defendants due to the rules on privity, Linden Gardens took action in their place. *Decision:* As the transfer was in the contemplation of both parties the original beneficiary could claim full damages on behalf of the third party.

	Exceptions
Implied trusts	Equity may hold that an implied trust has been created *Gregory and Parker v Willimans 1817* *The facts:* P owed money to G and W. He agreed with W to transfer his property to W if W would pay his (P's) debt to G. The property was transferred, but W refused to pay G. G could not sue on the contract between P and W. *Decision:* P could be regarded as a trustee for G, and G would therefore bring an action jointly with P.
Statutory exceptions	Road Traffic Act 1972: A person injured in a road accident may claim against the motorist's insurers. Married Woman's Property Act 1882: Permits husband and wife to insure his or her own life for the benefit of the other under a trust which the beneficiary can enforce. Contracts (Rights of Third Parties) Act 1999: see below.
Agency	In normal circumstances the agent discloses to a third party with whom he contracts that he is acting for a principal. The contract, when made, is between the principal and the third party. The agent has no liability under the contact and no right to enforce it. Agency is considered further in Chapter 12.
Covenants	A restrictive covenant may run with land *Tulk v Moxhay 1848* *The facts:* The claimant owned several plots of land in Leicester Square. He sold one to X, who agreed not to build on it, but to preserve it in its existing condition. It was sold on, eventually being purchased by the defendant, who, although he was aware of the restriction, proposed to build on it. The claimant sought an injunction. *Decision:* The injunction was granted.

5.2 Contracts (Rights of Third Parties) Act 1999

This Act has a fundamental effect on the rule of **privity of contract** by setting out the circumstances in which a third party has a right to enforce a contract term or have it varied or rescinded, and a right to all the remedies that are available for breach of contract. It brings the law in England, Wales and Northern Ireland into line with Scotland, most of the EU and the US. There is a two-limbed test for the circumstances in which a third party may enforce a contract term.

- Whether the contract itself expressly so provides
- Where the term confers a benefit on the third party, unless it appears that the contracting parties did not intend him to have the right to enforce it.

The third party must be expressly identified in the contract by name, class or description, but need not be in existence when the contract is made (for example, an unborn child or a future spouse). The Act enables a third party to take advantage of exclusion clauses as well as to enforce 'positive' rights.

Section 2 of the Act protects third parties from the original parties varying contract terms without their consent.

Under section 5, the promisor is protected from double liability. Damages awarded to the third party will be reduced by the amount of damages already awarded to the original promisee.

The Act does not confer third party rights in relation to a company's constitution, or employment contracts. So, for example, a customer of an employer cannot use this Act to enforce a term of a contract of employment against an employee.

6 Contract formation checklist

Essential element	Components	Definition	Rules	Exceptions
Agreement	Offer	'A definite promise to be bound on specific terms'	Cannot be vague Does not have to be made to particular person Must be distinguished from invitation to treat	
	+ Acceptance	'A positive act by a person to whom an offer has been made which, if unconditional, brings a binding contract into effect.'	May be express words, action or inferred from action, but not silence. Must be unconditional acceptance of terms (ie not counter-offer) Must be communicated to the offeror ⇨ Offer can only be accepted when it remains open – it may lapse in the following situations: (1) Rejection (2) Lapse of time (3) Revocation (4) Failure of condition (5) Death	Unless: (1) Offeror waives the need (2) Particular means of communi-cation prescribed (3) Under postal rule, a posted letter does not arrive acceptance remains valid.
Intention		'An agreement will only become legally binding if the parties intend that this will be so'	If the intention is expressed in the contract, that expression will be followed. If there is no ⇨ express intention in the agreement, the courts apply 'rebuttable presumptions:' (1) Family or social agreements not intended to be (2) Commercial agreements intended to be binding	No exceptions – but remember the presumptions are rebuttable – if you can prove otherwise, the courts will apply what you can prove.

Essential element	Components	Definition	Rules	Exceptions
Consideration	**Executed or Executory**	'A valuable consideration in the sense of the law may consist either in some right, interest, profit or benefit accruing to one party, or some forbearance detriment, loss or responsibility given, suffered or undertaken by the other.'	Must not be past ⟹	(1) Bills of exchange (2) Written confirmation (3) Implied promise to pay for a service
			Need not be adequate	
			Must be sufficient	
			Waiver of rights under a contract must be matched by consideration from the other party. ⟹	(1) Alternative consideration given (goods, early settlement) (2) Third party pays part – rest is cancelled (3) Doctrine of promissory estoppel
			Consideration must move from the promisee (privity of contract), only they then have rights in the contract ⟹	(1) Trusts (2) Statutory exceptions (Contracts (Rights of 3Ps Act) (3) Agency (4) Restrictive covenants

7 The electronic contract

FAST FORWARD

The **pace of technological change** raises issues for modern contract law. Problems arise as contracts are often **electronic**, are **digitally signed**, are **accepted by email** and consideration is often provided by **credit card**.

It could be said that the case of *Byrne v van Tienhoven*, dating from 1880, is an early example of an **electronic contract**. In that case, the sending of an acceptance by telegram was an important action in a chain of events leading to the formation of a contract. Since then, technology has permitted such actions to become almost **instantaneous**. Fax messages, e-mails and use of the internet may all play a part in the communication of offers and purported acceptances.

Exam focus point

If a scenario is presented involving **modern technology**, you will earn marks for applying your knowledge of the basic law of contract. There may well be very little case law in some areas – or none – but as long as you work through each element of the scenario in a logical manner, you should do well.

This is a potentially wide ranging topic and the law is still in its infancy. Below is a summary of the issues which will need to be considered.

(a) **In writing?** There are two main reasons why contracts need to be in writing.

    (i) A written contract provides evidence of the terms of the contract.

    (ii) The requirement of formality allows a weaker party to 'think twice' before entering into a transaction.

    An electronic contract meets the reasoning behind the requirement for writing, and can thus be said to be in writing.

(b) **Signed?** In 2000 the UK government passed legislation to give legal effect to 'digital signatures', thereby giving an electronic contract the same status as contracts in more traditional formats.

(c) **Timing of acceptance**. A contract comes into existence when an offer is accepted; in the case of acceptance by letter, this is when the letter is posted not when it is received. Internet e-mail shares many of the qualities of conventional mail – it is not usually instantaneous and may be subject to delay. Therefore the postal rule, with any problems arising from it, probably applies, although the point has not been tested.

(d) **Consideration**. Difficulties with credit card payments have slowed the growth of electronic commerce. The Internet is largely insecure, and this may cause problems when it comes to payment.

Activities on the internet are largely **unregulated** at the moment, but this is likely to change, as governments recognise the business opportunities available and the EU seeks to **protect consumers**. **Basic legal principles** must therefore be applied.

Of course, the internet is much more than simply a means of sending and receiving messages. As the commercial applications of the **world wide web** have been exploited, a new 'shop front' has been developed. Some sites are highly automated and software handles ordering, stock checking, payment processing and despatch confirmation without human involvement.

There are risks associated with leaving commercial transactions to automated IT programs. Eliminating human intervention and fully automating the sales process, for example, can increase the likelihood of errors. A notable recent example is the Argos website in the UK which offered television sets for £2.99, rather than £299.

The following are some of the **practical legal issues** that must be faced by a **seller** when contracting on-line.

- Websites should be constructed as shop windows, that is, **invitations to treat** rather than offers.
- **Terms and conditions** governing electronic transactions should be made explicit and clear.
- **An indication of interest** by a purchaser visiting the website should be understood by both parties to be **an offer**, not an acceptance, which the seller is then free to accept or reject.
- Sellers can continue to use **disclaimers of liability**, clearly displayed on the website, subject to the usual **consumer protection laws** on unfair terms.
- The **law and jurisdiction** governing the transaction should be made clear, for example, 'All transactions are governed by English law'.
- The seller should make sure that any **web pages do not contravene local laws** (for example, those relating to advertising standards) in the countries targeted.
- A **time limit** should be set for all offers made on the website, which should take account of potential delays in receiving emails.

Chapter Roundup

- **Consideration** is an **essential** part of most contracts. It is what each party brings to the contract.

- Consideration may be **executed** (an act in return for a promise) or **executory** (a promise in return for a promise). It may not be **past**, unless one of three recognised exceptions applies.

- The long-established rule is that consideration need **not be adequate** but it **must be sufficient**.

- The principle of **promissory estoppel** was developed in *Central London Property Trust v High Trees House 1947*. It means that in some cases where someone has made a promise they can be prevented from denying it.

- Various cases give us a set of rules to apply when determining whether the **parties** to a contract intended to be **legally bound** by it.

- As a general rule, only a person who is a party to a contract has enforceable rights or obligations under it. This is the doctrine of **privity of contract**. The Contracts (Rights of Third Parties) Act 1999 has had a fundamental effect on the doctrine.

- The **pace of technological change** raises issues for modern contract law. Problems arise as contracts are often **electronic**, are **digitally signed**, are **accepted by email** and consideration is often provided by **credit card**.

Quick Quiz

1   Distinguish between executed and executory consideration.

2   Past consideration, as a general rule, is not sufficient to make a promise binding.

    True   ☐

    False   ☐

3   **Fill in the blanks** in the statement below.

    Consideration need not be (1) ………………. but it must be (2) ……………….. .

4   **Fill in the blanks** in the statement below.

    If Alice promises Ben that (for a consideration provided by Ben) Alice will confer a benefit on Charlotte, then (1)………………. cannot at common law enforce Alice's promise. This is the doctrine of (2)…………………

5   What is the doctrine of promissory estoppel?

6   A promise of additional reward for the performance of existing duties is not generally binding.

    True   ☐

    False   ☐

Answers to Quick Quiz

1   Executed consideration is an *act* in return for a promise such as paying for goods when the shopkeeper hands them over. Executory consideration is a *promise* given for a promise, such as promising to pay for goods that the shopkeeper puts on order for you.

2   True. Past consideration is not valid consideration for a new contract.

3   (1) adequate, (2) sufficient

4   (1) Charlotte, (2) Privity of contract

5   If a creditor (Y) makes a promise (unsupported by consideration) to the debtor (X) that Y will not insist on the full discharge of the debt, and the promise is made with the intention that X should act on it and he does so, Y is estopped from retracting his promise, unless X can be restored to his original position.

6   True (as in *Stilk v Myrick*)

Now try the questions below from the Exam Question Bank

Number	Level	Marks	Time
Q6	Examination	10	18 mins
Q7	Examination	10	18 mins

Terms of contract

Topic list	Syllabus reference
1 Contract terms	B2 (a)
2 Express terms and implied terms	B2 (b)
3 Conditions and warranties	B2 (b)
4 Exclusion clauses	B2 (c)
5 The Unfair Contract Terms Act 1977	B2 (c)
6 The Unfair Terms in Consumer Contracts Regulations 1999	B2 (c)

Introduction

This chapter analyses the contents of a contract, specifically the different types of **contract term**.

You must be clear as to what **express terms** are and be able to distinguish them from mere **representations**. It is also important that you understand how terms can be **implied** into contracts and whether or not terms are **conditions** or **warranties**.

Once you have grasped these subjects you will be able to determine whether or not an organisation or individual has **breached** the terms of the contract and determine their liability (if any).

We complete the chapter by looking at **exclusion clauses**. You must be familiar with the legislation in this area, the effect of such clauses and how they are controlled.

Study guide

		Intellectual level
(B)	**The law of obligations**	
2	Content of contracts	
(a)	Distinguish terms from mere representation	2
(b)	Define the various contractual terms	1
(c)	Explain the effect of exclusion clauses and evaluate their control	2

Exam guide

You may be asked to explain contract terms, conditions and warranties and how they are brought into the contract. Scenario questions may require you to give advice as to whether a party can rely on an exclusion clause.

1 Contract terms

FAST FORWARD

Statements made by the parties may be classified as **terms or representations**. Different **remedies** attach to breach of a term and to misrepresentation respectively.

In addition to the final contract, many statements may be made during the process of negotiation that often lead to the formation of a contract. It is important to be able to establish whether what has been written or said actually amounts to a contract term or whether it is simply a representation. **Statements may be classified as terms or as representations**.

Key term

> A **representation** is something which induces the formation of a contract but which does not become a **term** of the contract. The importance of the distinction is that different remedies are available depending on whether a term is broken or a representation turns out to be untrue.

If something said in negotiations proves to be untrue, the party misled can claim for **breach of contract** if the statement became a **term** of the contract. If the pre-contract statement was merely a **representation** then the party misled can claim misrepresentation, resulting in a lesser remedy than for breach of contract. There are a number of factors that a court may consider when determining whether a statement is or is not a term.

The court will consider **when** the representation was made to assess whether it was designed as a contract term or merely as an incidental statement. The court will also look at the **importance** the recipient of the information attached to it.

> *Bannerman v White 1861*
>
> *The facts:* In negotiations for the sale of hops the buyer emphasised that it was **essential** to him that the hops should not have been treated with sulphur adding that, if they had, he would not even bother to ask the price. The seller replied explicitly that no sulphur had been used. It was later discovered that a small proportion of the hops (5 acres out of 300) had been treated with sulphur. The buyer refused to pay the price.
>
> *Decision:* The representation as to the absence of sulphur was intended to be a **term** of the contract.

> **Routledge v McKay 1954**
>
> *The facts:* The defendant, in discussing the possible sale of his motorcycle to the claimant, said on 23 October that the cycle was a 1942 model; he took this information from the registration document. On 30 October the parties made a written contract which did not refer to the year of the model and the purchaser had not indicated that the age of the cycle was of critical importance to him. The actual date was 1930.
>
> *Decision:* The buyer's claim for damages failed. The reference to a 1942 model was a **representation made prior** to the contract

If the statement is made by a person with **special knowledge** it is more likely to be treated as a contract term.

> **Dick Bentley Productions v Arnold Smith Motors 1965**
>
> *The facts:* The defendants sold the claimants a car which they stated to have done only 20,000 miles since a replacement engine and gear-box had been fitted. In fact the car had covered 100,000 miles since then and was unsatisfactory.
>
> *Decision:* The defendants' statement was a term of the contract and the claimants were entitled to damages.

> **Oscar Chess v Williams 1957**
>
> *The facts:* The defendant, when selling his car to the claimant car dealers, stated (as the registration book showed) that his car was a 1948 model and the dealers valued it at £280 in the transaction. In fact it was a 1939 model, worth only £175, and the registration book had been altered by a previous owner.
>
> *Decision:* The statement was a mere representation. The seller was not an expert and the buyer had better means of discovering the truth.

2 Express terms and implied terms

 FAST FORWARD

> As a general rule, the parties to a contract may include in the agreement whatever **terms** they choose. This is the principle of **freedom of contract**. Terms clearly included in the contract are **express terms**. The law may complement or replace terms by **implying** terms into a contract.

2.1 Express terms

Key term

> An **express term** is a term expressly agreed by the parties to a contract to be a term of that contract. In examining a contract, the courts will look first at the terms expressly agreed by the parties.

An apparently binding legal agreement must be **complete in its terms** to be a valid contract.

> **Scammell v Ouston 1941**
>
> *The facts:* The defendants wished to buy a motor-van from the claimants on hire-purchase. They placed an order 'on the understanding that the balance of purchase price can be had on hire-purchase terms over a period of two years'. The hire-purchase terms were never specified.
>
> *Decision:* The court was unable to identify a contract which it could uphold because the language used was so vague.

It is always possible for the parties to leave an essential term to be **settled by other means**, for example by an independent third party.

It may be agreed to sell at the open market price on the day of delivery, or to invite an arbitrator to determine a fair price. The price may be determined by the course of dealing between the parties.

Where an agreement appears vague or incomplete, the courts will seek to uphold it by looking at the **intention of the parties**: *Hillas & Co Ltd v Arcos Ltd 1932*. If the parties use standard printed conditions, some of which are inappropriate, such phrases may be disregarded.

Nicolene v Simmonds 1953

The facts: The claimant offered to buy steel bars from the defendant. A contract was made by correspondence, in which the defendant provided that 'the usual conditions of acceptance apply'. The defendant failed to deliver the goods and argued that there had been no explicit agreement.

Decision: The words should be disregarded. The contract was complete without these words; there were no usual conditions of acceptance.

2.2 Implied terms

FAST FORWARD

Terms may be implied by the **courts**, by **statute** or by **custom**.

There are occasions where certain terms are not **expressly** adopted by the parties. Additional terms of a contract may be **implied** by law: through custom, statute or the courts to bring efficacy to the contract. Implied terms may override express terms in certain circumstances such as where they are implied by statute.

Key term

An **implied term** can be defined as follows.

'A term deemed to form part of a contract even though not expressly mentioned. Some such terms may be implied by the courts as necessary to give effect to the presumed intentions of the parties. Other terms may be implied by statute, for example, the Sale of Goods Act.'

2.2.1 Terms implied by custom

The parties may enter into a contract subject to **customs** of their trade. Any express term overrides a term which might be implied by custom.

Hutton v Warren 1836

The facts: The defendant landlord gave the claimant, a tenant farmer, notice to quit the farm. He insisted that the tenant should continue to farm the land during the period of notice. The tenant asked for 'a fair allowance' for seeds and labour from which he received no benefit because he was to leave the farm.

Decision: By custom he was bound to farm the land until the end of the tenancy; but he was also entitled to a fair allowance for seeds and labour incurred.

Les Affreteurs v Walford 1919

The facts: A charter of a ship provided expressly for a 3% commission payment to be made 'on signing the charter'. There was a trade custom that it should only be paid at a later stage. The ship was requisitioned by the French government and so no hire was earned.

Decision: An express term prevails over a term otherwise implied by custom. The commission was payable on hire.

2.2.2 Terms implied by statute

Terms may be implied by statute. In some cases the statute permits the parties to contract out of the **statutory terms**. In other cases the statutory terms are obligatory, for example the protection given by the Sale of Goods Act 1979 to a consumer who buys goods from a trader cannot be taken away from him.

2.2.3 Terms implied by the courts

Terms may be implied if the court concludes that the parties intended those terms to apply to the contract.

The Moorcock 1889

The facts: The owners of a wharf agreed that a ship should be moored alongside to unload its cargo. It was well known that at low water the ship would ground on the mud at the bottom. At ebb tide the ship settled on a ridge concealed beneath the mud and suffered damage.

Decision: It was an implied term, though not expressed, that the ground alongside the wharf was safe at low tide since both parties knew that the ship must rest on it.

A term of a contract which is left to be implied and is not expressed is often something that goes without saying; so that, if while the parties were making their bargain an officious bystander were to suggest some express provision for it, they would say 'why should we put that in? That's obvious': This was put forward in *Shirlaw v Southern Foundries 1940*. The terms are required to give **efficacy** to the contract, that is, to make it work in practice.

The court may also imply terms because the court believes such a term to be a 'necessary incident' of this type of contract.

Liverpool City Council v Irwin 1977

The facts: The defendants were tenants in a tower block owned by the claimants. There was no formal tenancy agreement. The defendants withheld rent, alleging that the claimants had breached implied terms because *inter alia* the lifts did not work and the stairs were unlit.

Decision: Tenants could only occupy the building with access to stairs and/or lifts, so terms needed to be implied on these matters.

Where a term is implied as a 'necessary incident' it has precedent value and such terms will be implied into future contracts of the same type.

3 Conditions and warranties

FAST FORWARD

Statements which are classified as contract terms may be further categorised as **conditions** or **warranties**. A **condition** is a vital term going to the **root** of the **contract**, while a **warranty** is a term **subsidiary** to the main purpose of the **contract**. The remedies available for breach are different in each case.

Exam focus point

It is fundamental that students can explain and distinguish between conditions and warranties. The effects of their breach are different.

The terms of the contract are usually classified by their relative importance as **conditions** or **warranties**.

(a)   **A condition is a vital term**, going to the root of the contract, breach of which entitles the injured party to decide to treat the contract as **discharged** and to claim damages.

Key term

A **condition** can be defined as follows.

'An important term which is vital to a contract so that its breach will destroy the basis of the agreement. It may arise from an express agreement between the parties or may be implied by law.

(b)   **A warranty is a term subsidiary to the main purpose of the contract**, breach of which only entitles the injured party to claim damages.

Key term

> A **warranty** can be defined as follows.
>
> 'A minor term in a contract. If broken, the injured party must continue performance but may claim damages for the loss suffered.'

Poussard v Spiers 1876

The facts: Mme Poussard agreed to sing in an opera throughout a series of performances. Owing to illness she was unable to appear on the opening night and the next few days. The producer engaged a substitute who insisted that she should be engaged for the whole run. When Mme Poussard recovered, the producer declined to accept her services for the remaining performances.

Decision: Failure to sing on the opening night was a breach of condition which entitled the producer to treat the contract for the remaining performances as discharged.

Bettini v Gye 1876

The facts: An opera singer was engaged for a series of performances under a contract by which he had to be in London for rehearsals six days before the opening performance. Owing to illness he did not arrive until the third day before the opening. The defendant refused to accept his services, treating the contract as discharged.

Decision: The rehearsal clause was subsidiary to the main purpose of the contract.

Schuler v Wickham Machine Tool Sales 1973

The facts: The claimants entered into a contract with the defendants giving them the sole right to sell panel presses in England. A clause of the contract provided that the defendants' representative should visit six named firms each week to solicit orders. The defendants' representative failed on a few occasions to do so and the claimants claimed to be entitled to repudiate the agreement.

Decision: Such minor breaches by the defendants did not entitle the claimants to repudiate.

Classification may depend on the following issues.

(a)   **Statute** often identifies implied terms specifically as conditions or warranties. An example is the Sale of Goods Act 1979.

(b)   **Case law** may also define particular types of clauses as conditions, for example a clause as to the date of 'expected readiness' of a ship let to a charterer: *The Mihalis Angelos 1971*.

(c)   The court may construe what was the **intention of the parties** at the time the contract was made as to whether a broken term was to be a condition or a warranty: *Bunge Corporation v Tradax SA 1981*.

It is important to remember that if the injured party merely wants damages, there is **no** need to consider whether the term broken is a condition or a warranty, since either type of breach entitles the injured party to damages.

 Question   Conditions and warranties

Norma, a professional singer, enters into a contract to sing throughout a series of concerts. A term in the contract states that she must attend five rehearsals before the opening night. Norma falls ill and misses the last two rehearsals and the opening night. Is she in breach of contract? Give reasons.

Norma is in breach of contract as she has failed to fulfil the condition that she would sing on the opening night (*Poussard v Spiers 1876*). Had she just failed to attend the two rehearsals, this would have amounted to breach of warranty (*Bettini v Gye 1876*).

3.1 Innominate terms

FAST FORWARD

It may not be possible to determine whether a term is a condition or a warranty. Such terms are classified by the courts as **innominate terms**.

Traditionally, terms were either classified as conditions or warranties and the injured party could choose to end the contract only for breach of condition. Sometimes a warranty was broken with catastrophic results, yet the court could not permit the injured party to end the contract because the term broken was not a condition. More recently the courts have held that where the breach deprives the injured party of **substantially the whole benefit** of the contract the term broken can be called '**Innominate**' and the injured party can choose to end the contract even if it could not be regarded as a condition.

If the nature and effect of the breach is such as to deprive the injured party of most of his benefit from the contract then it will be treated as if the guilty party had breached a condition.

The doctrine was developed in:

Hong Kong Fir Shipping Co Ltd v Kawasaki Kisa Kaisha Ltd 1962

The facts: The defendants chartered a ship from the claimants for a period of 24 months. A term in the contract stated that the claimants would provide a ship which was 'in every way fitted for ordinary cargo service'. Because of the engine's age and the crew's lack of competence the ship's first voyage, from Liverpool to Osaka, was delayed for 5 months and further repairs were required at the end of it. The defendants purported to terminate the contract, so the claimants sued for breach; the defendants claimed that the claimants were in breach of a contractual condition.

Decision: The term was innominate and could not automatically be construed as either a condition or a warranty. The obligation of 'seaworthiness' embodied in many charterparty agreements was too complex to be fitted into one of the two categories.

The ship was still available for 17 out of 24 months. The consequences of the breach were not so serious that the defendants could be justified in terminating the contract as a result.

Exam focus point

Do not over emphasise innominate terms. Being able to provide an explanation is sufficient.

Breach

Phil agrees with Professional Cars plc that they are to provide a white Rolls Royce for his daughter's wedding. On the day the driver arrives in a black Ford Scorpio. Phil sends him away. What is the consequence?

Phil can sue Professional Cars plc for breach of contract. The company has not agreed to supply 'a car' but 'a white Rolls Royce'. Its failure to fulfil this term allows Phil to sue for breach if he wishes to claim damages, eg the cost of hiring another car. It does not matter if the term broken is a condition or a warranty.

To what is the injured party to a contract entitled in the event of breach of:

(a)   A condition by the other party?
(b)   A warranty by the other party?

Answer

(a)   He may choose to treat the contract as discharged and repudiate or terminate the contract, or alternatively he may go on with it and sue for damages.

(b)   He may claim damages only.

4 Exclusion clauses

FAST FORWARD

An **exclusion clause** may attempt to restrict one party's liability for breach of contract or for negligence.

To be enforceable, a term must be validly incorporated into a contract. Because most disputes about whether a term has been incorporated arise in the context of exclusion clauses, much of the relevant case law surrounds exclusion clauses. In this section, we will examine the ways in which the courts may determine:

(a)   Whether an exclusion clause (as a contract term) has been **validly incorporated** into the contract; and

(b)   If so, how the exclusion clause should be **interpreted**

Key term

An **exclusion clause** can be defined as follows.

'A clause in a contract which purports to exclude liability altogether or to restrict it by limiting damages or by imposing other onerous conditions. They are sometimes referred to as **exemption clauses**.

There has been strong criticism of the use of exclusion clauses in contracts made between manufacturers or sellers of goods or services and private citizens as consumers. The seller puts forward standard conditions of sale which the buyer may not understand, but which he must accept if he wishes to buy. With these so-called **standard form contracts**, the presence of exclusion clauses becomes an important consideration.

For many years the courts demonstrated the hostility of the common law to exclusion clauses by developing various rules of case law designed to restrain their effect. These are described in this section of the chapter. To these must also be added the considerable statutory safeguards provided by the **Unfair Contract Terms Act 1977** (UCTA). These are considered in the next section of this chapter.

The statutory rules do permit exclusion clauses to continue in some circumstances. Hence it is necessary to consider both the **older case law** and the **newer statutory rules**.

The **courts** have generally sought to protect consumers from the harsher effects of exclusion clauses in two ways.

(a)   Exclusion clauses must be **incorporated** into a contract before they have legal effect.
(b)   Exclusion clauses are **interpreted** strictly. This may prevent the application of the clause.

4.1 Incorporation of exclusion clauses

The courts protect customers from the harsher effects of exclusion clauses by ensuring that they are properly **incorporated** into a contract and then by **interpreting** them strictly.

The law seeks to protect customers (usually the weaker party to the contract) from the full force of exclusion clauses. They do this by applying the '**letter of the law'** to see if such clauses have been incorporated correctly. Where there is uncertainty the clauses may be excluded from the contract.

Such uncertainty can arise in several circumstances.

- The document containing notice of the clause must be an **integral part** of the contract.
- If the document is an integral part of the contract, a term may not usually be disputed if it is included in a document which a party has **signed**.
- The term must be put forward **before** the contract is made.
- If the contact is not signed, an exclusion clause is not a binding term unless the person whose rights it restricts was made **sufficiently aware** of it at the time of agreeing to it.
- **Onerous terms** must be sufficiently highlighted (it is doubtful whether this applies to signed contracts).

4.1.1 Contractual documents

Where the exclusion clause is contained in an unsigned document it must be shown that this document is an integral part of the contract and is one which could be expected to contain terms.

Chapelton v Barry UDC 1940

The facts: There was a pile of deck chairs and a notice stating 'Hire of chairs 2d per session of three hours'. The claimant took two chairs, paid for them and received two tickets which were headed 'receipt' which he put in his pocket. One of the chairs collapsed and he was injured. The defendant council relied on a notice on the back of the tickets by which it disclaimed liability for injury.

Decision: The notice advertising chairs for hire gave no warning of limiting conditions and it was not reasonable to communicate them on a receipt. The disclaimer of liability was not binding on the claimant.

Thompson v LMS Railway 1930

The facts: An elderly lady who could not read asked her niece to buy her a railway excursion ticket on which was printed 'Excursion: for conditions see back'. On the back it was stated that the ticket was issued subject to conditions contained in the company's timetables. These conditions excluded liability for injury.

Decision: The conditions had been adequately communicated and therefore had been accepted.

4.1.2 Signed contracts

If a person **signs** a document containing a term, he is held to have agreed to the term even if he had not read the document. But this is not so if the party who puts forward the document for signature gives a misleading explanation of the term's legal effect.

L'Estrange v Graucob 1934

The facts: The defendant sold to the claimant, a shopkeeper, a slot machine under conditions which excluded the claimant's normal rights under the Sale of Goods Act 1893. The claimant signed the document described as a 'Sales Agreement' and including clauses in 'legible, but regrettably small print'.

Decision: The conditions were binding on the claimant since she had signed them. It was not material that the defendant had given her no information of their terms nor called her attention to them.

> **Curtis v Chemical Cleaning Co 1951**
>
> *The facts:* The claimant took her wedding dress to be cleaned. She was asked to sign a receipt on which there were conditions that restricted the cleaner's liability and in particular placed on the claimant the risk of damage to beads and sequins on the dress. The document in fact contained a clause 'that the company is not liable for any damage however caused'. The dress was badly stained in the course of cleaning.
>
> *Decision:* The cleaners could not rely on their disclaimer since they had misled the claimant. She was entitled to assume that she was running the risk of damage to beads and sequins only.

4.1.3 Unsigned contracts and notices

Each party must be aware of the contract's terms before or **at the time of entering into the agreement** if they are to be binding.

> **Olley v Marlborough Court 1949**
>
> *The facts:* A husband and wife arrived at a hotel and paid for a room in advance. On reaching their bedroom they saw a notice on the wall by which the hotel disclaimed liability for loss of valuables unless handed to the management for safe keeping. The wife locked the room and handed the key in at the reception desk. A thief obtained the key and stole the wife's furs from the bedroom.
>
> *Decision:* The hotel could not rely on the notice disclaiming liability since the contract had been made previously and the disclaimer was too late.

Complications can arise when it is difficult to determine at exactly **what point in time** the contract is formed so as to determine whether or not a term is validly included.

> **Thornton v Shoe Lane Parking Ltd 1971**
>
> *The facts:* The claimant wished to park his car in the defendant's automatic car park. He had seen a sign saying 'All cars parked at owner's risk' outside the car park and when he received his ticket he saw that it contained words which he did not read. In fact these made the contract subject to conditions displayed obscurely on the premises. These not only disclaimed liability for damage but also excluded liability for injury. When he returned to collect his car there was an accident in which he was badly injured.
>
> *Decision:* The reference on the ticket to conditions was received too late for the conditions to be included as contractual terms. At any rate, it was unreasonable for a term disclaiming liability for personal injury to be presented so obscurely. Note that since the Unfair Contracts Terms Act 1977 the personal injury clause would be unenforceable anyway.

An exception to the rule that there should be prior notice of the terms is where the parties have had **consistent dealings** with each other in the past, and the documents used then contained similar terms.

> **J Spurling Ltd v Bradshaw 1956**
>
> *The facts:* Having dealt with a company of warehousemen for many years, the defendant gave it eight barrels of orange juice for storage. A document he received a few days later acknowledged receipt and contained a clause excluding liability for damage caused by negligence. When he collected the barrels they were empty and he refused to pay.
>
> *Decision:* It was a valid clause as it had also been present in the course of previous dealings, even though he had never read it.

If the parties have had previous dealings (but not on a consistent basis), then the person to be bound by the term must be **sufficiently aware** of it at the time of making the latest contract.

> **Hollier v Rambler Motors 1972**
>
> *The facts:* On three or four occasions over a period of five years the claimant had had repairs done at a garage. On each occasion he had signed a form by which the garage disclaimed liability for damage caused by fire to customers' cars. The car was damaged by fire caused by negligence of garage employees. The garage contended that the disclaimer had by course of dealing become an established term of any contract made between them and the claimant.
>
> *Decision:* The garage was liable. There was no evidence to show that the claimant knew of and agreed to the condition as a continuing term of his contracts with the garage.

4.1.4 Onerous terms

Where a term is particularly unusual and onerous it should be highlighted (although it is doubtful whether this applies to signed contracts). Failure to do so may mean that it does not become incorporated into the contract.

> **Interfoto Picture Library Ltd v Stiletto Visual Programmes Ltd 1988**
>
> *The facts:* 47 photographic transparencies were delivered to the defendant together with a delivery note with conditions on the back. Included in small type was a clause stating that for every day late each transparency was held a 'holding fee' of £5 plus VAT would be charged. They were returned 14 days late. The claimants sued for the full amount.
>
> *Decision:* The term was onerous and had not been sufficiently brought to the attention of the defendant. The court reduced the fee to one tenth of the contractual figure to reflect more fairly the loss caused to the claimants by the delay.

Question

Exclusion clause

Natasha hires a care from a car rental company. On arrival at their office she is given a form, which includes terms and conditions in small print on the back, and asked to sign it. She does so and pays the hire charge. When she gets into the car, she happens to look in the glove compartment and sees a document headed 'Limitation of Liability'. This states that the hire company will not be liable for any injury caused by a defect in the car unless this is as a result of the company's negligence. While Natasha is driving on the motorway, the airbag inflates and causes her to crash. She is badly injured. Assuming that negligence is not claimed, what is the status of the exclusion clause?

Answer

There must be prior notice of the presence of an exclusion clause. The answer here will depend on whether this exclusion was included in the original terms and conditions (and therefore merely reinforced by the later document) or not. The hire company's only other possible defence will be to show a consistent course of dealings with Natasha.

4.2 Interpretation of exclusion clauses

In deciding what an exclusion clause means, the courts interpret any ambiguity against the person who relies on the exclusion. This is known as the **contra proferentem rule**. Liability can only be excluded or restricted by clear words.

In the *Hollier* case above, the court decided that as a matter of interpretation the disclaimer of liability could be interpreted to apply:

*   Only to accidental fire damage or
*   To fire damage caused in any way including negligence.

It should therefore be interpreted against the garage in the **narrower sense** of (a) so that it did not give exemption from fire damage due to negligence. If a person wishes successfully to exclude or limit liability for loss caused by **negligence** the courts require that the word 'negligence', or an accepted synonym for it, should be included in the clause.

Alderslade v Hendon Laundry 1945

The facts: The conditions of contracts made by a laundry with its customers excluded liability for loss of or damage to customers' clothing in the possession of the laundry. By its negligence the laundry lost the claimant's handkerchief.

Decision: The exclusion clause would have no meaning unless it covered loss or damage due to negligence. It did therefore cover loss by negligence.

4.2.1 The 'main purpose' rule

When construing an exclusion clause the court will also consider the **main purpose rule**. By this, the court presumes that the clause was not intended to prevent the main purpose of the contract.

4.2.2 Fundamental breach

There is no doubt that at common law a **properly drafted** exclusion clause can cover any breach of contract.

Photo Productions v Securicor Transport 1980

The facts: The defendants agreed to guard the claimants' factory under a contract by which the defendant were excluded from liability for damage caused by any of their employees. One of the guards deliberately started a small fire which destroyed the factory and contents. It was contended that Securicor had entirely failed to perform their contract and so they could not rely on any exclusion clause in the contract.

Decision: There is no principle that total failure to perform a contract deprives the party at fault of any exclusion from liability provided by the contract. In this case the exclusion clause was drawn widely enough to cover the damage which had happened. As the fire occurred before the UCTA was in force, the Act could not apply here. But if it had done it would have been necessary to consider whether the exclusion clause was reasonable.

Exam focus point

Reliance on exclusion clauses is an everyday occurrence in business dealings and therefore is of great practical relevance.

---

5 The Unfair Contract Terms Act 1977

The Unfair Contract Terms Act 1977 aims to **protect consumers** (effectively individuals) when they enter contracts by stating that some exclusion clauses are **void**, and considering whether others are **reasonable**.

When considering the **validity** of exclusion clauses the courts have had to strike a balance between:

- The principle that parties should have complete **freedom to contract** on whatever terms they wish, and
- The need to **protect the public** from unfair exclusion clauses

Exclusion clauses do have a proper place in business. They can be used to allocate contractual risk, and thus to determine in advance who is to insure against that risk. Between businessmen with similar bargaining power exclusion clauses are a legitimate device. The main limitations are now contained in the Unfair Contract Terms Act 1977.

Before we consider the specific terms of UCTA, it is necessary to describe how its scope is restricted.

(a)   In general the Act only applies to clauses inserted into agreements by **commercial concerns or businesses**. In principle private persons may restrict liability as much as they wish.

(b)   The Act does not apply to some contracts, for example contracts of insurance or contracts relating to the transfer of an interest in land.

(c)   Specifically, the Act applies to:

(i)   clauses that attempt to limit liability for negligence;
(ii)   clauses that attempt to limit liability for breach of contract.

The Act uses two techniques for controlling exclusion clauses – some types of clauses are **void**, whereas others are subject to a **test of reasonableness**.

The main provisions can be summarised as follows:

(a)   Any clause that attempts to restrict liability for death or personal injury arising from negligence is **void**.

(b)   Any clause that attempts to restrict liability for other loss or damage arising from negligence is void unless it can be shown to be **reasonable**.

(c)   Any clause that attempts to limit liability for breach of contract, where the contract is based on standard terms or conditions, or where one of the parties is a consumer, is void unless it can be shown to be **reasonable**.

5.1 Clauses which are void

If an exclusion clause is made **void by statute** it is unnecessary to consider how other legal rules might affect it. There is simply no need to assess whether it is reasonable.

A clause is void by statute in the following circumstances.

- A clause which purports to exclude or limit liability for **death or personal injury** resulting from negligence is void: s 2(1) UCTA. This is the key circumstance to remember.

- A guarantee clause which purports to exclude or limit liability for loss or damage caused by a **defect** of the goods in **consumer use** is void: s 5 UCTA.

- In a contract for the sale or hire purchase of goods, a clause that purports to exclude the condition that the seller has a **right to sell** the goods is void: s 6(1) UCTA.

- In a contract for the sale of goods, hire purchase, supply of work or materials or exchange *with a consumer*, a clause that purports to exclude or limit liability for breach of the conditions relating to description, quality, fitness and sample implied by the Sale of Goods Act 1979 is void: s 6(2) and 7(2) UCTA.

5.2 Clauses which are subject to a test of reasonableness

If a clause is not automatically void, it is subject to a test of reasonableness. The main provisions of the Act that refer to this type of clause are set out in Sections 2, 3, 6 and 7 of the Act.

5.3 Exclusion of liability for negligence (s 2)

As we saw above, a person acting in the course of a business cannot, by reference to any contract term, restrict his liability for **death or personal injury** resulting from negligence. The clause containing the term is simply void. In the case of **other loss or damage**, a person cannot introduce a clause restricting his liability for negligence unless the term is **reasonable**.

5.4 Standard term contracts and consumer contracts (s 3)

The person who uses a standard-term contract in dealing with a **consumer** cannot, unless the term is **reasonable**, restrict liability for his own breach.

> **George Mitchell Ltd v Finney Lock Seeds Ltd 1983**
>
> *The facts:* The claimant ordered 30 pounds of Dutch winter cabbage seeds from the defendants. The defendant's standard term contract included an exclusion clause that limited their liability to a refund of the amount paid by the claimant. The wrong type of cabbage seed was delivered. The seed was planted over 63 acres, but when the crop came up it was not fit for human consumption. The claimant claimed £61,500 damages plus £30,000 interest.
>
> *Decision:* At common law the exclusion clause would have protected the defendant, but the court decided in favour of the claimant, relying exclusively on the statutory ground of reasonableness.

5.4.1 Consumers

Where a business engages in an activity which is merely incidental to the business, the activity will not be in the course of the business unless it is an integral part and carried on with a degree of regularity.

> **R & B Customs Brokers Ltd v United Dominions Trust Ltd 1988**
>
> *The facts:* The claimants, a company owned by Mr and Mrs Bell and operating as a shipping broker, bought a second-hand Colt Shogun. The car was to be used partly for business and partly for private use.
>
> *Decision:* This was a consumer sale, since the company was not in the business of buying cars.

5.5 Sale and supply of goods (ss 6-7)

Any contract (that is, consumer or non-consumer) for the sale or hire purchase of goods cannot exclude the implied condition that the seller has a **right to sell** the goods.

As we saw earlier when looking at clauses that are automatically void, a **consumer** contract for the sale of goods, hire purchase, supply of work or materials or exchange of goods cannot exclude or restrict liability for breach of the conditions relating to description, quality, fitness and sample implied by the Sale of Goods Act 1979 and the Supply of Goods and Services Act 1982. For a non-consumer contract, such exclusions are subject to a **reasonableness** test. The rules are set out in the following table.

	Exemption clauses in contracts for the sale of goods or supply of work or materials	
	Consumer transaction	**Non-consumer transaction**
Title	Void	Void
Description	Void	Subject to reasonableness test
Quality and suitability	Void	Subject to reasonableness test
Sample	Void	Subject to reasonableness test

5.6 The statutory test of reasonableness (s 11)

The term must be **fair and reasonable** having regard to all the circumstances which were, or which ought to have been, known to the parties when the contract was made. The burden of proving reasonableness lies on the person seeking to rely on the clause. Statutory guidelines have been included in the Act to assist the determination of reasonableness. For instance, the court will consider the following.

- The relative **strength** of the parties' bargaining positions.
- Whether any **inducement** (for example, a reduced price) was offered to the customer to persuade him to accept limitation of his rights.
- Whether the customer **knew or ought to have known** of the existence and extent of the exclusion clause.
- If failure to comply with a condition (for example, failure to give notice of a defect within a short period) excludes or restricts the customer's rights, whether it was reasonable to expect when the contract was made that compliance with the condition would be practicable.
- Whether the goods were made, processed or adapted to the **special order** of the customer (UCTA Sch 2).

> **Smith v Eric S Bush 1989**
>
> *The facts:* A surveyor prepared a report on a property which contained a clause disclaiming liability for the accuracy and validity of the report. In fact the survey was negligently done and the claimant had to make good a lot of defects once the property was purchased.
>
> *Decision:* In the absence of special difficulties, it was unreasonable for the surveyor to disclaim liability given the cost of the report, his profession and his knowledge that it would be relied upon to make a major purchase.

> **St Albans City and District Council v International Computers Ltd 1994**
>
> *The facts:* The defendants had been hired to assess population figures on which to base community charges (local government taxation). Their standard contract contained a clause restricting liability to £100,000. The database which they supplied to the claimants was seriously inaccurate and the latter sustained a loss of £1.3 million.
>
> *Decision:* The clause was unreasonable. The defendants could not justify this limitation, which was very low in relation to the potential loss. In addition, they had aggregate insurance of £50 million. The defendants had to pay full damages.

Question   UCTA

The Unfair Contract Terms Act 1977 limits the extent to which it is possible to exclude or restrict *business liability*. What do you understand by the phrase business liability?

Answer

Business liability is liability which arises from things done or to be done in the course of a business, or from the occupation of premises used for business purposes. Business includes a profession and the activities of any government department or public or local authority.

6 The Unfair Terms in Consumer Contracts Regulations 1999

FAST FORWARD

> The Unfair Terms in Consumer Contracts Regulations 1999 defines what is meant by an **unfair term**. They deal with consumer contracts and terms which have not been individually negotiated.

These regulations implemented an EU directive on unfair contract terms. UCTA 1977 continues to apply. There are now three layers of relevant law.

- The **common law**, which applies to all contracts, whether or not one party is a consumer
- **UCTA 1977**, which applies to all contracts and which has specific provisions for consumer contracts
- The **Regulations (UTCCR 1999)**, which only apply to consumer contracts and to terms which have not been individually negotiated

The new regulations apply to contracts for the supply of goods or services.

- They apply to terms in **consumer contracts**.

Key term

> A **consumer** is defined as 'a natural person who, in making a contract to which these regulations apply, is acting for purposes which are outside his business'.

- They apply to contractual terms which have **not** been **individually negotiated**.
- There are a number of **exceptions** including contracts relating to family law or to the incorporation or organisation of companies and partnerships and employment contracts.

A key aspect of the regulations is the definition of an unfair term.

Key term

> An **unfair term** is any term which causes a significant imbalance in the parties' rights and obligations under the contract to the detriment of the consumer.

In making an assessment of good faith, the courts will have regard to the following.

- The **strength of the bargaining positions** of the parties
- Whether the consumer had an **inducement** to agree to the term
- Whether the goods or services were sold or supplied to the **special order** of the consumer
- The extent to which the seller or supplier has dealt **fairly and equitably** with the consumer

The **effect** of the regulations is to render certain terms in consumer contracts unfair.

- Excluding or limiting liability of the seller when the consumer dies or is injured, where this results from an act or omission of the seller
- Excluding or limiting liability for partial or incomplete performance by the seller
- Making a contract binding on the consumer where the seller can still avoid performing the contract

Two forms of **redress** are available.

- A consumer who has concluded a contract containing an unfair term can ask the court to find that the unfair term should not be binding.
- A complaint, for example by an individual, a consumer group or a trading standards department can be made to the Director General of Fair Trading.

Chapter Roundup

- Statements made by the parties may be classified as **terms or representations**. Different **remedies** attach to breach of a term and to misrepresentation respectively.

- As a general rule, the parties to a contract may include in the agreement whatever **terms** they choose. This is the principle of **freedom of contract**. Terms clearly included in the contract are **express terms**. The law may complement or replace terms by **implying** terms into a contract.

- Terms may be implied by the **courts**, by **statute** or by **custom**.

- Statements which are classified as contract terms may be further categorised as **conditions** or **warranties**. A **condition** is a vital term going to the **root** of the **contract**, while a **warranty** is a term **subsidiary** to the main purpose of the **contract**. The remedies available for breach are different in each case.

- It may not be possible to determine whether a term is a condition or a warranty. Such terms are classified by the courts as **innominate terms**.

- An **exclusion clause** may attempt to restrict one party's liability for breach of contract or for negligence.

- The courts protect customers from the harsher effects of exclusion clauses by ensuring that they are properly **incorporated** into a contract and then by **interpreting** them strictly.

- The Unfair Contract Terms Act 1977 aims to **protect consumers** (effectively individuals) when they enter contracts by stating that some exclusion clauses are **void**, and considering whether others are **reasonable**.

- The Unfair Terms in Consumer Contracts Regulations 1999 defines what is meant by an **unfair term**. They deal with consumer contracts and terms which have not been individually negotiated.

1   Why is it important to distinguish between terms and representations?

2   A term may be implied into a contract by

i   Statute
ii   Trade practice unless an express term overrides it
iii   The court, to provide for events not contemplated by the parties
iv   The court, to give effect to a term which the parties had agreed upon but failed to express because
       it was obvious
v   The court, to override an express term which is contrary to normal custom

A   ii and iii only
B   i, ii and iv only
C   i, iv and v only
D   i, ii, iv and v only

3   **Fill in the blanks** in the statements below, using the words in the box.

A (1) .... is a vital term, going to the root of the contract, breach of which entitles the injured
party to treat the contract as (2) .... and claim (3) ....

A (4) .... is a term (5) .... to the main purpose of the contract.

The consequence of a term being classified as innominate is that the court must decide what is the actual
effect of its (6) ....

• breach	• condition	• subsidiary
• warranty	• damages	• discharged

4   Give an example of a statute which identifies implied terms specifically as conditions or warranties.

5   Terms implied by custom cannot be overridden

True   ☐

False   ☐

6   **Fill in the blanks** in the statement below, using the words in the box.

A contract is a consumer contract if the buyer neither makes the contract in course of (1) ....
nor holds himself out as doing so.

The other (2) .... does make the contract in course of (3) ....

In the case of a contract governed by the law of (4) ...., the goods are of a type ordinarily
supplied for (5) ....

• business	• sale of goods	• business
• party	• private use or consumption	

7   Match the laws to their jurisdictions under the law of contract

(a)   Common law   (1)   All contracts with specific provisions for consumer contracts
(b)   UCTA 1977   (2)   Applies only to consumer contracts and to non-negotiated terms
(c)   UTCCR 1999   (3)   All contracts

8   What is the 'contra proferentem' rule?

Answers to Quick Quiz

1   The importance of the distinction is that different remedies are available depending on whether a term is broken or a representation turns out to be untrue.

2   B. Courts will not imply factors outside the contemplation of the parties.

3   (1) condition (2) discharged (3) damages (4) warranty (5) subsidiary (6) breach

4   Sale of Goods Act 1979

5   False. Such terms can be overridden.

6   (1) business, (2) party, (3) business, (4) sale of goods, (5) private use or consumption

7   (a)   (3)
    (b)   (1)
    (c)   (2)

8   In deciding what an exclusion clause means, the courts interpret any ambiguity against the person at fault who relies on the exclusion.

Now try the questions below from the Exam Question Bank

Number	Level	Marks	Time
Q8	Examination	10	18 mins
Q9	Examination	10	18 mins

7

Breach of contract

Topic list	Syllabus reference
1 Discharge of contract	B3(a)
2 Breach of contract	B3(a)
3 Damages	B3(b)
4 Remoteness of damage	B3(b)
5 Measure of damages	B3(b)
6 Liquidated damages and penalty clauses	B3(b)
7 Other common law remedies	B3(c)
8 Equitable remedies	B3(c)

Introduction

Most contracts end with the intended result, however many contracts end with one party breaching the **terms** of the deal. This chapter examines what breach of contract is and what the remedies are for the innocent party.

Damages are **monetary compensation** for a loss. However, there are rules concerning what damages can be claimed for and how much should be awarded. **Liquidated damages** and **penalty clauses** are contractual terms that state how damages will be calculated so both parties agree to them in advance. You should be able to explain when these will and will not be enforced by the court.

There are also **equitable remedies** that can be claimed if damages are not suitable. You should be able to explain all of them.

Study guide

		Intellectual level
(B)	**The law of obligations**	
3	Breach of contract and remedies	
(a)	Explain the meaning and effect of breach of contract	2
(b)	Explain the rules relating to the award of damages	2
(c)	Analyse the equitable remedies for breach of contract	2

Exam guide

In scenario questions you may be asked to give advice as to whether or not one party can claim damages from another. Knowledge based questions may require you to explain the circumstances where damages and other remedies would be available.

1 Discharge of contract

> **FAST FORWARD**
>
> Contracts can be discharged through **agreement**, **frustration**, **performance** and **breach**.

Contracts can be **discharged** in four ways:

- **Agreement**. Where both parties agree to end the agreement and it is supported by consideration

- **Frustration**. Where performance of an obligation is impossible due to specific circumstances occurring after formation of the contract.

- **Performance**. The most common method of discharge. The contractual obligations are exactly or substantially met (all contract terms are performed).

- **Breach**. Where one party fails to meet its contractual obligations (see Section 2 below).

Exam focus point

> Your syllabus concentrates on **breach of contract** and does not require you to explain the other methods of discharge.

2 Breach of contract

> **FAST FORWARD**
>
> A party is said to be in breach of contract where, without **lawful excuse**, he does not perform his contractual obligations precisely.

A person sometimes has a lawful excuse not to perform contractual obligations, if:

- Performance is **impossible**, perhaps because of some unforeseeable event.
- He has tendered performance but this has been **rejected.**
- The **other party** has made it **impossible** for him to perform.
- The contract has been discharged through **frustration**.
- The parties have by **agreement** permitted **non-performance.**

Breach of contract gives rise to a secondary obligation to pay damages to the other party. However, the primary obligation to perform the contract's terms remains, unless the party in default has **repudiated** the contract. This may be before performance is due, or before it has been completed, and repudiation has been accepted by the injured party.

Repudiation can be defined as a breach of contract which entitles the injured party to end the contract if he so chooses.

2.1 Repudiatory breach

Breach of a **condition** in a contract or other repudiatory breach allows the injured party to **terminate** the contract unless the injured party elects to treat the contract as continuing and merely claim **damages** for his loss.

A **repudiatory breach** occurs where a party indicates, either by words or by conduct, that he does not intend to honour his contractual obligations or commits a breach of condition or commits a breach which has very serious consequences for the injured party. It usually occurs when performance is due.

It does not **automatically** discharge the contract – indeed the injured party has a choice.

- He can elect to treat the contract as repudiated by the other, **recover damages** and treat himself as being discharged from his primary obligations under the contract.
- He can elect to **affirm** the contract.

2.1.1 Types of repudiatory breach

Repudiatory breach arises in the following circumstances.

(a) **Refusal to perform (renunciation).** One party renounces his contractual obligations by showing that he has no intention to perform them: *Hochster v De la Tour 1853* (See below.)

(b) **Failure to perform an entire obligation.** An entire obligation is said to be one where complete and precise performance of it is a precondition of the other party's performance.

(c) **Incapacitation.** Where a party prevents himself from performing his contractual obligations he is treated as if he refused to perform them. For instance, where A sells a thing to C even though he promised to sell it to B, he is in repudiatory breach of his contract with B.

(d) **Breach of condition** (discussed in Chapter 6)

(e) **Breach of an innominate term** which has the effect of depriving the injured party of substantially the whole benefit of the contract (discussed in Chapter 6).

2.1.2 Anticipatory breach

If there is **anticipatory breach** (one party declares in advance that he will not perform his side of the bargain when the time for performance arrives) the other party may treat the contract as discharged forthwith, or continue with his obligations until actual breach occurs. His claim for damages will then depend upon what he has actually lost.

Repudiation may be **explicit** or **implicit**. A party may break a condition of the contract merely by declaring in advance that he will not perform it, or by some other action which makes future performance impossible. The other party may treat this as **anticipatory breach**

- Treat the contract as discharged forthwith
- At his option may allow the contract to continue until there is an actual breach

Hochster v De La Tour 1853

The facts: The defendant engaged the claimant as a courier to accompany him on a European tour commencing on 1 June. On 11 May he wrote to the claimant to say that he no longer required his services. On 22 May the claimant commenced legal proceedings for anticipatory breach of contract. The defendant objected that there was no actionable breach until 1 June.

Decision: The claimant was entitled to sue as soon as the anticipatory breach occurred on 11 May.

Where the injured party allows the contract to continue, it may happen that the parties are discharged from their obligations **without** liability by some other cause which occurs later.

If the innocent party elects to treat the contract as still in force, the former may continue with his preparations for performance and **recover the agreed price** for his services. Any claim for damages will be assessed on the basis of what the claimant has really lost.

White & Carter (Councils) v McGregor 1961

The facts: The claimants supplied litter bins to local councils, and were paid not by the councils but by traders who hired advertising space on the bins. The defendant contracted with them for advertising of his business. He then wrote to cancel the contract but the claimants elected to advertise as agreed, even though they had at the time of cancellation taken no steps to perform the contract. They performed the contract and claimed the agreed payment.

Decision: The contract continued in force and they were entitled to recover the agreed price for their services. Repudiation does not, of itself, bring the contract to an end. It gives the innocent party the choice of affirmation or rejection.

The Mihalis Angelos 1971

The facts: The parties entered into an agreement for the charter of a ship to be 'ready to load at Haiphong' (in Vietnam) on 1 July 1965. The charterers had the option to cancel if the ship was not ready to load by 20 July. On 17 July the charterers repudiated the contract believing (wrongly) that they were entitled to do so. The shipowners accepted the repudiation and claimed damages. On 17 July the ship was still in Hong Kong and could not have reached Haiphong by 20 July.

Decision: The shipowners were entitled only to nominal damages since they would have been unable to perform the contract and the charterers could have cancelled it without liability on 20 July.

2.1.3 Termination for repudiatory breach

To terminate for repudiatory breach the innocent party must **notify** the other of his decision. This may be by way of refusal to accept defects in performance, refusal to accept further performance, or refusal to perform his own obligations.

- He is not bound by his **future** or **continuing contractual obligations**, and cannot be sued on them.
- He need not **accept** nor pay for further performance.
- He can **refuse to pay** for partial or defective performance already received, unless the contract is severable.
- He can **reclaim money** paid to a defaulter if he can and does reject defective performance.
- He is **not discharged** from the contractual obligations which were due at the time of termination.

The innocent party can also claim **damages** from the defaulter. An innocent party who began to perform his contractual obligations but who was prevented from completing them by the defaulter can claim **reasonable** remuneration on a *quantum meruit* basis.

2.1.4 Affirmation after repudiatory breach

If a person is aware of the other party's repudiatory breach and of his own right to terminate the contract as a result but still decides to treat the contract as being in existence he is said to have **affirmed the contract**. The contract remains fully in force.

Point to note

Anticipatory breach occurs before the time that performance is due. Repudiatory breach usually occurs at the time of performance.

3 Damages

FAST FORWARD

Damages are a common law remedy and are primarily intended to restore the party who has suffered loss to the position he would have been in if the contract had been performed. The two tests applied to a claim for damages relate to **remoteness of damage** and **measure of damages**.

Key term

Damages are a common law remedy intended to restore the party who has suffered loss to the same position he would have been in if the contract had been performed. The two tests applied to a claim for damages relate to **remoteness of damage** and **measure of damages**.

Damages form the main remedy in actions for breach of contract, but there are others: injunctions and specific performance are the most important.

In a claim for damages the first issue is **remoteness of damage**. Here the courts consider how far down the sequence of cause and effect the consequences of breach should be traced before they should be ignored. Secondly, the court must decide how much money to award in respect of the breach and its relevant consequences. This is the **measure of damages**.

4 Remoteness of damage

FAST FORWARD

Remoteness of damage is tested by the **two limbs** of the rule in **Hadley v Baxendale 1854**.

- The first part of the rule states that the **loss must arise either naturally from the breach** or in a manner which the parties may reasonably be supposed to have contemplated when making the contract.

- The second part of the rule provides that a **loss outside the usual course of events** will only be compensated if the exceptional circumstances which caused it were within the defendant's **actual or constructive knowledge** when he made the contract.

Under the rule in *Hadley v Baxendale* damages may only be awarded in respect of loss as follows.

(a)   (i)   **The loss must arise naturally** from the breach.

       (ii)   The loss must arise **in a manner which the parties may reasonably be supposed to have contemplated**, in making the contract, as the probable result of the breach of it.

(b)   A loss outside the **natural course** of events will only be compensated if the exceptional circumstances are within the defendant's knowledge when he made the contract.

Hadley v Baxendale 1854

The facts: The claimants owned a mill at Gloucester whose main crank shaft had broken. They made a contract with the defendant for the transport of the broken shaft to Greenwich to serve as a pattern for making a new shaft. Owing to neglect by the defendant, delivery was delayed and the mill was out of action for a longer period. The defendant did not know that the mill would be idle during this interval. He was merely aware that he had to transport a broken millshaft. The claimants claimed for loss of profits of the mill during the period of delay.

Decision: Although the failure of the carrier to perform the contract promptly was the direct cause of the stoppage of the mill for an unnecessarily long time, the claim must fail since the defendant did not know that the mill would be idle until the new shaft was delivered. Moreover it was not a natural consequence of delay in transport of a broken shaft that the mill would be out of action. The miller might have a spare.

The defendant is liable only if he knew of the **special circumstances** from which the abnormal consequence of breach could arise.

> **Victoria Laundry (Windsor) v Newman Industries 1949**
>
> *The facts:* The defendants contracted to sell a large boiler to the claimants 'for immediate use' in their business of launderers and dyers. Owing to an accident in dismantling the boiler at its previous site delivery was delayed. The defendants were aware of the nature of the claimants' business and had been informed that the claimants were most anxious to put the boiler into use in the shortest possible space of time. The claimants claimed damages for normal loss of profits for the period of delay and for loss of abnormal profits from losing 'highly lucrative' dyeing contracts to be undertaken if the boiler had been delivered on time.
>
> *Decision:* Damages for loss of normal profits were recoverable since in the circumstances failure to deliver major industrial equipment ordered for immediate use would be expected to prevent operation of the plant. The claim for loss of special profits failed because the defendants had no knowledge of the dyeing contracts.

Contrast this ruling with the case below.

> **The Heron II 1969**
>
> *The facts:* K entered into a contract with C for the shipment of a cargo of sugar belonging to C to Basra. He was aware that C were sugar merchants but he did not know that C intended to sell the cargo as soon as it reached Basra. The ship arrived nine days late and in that time the price of sugar on the market in Basra had fallen. C claimed damages for the loss due to the fall in market value.
>
> *Decision:* The claim succeeded. It is common knowledge that market values of commodities fluctuate so that delay might cause loss.

If the type of loss caused is not **too remote** the defendant may be liable for serious consequences.

> **H Parsons (Livestock) v Uttley Ingham 1978**
>
> *The facts:* There was a contract for the supply and installation of a large storage hopper to hold pig foods. Owing to negligence of the defendant supplier the ventilation cowl was left closed. The pig food went mouldy. Young pigs contracted a rare intestinal disease, from which 254 died. The pig farmer claimed damages for the value of the dead pigs and loss of profits from selling the pigs when mature.
>
> *Decision:* Some degree of illness of the pigs was to be expected as a natural consequence. Since illness was to be expected, death from illness was not too remote.

5 Measure of damages

FAST FORWARD

The **measure of damages** is that which will **compensate for the loss incurred**. It is not intended that the injured party should profit from a claim. Damages may be awarded for financial and non-financial loss.

As a general rule, the amount awarded as damages is what is needed to put the claimant in the position he would have achieved if the contract had been performed. This is sometimes referred to as protecting the **expectation interest** of the claimant.

A claimant may alternatively seek to have his **reliance interest** protected; this refers to the position he would have been in had he not relied on the contract. This compensates for wasted expenditure.

The onus is on the defendant to show that the expenditure would **not** have been recovered if the contract had been performed.

> ### C & P Haulage v Middleton 1983
>
> *The facts:* The claimants granted to the defendant a 6-month renewable licence to occupy premises as an engineering workshop. He incurred expenditure in doing up the premises, although the contract provided that he could not remove any fixtures he installed. He was ejected in breach of the licence agreement 10 weeks before the end of a 6-month term. He sued for damages.
>
> *Decision:* The defendant could only recover nominal damages. He could not recover the cost of equipping the premises (as reliance loss) as he would not have been able to do so if the contract had been lawfully terminated.

If a contract is **speculative**, it may be unclear what profit might result.

> ### Anglia Television Ltd v Reed 1972
>
> *The facts:* The claimants engaged an actor to appear in a film they were making for television. He pulled out at the last moment and the project was abandoned. The claimants claimed the preparatory expenditure, such as hiring other actors and researching suitable locations.
>
> *Decision:* Damages were awarded as claimed. It is impossible to tell whether an unmade film will be a success or a failure and, had the claimants claimed for loss of profits, they would not have succeeded.

The general principle is to compensate for **actual financial loss**.

> ### Thompson Ltd v Robinson (Gunmakers) Ltd 1955
>
> *The facts:* The defendants contracted to buy a Vanguard car from the claimants. They refused to take delivery and the claimants sued for loss of profit on the transaction. There was at the time a considerable excess of supply of such cars over demand for them and the claimants were unable to sell the car.
>
> *Decision:* The market price rule (see below), which the defendants argued should be applied, was inappropriate in the current market as demand for such cars was so low as to effectively mean that no market for them existed. The seller had lost a sale and was entitled to the profit.

> ### Charter v Sullivan 1957
>
> *The facts:* The facts were the same as in the previous case, except that the sellers were able to sell every car obtained from the manufacturers.
>
> *Decision:* Only nominal damages were payable.

5.1 Market price rule

The measure of damages for breaches of contract for the sale of goods is usually made in relation to the **market price** of the goods. Where a seller fails to sell the goods, the buyer can go into the market and purchase **equivalent goods** instead. The seller would have to compensate the buyer for any additional cost the buyer incurred over the contract cost. The situation is reversed when the buyer fails to purchase the goods. The seller can sell the goods on the **open market** and recover any **loss of income** he incurred by having to sell the goods at a lower price than that he contracted to.

5.2 Non-financial loss

In some cases, damages have been recovered for mental distress where that is the main result of the breach. It is uncertain how far the courts will develop this concept. Contrast the cases below.

Jarvis v Swan Tours 1973

The facts: The claimant entered into a contract for holiday accommodation at a winter sports centre. What was provided was much inferior to the description given in the defendant's brochure. Damages on the basis of financial loss only were assessed at £32.

Decision: The damages should be increased to £125 to compensate for disappointment and distress because this was a contract the principle purpose of which was the giving of pleasure.

Alexander v Rolls Royce Motor Cars Ltd 1995

The facts: The claimant sued for breach of contract to repair his Rolls Royce motor car and claimed damages for distress and inconvenience or loss of enjoyment of the car.

Decision: Breach of contract to repair a car did not give rise to any liability for damages for distress, inconvenience or loss of enjoyment.

5.3 Cost of cure

Where there has been a breach and the claimant is seeking to be put in the position he would have been in if the contract had been performed, by seeking a sum of money to 'cure' the defect which constituted the breach, he may be denied the cost of cure if it is **wholly disproportionate** to the breach.

Ruxley Electronics and Construction Ltd v Forsyth 1995

The facts: A householder discovered that the swimming pool he had ordered to be built was shallower than specified. He sued the builder for damages, including the cost of demolition of the pool and construction of a new one. Despite its shortcomings, the pool as built was perfectly serviceable and safe to dive into.

Decision: The expenditure involved in rectifying the breach was out of all proportion to the benefit of such rectification. The claimant was awarded a small sum to cover loss of amenity.

5.4 Mitigation of loss

In assessing the amount of damages it is assumed that the claimant will take any reasonable steps to reduce or **mitigate** his loss. The burden of proof is on the defendant to show that the claimant failed to take a reasonable opportunity of mitigation.

Payzu Ltd v Saunders 1919

The facts: The parties had entered into a contract for the supply of goods to be delivered and paid for by instalments. The claimants failed to pay for the first instalment when due, one month after delivery. The defendants declined to make further deliveries unless the claimants paid cash in advance with their orders. The claimants refused to accept delivery on those terms. The price of the goods rose, and they sued for breach of contract.

Decision: The seller had no right to repudiate the original contract. But the claimants should have mitigated their loss by accepting the seller's offer of delivery against cash payment. Damages were limited to the amount of their assumed loss if they had paid in advance, which was interest over the period of pre-payment.

The injured party is not required to take **discreditable** or **risky measures** to reduce his loss since these are not 'reasonable'.

> *Pilkington v Wood 1953*
>
> *The facts:* The claimant bought a house in Hampshire, having been advised by his solicitor that title was good. The following year, he decided to sell it. A purchaser was found but it was discovered that the house was not saleable at the agreed price, as the title was not good. The defendant was negligent in his investigation of title and was liable to pay damages of £2,000, being the difference between the market value of the house with good title and its market value with defective title. The defendant argued that the claimant should have mitigated his loss by taking action against the previous vendor for conveying a defective title.
>
> *Decision:* This would have involved complicated litigation and it was not clear that he would have succeeded. The claimant was under no duty to embark on such a hazardous venture 'to protect his solicitor from the consequences of his own carelessness'.

Question   **Measure of damages**

Chana agrees to buy a car from Mike's Motors for £6,000. Mike paid £5,500 for the car. On the agreed day, Chana arrives at the dealers but refuses to accept or pay for the car. In the meantime, the car's market value has risen to £7,000. The following week Mike sells the car for £7,500. Mike claims against Chana for damages. How much is he likely to be awarded?

Answer

He is likely to be awarded nominal damages only, as he has incurred no loss.

6 Liquidated damages and penalty clauses

FAST FORWARD

> To avoid later complicated calculations of loss, or disputes over damages payable, the parties may include up-front in their contract a formula (**liquidated damages**) for determining the damages payable for breach.

Key term

> **Liquidated damages** can be defined as 'a fixed or ascertainable sum agreed by the parties at the time of contracting, payable in the event of a breach, for example, an amount payable per day for failure to complete a building. If they are a genuine attempt to pre-estimate the likely loss the court will enforce payment.'

> *Dunlop Pneumatic Tyre Co Ltd v New Garage & Motor Co Ltd 1915*
>
> *The facts:* The contract (for the sale of tyres to a garage) imposed a minimum retail price. The contract provided that £5 per tyre should be paid by the buyer if he resold at less than the prescribed retail price or in four other possible cases of breach of contract. He did sell at a lower price and argued that £5 per tyre was a 'penalty' and not a genuine pre-estimate of loss.
>
> *Decision:* As a general rule when a fixed amount is to be paid as damages for breaches of different kinds, some more serious in their consequences than others, that is not a genuine pre-estimate of loss and so it is void as a 'penalty'. In this case the formula was an honest attempt to agree on liquidated damages and would be upheld.

> *Ford Motor Co (England) Ltd v Armstrong 1915*
>
> *The facts:* The defendant had undertaken not to sell the claimant's cars below list price, not to sell Ford cars to other dealers and not to exhibit any Ford cars without permission. A £250 penalty was payable for each breach as being the agreed damage which the claimant would sustain.
>
> *Decision:* Since the same sum was payable for different kinds of loss it was not a genuine pre-estimate of loss and was in the nature of a penalty. Unlike the *Dunlop* case the figure set was held to be excessive.

A contractual term designed as a **penalty clause** to discourage breach is void and not enforceable. Relief from penalty clauses is an example of the influence of equity in the law of contract, and has most frequently been seen in consumer credit cases.

Key term

> A **penalty clause** can be defined as 'a clause in a contract providing for a specified sum of money to be payable in the event of a subsequent breach. If its purpose is merely to deter a potential difficulty, it will be held void and the court will proceed to assess unliquidated damages.'

> *Bridge v Campbell Discount Co 1962*
>
> *The facts:* A clause in a hire purchase contract required the debtor to pay on termination both arrears of payments due before termination and an amount which, together with payments made and due before termination, amounted to two thirds of the HP price, and additionally to return the goods.
>
> *Decision:* This was a penalty clause and void since, in almost all circumstances, the creditor would receive on termination more than 100% of the value of the goods.

We have seen that if a clause for liquidated damages is included in the contract it should be highlighted as an **onerous term**. In *Interfoto Picture Library Ltd v Stiletto Visual Programmes Ltd 1988* the defendants did not plead that the clause in question was a penalty clause and hence void, but it is probable that they could have done.

7 Other common law remedies

7.1 Action for the price

FAST FORWARD

A simple **action for the price** to recover the agreed sum should be brought if breach of contract is failure to pay the price. But property must have passed from seller to buyer, and complications arise where there is anticipatory breach.

If the breach of contract arises out of one party's failure to pay the contractually agreed price due under the contract, the creditor should bring a personal action against the debtor to recover that sum. This is a fairly straightforward procedure but is subject to two specific limitations.

The first is that an **action for the price** under a contract for the sale of goods may only be brought if property has passed to the buyer, unless the price has been agreed to be payable on a specific date: s 49 Sale of Goods Act 1979.

Secondly, whilst the injured party may recover an agreed sum due at the time of an anticipatory breach, sums which become due after the anticipatory breach may not be recovered unless he affirms the contract.

7.2 Quantum meruit

FAST FORWARD

A **quantum meruit** is a claim which is available as an alternative to damages. The injured party in a breach of a contract may claim the value of his work. The aim of such an award is to restore the claimant to the position he would have been in had the contract never been made. It is a **restitutory award**.

In particular situations, a claim may be made on a quantum meruit basis as an **alternative** to an action for damages for breach of contract.

Key term

The phrase **quantum meruit** literally means **'how much it is worth'**. It is a measure of the value of contractual work which has been performed. The aim of such an award is to restore the claimant to the position he would have been in if the contract had never been made, and is therefore known as a **restitutory award**.

Quantum meruit is likely to be sought where one party has already performed part of his obligations and the other party then repudiates the contract.

De Barnardy v Harding 1853

The facts: The claimant agreed to advertise and sell tickets for the defendant, who was erecting stands for spectators to view the funeral of the Duke of Wellington. The defendant cancelled the arrangement without justification.

Decision: The claimant might recover the value of services rendered.

In most cases, a quantum meruit claim is needed because the other party has unjustifiably prevented performance: *Planché v Colburn 1831*.

Because it is **restitutory**, a quantum meruit award is usually for a **smaller amount** than an award of damages. However where only **nominal damages** would be awarded (say because the claimant would not have been able to perform the contract anyway) a quantum meruit claim would still be available and would yield a **higher amount**.

8 Equitable remedies

8.1 Specific performance

FAST FORWARD

An order for **specific performance** is an equitable remedy. The party in breach is ordered to perform his side of the contract. Such an order is only made where damages are inadequate compensation, such as in a sale of land, and where actual consideration has passed.

The court may at its **discretion** give an equitable remedy by ordering the defendant to perform his part of the contract instead of letting him 'buy himself out of it' by paying damages for breach.

Key term

Specific performance can be defined as 'an order of the court directing a person to perform an obligation. It is an equitable remedy awarded at the discretion of the court when damages would not be an adequate remedy. Its principal use is in contracts for the sale of land but may also be used to compel a sale of shares or debentures. It will never be used in the case of employment or other contracts involving personal services.'

An order will be made for specific performance of a contract for the **sale of land** since the claimant may need the land for a particular purpose and would not be adequately compensated by damages for the loss of his bargain.

The order will **not** be made if it would require performance over a period of time and the court could not ensure that the defendant did comply fully with the order. Therefore specific performance is not ordered for contracts of **employment** or **personal service** nor usually for building contracts.

8.2 Injunction

FAST FORWARD

An **injunction** is a discretionary court order and an equitable remedy, requiring the defendant to observe a negative condition of a contract.

Key term

> An **injunction** is a discretionary court order and an equitable remedy, requiring the defendant to observe a negative restriction of a contract.

An injunction may be made to **enforce** a contract of **personal service** for which an order of specific performance would be refused.

> *Warner Bros Pictures Inc v Nelson 1937*
>
> *The facts:* The defendant (the film star Bette Davis) agreed to work for a year for the claimants and not during the year to work for any other producer nor 'to engage in any other occupation' without the consent of the claimants. She came to England during the year to work for a British film producer. The claimants sued for an injunction to restrain her from this work and she resisted arguing that if the restriction were enforced she must either work for them or abandon her livelihood.
>
> *Decision:* The court would not make an injunction if it would have the result suggested by the defendant. But the claimants merely asked for an injunction to restrain her from working for a British film producer. This was one part of the restriction accepted by her under her contract and it was fair to hold her to it to that extent.

An injunction is limited to **enforcement** of **contract terms** which are in substance negative restraints.

> *Metropolitan Electric Supply Co v Ginder 1901*
>
> *The facts:* The defendant contracted to take all the electricity which he required from the claimants. They sued for an injunction to restrain him from obtaining electricity from another supplier.
>
> *Decision:* The contract term (electricity only from the one supplier) implied a negative restriction (no supplies from any other source) and to that extent it could be enforced by injunction.

An injunction would **not** be made merely to **restrain** the defendant from acts inconsistent with his positive obligations.

> *Whitwood Chemical Co v Hardman 1891*
>
> *The facts:* The defendant agreed to give the whole of his time to his employers, the claimants. In fact he occasionally worked for others. The employers sued for an injunction to restrain him.
>
> *Decision:* By his contract he merely stated what he would do. This did not imply an undertaking to abstain from doing other things.

8.2.1 Mareva or 'freezing' injunctions

The Mareva injunction is named from the case of *Mareva Compania Naviera SA v International Bulkcarriers SA 1975*, but it has now been given **statutory effect** by s 37 Supreme Court Act 1981. If the claimant can convince the court that he has a good case and that there is a danger of the defendant's assets being exported or dissipated, he may be awarded an injunction which restricts the defendant's dealing with the assets.

8.3 Rescission

Strictly speaking the equitable right to **rescind** an agreement is not a remedy for breach of contract – it is a right which exists in certain circumstances, such as where a contract is **voidable**.

Rescinding a contract means that it is cancelled or rejected and the parties are restored to their pre-contract condition. Four conditions must be met.

- It must be possible for each party to be returned to the pre-contract condition *(restitutio in integrum)*.
- An innocent third party who has acquired rights in the subject matter of the contract will prevent the original transaction being rescinded.
- The right to rescission must be exercised within a reasonable time of it arising.
- Where a person affirms a contract expressly or by conduct it may not then be rescinded.

Exam focus point

> You may be asked for a general discussion of remedies for breach of contract. Alternatively, you may be asked whether a particular remedy, say specific performance, is appropriate in any given situation.

Chapter Roundup

- Contracts can be discharged through **agreement**, **frustration**, **performance** and **breach**.

- A party is said to be in breach of contract where, without **lawful excuse**, he does not perform his contractual obligations precisely.

- **Breach** of a **condition** in a contract or other repudiatory breach allows the injured party to **terminate** the contract unless the injured party elects to treat the contract as continuing and merely claim **damages** for his loss.

- If there is **anticipatory breach** (one party declares in advance that he will not perform his side of the bargain when the time for performance arrives) the other party may treat the contract as discharged forthwith, or continue with his obligations until actual breach occurs. His claim for damages will then depend upon what he has actually lost.

- **Damages** are a common law remedy intended to restore the party who has suffered loss to the position he would have been in had the contract been performed. The two tests applied to a claim for damages relate to **remoteness of damage** and **measure of damages**.

- **Remoteness of damage** is tested by the **two limbs** of the rule in **Hadley v Baxendale 1854**.

    - The first part of the rule states that the **loss must arise either naturally from the breach** or in a manner which the parties may reasonably be supposed to have contemplated when making the contract.

    - The second part of the rule provides that a **loss outside the usual course of events** will only be compensated if the exceptional circumstances which caused it were within the defendant's **actual or constructive knowledge** when he made the contract.

- The **measure of damages** is that which will **compensate for the loss incurred**. It is not intended that the injured party should profit from a claim. Damages may be awarded for financial and non-financial loss.

- To avoid later complicated calculations of loss, or disputes over damages payable, the parties may include up-front in their contract a formula (**liquidated damages**) for determining the damages payable for breach.

- A simple **action for the price** to recover the agreed sum should be brought if breach of contract is failure to pay the price. But property must have passed from seller to buyer, and complications arise where there is anticipatory breach.

- A **quantum meruit** is a claim which is available as an alternative to damages. The injured party in a breach of a contract may claim the value of his work. The aim of such an award is to restore the claimant to the position he would have been in had the contract never been made. It is a **restitutory** award.

- An order for **specific performance** is an equitable remedy. The party in breach is ordered to perform his side of the contract. Such an order is only made where damages are inadequate compensation, such as in a sale of land, and where actual consideration has passed.

- An **injunction** is a discretionary court order and an equitable remedy, requiring the defendant to observe a negative conditions of a contract.

1   **Fill in the blanks** in the statements below, using the words in the box.

(1) ……………….. are a (2) ……………….. remedy designed to restore the injured party to the position he would have been in had the contract been (3) ………………..

A loss outside the natural course of events will only be compensated if the (4) ……………….. circumstances are within the (5) ………………..'s knowledge at the time of making the contract.

In assessing the amount of damage it is assumed that the (6) ……………….. will (7) ……………….. his loss.

A contractual term designed as a (8) ……………….. is (9) ……………….. .

• mitigate	• performed	• claimant
• penalty clause	• exceptional	• damages
• common law	• void	• defendant

2   **Fill in the blanks** in the statements below.

When anticipatory breach occurs, the injured party has two options. These are

(1) ………………..

(2) ………………..

3   What is the two-limbed rule set out in *Hadley v Baxendale*?

4   The amount awarded as damages is what is needed to put the claimant in the position he would have achieved if the contract had been performed. What interest is being protected here?

expectation
reliance

5   A court will never enforce a liquidated damages clause, as any attempt to discourage breach is void.

True   ☐

False   ☐

6   Are each of the following remedies based on (i) equity or (ii) common law?

(a)   Quantum meruit
(b)   Injunction
(c)   Action for the price
(d)   Rescission
(e)   Specific performance

7   What are the two limitations on the creditor's right to bring an action for the price?

8   What four conditions must be met for rescission to be possible?

1. (1) damages   (2) common law   (3) performed
   (4) exceptional   (5) defendant   (6) claimant
   (7) mitigate   (8) penalty clause   (9) void

2. (1) treat the contract as discharged forthwith
   (2) allow the contract to continue until there is an actual breach

3. (i) The loss must arise naturally from the breach

   (ii) The loss must arise in a manner which the parties may reasonably be supposed to have contemplated when making the contract was made.

4. Expectation

5. False. Courts will enforce liquidated damages clauses if they are genuine.

6. (a) Common law
   (b) Equity
   (c) Common law
   (d) Equity
   (e) Equity

7. (i) An action for the price under a contract for the sale of goods may only be brought if property has passed (or price is payable on a specified date).

   (ii) Sums which become due after an anticipatory breach may not be recovered unless the creditor has affirmed the contract.

8. (a) It must be possible for each party to be returned to the pre-contract condition *(restitutio in integrum)*.

   (b) An innocent third party who has acquired rights in the subject matter of the contract will prevent the original transaction being rescinded.

   (c) The right to rescission must be exercised within a reasonable time of it arising.

   (d) Where a person affirms a contract expressly or by conduct it may not then be rescinded.

Now try the questions below from the Exam Question Bank

Number	Level	Marks	Time
Q10	Examination	10	18 mins
Q11	Examination	10	18 mins

The law of torts

Topic list	Syllabus reference
1 Tort and other wrongs	B4(a), B4(b)
2 The tort of negligence	B4(b)
3 Duty of care	B4(c)
4 Breach of duty of care	B4(c)
5 Causality and remoteness of damage	B4(d)
6 Defences to negligence	B4(e)

Introduction

In this chapter we introduce the law of torts.

Torts are **wrongful acts** against an **individual**, a **company** or their **property** that gives rise to a **civil liability** against the person who committed them.

There are a number of torts, however **negligence** is the one that will concern you most in your studies.

Your syllabus requires you to understand the **nature** of torts and to explain the **factors** that must be present for claims to succeed. By focussing on the rules and their related **cases** you will be able to apply them to any case given to you in an exam question.

Study guide

		Intellectual level
(B)	**The law of obligations**	
4	The law of torts	
(a)	Explain the meaning of tort	2
(b)	Identify examples of torts including 'passing off' and negligence	2
(c)	Explain the duty of care and its breach	2
(d)	Explain the meaning of causality and remoteness of damage	2
(e)	Discuss defences to actions in negligence	2

Exam guide

There are a number of ways tort could be examined. Scenario questions may require you to identify whether a tort has been committed, whether a duty of care exists or if there is sufficient link between the actions and resulting damage for liability to be established. Other questions may require you to explain the different types of tort and the circumstances that create a liability for damages.

1 Tort and other wrongs

> **FAST FORWARD**
>
> The law gives various rights to persons. When such a right is infringed the wrongdoer is liable in **tort**.

1.1 Tort

Tort is distinguished from other legal wrongs.

(a) It is **not** a **breach of contract**, where the obligation which is alleged to have been breached arose under an agreement between two parties.

(b) It is **not** a **crime**, where the object of proceedings is to punish the offender rather than compensate the victim.

Key term

> A **tort** is a civil wrong and the person wronged sues in a **civil court** for compensation or an injunction. The claimant's claim generally is that he has suffered a loss such as personal injury at the hands of the defendant and the defendant should pay damages.
>
> **In tort no previous transaction or contractual relationship need exist**: the parties may be complete strangers as when a motorist knocks down a pedestrian in the street. The claim in tort is based on the general law of duties and rights.

Notwithstanding the distinction made above, note that the same event can easily give rise to more than one legal liability.

1.2 Types of tort

The nature of tort can best be understood by examining examples of torts.

1.2.1 Trespass to land

Trespass to land involves **one** or a **combination** of the following acts without lawful justification:

- **Entering** land that is owned by the claimant
- **Remaining** on the land
- **Placing** objects or projections onto the land

Liability for trespass is **strict**, which means that even if the action is accidental or no damage results from it, the trespasser is still liable. There is a fundamental right to the privacy of the home under English law.

1.2.2 Nuisance

Landowners have the right to use their land as they see fit and not to have their land interfered with. Nuisance occurs where the use of land by one occupier causes **damage** to a neighbouring occupier or their land.

There are two types of nuisance, **private** and **public**.

(a) **Private nuisance**

This is the 'unlawful interference with a person's use, or enjoyment of land, or some right or in connection with it' (*Winfield and Jolowicz*).

Cases of private nuisance often involve neighbours and are caused by noise, smell, vibrations, animals, trees and incursions by other such items. Judging liability is a **balancing act**, occupiers are entitled to 'reasonable comfort' but no more.

(b) **Public nuisance**

Public nuisances are not related to private nuisance as they are created by statute and are therefore **criminal offences**. Examples include obstructing the highway, takeaway restaurants creating litter and odours and 'raves' that attract hundreds of people late at night creating noise and disturbance to a wide area.

These nuisances are 'acts or omissions that materially affect the reasonable comfort and convenience of the life of a class of Her Majesty's subjects ' *Att.-Gen v P.Y.A. Quarries Ltd 1957*. The key point to realise is that the claimant is **not** required to have an **interest in land** before being entitled to sue, unlike private nuisances.

The **number** of people that have to be affected before a liability under public nuisance is created is a question of fact. However the claimant does not have to prove the whole community was affected, just that a representative cross-section was inconvenienced.

1.2.3 Trespass to the person

The acts of **battery**, **assault** and **false imprisonment** are commonly considered within the scope of trespass to the person. You should note that the acts often result in a criminal action against the defendant as well.

(a) **Battery**

Battery involves the **intentional** bringing of a material object into contact with another person. It is not just restricted to violent acts, but can also include non-violent acts such as the application of 'tone rinse' to a scalp – *Nash v Sheen 1953*. For liability to be created it is just the **act** that must be intentional – not the injury.

(b) **Assault**

Assault is the intentional act of putting another in **reasonable fear or apprehension of immediate battery**. Words may not enough to create a liability unless they are accompanied by menacing or threatening actions. For example, telling someone you will shoot them may not be classed as assault unless you are pointing a gun at them as well. The claimant does not have to prove the defendant intended to cause battery, it is sufficient to prove that they were **in reasonable fear** of it. Therefore pointing an unloaded gun constitutes assault even there is no intention to cause injury.

(c) **False imprisonment**

False imprisonment involves **unlawfully arresting**, **imprisoning** or **preventing a person from leaving** from where they are. The claimant does not have to prove damage was caused as it was their liberty that was taken from them.

Describe the difference between assault and battery.

Answer

Battery is the intentional action of bringing a material object into contact with another person. Assault involves putting a person in reasonable fear of battery through words and actions.

1.2.4 Defamation

The **expression** or **publication** of **false** or **defamatory statements** that is not lawfully justified are known collectively as defamation. In other words, defamation involves the **ridicule** of an individual or holding them in **contempt**. The words **libel** and **slander** are often used to describe this tort. In legal terms, libel refers to **visible** acts such as writing, pictures and even effigies. Slanderous acts are those that are **spoken** or **gestured**. You should note that **libel** is a **criminal act** which will be actionable in all cases and **slander** is a **civil injury** and in almost all cases damage must be proved.

1.2.5 Deceit, injurious falsehood and 'passing-off'

Deceit is a wrong whereby the claimant is **mislead** into taking actions that are to his detriment. A typical example of deceit is the con-artist who encourages an individual to pay him money for goods that he has no intention of supplying.

Injurious falsehood involves the defendant making **false statements** about the claimant that cause the claimant damage through the actions of others. A key example in the business context is the tort of **passing-off.**

Passing-off is the use of a name, mark or description by one business that **misleads a consumer** to believe that their business is that of another. This tort often occurs when expensive 'designer' products such as watches or clothing are copied and sold as 'originals' to unsuspecting customers.

The development of the **internet** in recent years has seen the routine selling of domain names to those who wish to buy them. This has created the opportunity for individuals to set up a website that has the intention of mimicking an established brand and stealing their customers.

We shall return to the tort of 'passing-off' in more detail in Chapter 15 where we consider the impact it has on the choice of company names.

1.2.6 Negligence

The number of actions under negligence far exceeds the number under the other torts. In simple terms the **carelessness** of an individual or company causes damage (physical or financial) to the claimant. Negligent acts tend to be **inadvertent** or **reckless**, but not normally intentional.

We shall be studying negligence in more detail later in Section 2.

Question

John has run his fish and chip shop called ' Fry and Fish' for the last ten years. He finds out that a new fish and chip shop called 'Fish and Fries' run by Kevin has recently opened round the corner from him. Angry that he may lose custom he arranges for leaflets to be printed that state '... Kevin of Fish and Fries hates fish and everyone who eats it!....' John distributes the leaflets to homes in the vicinity of the shops even though he knows the statement to be untrue.

Which torts may have been committed?

The first tort that must be considered is passing-off. Kevin's shop has a similar name to John's but it is unlikely that it would mislead customers to think that his shop is John's. Therefore no tort has been committed.

John's printed statement is unlawful, holds Kevin to ridicule and is therefore defamatory. The fact that it is written makes it libellous rather than slanderous.

2 The tort of negligence

FAST FORWARD

Negligence is the most important modern tort. To succeed in an action for negligence the claimant must prove that:

- The defendant had **a duty of care** to avoid causing injury, damage or loss
- There was **a breach of that duty** by the defendant
- *In consequence* the claimant suffered **injury, damage or loss**

2.1 Definition

There is a **distinct tort of negligence** which is causing loss by a failure to take reasonable care when there is a duty to do so. This is the most important and far reaching modern tort.

FAST FORWARD

The term negligence is used to describe **carelessly** carrying out an **act** and breaking a **legal duty of care** owed to another causing them **loss or damage.**

Exam focus point

You must be aware of the academic requirements for negligence to be proved. The criteria for a successful negligence action are fundamental and should be learnt by all students.

3 Duty of care

FAST FORWARD

In the landmark case of *Donoghue v Stevenson 1932* the House of Lords ruled that a person might **owe a duty of care to another with whom he had no contractual relationship** at all. The doctrine has been refined in subsequent rulings, but the principle is unchanged.

3.1 The basic rule

The question of whether or not a duty of care exists in any situation is generally decided by the courts on a **case by case basis**, with each new case setting a precedent based on its own particular facts.

In the case described below, the House of Lords was attempting to establish a general duty that could be applied to all subsequent cases and situations.

Donoghue v Stevenson 1932

The facts: A purchased a bottle of ginger beer for consumption by B. B drank part of the contents, which contained the remains of a decomposed snail, and became ill. The manufacturer argued that as there was no contract between himself and B he owed her no duty of care and so was not liable.

Decision: The House of Lords laid down the general principle that every person owes a duty of care to his 'neighbour', to 'persons so closely and directly affected by my act that I ought reasonably to have them in contemplation as being so affected'.

3.2 Development of the doctrine

This narrow doctrine has been much refined over the years since the snail made its celebrated appearance. For any duty of care to exist, it was stated in *Anns v Merton London Borough Council 1977* that two stages must be tested:

- Is there sufficient **proximity** between the parties, such that the harm suffered was **reasonably foreseeable**?

- Should the duty be **restricted** or **limited** for reasons of economic, social or public policy?

The latest stage in the doctrine's development came in *Caparo Industries plc v Dickman 1990*. We shall come back to this case when we study the duty of care of accountants and auditors, however it established a three stage test for establishing a duty of care that still stands:

- Was the harm **reasonably foreseeable**?
- Was there a relationship of **proximity** between the parties?
- Considering the circumstances, is it **fair, just and reasonable** to impose a duty of care?

4 Breach of duty of care

FAST FORWARD

The second element that must be proven by a claimant in an action for negligence is that there was a **breach of the duty** of care by the defendant.

4.1 The basic rule

Breach of duty of care is the second issue to be considered in a negligence claim. The standard of reasonable care requires that the person concerned should do what a **reasonable man** would do. This will also mean the reasonable **employer**, or the reasonable **adviser**.

The following factors should be considered when deciding if a duty of care has been breached:

(a) **Probability of injury**

It is presumed that a reasonable man takes **greater precautions** when the risk of injury is high. Therefore when the risk is higher the defendant must do more to meet his duty. In *Glasgow Corporation v Taylor 1992* a local authority was held to be negligent when children ate poisonous berries in a park. A warning notice was not considered to be sufficient to protect children.

(b) **Seriousness** of the risk

The young, old or disabled may be prone to more serious injury than a fit able-bodied person. The **'egg-shell skull'** rule means that you must take your victim as they are. Where the risk to the vulnerable is high, the level of care required is raised.

Paris v Stepney Borough Council 1951

The facts: P was employed by K on vehicle maintenance. P had already lost the sight of one eye. It was not the normal practice to issue protective goggles since the risk of eye injury was small. A chip of metal flew into P's good eye and blinded him.

Decision: There was a higher standard of care owed to P because an injury to his remaining good eye would blind him.

(c) Issues of **practicality and cost**

It is not always reasonable to ensure all possible precautions are taken. Where the **cost** or **disruption** caused to eliminate the danger far **exceeds the risk** of it occurring it is likely that defendants will be found not to have breached their duty if they do not implement them.

> **Latimer v AEC Ltd 1952**
>
> *The facts*: The defendants owned a factory that become flooded after a period of heavy rain. The water mixed with oil on the factory floor causing it to become very slippery. Sawdust was applied to the majority of the areas affected, but the claimant slipped on one of the few areas that was not treated.
>
> *Decision:* The defendant did all that was necessary to reduce the risk to its employees and was not held liable. The only other option was to close the factory, however no evidence could be provided that would indicate a reasonable employer would have done taken that course of action. Closing the factory would have outweighed the risk to the employees.

(d)   **Common practice**

Where an individual can prove their actions were in line with **common practice** or **custom** it is likely that they would have met their duty of care. This is unless the common practice itself is found to be negligent.

(e)   **Social benefit**

Where an action is of **some benefit** to society, defendants may be **protected** from liability even if their actions create risk. For example, a fire engine that speeds to a major disaster provides a social benefit that may outweigh the greater risk to the public.

(f)   **Professions and skill**

Persons who hold themselves out to possess a particular skill should be judged on what a **reasonable person possessing the same skill** would do in the situation rather than that of a reasonable man. Professions are able to set their own **standards of care** for their members to meet and therefore members should be judged against these standards rather than those laid down by the courts.

4.2 Res ipsa loquitur

In some circumstances the claimant may argue that the **facts speak for themselves** (*res ipsa loquitur*) – want of care being the only possible explanation for what happened, negligence on the part of the defendant must be presumed.

Key term

> **Res ipsa loquitur** can be defined as: 'The thing speaks for itself'. If an accident occurs which appears to be most likely caused by negligence, the court may apply this maxim and infer negligence from mere proof of the facts. The burden of proof is reversed and the defendant must prove that s/he was not negligent.

The claimant must demonstrate the following to rely on this principle:

(a)   The thing which caused the injury was under the **management and control** of the defendant.

(b)   The accident was such as would not occur if those in control used **proper care**. Therefore in *Richley v Fould 1965* the fact that a car skidded to the wrong side of the road was enough to indicate careless driving.

4.3 Example

In *Mahon v Osborne 1939* a surgeon was required to prove that leaving a swab inside a patient after an operation was not negligent.

5 Causality and remoteness of damage

FAST FORWARD

Finally the claimant must demonstrate that he suffered injury or loss as a **result** of the breach.

5.1 Damage or loss

This is the third element of a negligence claim. A claim for compensation for negligence will not succeed if **damage** or **loss** is not proved.

A person will only be compensated if he has suffered actual loss, injury, damage or harm **as a consequence** of another's actions. Examples of such loss may include:

- Personal injury
- Damage to property
- Financial loss which is directly connected to personal injury, for example, loss of earnings
- Pure financial loss is rarely recoverable

5.2 The 'But for' test

To satisfy the requirement that harm must be caused by another's actions, the **'But for' test** is applied. The claimant must prove that if it was not 'but for' the other's actions they would not have suffered damage. Therefore claimants are **unable** to claim for any harm that would have happened to them **anyway** irrespective of the defendant's actions.

Barnett v Chealsea and Kensington HMC 1969

The facts: A casualty doctor sent a patient home without treatment, referring him to his own doctor. The patient died of arsenic poisoning.

Decision: Whilst the doctor was held negligent, the negligence did not cause the patient's death as they would have died anyway.

5.2.1 Multiple causes

The courts often have difficulty in determining **causation** where there are a number of possible causes of injury including the negligent act. The courts must decide on the **facts** if the negligent act was the one that most likely caused the injury.

Wilsher v Essex AHA 1988

The facts: A premature baby suffered blindness after birth. It was claimed that a doctor failed to notice that the baby received high doses of oxygen and this caused the blindness.

Decision: Evidence was provided that there was six possible causes of the blindness including the one claimed. However, the court could not ascertain which of the six actually occurred and therefore could not create a direct causal link.

The case below indicates the court's flexibility when applying legal principles in **exceptional** cases.

Fairchild v Glenhaven Funeral Services Ltd & Others 2002

The facts: The claimants all contracted a disease caused by contact with asbestos over extended periods of time with several different employers. The defence claimed that the disease could be contracted by exposure to one asbestos fibre and as the claimants were employed by a number of employers it could not be established at which employer they contracted the disease.

> *Decision:* The House of Lords held that all the employers (who had failed to take reasonable care), contributed to the cause and were all liable.

5.3 Novus actus intervieniens

Courts will only impart liability where there is a cause of events that are a **probable** result of the defendant's actions. Defendant's will not be liable for damage when the chain of events is broken. There are **three types** of intervening act that will break the chain of causation.

5.3.1 Act of the claimant

The actions of the claimant themselves may **break** the chain of causation. The rule is that where the act is **reasonable** and in the **ordinary course of things** an act by the claimant will not break the chain.

> *McKew v Holland, Hannen and Cubbitts (Scotland) Ltd 1969*
>
> *The facts:* The claimant had a leg injury which was prone to causing his leg to give way from time to time. Whilst at work he failed to ask for assistance when negotiating a flight of stairs. He fell and was injured as a result.
>
> *Decision:* The fact that the claimant failed to seek assistance was unreasonable and was sufficient to break the chain of causality.

5.3.2 Act of a third party

Where a **third party** intervenes in the course of events the defendant will normally only be liable for damage **until** the intervention.

> *Lamb v Camden LBC 1981*
>
> *The facts:* The defendant negligently caused a house to be damaged, and as a result it had to be vacated until it could be repaired. During the vacant period, squatters took up residence and the property suffered further damage.
>
> *Decision:* Intrusion by squatters was a possibility that the defendant should have considered, but it was not held to be a likely event. Therefore the defendant should not be liable for the additional damage caused by the intervening actions of the squatters.

5.3.3 Natural events

The chain of causality is **not automatically** broken due to an intervening natural event. In situations where the breach puts the claimant at risk of **additional** damage caused by a natural event the chain will not be broken. However, where the natural event is **unforeseeable**, the chain will be broken.

> *Carslogie Steamship Co Ltd v Royal Norwegian Government 1952*
>
> *The facts:* A ship owned by the claimants was damaged as a result of the defendant's negligence and required repair. During the trip to the repair site the ship was caught in severe weather conditions that resulted in additional damage being caused and therefore a longer repair time was required. The claimants claimed loss of charter revenue for the period the ship was out of action for repairs caused by the original incident.

> *Decision:* The House of Lords held that the defendants were liable for loss of profit suffered as result of the defendants' wrongful act only. Whilst undergoing repairs, the ship ceased to be a profit-earning machine as the weather damage had rendered her unseaworthy. The weather conditions created an intervening act and the claimants had sustained no loss of profit due to the ship being out of action as it would have been unavailable for hire anyway due to the weather damage.

5.4 Remoteness of damage

Even where causation is proved, a negligence claim can still fail if the damage caused is *'too remote'*. The test of **reasonable foresight** developed out of *The Wagon Mound (1961)*. Liability is limited to damage that a **reasonable man** could have foreseen. This does not mean the exact event must be foreseeable in detail, just that the eventual outcome is foreseeable.

> *The Wagon Mound 1961*
>
> *The facts:* A ship was taking on oil in Sydney harbour. Oil was spilled onto the water and it drifted to a wharf 200 yards away where welding equipment was in use. The owner of the wharf carried on working because he was advised that the sparks were unlikely to set fire to furnace oil. Safety precautions were taken. A spark fell onto a piece of cotton waste floating in the oil, thereby starting a fire which damaged the wharf. The owners of the wharf sued the charterers of the Wagon Mound.
>
> *Decision:* The claim must fail. Pollution was the foreseeable risk: fire was not.

The House of Lords decided in the case of *Jolley v London Borough of Sutton 2000* that the remoteness test can be passed if **some** harm is foreseeable even if the exact nature of the injuries could not be.

> *Jolley v London Borough of Sutton 2000*
>
> *The facts:* The defendants should have removed a boat which had been dumped two years previously. A teenage boy was injured while attempting to repair it.
>
> *Decision:* Even though the precise incident was not foreseeable, the authority should have foreseen that some harm could be caused since they knew children regularly played on the abandoned boat.

6 Defences to negligence

FAST FORWARD

The amount of damages awarded to the claimant can be reduced if it is shown that he **contributed** to his injury. The defendant can be **exonerated** from paying damages if it can be proved that the claimant **expressly** or **impliedly** consented to the risk.

6.1 Contributory negligence

A court may **reduce** the amount of damages paid to the claimant if the defendant establishes that they **contributed** to their own **injury** or **loss**, this is known as **contributory negligence**.

> *Sayers v Harlow UDC 1958*
>
> *The facts:* The claimant was injured whilst trying to climb out of a public toilet cubicle that had a defective lock.
>
> *Decision:* The court held that the claimant had contributed to her injuries by the method by which she had tried to climb out.

If the defendant proves that the claimant was at least **partially** at fault, courts will reduce the damages awarded to them by a **percentage** that is **just** and **reasonable**. This percentage is calculated according to what is established as the **claimant's share of the blame**. This is typically in the range of 10% to 75%, however it is possible to reduce the claim by up to 100% *Jayes v IMI (Kynoch) Ltd 1985.*

6.2 Volenti non fit injuria

Where a defendant's actions carry the risk of a tort being committed they will have a defence if it can be proved that the claimant consented to the risk. *Volenti non fit injuria* literally means the **voluntary acceptance** of the **risk of injury**.

This defence is available to the defendant where both parties have **expressly** consented to the risk (such as waiver forms signed by those taking part in dangerous sports), or it may be **implied** by the **conduct** of the claimant.

ICI v Shatwell 1965

The facts: The claimant and his brother disregarded safety precautions whilst using detonators, resulting in injury to the claimant.

Decision: The court upheld the defence of *volenti non fit injuria*. The claimant disregarded his employer's statutory safety rules and consented to the reckless act willingly.

An **awareness** of the risk **is not sufficient to establish consent**. For this defence to be successful the defendant must **prove** that the claimant was **fully informed** of the **risks** and that they consented to them.

This point was made in *Dann v Hamilton 1939* where a girl passenger in a car driven by a drunk driver was injured. The defendant established that she was aware of the risk but could offer no evidence that she consented to it. As a result of this case the defence of *volenti* is unlikely to succeed in cases where consent is **implied**.

Chapter Roundup

- The law gives various rights to persons. When such a right is infringed the wrongdoer is liable in **tort**.

- **Negligence** is the most important modern tort. To succeed in an action for negligence the claimant must prove that:

    - The defendant had **a duty of care** to avoid causing injury, damage or loss
    - There was **a breach of that duty** by the defendant
    - *In consequence* the claimant suffered **injury, damage or loss**

- The term negligence is used to describe **carelessly** carrying out an **act** and breaking a **legal duty of care** owed to another causing them **loss or damage.**

- In the landmark case of *Donoghue v Stevenson 1932* the House of Lords ruled that a person might **owe a duty of care to another with whom he had no contractual relationship** at all. The doctrine has been refined in subsequent rulings, but the principle is unchanged.

- The second element that must be proven by a claimant in an action for negligence is that there was a **breach of the duty** of care by the defendant.

- Finally the claimant must demonstrate that he suffered injury or loss as a **result** of the breach.

- The amount of damages awarded to the claimant can be reduced if it is shown that he **contributed** to his injury. The defendant can be **exonerated** from paying damages if it can be proved that the claimant expressly or impliedly consented to the risk.

Quick Quiz

1   In tort no previous transaction or contractual relationship need exist.

   True ☐

   False ☐

2   The 'neighbour' principle was established by the landmark case

   A   Caparo v Dickman 1990
   B   Anns v Merton London Borough Council 1977
   C   Donogue v Stevenson 1932
   D   The Wagon Mound 1961

3   When the court applies the maxim *res ipsa loquitur*, it is held that the facts speak for themselves and the defendant does not have to prove anything, since the burden of proof is on the claimant.

   True ☐

   False ☐

4   **Fill in the blanks** in the statements below.

   Which three things must a claimant prove to succeed in an action for negligence?

   The defendant owed the claimant a (1)............... ....

   These was a (2)....... of the (3)........... by the defendant

   In (4)......................... the claimant suffered (5)............., (6)............. or (7).............

5   Which of the following would prevent a claim for negligence from being successful?

   (a)   The claimant acted unreasonably.
   (b)   The defendant caused the harm to the claimant.
   (c)   A third party is the actual cause of harm.
   (d)   The parties were proximate and the harm suffered was reasonably foreseeable.
   (e)   An intervening act broke the 'chain of causation'.
   (f)   The duty of care was restricted by public policy.

6   Briefly describe the defence of volenti non fit injura.

7   Under which circumstance will a court reduce the award of damages to a claimant?

   A   The claimant intervened in the chain of causality
   B   A natural event occurred which caused additional damage
   C   The claimant contributed to the loss he suffered
   D   The defendant acknowledged he was to blame

Answers to Quick Quiz

1   True. No transaction or relationship is needed.

2   C. Donogue v Stevenson 1932

3   False. The burden of proof under *res ipsa loquitur* is reversed, the defendant must prove that he was not negligent.

4   (1)   duty of care
     (2)   breach
     (3)   duty
     (4)   consequence
     (5)   injury
     (6)   loss
     (7)   damage

5   (a), (c), (e), (f)

6   Volenti non fit injura is a valid defence to a negligence claim where the claimant expressly or impliedly consented to the risk.

7   C. The correct answer describes contributory negligence. Options A and B are intervening acts that break the chain of causality.

Now try the questions below from the Exam Question Bank

Number	Level	Marks	Time
Q12	Examination	10	18 mins

Professional negligence

Topic list	Syllabus reference
1 Professional advice	B5(a)
2 The Caparo decision	B5(a)

Introduction

In this chapter we complete our study of negligence with **professional negligence** and the duty of care owed by **accountants** and **auditors**.

As accountants we are likely to have a **contractual relationship** with our clients that affords them protection if we give negligent advice. However, other people such as shareholders who may also rely on our work have no contractual relationship with us and case law has developed over the years that determines what duty of care is owed to them.

Your syllabus requires you to **explain** and **analyse** the **duty of care** owed by accountants and auditors, so you must ensure that you understand the **implications** of the Caparo and other cases.

Study guide

		Intellectual level
(B)	**The law of obligations**	
5	Professional negligence	
(a)	Explain and analyse the duty of care of accountants and auditors	2

Exam guide

You may be required to explain the issues of negligence and duty of care that are specific to accountants and auditors. Scenario questions may focus on whether or not liability can be established against them.

1 Professional advice

FAST FORWARD

> Professional individuals and organisations have a special relationship with their clients and those who rely on their work. This is because they act in an **expert capacity**.

1.1 Development

This section seeks to demonstrate how the law relating to negligent professional advice, and in particular **auditors**, has been developed through the operation of precedent, being refined and explained with each successive case that comes to court. It illustrates the often step-by-step development of English law, which has gradually refined the principles laid down in *Donoghue v Stevenson* and *Anns v Merton London Borough Council* to cover **negligent misstatements** which cause financial loss.

1.2 The special relationship

Before 1963, it was held that any liability for careless statements was limited in scope and depended upon the existence of a **contractual** or **fiduciary relationship** between the parties. Lord Denning's tests of a further (later termed 'special') relationship were laid down in the Court of Appeal in his dissenting judgement on *Candler v Crane, Christmas & Co 1951*

FAST FORWARD

> According to Lord Denning, to establish a **special relationship** the person who made the statement must have done so in some professional or expert capacity which made it likely that others would rely on what he said. This is the position of an adviser such as an accountant, banker, solicitor or surveyor.

It follows that a duty could not be owed to complete strangers, but Lord Denning also stated at the time: 'Accountants owe a duty of care not only to their own clients, but also to **all those whom they know will rely on their accounts** in the transactions for which those accounts are prepared.' This was to prove a significant consideration in later cases.

However, Lord Denning's view was a dissenting voice in 1951 in the *Candler* case, where the Court of Appeal held that the defendants were **not** liable (for a bad investment based upon a set of negligently prepared accounts) because there was no direct contractual or fiduciary relationship with the claimant investor.

It was twelve years later that the **special relationship** was accepted as a valid test. Our starting point is the **leading case** on negligent misstatement, outlined below, which was the start of a **new judicial approach** to cases involving negligent misstatement. You must make sure that you are familiar with it.

> *Hedley Byrne & Co Ltd v Heller and Partners Ltd 1963*
>
> *The facts:* HB were advertising agents acting for a new client, Easipower Ltd. HB requested information from Easipower's bank (HP) on its financial position. HP returned non-committal replies, which expressly disclaimed legal responsibility, and which were held to be a negligent misstatement of Easipower's financial resources.
>
> *Decision:* While HP were able to avoid liability by virtue of their disclaimer, the House of Lords went on to consider whether there ever could be a duty of care to avoid causing financial loss by negligent misstatement where there was no contractual or fiduciary relationship. It decided (as *obiter dicta*) that HP were guilty of negligence having breached the duty of care, because a special relationship did exist. Had it not been for the disclaimer, a claim for negligence would have succeeded.

In reaching the decision in *Hedley Byrne*, Lord Morris said the following:

> '*If someone possessed of a special skill undertakes….to apply that skill for the assistance of another person who **relies** on that skill, a duty of care will arise….If, in a sphere in which a person is so placed that others could reasonably rely on his skill….a person takes it on himself to give information or advice to….another person who, as he **knows or should know**, will place reliance on it, then a duty of care will arise.*'

Point to note

> As you already know from your studies in Chapter 2, *obiter dicta* such as those made in 1963 do not form part of the *ratio decidendi*, and are not binding on future cases. They will, however, be **persuasive**.

Note that at the time liability did not extend to those who the advisor might merely **foresee as a possible user** of the statement.

However in a subsequent case, the courts extended potential liability, and started to take account of third parties not known to the adviser. The following case echoed the principles laid down in *Anns* (see Chapter 8) and addressed the question of **reasonable foresight** being present to create a duty of care.

> *JEB Fasteners Ltd v Marks, Bloom & Co 1982*
>
> *The facts:* The defendants, a firm of accountants, prepared an audited set of accounts showing overvalued stock and hence inflated profit. The auditors knew there were liquidity problems and that the company was seeking outside finance. The claimants were shown the accounts; they took over the company for a nominal amount, since by that means they could obtain the services of the company's two directors. At no time did MB tell JEB that the stock value was inflated. With the investment's failure, JEB sued MB, with the following claims.
>
> (a)   The accounts had been prepared negligently.
>
> (b)   They had relied on those accounts.
>
> (c)   They would not have invested had they been aware of the company's true position.
>
> (d)   MB owed a duty of care to all persons whom they could reasonably foresee would rely on the accounts.
>
> *Decision:* Even though JEB had relied on the accounts (b), they would not have acted differently if the true position had been known (c), since they had really wanted the directors and not the company. Hence the accountants were not the cause of the consequential harm and were not liable. Significantly (although this did not affect the decision as to liability) it was the judge's view that MB did indeed owe a duty of care through foresight (d) and had been negligent in preparing the accounts (a).

Decisions since *JEB Fasteners* have, however, shied away from the foresight test and gone back to looking at whether the adviser has **knowledge of the user** and the **use to which the statement will be put**.

2 The Caparo decision

> The **Caparo case** is fundamental to understanding professional negligence. It was decided that **auditors do not owe a duty of care to the public at large** or to **shareholders increasing their stakes**.

This important and controversial case made considerable changes to the tort of negligence as a whole, and the negligence of **professionals** in particular. It set a precedent which forms the basis for courts when considering the liability of professional advisers.

Caparo Industries plc v Dickman and Others 1990

The facts: Caparo, which already held shares in Fidelity plc, bought more shares and later made a takeover bid, after seeing accounts prepared by the defendants that showed a profit of £1.3m. Caparo claimed against the directors (the brothers Dickman) and the auditors for the fact that the accounts should have shown a loss of £400,000. The claimants argued that the auditors owed a duty of care to investors and potential investors in respect of the audit. They should have been aware that a press release stating that profits would fall significantly had made Fidelity vulnerable to a takeover bid and that bidders might well rely upon the accounts.

Decision: The auditor's duty did not extend to potential investors nor to existing shareholders increasing their stakes. It was a duty owed to the body of shareholders as whole.

In the *Caparo* case the House of Lords decided that there were **two** very different situations facing a person giving professional advice.

(a)   Preparing information in the knowledge that a **particular person** was contemplating a transaction and would rely on the information in deciding whether or not to proceed with the transaction (the 'special relationship').

(b)   Preparing a statement for **general circulation**, which could forseeably be relied upon by persons unknown to the professional for a variety of different purposes.

It was held therefore that a public company's auditors owe **no duty of care to the public at large** who rely on an audit report when deciding to invest – and, in purchasing additional shares, an existing shareholder is in no different position to the public at large.

In *MacNaughton (James) Papers Group Ltd v Hicks Anderson & Co 1991*, it was stated that it was necessary to examine each case in the light of the following.

*   Foreseeability
*   Proximity
*   Fairness

This is because there could be **no single overriding principle** that could be applied to all individual cases. Lord Justice Neill set out the matters to be taken into account in considering this.

*   The purpose for which the statement was **made**
*   The purpose for which the statement was **communicated**
*   The **relationship** between the maker of the statement, the recipient and any third party
*   The **size** of any class to which the recipient belonged
*   The **state of knowledge** of the maker
*   Any **reliance** by the recipient

2.1 Non-audit role

The duty of care of accountants is held to be higher when advising on takeovers than when auditing. The directors and financial advisors of the target company in a contested takeover bid owe a duty of care to a **known** takeover bidder in respect of financial statements prepared for the purpose of contesting the bid: *Morgan Crucible Co plc v Hill Samuel Bank Ltd and others 1990*.

2.2 The law since *Caparo*

A more recent case highlighted the need for a cautious approach and careful evaluation of the circumstances when giving **financial advice**, possibly with the need to issue a disclaimer.

ADT Ltd v BDO Binder Hamlyn 1995

The facts: Binder Hamlyn was the joint auditor of BSG. In October 1989, BSG's audited accounts for the year to 30 June 1989 were published. Binder Hamlyn signed off the audit as showing a true and fair view of BSG's position. ADT was thinking of buying BSG and, as a potential buyer, sought Binder Hamlyn's confirmation of the audited results. In January 1990, the Binder Hamlyn audit partner attended a meeting with a director of ADT. This meeting was described by the judge as the 'final hurdle' before ADT finalised its bid for BSG. At the meeting, the audit partner specifically confirmed that he 'stood by' the audit of October 1989. ADT proceeded to purchase BSG for £105m. It was subsequently alleged that BSG's true value was only £40m. ADT therefore sued Binder Hamlyn for the difference, £65m plus interest.

Decision: Binder Hamlyn assumed a responsibility for the statement that the audited accounts showed a true and fair view of BSG which ADT relied on to its detriment. Since the underlying audit work had been carried out negligently, Binder Hamlyn was held liable for £65m. The courts expect a higher standard of care from accountants when giving advice on company acquisitions since the losses can be so much greater.

This situation was different from *Caparo* since the court was specifically concerned with the **purpose of the statement made at the meeting**. Did Binder Hamlyn **assume any responsibility** as a result of the partner's comments? The court decided that it did. The court did not need to consider the question of duty to individual shareholders, because *Caparo* had already decided that there was none.

Following the *ADT* case, another case tested the court's interpretation.

NRG v Bacon and Woodrow and Ernst & Young 1996

The facts: NRG alleged that the defendants had failed to suggest the possibility that certain companies it was targeting might suffer huge reinsurance losses. They had also failed to assess properly whether these losses could be protected against, because defective actuarial methods had been used. As a result, it overpaid for these companies by £255m.

Decision: The judge observed that accountants owe a higher standard of care when advising on company purchases, because the potential losses are so much greater, following *ADT*. However, applying this higher standard of care to the facts, it was decided that NRG had received the advice that any competent professional would have given, because the complex nature of the losses that the companies were exposed to were not fully understood at the time. In addition, the use of defective actuarial methods had not led directly to the losses, because NRG would have bought the companies anyway.

There have been some other **important clarifications** of the law affecting accountants' liability in the area of responsibility towards non-clients. The following two cases both concern auditors' liability to group companies.

Barings plc v Coopers & Lybrand 1997

The facts: Barings collapsed in 1995 after loss-making trading by the general manager of its Singapore subsidiary, BFS. BFS was audited by the defendant's Singapore firm, which provided Barings directors with consolidation schedules and a copy of the BFS audit report. The defendant tried to argue that there was no duty of care owed to Barings, only to BFS.

Decision: A duty of care was owed to Barings, as the defendants must have known that their audit report and consolidation schedules would be relied upon at group level.

> *BCCI (Overseas) Ltd v Ernst & Whinney 1997*
>
> *The facts:* In this case, the defendants audited the group holding company's accounts, but not those of the claimant subsidiary. The claimant tried to claim that the defendants had a duty of care to them.
>
> *Decision:* No duty of care was owed to the subsidiary because no specific information is normally channelled down by a holding company's auditor to its subsidiaries.

UK accountancy firms have been investigating ways of limiting liability in the face of increasing litigation. KPMG, for example, incorporated its audit practice in 1995.

In 2000, the Limited Liability Partnerships Act 2000 was passed, and limited liability partnerships have been permitted under law since 2001.

This protects the partners of accountancy firms from the financial consequences of negligent actions as their liability to third parties (previously unlimited) can now be limited. We shall see more of this in Chapter 13 on business associations.

Exam focus point

> All the above cases are extremely important. Ensure you learn them all.

Chapter Roundup

- Professional individuals and organisations have a special relationship with their clients and those who rely on their work. This is because they act in an **expert capacity**.

- According to Lord Denning, to establish a **special relationship** the person who made the statement must have done so in some professional or expert capacity which made it likely that others would rely on what he said. This is the position of an adviser such as an accountant, banker, solicitor or surveyor.

- The **Caparo case** is fundamental to understanding professional negligence. It was decided that **auditors do not owe a duty of care to the public at large** or to **shareholders increasing their stakes**.

1   In no more than 40 words, explain why the decision in *ADT Ltd v Binder Hamlyn* was different from *Caparo*.

2   In no more than 30 words, explain how a 'special relationship' is defined in the context of professional advice.

3   'A public company's auditors owe no duty of care to the public at large who rely on the audit report in deciding to invest.'

This is the decision from *Caparo*.

True ☐
False ☐

4   The duty of care owed by accountants is greater when advising on take-overs than when auditing.

True ☐
False ☐

5   Which of the following is a realistic method that accountancy firms can use to limit their liability.

A   Form a limited liability partnership
B   Avoid giving professional advice
C   Form a limited liability collective
D   Take legal advice before giving professional advice

Answers to Quick Quiz

1   Binder Hamlyn was held to have specifically assumed responsibility for its statements at a meeting held to discuss the audited results, which made it liable outside the usual sphere laid down by Caparo.

2   The person who makes the statement does so in some professional or expert capacity, making it likely that another will rely on what they say.

3   True. Auditors do not owe a duty of care to the public at large.

4   True. This was the decision in *Morgan Crucible Co plc v Hill Samuel Bank Ltd and others 1990*

5   A. Option C is a made up organisation, options B and D are unrealistic.

Now try the question below from the Exam Question Bank

Number	Level	Marks	Time
Q13	Examination	10	18 mins

Employment law

10

Employment contract

Topic list	Syllabus reference
1 What is an employee?	C1(a)
2 Why does it matter?	C1(a)
3 Employment contract: basic issues	C1(b)
4 Common law duties	C1(b)
5 Statutory duties	C1(b)
6 Varying the terms of an employment contract	C1(b)
7 Continuous employment	C1(b)

Introduction

We begin our study of employment law by looking at the **distinction** between the **employed** and the **self-employed**. This distinction is very important as it has implications regarding employee **rights** and **liabilities**.

The chapter continues by examining the **contents** of an employment contract. Like any other contract it may include **express** and **implied terms** and you should be able to explain how these terms are included.

Employers and employees owe certain **duties** to one another; breach of these duties may result in legal action against the party who breached their duty. Learn these duties and the supporting case law as they are an important part of your syllabus.

Statutory references in this chapter are to the Employment Rights Act 1996 (ERA 1996) unless otherwise noted.

Study guide

		Intellectual level
(C)	**Employment law**	
1	Contract of employment	
(a)	Distinguish between employees and the self-employed	2
(b)	Explain the nature of the contract of employment and give examples of the main duties placed on the parties to such a contract.	2

Exam guide

Questions may be set that require you to explain the differences between the employed and the self-employed and the implications to an individual of being classed as one or the other.

You may also be requested to explain the various duties that employees and employers have to each other.

1 What is an employee?

FAST FORWARD

It is important to distinguish between a **contract of service** (employment) and a **contract for services** (independent contractor). Each type of contract has different rules for taxation, health and safety provisions, protection of contract and vicarious liability in tort and contract.

A contract of service is **distinguished** from a contract for services usually because the parties **express** the agreement to be one of service. This does not always mean that an employee will not be treated as an independent contractor by the court, however; much depends on the three tests.

- Control test
- Integration test
- Economic reality test

A general rule is that an employee is someone who is employed under a **contract of service**, as distinguished from an independent contractor, who is someone who works under a **contract for services**.

However, it is important to note that some statutory provisions apply to 'workers' and this term is wider than 'employees' and includes those personally performing work or services unless truly self-employed.

Key terms

An **employee** is 'an individual who has entered into, or works under a contract of employment'. (ERA 1996)

A **contract of employment** is 'a contract of service or apprenticeship, whether express or implied, and (if it is express) whether it is oral or in writing.'

In practice this distinction depends on many factors. As we will discuss in Section 2 it can be very important to know whether an individual is an employee or an independent contractor. The courts will apply a series of **tests**.

Primarily, the court will look at the **reality of the situation**. This may be in spite of the form of the arrangement.

> **Ferguson v John Dawson & Partners 1976**
>
> *The facts*: A builder's labourer was paid his wages without deduction of income tax or National Insurance contributions and worked as a self-employed contractor providing services. His 'employer' could dismiss him, decide on which site he would work, direct him as to the work he should do and also provided the tools which he used. He was injured in an accident and sued his employers on the basis that they owed him legal duties as his employer.
>
> *Decision*: On the facts taken as a whole, he was an employee working under a contract of employment.

Where there is some **doubt** as to the nature of the relationship the courts will then look at any **agreement between the parties**.

> **Massey v Crown Life Assurance 1978**
>
> *The facts*: The claimant was originally employed by an insurance company as a departmental manager; he also earned commission on business which he introduced. At his own request he changed to a self-employed basis. Tax and other payments were no longer deducted by the employers but he continued to perform the same duties. The employers terminated these arrangements and the claimant claimed compensation for unfair dismissal.
>
> *Decision*: As he had opted to become self-employed and his status in the organisation was consistent with that situation, his claim to be a dismissed employee failed.

It can still be unclear whether a person is an employee or an independent contractor. Historically, the tests of **control, integration** into the employer's organisation, and **economic reality** (or the multiple test) have been applied in such cases.

The fundamental prerequisite of a contract of employment is that there must be **mutual obligations** on the employer to provide, and the employee to perform, work.

1.1 The control test

The court will consider whether the employer has **control** over the way in which the employee performs his duties.

> **Mersey Docks & Harbour Board v Coggins & Griffiths (Liverpool) 1947**
>
> *The facts:* Stevedores hired a crane with its driver from the harbour board under a contract which provided that the driver (appointed and paid by the harbour board) should be the employee of the stevedores. Owing to the driver's negligence a checker was injured. The case was concerned with whether the stevedores or the harbour board were vicariously liable as employers.
>
> *Decision:* It was decided that the issue must be settled on the facts and not on the terms of the contract. The stevedores could only be treated as employers of the driver if they could control in detail how he did his work. But although they could instruct him what to do, they could not control him in how he operated the crane. The harbour board (as 'general employer') was therefore still the driver's employer.

1.2 The integration test

The courts consider whether the employee is so skilled that he cannot be controlled in the performance of his duties. Lack of control indicates that an employee is **not integrated** into the employer's organisation, and therefore not employed.

> **Cassidy v Ministry of Health 1951**
>
> *The facts:* The full-time assistant medical officer at a hospital carried out a surgical operation in a negligent fashion. The patient sued the Ministry of Health as employer. The Ministry resisted the claim arguing that it had no control over the doctor in his medical work.

> *Decision:* In such circumstances the proper test was whether the employer appointed the employee, selected him for his task and so integrated him into the organisation. If the patient had chosen the doctor the Ministry would not have been liable as employer. But here the Ministry (the hospital management) made the choice and so it was liable.

The control and integration tests are important, but **no longer decisive** in determining whether a person is an employee.

1.3 The multiple (economic reality) test

Courts also consider whether the employee was **working on his own account** and this requires numerous factors to be taken into account.

> *Ready Mixed Concrete (South East) v Ministry of Pensions & National Insurance 1968*
>
> *The facts*: The driver of a special vehicle worked for one company only in the delivery of liquid concrete to building sites. He provided his own vehicle (obtained on hire purchase from the company) and was responsible for its maintenance and repair. He was free to provide a substitute driver. The vehicle was painted in the company's colours and the driver wore its uniform. He was paid gross amounts (no tax etc deducted) on the basis of mileage and quantity delivered as a self-employed contractor. The Ministry of Pensions claimed that he was in fact an employee for whom the company should make the employer's insurance contributions.
>
> *Decision*: In such cases the most important test is whether the worker is working on his own account. On these facts the driver was a self-employed transport contractor and not an employee.

In the above case, Mackenna J held that a contract of service existed where:

- There is **agreement** from the worker that they will provide work for their master in exchange for remuneration.
- The worker agrees either expressly or impliedly that their master can exercise **control** over their performance.
- There are other **factors** included in the contract that make it **consistent** with a contract for service.

The fact that the drivers could appoint a **replacement** for themselves was a major factor in the decision that found them as contractors rather than employees.

1.4 Agency workers

The status of agency workers has been the subject of numerous cases in recent years as the numbers employed under such contracts has increased. Two key cases have considered **length of service** of agency workers and **control** that the client of the agency has over the worker.

(a)   **Length of service**

In *Franks v Reuters Ltd 2003*, the agency worker had been providing services to the client for some **six years** engaged in a variety of jobs, and was effectively so thoroughly integrated with the employer's organisation as to be **indistinguishable** from the employer's staff.

Mummery LJ, said that an *'implied contract of employment did not arise simply by virtue of the length of the employment, but it could well be a factor in applying the overall tests appropriate to establish (or otherwise) an employment status'.*

The case was remitted to the tribunal for further consideration, but the length of an assignment of an agency worker clearly has implications for the development of other indications of an employment relationship, with those utilising the services of the worker forgetting the true nature of the relationship and behaving towards the work as if he or she was an employee. It may be that at this point the relevant approach also starts to involve the 'integration' test'.

(b) **Control over the worker**

Where the client of the agency has **sufficient control** over the employee provided by the agency, it could be held that they are in fact the true employer.

Motorola v Davidson and Melville Craig 2001

The facts: Davidson was contracted with the Melville Craig agency and was assigned to work for Motorola. Both the agency and Motorola had agreed that Davidson could be sent back to the agency if his work was unacceptable. Following a disciplinary hearing Davidson was found unacceptable and returned to the agency. Davidson took Motorola to an employment tribunal for unfair dismissal.

Decision: Motorola had sufficient control over Davidson to make them the employer. It was held that the court should look beyond the pure legal situation and look at the practical control aspects in such cases as well.

1.5 Relevant factors

Significant factors that you should consider when deciding whether or not a person is employed or self-employed are as follows.

- Does the employee use his **own tools and equipment** or does the employer provide them?
- Does the alleged employer have the power to **select or appoint** its employees, and may it dismiss them?
- **Payment of salary** is a fair indication of there being a contract of employment.
- **Working for a number of different people** is not necessarily a sign of self-employment. A number of assignments may be construed as 'a series of employments'.

In difficult cases, courts will consider whether the employee can **delegate** all his obligations, whether there is restriction as to place of work, whether there is a **mutual obligation** and whether holidays and hours of work are agreed.

O'Kelly v Trusthouse Forte Plc 1983

The facts: The employee was a 'regular casual' working when required as a waiter. There was an understanding that he would accept work when offered and that the employer would give him preference over other casual employees. The employment tribunal held that there was no contract of employment because the employer had no obligation to provide work and the employee had no obligation to accept work when offered.

Decision: The Court of Appeal agreed with this finding. Whether there is a contract of employment is a question of law but it depends entirely on the facts of each case; here there was no 'mutuality of obligations' and hence no contract.

The decision whether to classify an individual as an employee or not is also influenced by **policy considerations**. For example, an employment tribunal might regard a person as an employee for the purpose of unfair dismissal despite the fact that the tax authorities treated him or her as self-employed

---

Airfix Footwear Ltd v Cope 1978

The facts: The case concerned a classic outworking arrangement under which the applicant (having been given training and thereafter supplied with the necessary tools and materials) generally worked five days a week making heels for shoes manufactured by the respondent company. She was paid on a piece work basis without deduction of income tax or NIC.

Decision: Working for some seven years, generally for five days a week, resulted in the arrangement being properly classified as employment under a contract of employment.

---

2 Why does it matter?

FAST FORWARD

The distinction between **employed** and **self-employed** is important as to whether certain **rights** are available to an individual and how they are treated for **tax purposes**.

The first thing that it is important to note is that much of the legislation which gives protection to employees **extends further than employees**. Much of it is drafted to cover 'workers' which has a wide definition to cover most people providing services to others outside of the course of (their own) business.

This has reduced the importance of the distinction between employee and independent contractor in this area.

However, there are several other **practical reasons** why the distinction between a contract of service and a contract for services is important.

SIGNIFICANCE OF THE DISTINCTION		
	Employed	**Self-employed**
Social security	Employers must pay secondary Class 1 contributions on behalf of employees Employees make primary Class 1 contributions There are also differences in statutory sick pay and levies for industrial training purposes	Independent contractors pay Class 2 and 4 contributions
Taxation	Deductions must be made by an employer for income tax under PAYE (Schedule E) from salary paid to employee	The self-employed are taxed under Schedule D and are directly responsible to the HM Revenue and Customs for tax due
Employment protection	There is legislation which confers protection and benefits upon employees under a contract of service, including • Minimum periods of notice • Remedies for unfair dismissal	Employment protection is not available for contractors
Tortious acts	Employers are generally vicariously liable for tortious acts of employees, committed in the course of employment	Liability of the person hiring an independent contractor, for the contractors' acts, is severely limited unless there is strict liability
Implied terms	There are rights and duties implied by statute for employers and employees This will affect things such as copyrights and patents	These implied rights and duties do not apply to such an extent to a contract for services.
VAT	Employees do not have to register for or charge VAT	An independent contractor may have to register for, and charge VAT
Bankruptcy	In liquidation, an employee has preferential rights as a creditor for payment of outstanding salary and redundancy payments, up to certain limits	Contractors are treated as non-preferential creditors if their employer is liquidated

SIGNIFICANCE OF THE DISTINCTION		
	Employed	**Self-employed**
Health and safety	There is significant common law and regulation governing employers' duties to employees with regard to health and safety	The common law provisions and much of the regulation relating to employees also relates to independent contractors

Exam focus point

If you are asked about the importance of the distinction between employees and independent contractors in the exam, make sure that you highlight the fact that it is important for the **practical reasons** given above, but also that the recent **legislative trend** has been to extend protection to 'workers' beyond the traditional definition of employees.

3 Employment contract: basic issues

FAST FORWARD

There are no particular legal rules relating to the commencement of employment – it is really **just like any other contract** in requiring offer and acceptance, consideration and intention to create legal relations.

The definition of an employment contract was given in Section 1. To recap, it is a contract of service which may be **express** or **implied**. If express, it can be either **oral** or **written**. In essence, then, an employment contract can be a simple, straightforward agreement. The contact must, of course, comply with the usual rules relating to the formation of a valid contract.

Question

Essential elements of a contract of employment

As with any other contract, agreements for employment require offer and acceptance, consideration and the intention to create legal relations. How are these three essential elements manifested in a contract of employment?

Answer

Generally the offer comes from the employer and acceptance from the employee, who may write a letter or simply turn up for work at an agreed time. Consideration comprises the promises each party gives to the other – a promise to work for a promise to pay. If there is no consideration, a deed must be executed for there to be a contract of employment. The intention to create legal relations is imputed from the fact that essentially employment is a commercial transaction.

At the one extreme, an employment contract may be a **document** drawn up by solicitors and signed by both parties; at the other extreme it may consist of a **handshake** and a 'See you on Monday'. In such cases the court has to clarify the agreement by determining what the parties must be taken to have agreed.

Senior personnel may sign a contract specially drafted to include terms on **confidentiality** and **restraint of trade**. Other employees may sign a standard form contract, exchange letters with the new employer or simply agree terms orally at interview.

Each of these situations will form a valid contract of employment, subject to the requirements outlined below as to written particulars, as long as there is **agreement** on **essential terms** such as hours and wages. We will consider some of these essential terms in the following sections. Nor should it be forgotten that even prior to employment commencing the potential employer has legal obligations, for example not to discriminate in recruitment.

3.1 Implied terms

Implied terms usually arise out of **custom** and **practice** within a profession or industry. In *Henry v London General Transport Services Ltd 2001* it was held that four requirements should be met before such terms can be read into a contract.

- The terms must be **reasonable**, **certain** and **notorious**
- They must represent the **wishes** of both parties
- **Proof** of the custom or practice must be provided by the party seeking to rely on the term
- A **distinction** must be made between implying terms that make **minor** and **fundamental** changes to the terms of the contract

3.2 Requirement for written particulars

Within two months of the beginning of the employment the employer must give to an employee a written **statement of prescribed particulars** of his employment: s 1.

The statement should identify the following.

- The names of **employer** and **employee**
- The **date** on which employment began
- Whether any service with a previous employer forms part of the employee's **continuous period** of employment
- **Pay** – scale or rate and intervals at which paid
- **Hours** of work (including any specified 'normal working hours')
- Any **holiday** and **holiday pay** entitlement
- **Sick leave** and **sick pay** entitlement
- **Pensions** and pension **schemes**
- Length of **notice** of termination to be given on either side
- The **title** of the job which the employee is employed to do (or a brief job description)

A 'principal statement', which must include the **first six items** above and the title of the job, must be provided, but other particulars may be given by way of separate documents.

If the employee has a **written contract of employment** covering these points and has been given a copy it is not necessary to provide him with separate written particulars.

The written particulars must also contain details of **disciplinary procedures** and **grievance procedures** or reference to where they can be found; s35 Employment Act 2002.

If the employer fails to comply with these requirements the employee may apply to an **employment tribunal** for a declaration of what the terms should be: s 11. S38 Employment Act 2002 allows a tribunal to award compensation to an employee claiming unfair dismissal if the particulars are incomplete.

Question	Employee or independent contractor?

Charles saw a sign advertising vacancies at a local building site. He contacted the foreman and was told that he would be required but that, because work depended on the weather conditions, he would not be given an employment contract – he would be accountable for his own income tax and National Insurance. The foreman added that he would be provided with tools and that at the beginning of each day he would be told which site he would work on that day. Lateness or theft of materials would lead to his dismissal.

Is Charles an employee?

Charles is an employee. Even though he does not receive an employment contract the facts indicate a contract of service since he is controlled by the employer in that the latter provides tools, tells him where to work and reserves the right to dismiss him.

4 Common law duties

FAST FORWARD

The **employer** has an implied **duty at common law** to take **reasonable care** of his employees; he must select proper staff, materials and provide a safe system of working.

The **employee** has a duty to exercise **care and skill** in performance of his duties.

4.1 Employee's duties

The employee has a **fundamental duty of faithful service** to his employer. All other duties are features of this general duty.

> *Hivac Ltd v Park Royal Scientific Instruments Ltd 1946*
>
> *The facts:* In their spare time certain of the claimant's employees worked for the defendant company, which directly competed with the claimant.
>
> *Decision:* Even though the employees had not passed on any confidential information, they were still in breach of their duty of fidelity to the claimants.

This duty also extends after the employment where **trade secrets** are concerned. Employees will be in breach of their duty if they disclose such secrets to their new employer. The **facts of the case** and the **nature of employment** should be considered when making a decision, for example customer lists of a chicken selling business was not considered a trade secret when a sales manager set up his own competing organisation *(Faccenda Chicken Ltd v Fowler 1986)*

The **implied** duties of the employee include the following.

- **Reasonable competence** to do his job.
- **Obedience** to the employer's instructions unless they require him to do an unlawful act or to expose himself to personal danger (not inherent in his work) or are instructions outside the employee's contract.

> *Pepper v Webb 1969*
>
> *The facts:* The defendant, a gardener refused to obey instructions from his employer regarding planting in the garden. He also swore at him.
>
> *Decision:* The gardener was in breach of his implied duty to obey as the instructions were lawful and reasonable.

- **Duty to account for all money and property** received during the course of his employment.

> *Boston Deep Sea Fishing and Ice Co v Ansell 1888*
>
> *The facts:* The defendant, who was managing director of the claimant company, accepted personal commissions from suppliers on orders which he placed with them for goods supplied to the company. He was dismissed and the company sued to recover from him the commissions.
>
> *Decision:* The company was justified in dismissing the claimant and he must account to it for the commissions.

- **Reasonable care and skill** in the performance of his work: *Lister v Romford Ice and Cold Storage Co 1957.* What is reasonable depends on the degree of skill and experience which the employee professes to have.

- **Personal service** – the contract of employment is a personal one and so the employee may not delegate his duties without the employer's express or implied consent.

4.2 Employer's duties

There is an overriding **duty of mutual trust and confidence** between the employer and the employee. Examples of where this duty have been breached include:

- A director calling his secretary 'an intolerable bitch on a Monday morning' – *Isle of Wight Tourist Board v Coombes 1976*
- Failure to investigate a sexual harassment claim – *Bracebridge Engineering v Darby 1990*

The employer usually also has the following duties at common law:

- To **pay remuneration** to employees. If there is no rate fixed by the parties, this duty is to pay **reasonable** remuneration. There is statutory provision for this, see Section 5.
- To **indemnify the employee** against expenses and losses incurred in the course of employment.
- To take care of the employees' **health and safety** at work. This is also provided for in statute.
- To **provide work**, where
  - Employee is an apprentice
  - Employee is paid with reference to work done
  - The opportunity to work is the essence of the contract (for example, for actors)
  - There is work available to be done (subject to contractual terms to the contrary) **and** the relevant employee is a skilled worker who needs work to preserve his or her skills – *William Hill Organisation v Tucker 1998*
  - There is no breach of duty if there is **no work** available and the employer continues to pay its employees. However, if an employee was appointed to a **particular role** and no work was provided there may be a breach of duty to provide work if it denies the employee the opportunity to maintain his skills – *Collier v Sunday Referee Publishing Co Ltd 1940*

There is no duty to provide a **reference** when employees leave service. Employers may be liable under negligence for not taking reasonable care over accuracy and fairness if they do provide one *(Cox v Sun Alliance Life 2001)*

The importance of these common law implied duties on both parties is that:

(a) **Breach of a legal duty**, if it is important enough, may entitle the injured party to treat the contract as **discharged** and to claim damages for breach of contract at common law; and

(b) In an employee's claim for compensation for unfair dismissal, the employee may argue that it was a case of **constructive dismissal** by the employer, or the employer may seek to justify his express dismissal of the employee by reference to his conduct. We shall discuss constructive dismissal in Chapter 11.

5 Statutory duties

FAST FORWARD

Statute implies terms into employment contracts, which may not usually be overridden, regarding pay, maternity leave and work-life balance generally, time off, health and safety and working time.

Various matters are implied into contracts of employment by statute. Some of them build upon the **basic matters** covered by common law above. Most of the employment statutes in this area implement European Directives on employment law issues. The employer has statutory duties in the following areas:

- Pay
- Time off work
- Maternity rights and the 'work-life balance'
- Health and safety
- Working time

5.1 Pay

There are two key pieces of legislation in relation to pay. These are the **Equal Pay Act 1970** and the **National Minimum Wage Act 1998**.

5.1.1 Equal Pay Act 1970

Under this Act, contractual **employment terms should be at least as favourable as those given to an employee of the opposite sex**. The Act covers terms such as sick pay, holiday pay and working hours, and it applies to all forms of full-time and part-time work.

Hayward v Cammell Laird Shipbuilders 1986

The facts: The House of Lords upheld the claim of a canteen cook to equal pay with painters, joiners and thermal insulation engineers employed in the same shipyard on the ground that her work was of equal value.

Decision: Overall the applicant was considered to be employed on work of equal value. Hayward's application was the first successful claim for equal pay for work of equal value.

A difference in pay which is connected with economic factors affecting the efficient carrying on of the employer's business or other activity may well be relevant: *Rainey v Greater Glasgow Health Board 1987*. Examples are as follows.

- Greater length of service is a material factor: *Capper Pass v Lawton 1977*.
- Working at different times of day is not a material factor: *Dugdale v Kraft Foods 1977*.
- A distinction in hourly pay between workers in London and those based in (the cheaper area of) Nottingham is based on a material factor: *NAAFI v Varley 1976*.
- 'Market forces' do not necessarily amount to a genuine material factor: *Ratcliffe & Others v North Yorkshire County Council 1995*.

5.1.2 National Minimum Wage Act 1998

A national minimum wage was introduced in the UK in 1999. The current **hourly rate** (from October 2008) is £5.73. For persons between the ages of 18 and 21, the rate is £4.77 and for 16-17 year olds it is £3.53.

5.1.3 Other matters

Employers are obliged to provide an itemised pay statement: s 8.

5.2 Time off work

In addition to the rights relating to maternity and parental leave discussed below, statute lists several occasions when an employee has a right to time off work.

(a)   **Trade union officials** are entitled to time off on full pay at the employer's expense to enable them to carry out **trade union duties**: ss 168-169 Trade Union and Labour Relations (Consolidation) Act 1992.

(b)   An employee who has been given notice of dismissal for **redundancy** may have time off to look for work or to arrange training for other work.

(c)   A member of a recognised independent **trade union** may have time off work (without statutory right to pay) for **trade union activities**, for example, attending a branch meeting: s 170 TULRCA 1992.

(d)   Employees also have a duty to allow an employee to have reasonable time off to carry out certain **public duties**, for example performing his duties as a magistrate. There is **no statutory provision** entitling an employee to time off for jury service, but prevention of a person from attending as a juror is contempt of court.

5.3 Maternity rights and the 'work-life balance'

A woman who is pregnant is given substantial rights under statute, including:

*   A right to **time off work** for ante-natal care
*   The right to **ordinary maternity leave**
*   The right to **additional maternity leave**
*   The right to **maternity pay**
*   The right to **return to work** after maternity leave
*   If dismissed, a claim for **unfair dismissal** (this will be discussed in Chapter 11)

Much recent employment legislation, including provisions introduced by the Employment Act 2002, has been concerned with the introduction of **family-friendly** employment policies. There has been a specific focus on the so-called **'work-life balance'**. The law has developed as a result in the areas of:

*   Maternity leave and pay
*   Paternity leave
*   Rights of adoptive parents
*   A right to request flexible working

5.3.1 Ante-natal care

An employee has a right not to be unreasonably refused time off for ante-natal care during working hours. She is also entitled to pay during such an absence. There is **no minimum qualifying period**, ss 55-57 Employment Rights Act 1996.

5.3.2 Maternity leave

Every woman is given the right to **ordinary maternity leave** which is **twenty-six weeks** long, subject to her satisfying conditions for giving her employer notice of her intentions. A woman who has been continuously employed for 26 weeks has a right to **additional maternity leave**, which allows the employee a further period of **twenty-six weeks' leave**. This means that the total period of statutory maternity leave is 52 weeks.

An employee on **ordinary** maternity leave has the **right to return to work** in the job she had before her absence, with her seniority, pension and similar rights which she would have had if she had not been absent and on no less favourable terms than if she had not been absent: s 71.

An employee on **additional** maternity leave has the same rights, except if it is **not practicable** for her to return to the job she had before, she has the right to another job which is **suitable and appropriate** to her, on the same or better status, terms and conditions.

5.3.3 Maternity pay

Statutory maternity pay is paid during an employee's ordinary maternity leave. Additional maternity leave is unpaid. The employee must have at least 26 weeks of continuous employment and her average earnings must be above a certain level (otherwise she may be entitled to claim **maternity allowance** instead). SMP is paid at the following rate:

(a)   For the first six weeks, 90% of salary,

(b)   For the remainder of ordinary maternity leave, the lower of £100 per week or 90% of her average weekly earnings.

5.3.4 Paternity leave

New fathers have rights to paternity leave and pay, the employee claiming the right must:

- Be the biological father of the child or the mother's husband or partner;
- Have or expect to have responsibility for the child's upbringing;
- Have 26 weeks' continuous service.

Eligible employees will be entitled to take either **one week** or **two consecutive** weeks paid paternity leave. The leave must be completed within 56 days of the actual birth of the child.

Statutory Paternity Pay will be paid during the paternity leave. This will be paid at the lower of £100 per week or 90% of the employee's average weekly earnings. These rights are **in addition to** the existing parental leave provisions (see below) which allow up to 13 weeks of **unpaid** paternity leave for each child under 5 years old, provided that the employee has one year's continuous service.

5.3.5 Adoptive parents

The family-friendly employment policies introduced by the Employment Act 2002 extend to adoptive parents, who have similar rights to those provided under the maternity provisions. There is a right to **statutory adoption leave** (SAL) and **statutory adoption pay** (SAP). Statutory adoption leave may consist of 26 weeks of ordinary adoption leave and 26 weeks of additional adoption leave.

Adoptive parents' rights extend to one of the adopting couple but not to both. The adopting parent must have 26 weeks of continuous employment. Leave is not available in cases of step family adoption, adoption by existing step parents or extended family adoption.

5.3.6 Flexible working

Employees have the **right**:

- To apply for a change in terms and conditions of employment in respect of hours, time and place of work and
- Not to be unreasonably refused.

To be **eligible** to apply for flexible working, the employee must:

- Have a child under six years of age (or under 18 if the child is disabled)
- Have been continuously employed for 26 weeks at the date of the application
- Have, or expect to have, responsibility for the child's upbringing
- Be making the application in order to care for the child and
- Not have made another application for flexible working in the previous 12 months

There is a detailed set of procedures for the submission of an application, the provision of a response by the employer and, if necessary, any subsequent appeal by the employee. If a request is granted, any changes are regarded as **permanent contract changes**. The employer may reasonably refuse a request on the grounds of:

- The burden of additional cost
- A detrimental effect on ability to meet customer demand
- An inability to re-organise the work amongst existing staff or to recruit additional staff
- A detrimental impact on quality or performance
- Insufficiency of work during the periods the employee proposes to work or
- Planned structural changes

The given business reasons may not be contested by the employee. The only grounds for complaint are either that the employer has **failed** to follow the procedures properly or that the decision to reject an application was based on incorrect facts. If the body to which a complaint is made (an employment tribunal or ACAS) upholds the complaint it may award **compensation** up to a maximum of 8 weeks' pay but can not order the employer to implement the request for flexible working.

5.3.7 Parental leave

Any employee with a year's continuous service who has responsibility for a child is entitled to **unpaid parental leave** to care for that child: s 7 Employment Relations Act 1999.

The period allowed is 13 weeks for each child born or adopted after 15 December 1999. The entitlement ceases after the child is 5 years old, or on the 5th anniversary of the child being adopted. If the child is disabled (entitled to disability allowance), the right ceases after the child's eighteenth birthday.

The leave may not be taken in periods of less than one week, unless the child is disabled.

5.4 Health and safety

The key legislation under which an employer has a duty to his employees with regard to **health and safety** is the Health and Safety at Work Act 1974, which has been augmented by subsequent regulations, notably the Health and Safety at Work Regulations 1999. This Act makes it the duty of every employer to ensure the health, safety and welfare of his employees, as far as is practicable.

This general duty includes the following issues:

- Provide and maintain plant and systems of work which are safe and without risk
- Make arrangements to ensure safe use, handling, storage and transport of articles/substances
- Provide adequate information, instruction, training and supervision
- Maintain safe places of work and ensure that there is adequate access in and out
- Provide a safe and healthy working environment

5.4.1 Employment rights

The contract of employment contains an implied right not to be subjected to detriment by the employer on grounds of health and safety: s 44(1). Specifically, the employee has a right not to be subjected to detriment on the ground that he intended to or did:

- Carry out activities designated to him in connection with preventing/reducing health and safety risks at work
- Perform duties as a representative of workers on issues of health and safety
- Take part in consultation with the employer under the Health and Safety (Consultation with Employees) Regulations 1996
- Leave his place of work or refused to work in circumstances which he reasonably believed to be serious or imminent and he could not reasonably be expected to avert
- Take appropriate steps to protect himself or others from circumstances of danger which he believed to be serious and imminent

5.5 Working time

The Working Time Regulations 1998 provide broadly that a worker's **average working time in a seventeen week period,** (including overtime) shall **not exceed 48 hours for each 7 days period**, unless the worker has agreed in writing that this limit shall not apply.

The Regulations also give every worker the **right to paid annual leave**, which shall be a minimum of four weeks long. The employer may be able to specify when such holiday can or cannot be taken, but must give the employees notice of such occasions.

There are special rules relating to Sunday working.

6 Varying the terms of an employment contract

FAST FORWARD

A contract of employment can only be **varied** if the contract **expressly** gives that right, or if all parties consent to the variation.

It should be clear, from your earlier studies of general contract law, that a change in contract terms **can only be made with the consent of both parties** to the contract.

- Some terms are negotiated on a **collective** basis between employer and union(s).
- Some terms are negotiated **individually.**
- Some terms are implied by **statute.**

6.1 Varying terms without changing the contract

There may be circumstances in which an employer can vary the terms of an employment contract without actually needing to vary the contract itself. For example, there may be an **express term** in the contract which itself gives rights of variation, for example to allow a change in area of work.

Alternatively, an **implied term** may act to vary the contract.

(a) A sales representative may be required to take responsibility for such area as his employer considers necessary in order to meet changing market conditions

(b) Terms may also be implied by custom, for example, where a steel erector is required at the request of his employer to change sites: *Stevenson v Teeside Bridge & Engineering Co Ltd 1971*

6.2 Changing the existing contract

The existing contract can be changed by **consent**. Consent might be demonstrated by **oral agreement** to new terms, by the **signing** of a new statement of terms and conditions or by the employee showing acceptance by **working** under the new terms.

If an employer does not obtain **willing agreement** to a variation but the employer changes the contract anyway, the employee has a number of options.

- He may consent.
- He may stay in employment but make it clear by that he does not accept the variation.
- He may resign and claim constructive dismissal. (See Chapter 11)

6.3 Signing a new contract

The third option open to the employer is to give contractual notice to the employee and then offer a new contract on the new terms. This opens the employer to a **potential claim** for unfair dismissal. It is generally best for the employer to obtain consent to vary the terms of an existing contract.

7 Continous employment

FAST FORWARD

Many rights given to employees under the **Employment Rights Act 1996** are only available if an employee has a specified period of **continuous employment**.

You may have noticed references to 'continuous employment' in the previous sections. Most of the employment protection discussed here and in the following chapter is given to an employee who has one year's continuous service.

Exam focus point

You need to learn that one year's continuous service is required to qualify for employment protection and then learn the **exceptions** to this rule which are pointed out for you where they are discussed.

There are provisions in statute for how the year's continuous service should be calculated, and what counts as service and what does not. **The basic rule is that a year is twelve calendar months.**

Certain weeks might not be taken into account in calculating continuous service, but they do not break the period of continuous service. This might be the case if the employee takes part in a strike, or is absent due to service in the armed forces.

 Illustration

If Ben was employed for 8 months and then was given leave to do some service in the army for 5 months, on his return to the employer he would have been employed for 13 calendar months.

However, until he completes another 4 months of service he will not be eligible for the employment protection given to those employees with a year's continuous service. Once he has completed those 4 months, the 8 months prior and the 4 months subsequent to the armed service will count as continuous service, despite being split by a period away from the employer.

7.1 Transfer of undertakings

Another factor that impacts on continuous service is when a business or undertaking is transferred by one person to another. Where the business is transferred, so that an employee works for a new employer, this change represents **no break in the continuous service of the employee** (Transfer of Undertaking Regulations 1981).

Chapter Roundup

- It is important to distinguish between a **contract of service** (employment) and a **contract for services** (independent contractor). Each type of contract has different rules for taxation, health and safety provisions, protection of contract and vicarious liability in tort and contract.

- A contract of service is **distinguished** from a contract for services usually because the parties **express** the agreement to be one of service. This does not always mean that an employee will not be treated as an independent contractor by the court, however; much depends on the three tests.
    - Control test
    - Integration test
    - Economic reality test

- The distinction between **employed** and **self-employed** is important as to whether certain **rights** are available to an individual and how they are treated for **tax purposes**

- There are no particular legal rules relating to the commencement of employment – it is really **just like any other contract** in requiring offer and acceptance, consideration and intention to create legal relations.

- The **employer** has an implied **duty at common law** to take **reasonable care** of his employees; he must select proper staff, materials and provide a safe system of working.

- The **employee** has a duty to exercise **care and skill** in performance of his duties.

- **Statute** implies terms into employment contracts, which may not usually be overridden, regarding pay, maternity leave and work-life balance generally, time off, health and safety and working time.

- A contract of employment can only be **varied** if the contract **expressly** gives that right, or if all parties consent to the variation.

- Many rights given to employees under the **Employment Rights Act 1996** are only available if an employee has a specified period of **continuous employment**.

1   **Fill in the blanks** in the statements below

What tests are applied by the courts to answer these questions?

Has the employer control over the way in which the employee performs his duties? (1) ....

Is the skilled employee part of the employer's organisation? (2) ....

Is the employee working on his own account? (3)....................

2   Is working for a number of different people an automatic sign of self employment?

True [ ]

False [ ]

3   Give five reasons why the distinction between employed and self employed workers is important.

4   A 'principal statement' must include the following (tick all that apply)

(a)   Names of parties [ ]

(b)   Job title [ ]

(c)   Date employment began [ ]

(d)   Notice details [ ]

(e)   Details of continuous employment [ ]

(f)   Pay details [ ]

(g)   Pensions and pension scheme details [ ]

(h)   Holiday entitlement [ ]

5   What is an employee's fundamental duty?

6   How can an employee show acceptance when the terms of their employment contract have changed?

(i)   Signing a wholly new contract
(ii)   Working under the new terms
(iii)   Agreeing verbally

A   (iii) only
B   (i) and (ii) only
C   (ii) and (iii) only
D   (i), (ii) and (iii)

1   (1)   control test
    (2)   integration test
    (3)   multiple (economic reality) test

2   False. Other facts will be considered.

3   Social security
    Taxation
    Employment protection
    Tortious acts
    Health and safety
    (also implied terms, VAT, rights in bankruptcy)

4   (a) (c) (e) (f) (h). The other options must be included in the written statement of prescribed particulars but are not included in a 'principle statement'.

5   Faithful service to his employer

6   D. All the options are acceptable methods of showing agreement to the new terms.

Now try the question below from the Exam Question Bank

Number	Level	Marks	Time
Q14	Examination	10	18 mins

11

Dismissal and redundancy

Topic list	Syllabus reference
1 Termination by notice	C2(a)
2 Termination of employment by breach of contract	C2(a)
3 Wrongful dismissal	C2(a)
4 Remedies for wrongful dismissal	C2(c)
5 Unfair dismissal	C2(a)
6 Unfair dismissal – justification of dismissal	C2(a)
7 Remedies for unfair dismissal	C2(c)
8 Redundancy	C2(b), C2(c)

Introduction

Statutory references in this chapter are to the Employment Rights Act 1996 unless otherwise noted.

Ending an employment contract can be a traumatic time for all involved and it can result in legal action. Both employees and employers must know their rights and obligations to minimise the risk of such action.

Study guide

		Intellectual level
(C)	**Employment law**	
2	Dismissal and redundancy	
(a)	Distinguish between wrongful and unfair dismissal including constructive dismissal	2
(b)	Explain what is meant by redundancy	2
(c)	Discuss the remedies available to those who have been subject to unfair dismissal or redundancy	2

Exam guide

Questions are likely to focus on distinguishing wrongful, unfair and constructive dismissal and advising a client of the potential remedies.

Redundancy questions may require you to advise a company on what it must do to ensure it follows the correct procedures when making employees redundant. Be prepared to calculate compensation and redundancy packages.

1 Termination by notice

FAST FORWARD

When an employment contract is terminated by notice there is **no** breach of contract unless the **contents** of the notice (such as notice period) are themselves in breach.

A contract of employment may be terminated by **notice**. The following rules apply.

(a)   The period of notice given must **not be less than the statutory minimum,** whatever the contract may specify.

(b)   It **may be given without specific reason** for so doing, unless the contract requires otherwise.

(c)   If the contract states that notice may **only be given in specific circumstances** then generally it may **not** be given for any other reason.

> *McClelland v Northern Ireland General Health Services Board 1957*
>
> *The facts:* The claimant's contract gave the employer a right to terminate his employment for misconduct or inefficiency.
>
> *Decision:* There was no contractual right of termination for redundancy – it was a breach of contract to do so.

Although there is no breach of contract, termination by notice or non-renewal qualifies as 'dismissal' under the statutory code. This means that the employee may be entitled to compensation for unfair dismissal (see Section 7).

Statute imposes a **minimum period of notice** of termination to be given on either side.

1.1 Minimum period of notice

FAST FORWARD

Where employment is **terminated by notice** the period given must **not be less** than the **statutory minimum**.

If an employer terminates the contract of employment by giving notice, the **minimum period of notice** to be given is determined by the employee's length of continuous service in the employer's service as follows: s 86.

(a)   An employee who has been continuously employed for **one month or more** but less than one year is entitled to not less than **one week's** notice.

(b)   An employee who has been continuously employed for **two years or more** but less than twelve years is entitled to **one week's notice for each year of continuous employment.**

(c)   Any employee who has been employed for **twelve years** or more is entitled to not less than **twelve weeks'** notice.

If the **employee** gives notice, the minimum period required is **one week** if he has been employed for at least one month.

The notice must specify the **date of its expiry**. Either party may waive his entitlement to notice or accept a sum in lieu of notice.

The statutory rules on length of notice merely prescribe a **minimum**. If the contract provides for a longer period, notice must be given in accordance with the contract.

During the period of notice an employee is entitled to pay at a rate not less than the average of his earnings over the previous twelve weeks.

If the employee is **dismissed** in any way he may request his employer gives him a **written statement of the reasons** for his dismissal and **the employer must provide it** within fourteen days. The statement must contain at the least a simple summary of the reasons for dismissal and can be used as **admissible evidence** before an employment tribunal: s 92.

Dismissal is the word used to describe termination of an employment contract by the employer. This term is used in several ways, which we shall investigate through the rest of this chapter. Here are a few definitions relating to dismissal.

Summary dismissal is where the employer dismisses the employee without notice. He may do this if the employee has committed a serious breach of contract.

Constructive dismissal is where the employer commits a breach of contract, thereby causing the employee to resign. By implication, this is also dismissal without notice.

Wrongful dismissal is a common law concept arising in specific circumstances. It gives the employee an action for breach of contract.

Unfair dismissal is a statutory concept introduced by employment protection legislation. As a rule, every employee has the right not to be unfairly dismissed: s 54.

Correspondingly, **fair dismissal** is a statutory concept where a person has been dismissed as a result of a fair reason under legislation.

Note that the distinction between wrongful and unfair dismissal depends not so much upon the nature of the dismissal, as on the **remedies available**.

2 Termination of employment by breach of contract

Breach of the employment contract occurs where there is **summary dismissal, constructive dismissal, inability** on the employer's side to **continue employment**, or **repudiation** of the contract by the employee.

An employment contract is **terminated by breach in the following circumstances**.

- Summary dismissal
- Constructive dismissal
- Inability on the employer's behalf to continue
- Repudiation of the contract by the employee

The concepts of summary dismissal and constructive dismissal are both examples of dismissal without proper notice. A dismissal with proper notice is generally held to be lawful, unless it is shown to be wrongful or unfair.

However, under the ERA 1996, the reason for dismissal has to be determined in relation to both when the notice is given and when the employment is terminated.

2.1 Summary dismissal

Summary dismissal occurs where the employer dismisses the employee without notice. He may do this if the employee has committed a serious breach of contract and, if so, the employer incurs no liability.

If, however, he has **no sufficient justification** the employer is liable for **breach of contract** and the employee may claim a remedy for wrongful dismissal. Whether the employee's conduct justifies summary dismissal will vary according to the circumstances of the case.

Wilson v Racher 1974

The facts: A gardener swore at his employer using extreme obscenities.

Decision: His action for wrongful dismissal succeeded, as the employer's own conduct had provoked the outburst. This was a solitary outburst following a history of diligence and competence.

Contrast this with *Pepper v Webb 1969* that we saw in the previous chapter. The decision in this case favoured the employer as the incident also included a refusal to obey a reasonable and lawful instruction by the employee.

2.2 Constructive dismissal

Constructive dismissal occurs where the employer, although willing to continue the employment, repudiates some **essential term** of the contract, for example by the imposition of a complete change in the employee's duties, and the employee resigns. The employer is liable for breach of contract.

2.2.1 Establishing constructive dismissal

To establish constructive dismissal, an **employee** must show that:

- His employer has committed a serious breach of contract (a repudiatory breach).
- He left because of the breach.
- He has not 'waived' the breach, thereby affirming the contract.

Examples of breaches of contract which have lead to claims of constructive dismissal include the following.

- A reduction in pay: *Industrial Rubber Products v Gillon 1977*
- A complete change in the nature of the job: *Ford v Milthorn Toleman Ltd 1980*
- A failure to follow the prescribed disciplinary procedure: *Post Office v Strange 1981*
- A failure to provide a suitable working environment: *Waltons and Morse v Dorrington 1997*
- A failure to implement a proper procedure: *WA Goold (Pearmak) Ltd v McConnell & Another 1995*

The breach must be a serious one.

Western Excavating (ECC) Ltd v Sharp 1978

The facts: The defendant was suspended without pay for misconduct. This caused him financial difficulties, and so he applied for an advance against holiday pay but was refused. He then left and claimed for constructive dismissal.

Decision: The employers had not repudiated the contract and so there had been no dismissal.

2.3 Employer's inability to continue employment

If a personal employer dies, an employing firm of partners is dissolved, an employing company is compulsorily wound up, a receiver is appointed or the employee's place of employment is permanently closed, the employer may become unable to continue to employ the employee.

2.4 Repudiation of the contract by the employee

Resignation, striking or failing to perform the contract and to observe its conditions, is breach of contract by the employee. The employer may dismiss him or treat the contract as discharged by the employee's breach.

3 Wrongful dismissal

FAST FORWARD

Where the employer has **summarily dismissed** an employee without notice (as where the employer becomes insolvent), there may be a claim for **damages** at common law for **wrongful dismissal**.

An action for wrongful dismissal, since it derives from the employee's **common law** rights in contract, must be brought in the county court or the High Court. Claimants must show that they were **dismissed in breach of contract**, for example with less than the statutory minimum period of notice and that they have **as a result suffered loss.**

As the action is taken for a breach of contract, the courts will usually only award damages for the loss of notice period. This was confirmed in *Johnson v Unisys Ltd 2001*. The claimant was refused damages for breach of implied contractual terms that he said damaged his mental health.

A dismissal will not be wrongful if it is **justified**.

3.1 Justification of dismissal

The following have been taken as justifiable circumstances.

(a) **Wilful disobedience** of a lawful order suffices if it amounts to wilful and serious defiance of authority.

(b) **Misconduct**, in connection with the business or outside it if it is sufficiently grave. For example, acceptance of a secret commission, disclosure of confidential information, assault on a fellow employee or even financial embarrassment of an employee in a position of trust (*Pearce v Foster 1886* – stockbroker's clerk who incurred heavy gambling losses).

(c) **Dishonesty**, where the employee is in a position of particular trust.

(d) **Incompetence or neglect**, insofar as the employee lacks or fails to use skill which he professes to have.

(e) **Gross negligence**, depending on the nature of the job.

(f) **Immorality**, only if it is likely to affect performance of duties or the reputation of the business.

(g) **Drunkenness**, only if it occurs in aggravated circumstances such as when driving a vehicle or a train, or is repeated: *Williams v Royal Institute of Chartered Surveyors 1997*.

4 Remedies for wrongful dismissal

FAST FORWARD

Generally, the **only effective remedy** available to a **wrongfully dismissed** employee is a claim for **damages** based on the **loss of earnings**. The measure of damages is usually the sum that would have been earned if **proper notice** had been given.

As with any other case of compensation, the wronged party is expected to **mitigate** his loss by, say, seeking other employment.

Where breach of contract leaves the employer as the injured party, he may dismiss the employee and withhold wages. The employer may recover confidential papers, or apply for an injunction to enforce a valid restrictive covenant: *Thomas Marshall (Exporters) v Guinle 1978*.

Employment tribunals have jurisdiction to deal with wrongful dismissal cases, which formerly had to be heard in the civil courts.

5 Unfair dismissal

FAST FORWARD Certain employees have a right not to be **unfairly dismissed**. Breach of that right allows an employee to claim compensation from a tribunal. To claim for unfair dismissal, the employee must satisfy certain criteria.

Unfair dismissal is an extremely important element of employment protection legislation.

The remedies available following a successful action for **wrongful dismissal** are **limited to damages** compensating for the sum which would have been earned **if proper notice had been given.**

Legislation seeks to **widen the scope of protection** and **increase the range of remedies** available to an employee who has been unfairly dismissed. Under the terms of the **Employment Rights Act 1996**, the top rate of compensation for proven unfair dismissal is £63,000). This cap does not apply to those dismissed for 'whistleblowing', which falls under the Public Interest Disclosure Act 1998.

5.1 Scope

Every **included employee who qualifies** under the criteria (a) and (b) below has a statutory right not to be unfairly dismissed: s 94. Certain categories of employee are **excluded** from the statutory unfair dismissal code.

- Persons employed to work **outside Great Britain**
- Employees dismissed while taking **unofficial strike** or other industrial action
- Other categories, including members of the police

In order to obtain compensation or other remedies for unfair dismissal the employee must satisfy several criteria.

(a) Have been **continuously employed for one year** whether full-time or part-time.

(b) Have been **dismissed.** This may have to be determined by the tribunal, for example if the employee resigned claiming constructive dismissal.

(c) Have been **unfairly** dismissed. Dismissal may be unfair even though it is not a breach of contract by the employer.

There are some **exceptions** to the one year's continuous service qualification. These are:

- Where the matter concerns a **safety representative** being penalised for carrying out legitimate health and safety activities
- Where an employee is being **denied a statutory** right (for example an unlawful deduction from wages)
- Where the employee is **pregnant**

Exam focus point

> You should learn these exceptions to the continuous service rule.

The **effective date** of **dismissal** is reckoned as follows.

- Where there is termination by notice, the date on which the notice expires
- Where there is termination without notice, the date on which the termination takes effect
- Where an employee's fixed term contract is not renewed, the date on which that term expires

5.2 Making a claim

There are four steps to making a claim for **compensation** for unfair dismissal.

Step 1   The **employee** must **apply to a tribunal** within **three months** of dismissal

Step 2   The **employee** must **show** that he is a **qualifying employee** and that he has in fact been **dismissed**.

Step 3   Then the **employer** must **demonstrate** (prove):

(a)   What was the alleged **only or principal reason** for dismissal

(b)   That it was one of the reasons listed in s 96 (discussed in Section 6.1 below) or was otherwise a '**substantial reason** of a kind such as to be capable of justifying the dismissal of an employee' in this position.

Step 4   Then the tribunal must decide if the principal reason did in fact justify the dismissal and whether the employer acted reasonably in treating the reason as sufficient.

If the employer cannot show that the principal reason allegedly justifying the dismissal was one of the fair reasons given in statute (these are discussed in Section 6.1), the dismissal is unfair.
Dismissal may be identified in three separate circumstances.

(a)   **Actual dismissal** can usually be clearly recognised from the words used by an employer.

(b)   **Constructive dismissal**, as described earlier, involves a fundamental breach of the employment contract by the employer.

(c)   **Expiry of a fixed-term contract** without renewal amounts to a dismissal.

The employee must show that he has in fact been dismissed. The courts often have to debate whether or not the use of abusive language by employers constitutes mere abuse or indicates dismissal.

5.3 The reason for dismissal

The fair reasons for dismissal are discussed in Section 6.1. As noted above, if the principal reason for dismissal is not one of those fair reasons, then dismissal will be unfair.

However, even if the employer shows that he dismissed the employee for a reason which is recognised as capable of being sufficient, **a tribunal may still decide that the dismissal was unfair**. It may do this if it considers that on the basis of **equity and the merits** of the case, **the employer acted unreasonably** in dismissing the employee: s 98.

5.3.1 Reasonableness of employer

The **employment tribunal** is required to review the circumstances and to decide whether it was reasonable to dismiss the employee for the reasons given.

Determining whether the employer has acted reasonably requires the tribunal to ask:

- Has the correct **procedure** been applied?
- Did the employer take all **circumstances** into consideration?
- What would any **reasonable employer** have done?

The employer does not act reasonably unless he **takes account of the relevant circumstances**. If an inexperienced employee is struggling to do his work, the employer is expected to help by advice or supervision in the hope that he may improve.

The emphasis placed on giving one or more warnings before dismissing is partly so that the employee may heed the warning and amend his conduct or his performance.

5.3.2 Disciplinary procedure

Since October 2004 there have been statutory rules for dealing with **disciplinary** and **grievance procedures**. These provisions form part of an employee's contract of employment.

The standard statutory procedure for dismissal (and disciplinary) cases sets out **three steps**.

- There must be a **statement** of the **grounds for the action** and an invitation to a meeting
- The **nature** of the **meeting**
- An **appeal stage**

Where dismissal has already taken place, the employer must provide details of the grounds for the dismissal and permit the employee to appeal that decision.

These procedures (set out in the Employment Act 2002) have three general requirements

- The **timing** and **location** of any **meeting** must be **reasonable**
- The meeting must be **conducted** in such a way as to allow both the employer and the employee to explain their case
- If there is more than one meeting the employer should, if reasonably practicable, be represented by a more **senior person** then at the first meeting

All steps in the procedure should also be taken without unreasonable delay.

If either party fails to comply with the relevant procedures then neither party has to comply with the rest of the procedures. Under s 98A a dismissal will also be **automatically** unfair if the employer fails to comply with the procedures but the employer may still be able to prove the dismissal was reasonable. To do this he must show the employee would have been dismissed even if the procedure had been followed.

5.3.3 Warnings

Except in severe cases it is **not reasonable for an employer to dismiss an employee without first warning him** that if he continues or repeats his behaviour he is likely to be dismissed.

Newman v T H White Motors 1972

The facts: An employee used foul language to a trainee. The employer asked him not to do so. When he persisted the employer dismissed him.

Decision: This was an unreasonable and therefore unfair dismissal. The employer must make it clear to the employee that he risks dismissal if he persists.

5.3.4 Concluding on reasonableness

In reaching its conclusion on the issue of reasonableness, **the tribunal should not substitute what it would have done if placed in the employer's situation**. It is necessary to set the rights and interests of the employee against the interests of the employer's business and then decide whether **any reasonable employer could have come to a different conclusion**.

Unreasonableness and breach of contract by the employer must be distinguished. Some unreasonable conduct by the employer may be serious enough to repudiate the contract, and if the employee leaves he can claim for constructive dismissal by the employer.

If the employer acts unreasonably but in a manner which does not amount to repudiation of the contract, any resigning employee cannot claim constructive dismissal: *Western Excavating (ECC) Ltd v Sharp 1978*.

6 Unfair dismissal – justification of dismissal

Dismissal must be **justified** if it is related to the employee's capability or qualifications, the employee's conduct, redundancy, legal prohibition or restriction on the employee's continued employment or some other substantial reason.

Dismissal is **automatically unfair** if it is on the grounds of trade union membership or activities, refusal to join a trade union, pregnancy, redundancy when others are retained, a criminal conviction which is 'spent' under the Rehabilitation of Offenders Act 1974 or race or sex.

6.1 Potentially fair reasons for dismissal

To justify dismissal as fair dismissal, employers must show their **principal reason** relates to either:

(a) The **capability or qualifications** of the employee for performing work of the kind which he was employed to do

(b) The **conduct** of the employee

(c) **Redundancy**

(d) **Legal prohibition** or restriction that prevents the employee from lawfully working in the position which he held. For example, if a doctor is struck off the relevant professional register, or an employee loses his driving licence which he needs to be able to do his job.

(e) **Some other substantial reason** which justifies dismissal

6.1.1 Capability/qualifications

If the employer dismisses for want of capability on the part of the employee, the employer has to establish that fault.

- What does the contract require?
- What is the general standard of performance of his employees in this trade?
- What is the previous standard of performance of the dismissed employee himself?

If the employee is incompetent it must be of such a nature and quality as to justify dismissal. For example a shop manageress who left her shop dirty and untidy and who failed to maintain cash registers: *Lewis Shops Group Ltd v Wiggins 1973*.

'**Capability** is to be assessed by reference to skills, aptitude, health or any other physical or mental quality. '**Qualification**' means any academic or technical qualifications relevant to the position that the employee holds': s 98(3).

'**Reasonableness**' on the part of the employer is required, for example:

- **Consultation** with the employee to determine areas of difficulty
- Allowing a **reasonable time** for improvement
- Providing **training** if necessary
- Considering **all alternatives** to dismissal

If the employer relies on **ill health** as the grounds of incapability there must be **proper medical evidence**. The employer is entitled to consider his own business needs. A reasonable procedure involves cautions, confrontation with records and the granting of a period for improvement.

International Sports Ltd v Thomson 1980

The facts: The employee had been away from work for around 25% of the time, suffering from a number of complaints all of which were certified by medical certificates. She received a number of warnings. Prior to dismissal the company consulted their medical adviser. As the illnesses were unrelated and unverifiable, he did not consider an examination worthwhile. She was dismissed.

Decision: The dismissal was fair.

6.1.2 Misconduct

It is usual to apply the common law distinction between **gross misconduct**, which justifies summary dismissal on the first occasion and **ordinary misconduct**, which is not usually sufficient grounds for dismissal unless it is persistent.

Illustration

Assault on a fellow employee, conduct exposing others to danger (for example, smoking in an area prohibited for safety reasons), unpleasant behaviour towards customers and persistent absences from work have been treated as sufficient misconduct to justify dismissal.

6.1.3 Redundancy

If an employee is dismissed mainly or only on the ground of **redundancy**, he may claim remedies for unfair dismissal if he can show one of the following.

(a)   There were other employees in similar positions who might have been made redundant and that **selection for redundancy was in breach of a customary arrangement or agreed procedure**.

(b)   He was selected for a reason connected with **trade union membership**.

A redundancy selection procedure should be in conformity with **good industrial relations practice** which requires consultation and objective criteria of selection. The criteria set out by the EAT in *Williams v Compair Maxam Ltd 1982* have been accepted as standards of behaviour.

(a)   The employer should give as much **warning** as possible of impending redundancies.

(b)   The employer should **consult with the trade union** as to the best means of achieving the desired management result. In *Mugford v Midland Bank plc 1997* it was held that even when an employer consults a trade union over the selection criteria for redundancy, the employer must still consult the individuals to be made redundant before a final decision is taken.

(c)   It should be possible to check **criteria** for selection against such things as attendance records, efficiency at the job and length of service.

(d)   The employer should ensure that the selection is made **fairly**.

(e)   The employer should consider whether an **offer of alternative employment** can be made.

Redundancy is discussed further in Section 8.

6.1.4 Other substantial reason

The category of **other substantial reason** permits the employer to rely on some factor which is unusual and likely to affect him adversely. An employer has justified dismissal on specific grounds.

(a)   The employee was married to one of his competitors.

(b)   The employee refused to accept a reorganisation. For example, a change of shift working made in the interests of the business and with the agreement of a large majority of other employees.

6.1.5 Automatically fair reasons for dismissal

Other reasons are designated as being **automatically fair** by legislation.

*   Taking part in **unofficial industrial action**
*   Being a **threat to national security** (to be certified by the government)

An employee who strikes or refuses to work normally may be fairly dismissed unless the industrial action has been **lawfully organised** under the protection conferred by the Employment Relations Act 1999. Where dismissal results from a lock-out or a strike, the tribunal cannot deal with it as a case of alleged unfair dismissal unless victimisation is established.

6.1.6 Automatically unfair reasons for dismissal

Some reasons are automatically unfair (known as **'inadmissible reasons'**). Examples include:

- Pregnancy or other maternity-related grounds
- A spent conviction under the Rehabilitation of Offenders Act 1974
- Trade union membership or activities
- Dismissal on transfer of an undertaking (unless there are 'economic, technical or organisational reasons' justifying the dismissal)
- Taking steps to avert danger to health and safety at work
- Seeking to enforce rights relating to the national minimum wage
- Exercising rights under the Working Time Regulations 1998
- Refusing or opting out of Sunday working (in the retail sector)
- Making a protected disclosure order under the Public Interest Disclosure Act 1998.

Dismissal on grounds of pregnancy or pregnancy-related illness is automatically unfair, **regardless of length of service** as it amounts to **gender discrimination.**

6.2 Proving what was the reason for dismissal

The employer may be required to give to the employee a **written statement** of the **reason for dismissal**: s 92.

If an employee is dismissed for trying to **enforce his employment rights**, by for example asking for a written statement of particulars or an itemised pay statement, he may claim unfair dismissal **regardless of the length of service** and hours worked.

Question	Wrongful and unfair dismissal

What is the difference between wrongful dismissal and unfair dismissal?

Answer

Wrongful dismissal is a common law concept arising in specific circumstances and which gives the employee an action for breach of contract, for example where insufficient notice has been given.

Unfair dismissal is a statutory concept introduced by employment protection legislation. As a rule, every employee has the right not to be unfairly dismissed: s 54. Note that the distinction between wrongful and unfair dismissal depends not so much upon the nature of the dismissal, as on the remedies available.

7 Remedies for unfair dismissal

FAST FORWARD

Remedies for **unfair dismissal** include:
- **Reinstatement**
- **Re-engagement**
- **Compensation**

An employee who alleges unfair dismissal must present his complaint to an **employment tribunal** within three months of the effective date of termination. The dispute is referred to a Conciliation Officer and only comes before the tribunal if his efforts to promote a settlement fail.

7.1 Reinstatement

If unfair dismissal is established, the tribunal first considers the possibility of making an order for reinstatement.

> **Reinstatement** is return to the same job without any break of continuity: s 114.

7.2 Re-engagement

The tribunal may alternatively order **re-engagement**. The new employment must be comparable with the old or otherwise suitable.

> **Re-engagement** means that the employee is given new employment with the employer (or his successor or associate) on terms specified in the order.

In deciding whether to exercise these powers, the tribunal must take into account whether the complainant wishes to be reinstated and, whether it is practicable and just for the employer to comply. **Such orders are in fact very infrequent**.

The Employment Appeal Tribunal has ruled that an order for re-engagement should not be made if there has been a breakdown in confidence between the parties: *Wood Group Heavy Industrial Turbines Ltd v Crossan 1998*. In this case the employee was dismissed following allegations of drug dealing on company premises and time-keeping offences.

7.3 Compensation

If the tribunal does not order reinstatement or re-engagement the tribunal may award **compensation**, which may be made in three stages as follows.

(a)   A **basic award** calculated as follows. Those aged 41 and over receive one and a half weeks' pay (up to a current (from February 2008) maximum of £330 gross per week) for each year of service up to a maximum of 20 years. In other age groups the same provisions apply, except that the 22-40 age group receive one week's pay per year and the under 22 age group receive half a week's pay.

(b)   A **compensatory award** (taking account of the basic award) for any additional loss of earnings, expenses and benefits on common law principles of damages for breach of contract: s 124. This is limited to £63,000 by the Employment Rights Act 1996.

(c)   If the employer does not comply with an order for reinstatement or re-engagement and does not show that it was impracticable to do so a **punitive additional award** is made of between 26 and 52 weeks' pay (again subject to the £330 per week maximum).

The tribunal may reduce the amount of the award in any of the following circumstances.

- If the employee **contributed** in some way to his own dismissal: s 123(6)
- If he has **unreasonably refused** an offer of reinstatement
- If it is **just and equitable** to reduce the basic award by reason of some matter which occurred before dismissal: s 123(1)

Question   Non-renewal of fixed term contract

Nick commences employment under a three-year contract with Equis Ltd on 1 August 20X6. On 30 June 20X9 he is given notice that the contract is not to be renewed. Assuming that he has a case, what claims may he bring against Equis Ltd?

For the purposes of the Act, dismissal occurs when a fixed term contract is not renewed even though such an eventuality is implicit in the fact that the agreement has a fixed term. Nick is therefore entitled to claim for redundancy pay and/or compensation for unfair dismissal if he can prove the requisite facts. However, non-renewal cannot give rise to a claim for wrongful dismissal, which is only possible when there has been summary dismissal or dismissal with less than the required period of notice.

8 Redundancy

FAST FORWARD

Dismissal is caused by **redundancy** when the employer has ceased to carry on the business in which the employee has been employed or the business no longer needs employees to carry on that work. In these circumstances, dismissal is **presumed** by the courts to be by redundancy unless otherwise demonstrated.

An employee may claim a redundancy payment where he is

- Dismissed by his employer by reason of redundancy
- Laid off or kept on short time

8.1 What is redundancy?

Key term

A dismissal is treated as caused by **redundancy** if the only or main reason is that:

- The employer has ceased, or intends to cease, to carry on the business (or the local establishment of the business) in which the employee has been employed

- The requirements of that business for employees to carry on the work done by the employee have ceased or diminished (or are expected to): s 139 (1)

If the employee's contract has a **mobility clause** (a clause that allows the employer to change the place of work) there is no redundancy if the employee is relocated. However, in some cases it might be classed as constructive dismissal.

A key test for determining whether or not an employee is redundant is to see whether there has been a reduction of the employers' requirements for employees to work **at the place where the person concerned is employed**.

High Table Ltd v Horst and Others 1997

The facts: High Table Ltd, contract caterers, employed waitresses who had worked for several years at one company. The client company told High Table that the waitresses were no longer required, so they were dismissed by High Table on the grounds of redundancy. The waitresses, who had mobility clauses in their contracts, alleged unfair dismissal since High Table had not tried to re-employ them somewhere else.

Decision: The Court of Appeal ruled against them, saying that the place of work was at the client company premises and the dismissals were for genuine redundancy.

In considering whether the requirements of the business for staff have diminished, it is the **overall** position which must be considered. If for example A's job is abolished and A is moved into B's job and B is dismissed, that is a case of redundancy although B's job continues.

In *British Broadcasting Corporation v Farnworth 1998* a radio producer's fixed term contract was not renewed and the employer advertised for a radio producer with more experience. It was held by the EAT that the less experienced radio producer was indeed redundant as the requirement for her level of services had diminished.

If the employer reorganises his business or alters his methods so that the same work has to be done by different means which are beyond the capacity of the employee, that is not redundancy.

> *North Riding Garages v Butterwick 1967*
>
> *The facts*: A garage reorganised its working arrangements so that the workshop manager's duties included more administrative work . He was dismissed when it was found he could not perform these duties.
>
> *Decision*: His claim for redundancy pay must fail since it was not a case of redundancy.

> *Vaux and Associated Breweries v Ward 1969*
>
> *The facts*: The owners of a public house renovated their premises and as part of the new image they dismissed the middle-aged barmaid and replaced her with a younger employee.
>
> *Decision*: The claim for redundancy pay must fail since the same job still existed.

Exam focus point

> Like unfair dismissal, redundancy is likely to be a popular topic. Link your studies on redundancy and unfair dismissal to the material on remedies.

8.2 Calculation of redundancy pay

Redundancy pay is calculated on the same basis as the basic compensation for unfair dismissal.

8.3 Exceptions to the right to redundancy payment

A person is excluded from having a right to redundancy payment where

- They do not fit the **definition** of 'employee' given in statute
- They have not been **continuously employed** for **two** years
- They have been or could be dismissed for **misconduct**
- An offer to **renew the contract** is unreasonably **refused**
- Claim is made **out of time** (after six months)
- The employee leaves before being made redundant having been notified of the possibility of redundancies

8.3.1 Misconduct of the employee

An employee who is dismissed for **misconduct** is **not entitled to redundancy pay** even though he may become redundant.

> *Sanders v Neale 1974*
>
> *The facts*: In the course of a dispute employees refused to work normally. The employer dismissed them and closed down his business. The employees claimed redundancy pay.
>
> *Decision*: The claim must be dismissed since the employees had repudiated the contract before the employer's decision to close down made them redundant.

An employee can be dismissed for misconduct but still claim redundancy pay in the event of a strike.

- After receiving notice of termination of the contract from the employer
- After the employee has given notice claiming redundancy pay on account of lay-off or short time

8.3.2 Offer of further employment

The employer may offer a redundant employee **alternative** employment for the future. **If the employee then unreasonably refuses the offer, he loses his entitlement to redundancy pay**: s 141.

The offer must be of alternative employment **in the same capacity**, at the same place and on the same terms and conditions as the previous employment. It should not be perceived as being lower in status: *Cambridge District Co-operative Society v Ruse 1993.*

When there is a difference between the terms and conditions of a new contract and the previous contract, the employee is entitled to a **four week trial** period in the new employment. If either party terminates the new contract during the trial period, it is treated as a case of dismissal for redundancy at the expiry date of the previous employment. The employee can also still bring claims for unfair dismissal: *Trafalgar House Services Ltd v Carder 1997.*

8.4 Lay-off and short time

An employee's exact remuneration may depend on the employer providing work. He is 'laid off' in any week in which he earns nothing by reason of lack of work or he is 'kept on short time', which is any week in which he earns less than half a normal week's pay: s 86.

When an employee is **laid off** or **kept on short time** for four or more consecutive weeks, or six weeks in a period of thirteen weeks he **may claim redundancy** pay by giving notice to the employer of his intention to claim.

In addition to his notice of claim the employee must also give notice to the employer to terminate the contract of employment: s 150(1).

8.5 Strike action

Employees involved in **strike action after** redundancy notice is served **will** be entitled to redundancy payments. However, if they are **on strike** when the notice is served they will **not** be eligible for the payment.

Chapter Roundup

- When an employment contract is terminated by notice there is **no** breach of contract unless the **contents** of the notice (such as notice period) are themselves in breach.

- Where employment is **terminated by notice** the period given must **not be less** than the **statutory minimum**.

- **Breach of the employment contract** occurs where there is **summary dismissal**, **constructive dismissal**, **inability** on the employer's side to **continue employment**, or **repudiation** of the contract by the employee.

- Where the employer has **summarily dismissed** an employee without notice (as where the employer becomes insolvent), there may be a claim for **damages** at common law for **wrongful dismissal**.

- Generally, the only **effective remedy** available to a **wrongfully dismissed** employee is a claim for **damages** based on **the loss of earnings**. The measure of damages is usually the sum that would have been earned if **proper notice** had been given.

- Certain employees have a right not to be **unfairly dismissed**. Breach of that right allows an employee to claim compensation from a tribunal. To claim for unfair dismissal, the employee must satisfy certain criteria.

- Dismissal must be **justified** if it is related to the employee's capability or qualifications, the employee's conduct, redundancy, legal prohibition or restriction on the employee's continued employment or some other substantial reason.

- Dismissal is **automatically unfair** if it is on the grounds of trade union membership or activities, refusal to join a trade union, pregnancy, redundancy when others are retained, a criminal conviction which is 'spent' under the Rehabilitation of Offenders Act 1974 or race or sex.

- Remedies for **unfair dismissal** include:

    - **Reinstatement**
    - **Re-engagement**
    - **Compensation**

- Dismissal is caused by **redundancy** when the employer has ceased to carry on the business in which the employee has been employed or the business no longer needs employees to carry on that work. In these circumstances, dismissal is **presumed** by the courts to be by redundancy unless otherwise demonstrated.

1   How much notice is an employee with 5 years' continuous service entitled to?

2   If an employer cannot continue with the employment contract because the company has gone into liquidation, does that constitute breach of contract?

Yes   ☐

No   ☐

3   Is summary dismissal ever justified? If so, when?

4   **Fill in the blanks** below, using the words in the box.

To claim (1) .... for unfair dismissal, three issues have to be considered.

The employee must show that he is a (2) .... employee and that he has been (3) ....

The (4) .... must show what the (5) .... was for dismissal

Application has to be made to the (6) .... within (7) .... months of the dismissal

• qualifying	• dismissed	• employer
• reason	• three	• compensation
• employment tribunal		

5   Expiry of a fixed term contract without renewal amounts to a dismissal

True   ☐

False   ☐

6   Which of the following is *not* a question that a tribunal, when considering an employer's reasonableness in an unfair dismissal claim, will want to answer?

A   What would a reasonable employer have done?
B   Has the correct procedure been applied?
C   Has any employee been dismissed in this way before?
D   Did the employer take all circumstances into consideration?

7   Give an automatically fair reason for dismissal.

8   Which is the most common remedy awarded for unfair dismissal?

compensation
re-engagement
re-instalment

9   An employee is not entitled to redundancy pay if he resigns voluntarily before being made redundant even if he was aware of the possibility of redundancy.

True   ☐

False   ☐

1   5 weeks (1 week for each year's continuous service)

2   Yes. The contract is effectively repudiated.

3   Yes, in cases of serious breach of contract by the employee

4   (1) compensation (2) qualifying (3) dismissed (4) employer (5) reason (6) employment tribunal (7) three

5   True. Non-renewal constitutes dismissal.

6   C. The question is irrelevant to the employee's situation

7   Being a threat to national security (alternatively, taking part in unofficial industrial action)

8   Compensation, as in most cases the working relationship would have been irrevocably damaged

9   True, as he is not being made redundant

Now try the questions below from the Exam Question Bank

Number	Level	Marks	Time
Q15	Examination	10	18 mins

The formation and constitution of business organisations

Agency law

Topic list	Syllabus reference
1 Role of agency and agency relationships	D1(a)
2 Formation of agency	D1(b)
3 Authority of the agent	D1(c)
4 Relations between agents and third parties	D1(d)

Introduction

In this chapter we examine how an **agency relationship** arises and how the **agent's authority** is acquired and defined. Agency is the foundation of most business relationships where more than one person engages in commerce together. Examples include **partnerships** and **companies**, which we shall introduce in the next chapter.

'Agents' are employed by **'principals'** to perform tasks which the principals cannot or do not wish to perform themselves. This is often because the principal does not have the time or expertise to carry out the task.

If business people did not employ the services of agents, they would be weighed down by the contractual details, and would probably get little else done!

When parties enter into an **agency arrangement**, the principal gives a measure of authority to the agent to carry out tasks on his behalf. We shall look at the extent and limits of that authority in Section 3.

The agent **contracts and deals with third parties** on behalf of the principal. We shall look at the relationship between agents and the third parties they deal with in Section 4.

Study guide

		Intellectual level
(D)	**The formation and constitution of business organisations**	
1	Agency law	
(a)	Define the role of the agent and give examples of such relationships paying particular regard to partners and company directors	2
(b)	Explain how the agency relationship is established	2
(c)	Define the authority of the agent	2
(d)	Explain the potential liability of both principal and agent	2

Exam guide

Agency may form a knowledge question requiring you to explain what agents are, how agency relationships are established and their authority and liability to others.

1 Role of agency and agency relationships

FAST FORWARD

> **Agency** is a relationship which exists between two legal persons (the **principal** and the **agent**) in which the function of the agent is to form a **contract between his principal and a third party**. Partners, company directors, factors, brokers and commercial agents are all acting as agents.

Agency is a very important feature of modern commercial life. It can be represented diagrammatically as follows:

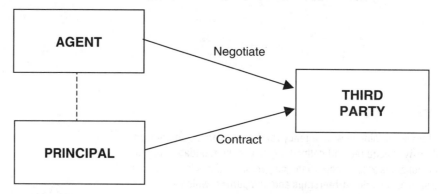

For instance Pendo may ask Alan to take Pendo's shoes to be repaired. Pendo and Alan expressly agree that Alan is to do this on Pendo's behalf. In other words, Alan becomes her agent in making a contract between Pendo and Thierry, the shoe repairer, for her shoes to be mended.

1.1 Types of agent

In practice, there are many examples of agency relationships, to which you are probably aware of in everyday life, although you might not know that they illustrate the law of agency. The most important agency relationships for the F4 syllabus are those of partners and company directors.

Types of agent	
Partners	This is a particularly important example of agents in your syllabus, and we shall look at it in more detail in Chapter 13. For now, you should know that participants in a partnership (for example, if you work for a firm of accountants) are agents of each other.

Types of agent	
Company directors	This is another important example of agency in your syllabus. As we shall discuss in Chapter 19, directors act as agents of the company.
Factors	A factor, sometimes called a mercantile agent, is a person whose job is to sell or buy goods on behalf of another person. For example, motor dealers are often factors.
Brokers	A broker may operate in many trades. He is essentially an intermediary who arranges contracts in return for commission. For example, an insurance broker.
Auctioneers	Auctioneers are agents authorised to sell property at auction on behalf of the seller. When an auctioneer accepts a bid from a buyer, he becomes the agent of the buyer for the purpose of making a record of the sale.
Commercial agents	A commercial agent is an independent agent who has continuing authority in connection with the sale or purchase of goods.

2 Formation of agency

FAST FORWARD

The relationship of principal and agent is created by **mutual consent** in the vast majority of cases. This **agreement does not have to be formal or written**.

The mutual consent comes about usually by **express agreement**, even if it is informal. However, it may also be **implied agreement**, due to the **relationship** or **conduct** of the parties.

2.1 Express agreement

This is where the agent is **expressly appointed** by the principal. This may be orally, or in writing. In most commercial situations, the appointment would be made in writing to ensure that everything was clear. An agent expressly appointed by the principal has **actual authority**, which we shall look at in Section 3.

2.2 Implied agreement

An agency relationship between two people may be implied by their **relationship** or by their **conduct**.

Illustration

If an employee's duties include making contracts for his employer, say by ordering goods on his account, then they are, by implied agreement, the agent of the employer for this purpose. An agent authorised in this way is said to have implied authority.

2.3 Ratification of an agent's act: retrospective agreement

FAST FORWARD

A principal may subsequently **ratify** an act of an agent retrospectively.

An agency relationship may be created retrospectively, by the 'principal' **ratifying** the act of the 'agent'. Therefore it is created after the 'agent' has formed a contract on behalf of the 'principal'. If the principal agrees to the acts of the agent after the event, he may approve the acts of the agent and make it as if they had been principal and agent at the time of the contract.

The conditions for ratification are:

- The principal must have **existed** at the time of the contract made by the agent
- The principal must have had **legal capacity** at the time the contract was made
- The ratification must take place **within reasonable time**
- He ratifies the contract in its **entirety**
- He **communicates** his ratification to the third party sufficiently clearly

Once a contract has been ratified by the principal, the effect is that it is as if the agency relationship had been **expressly formed before** the contract made by the agent took place.

2.4 Formation of agency agreement without consent

An agency may be created, or an agent's authority may be extended, without express consent. This happens **by estoppel**, when the principal **'holds out'** a person to be his agent, and when there is an **agent of necessity**.

2.4.1 Implied agreement

In some cases, an agency created by implied agreement might result in the agent having **more implied authority** than the principal might have consented to. Authority shall be discussed in Section 3.

2.4.2 Agent by estoppel

An agency relationship may be formed by implication when the **principal holds out to third parties** that a person is his agent, even if the principal and the 'agent' do not agree to form such a relationship. In such a case, the principal is estopped from denying the agent's apparent/ostensible authority (see Section 3), hence the name **'agent by estoppel'**. An agency relationship is not so formed if it is the 'agent' who creates the impression that he is in an agency relationship with a 'principal'.

2.4.3 Agent by necessity

In some rare situations, it may be necessary for a person to take action in respect of someone else's goods in an **emergency situation**. That person can become an **agent of necessity** of the owner of the goods, as he takes steps in respect of the goods.

 Illustration

A seller is shipping frozen goods to a buyer in another country. While the ship is docked, the freezers in the ship break down and the relevant part required to fix them cannot be obtained. If the ship's captain (acting as the agent of necessity) cannot make contact with the owner of the goods, he might, of necessity, sell the goods while they are still frozen, rather than allow them to spoil by defrosting.

This is particularly rare, because it would only occur when the 'agent' could not make contact with the 'principal', which in the modern world is **extremely unlikely**.

This principle is a historic part of English shipping and merchant law and you should be aware that it might be possible, but do not worry about the other details of the doctrine.

3 Authority of the agent

If an agent acts within the limits of his authority, any contract he makes on the principal's behalf is **binding** on both principal and third party. The extent of the agent's authority may be **express, implied** or **ostensible**. Express and implied authority are both forms of **actual authority**.

A principal does not give the agent unlimited authority to act on his behalf. A **contract** made by the agent is **binding** on the principal and the other party **only if** the **agent was acting within the limits of his authority** from his principal.

In analysing the limits of an agent's authority, three distinct sources of authority can be identified:

- Express authority
- Implied authority
- Ostensible authority

3.1 Express authority

Express authority is a matter between principal and agent. This is authority explicitly given by the principal to the agent to perform particular tasks, along with the powers necessary to perform those tasks.

The extent of the agent's express authority will depend on the **construction of the words used on his appointment**. If the appointment is in **writing**, then the document will need to be examined. If it is oral, then the scope of the agent's authority will be a matter of evidence.

If the agent contracts outside the scope of his express (actual) authority, he may be **liable** to the principal and the third party for **breach of warrant of authority**.

Illustration

A board of directors may give an individual direct express authority to enter the company into a specific contract. The company would be bound to this contract, but not to one made by the individual director outside the express authority.

3.2 Implied authority

Where there is no express authority, authority may be **implied** from the **nature** of the agent's activities or from what is **usual** or **customary** in the **circumstances**.

Between principal and agent the latter's express authority is paramount. The agent cannot contravene the principal's express instructions by claiming that he had implied authority for acting in the way he did.

As far as **third parties** are concerned, they are entitled to assume that the agent has implied usual authority unless they know to the contrary.

> *Watteau v Fenwick 1893*
>
> *The facts:* The owner of a hotel (F) employed the previous owner (H) to manage it. F forbade H to buy cigars on credit but H did buy cigars from W. W sued F who argued that he was not bound by the contract, since H had no actual authority to make it, and that W believed that H still owned the hotel.
>
> *Decision:* It was within the usual authority of a manager of a hotel to buy cigars on credit and F was bound by the contract (although W did not even know that H was the agent of F) since his restriction of usual authority had not been communicated.

> *Hely-Hutchinson v Brayhead Ltd 1968*
>
> *The facts:* The chairman and chief executive of a company acted as its *de facto* managing director, but he had never been formally appointed to that position. Nevertheless, he purported to bind the company to a particular transaction. When the other party to the agreement sought to enforce it, the company claimed that the chairman had no authority to bind it.
>
> *Decision:* Although the director derived no authority from his position as chairman of the board, he did acquire authority from his position as chief executive. Therefore the company was bound by the contract as it was within the implied authority of a person holding such a position.

3.3 Actual authority

Express and implied authority are sometimes referred to together as **actual authority**. This distinguishes them from **ostensible** or **apparent authority**, which is discussed next in this section.

> **Actual authority** is a legal relationship between principal and agent created by a consensual agreement between them.

3.4 Apparent/ostensible authority

> An agent's **apparent** or **ostensible authority** may be greater than his express or implied authority. This occurs where a **principal** holds it out to be so to a third party, who relied on the representation and altered his position as a result. It may be **more extensive** than what is usual or incidental.

The **ostensible** (or **apparent**) authority of an agent is what a principal **represents** to other persons that he has given to the agent (authority by '**holding out**'). As a result, an agent with **express** or **implied** authority which are limited can be held in practice to have a more extensive authority.

Apparent/ostensible authority usually arises either

(a)   where the **principal** has **represented** the agent as having authority even though he has not actually been appointed

(b)   where the **principal** has **revoked** the agent's **authority** but the **third party** has **not had notice** of this: *Willis Faber & Co Ltd v Joyce 1911.*

Illustration

A principal employs a stockbroker to sell shares. It is an implied term of the arrangement between them that the broker shall (unless otherwise agreed) have **actual authority** to do what is usual in practice for a broker selling shares for a client (but no more than that). Any person dealing with the broker is entitled to assume (unless informed to the contrary) that the broker has the usual authority of a broker acting for a client.

3.4.1 The extent of ostensible authority

Ostensible authority (unlike implied authority) is not restricted to what is usual and incidental. The principal may expressly or by inference from his conduct **confer on the agent any amount of ostensible authority**.

3.4.2 Example: partnership

A **partner** has considerable but **limited implied authority** by virtue of being a partner. If, however, the other partners allow him to exercise greater authority than is implied, they have represented that he has wider authority. They will be bound by the contracts which he makes within the limits of this **ostensible authority**.

3.4.3 Example: companies

Freeman & Lockyer v Buckhurst Park Properties (Mangal) Ltd 1964

The facts: K and H carried on business as property developers through a company which they owned in equal shares. Each appointed another director, making four in all. H lived abroad and the business of the company was left entirely under the control of K. As a director K had no actual or apparent authority to enter into contracts as agent of the company, but he did make contracts as if he were a managing director without authority to do so. The other directors were aware of these activities but had not authorised them. The claimants sued the company for work done on K's instructions.

> *Decision:* There had been a representation by the company through its board of directors that K was the authorised agent of the company. The board had authority to make such contracts and also had power to delegate authority to K by appointing him to be Managing Director. Although there had been no actual delegation to K, the company had by its acquiescence led the claimants to believe that K was an authorised agent and the claimants had relied on it. The company was bound by the contract made by K under the principle of 'holding out' (or estoppel). The company was estopped from denying (that is, not permitted to deny) that K was its agent although K had no actual authority from the company.

It can be seen that it is the conduct of the 'principal' which creates ostensible authority. It does not matter whether there is a pre-existing agency relationship or not.

Exam focus point

> This is important – ostensible authority arises in two distinct ways. It may arise where a **person makes a representation to third parties** that a particular person has the authority to act as their agent without actually appointing them as their agent. Alternatively, it may arise where a **principal has previously represented to a third party** that an agent has authority to act on their behalf.

3.4.4 Representations creating ostensible authority

The **representation must be made by the principal or an agent acting on his behalf.** It cannot be made by the agent who is claiming ostensible authority. *Armagas Ltd v Mundogas SA, The Ocean Frost 1986.*

It must be a **representation of fact, not law**, and must be **made to the third party**. This distinguishes ostensible authority from actual authority, where the third party need know nothing of the agent's authority.

3.4.5 Reliance on representations

It must be shown that the **third party relied on the representation**. If there is no causal link between the third party's loss and the representation, the third party will not be able to hold the principal as liable.

 Illustration

If the third party did not believe that the agent had authority, or if they positively knew they did not, then ostensible authority cannot be claimed. This is true even if the agent appeared to have authority.

3.4.6 Alteration of position following a representation

It is enough that the third party **alters his position as a result of reliance on the representation**. He does not have to suffer any detriment as a result, but damages would in such an event be minimal.

 Question   Ostensible authority

Give three examples of occasions when ostensible authority may arise.

Answer

- Where a person allows another person, who is not his agent, to appear as if he is.
- Where a principal allows his agent to give the impression that he has more extensive authority than is really the case.
- Where, following termination of the agency relationship, a principal allows his former agent to continue to appear to be his agent.

3.5 Revocation of authority

Where a principal has represented to a third party that an agent has authority to act, and has subsequently **revoked the agent's authority**, this may be **insufficient to escape liability**. The principal should inform third parties who have previously dealt with the agent of the change in circumstances. This is particularly relevant to partnerships and the position when a partner leaves a partnership.

We shall look at partnership in the next chapter.

3.6 Termination of agency

Agency is terminated by **agreement** or by **operation of law** (death, insanity, insolvency).

Agency is terminated when the **parties agree** that the relationship should end.

It may also be terminated by **operation of law** in the following situations:

- Principal or agent dies
- Principal or agent becomes insane
- Principal becomes bankrupt, or agent becomes bankrupt and this interferes with his position as agent

Termination brings the **actual authority** of the agent to an end. However, third parties are allowed to enforce contracts made later by the 'agent' until they are actively or constructively informed of the termination of the agency relationship.

4 Relations between agents and third parties

An agent usually has **no liability** for a contract entered into as an agent, nor any **right to enforce it**. Exceptions to this: when an agent is **intended** to have liability; where it is **usual business practice** to have liability; when the agent is actually acting on his own behalf; where agent and principal have joint liability.

A third party to a contract entered into with an agent acting outside his ostensible authority can sue for breach of **warranty of authority**.

4.1 Liability of the agent for contracts formed

An agent contracting for his principal within his actual and/or apparent authority generally **has no liability** on the contract and **is not entitled to enforce it**. However, there are **circumstances** when the **agent will be personally liable** and can enforce it.

(a) When he **intended to undertake personal liability** – for example where he signs a contract as party to it without signifying that he is an agent.

(b) Where it is **usual business practice or trade custom** for an agent to be liable and entitled.

(c) Where the agent **is acting on his own behalf** even though he purports to act for a principal.

Where an agent enters into a **collateral contract** with the third party with whom he has contracted on the principal's behalf, there is separate liability and entitlement to enforcement on that collateral contract.

It can happen that there is **joint liability** of agent and principal. This is usually the case where an agent did not disclose that he acted for a principal.

4.2 Breach of warranty of authority

An agent who **exceeds his ostensible authority** will generally have **no liability to his principal**, since the latter will not be bound by the unauthorised contract made for him. But the agent **will be liable** in such a case **to the third party** for breach of warranty of authority.

Chapter Roundup

- **Agency** is a relationship which exists between two legal persons (the **principal** and the **agent**) in which the function of the agent is to form a **contract between his principal and a third party**. Partners, company directors, factors, brokers and commercial agents are all acting as agents.

- The relationship of principal and agent is created by **mutual consent** in the vast majority of cases. This **agreement does not have to be formal or written**.

- The mutual consent comes about usually by **express agreement**, even if it is informal. However, it may also be **implied agreement**, due to the **relationship** or **conduct** of the parties.

- A principal many later **ratify** an act of an agent retrospectively.

- An agency may be created, or an agent's authority may be extended, without express consent. This happens **by estoppel**, when the principal **'holds out'** a person to be his agent, and when there is an **agent of necessity**.

- If an agent acts within the limits of his authority, any contract he makes on the principal's behalf is **binding** on both principal and third party. The extent of the agent's authority may be **express, implied** or **ostensible**. Express and implied authority are both forms of **actual authority**.

- An agent's **ostensible authority** may be greater than his express or implied authority. This occurs where a **principal** holds it out to be so to a third party, who relied on the representation and altered his position as a result. It may be **more extensive** than what is usual or incidental.

- Agency is terminated by **agreement** or by **operation of law** (death, insanity, insolvency).

- An agent usually has **no liability** for a contract entered into as an agent, nor any **right to enforce it**. Exceptions to this: when an agent is **intended** to have liability; where it is **usual business practice** to have liability; when the agent is actually acting on his own behalf; where agent and principal have joint liability.

  A third party to a contract entered into with an agent acting outside his ostensible authority can sue for breach of **warranty of authority**.

1   **Fill in the blanks** in the statements, using the words in the boxes below.

Agency is the (1)........................ which exists between two (2)....................... persons
(3)...........................and the agent, in which the function of the agent is to form a
(4)................................ between his (5)............................. and a
(6).................................

•	relationship	•	contract	•	legal
•	third party	•	principal	•	principal

2   A principal may, in certain circumstances, ratify the acts of the agent which has retrospective effect.

True   ☐

False ☐

3   What is the best definition of ostensible authority?

(a)   The authority which the principal represents to other persons that he has given to the agent.

(b)   The authority implied to other persons by the agent's actions.

4   What point of law is explained in the case of *Freeman & Lockyer v Buckhurst Park Properties (Mangal) Ltd 1964?*

5   Which of the following are circumstances where an agent may enforce a contract?

(a)   Where the agent is intended to take personal liability
(b)   Where it is usual business practice to allow enforcement
(c)   Where the agent acts on his own behalf even if he purports to act for a principle

(i)   (a), (b)
(ii)   (b), (c)
(iii) (a), (c)
(iv)   (a), (b) and (c)

1   (1)   relationship   (2)   legal   (3)   principal
    (4)   contract   (5)   principal   (6)   third party

2   True. Principals may ratify retrospectively.

3   (a). The key word is represents.

4   A director may have ostensible authority to contract, if although he does not have their express permission, the other directors are aware that contracts are being made and do nothing to prevent it.

5   (iv). They are all valid circumstances.

Now try the question below from the Exam Question Bank			
Number	**Level**	**Marks**	**Time**
Q16	Examination	10	18 mins

13

Organisations and legal personality

Topic list	Syllabus reference
1 Sole traders	D3(a)
2 Partnerships	D2(a) – (e)
3 Limited liability partnerships	D2(a), (d)
4 A company's legal identity	D3(a)
5 Limited liability of members	D3(b)
6 Types of company	D3(c)
7 Additional classifications	D3(c)
8 Effect of legal personality	D3(d)
9 Ignoring separate personality	D3(e)
10 Comparison of companies and partnerships	D3(a)

Introduction

Partnerships are a common form of business organisation and we are commonly used for **small businesses** and some **professional businesses**, for example accountants.

Partnerships are a group of individuals who have an **agency** relationship with each other. We shall look at how partnerships are **formed** and later **terminated**, then at how **relationships** with other partners and with third parties work. We shall also consider the issues that arise when deciding whether to trade as a **company** or a **partnership**.

We will then introduce companies as business vehicles that are distinct from sole traders and partnerships. The key difference between them is the concept of **separate legal personality**. This chapter outlines this doctrine, and also discusses its implications (primarily **limited liability** for members) and the exceptions to it (lifting the **veil of incorporation**).

In Section 6 we shall look at the different types of company that can be used to carry out business.

Study guide

(D)	**The formation and constitution of business organisations**	
2	Partnerships	
(a)	Demonstrate a knowledge of the legislation governing the partnership, both unlimited and limited	1
(b)	Discuss how partnerships are established	2
(c)	Explain the authority of partners in relation to partnership activity	2
(d)	Analyse the liability of various partners for partnership debts	2
(e)	Explain the way in which partnerships can be brought to an end	2
3	Corporations and legal personality	
(a)	Distinguish between sole traders, partnerships and companies	2
(b)	Explain the meaning and effect of limited liability	2
(c)	Analyse different types of companies, especially private and public companies	2
(d)	Illustrate the effect of separate personality	2
(e)	Recognise instances where separate personality will be ignored	2

Exam guide

Partnership can form a question on its own and as it is the form of organisation used by accountants in practice, it will always be highly examinable.

You must be able to compare and contrast companies and partnerships, and to advise parties starting up in business which would be the best form of business organisation for them.

> **Statutory references in Chapters 13 to 20 are to the Companies Act 2006 unless otherwise stated.**

1 Sole traders

FAST FORWARD

In a **sole tradership**, there is no legal distinction between the individual and the business.

1.1 Introduction

A sole trader owns and runs a business. They contribute capital to start the enterprise, run it with or without employees, and earn the profits or stands the losses of the venture.

Sole traders are found mainly in the retail trades (local newsagents), small scale service industries (plumbers), and small manufacturing and craft industries. An accountant may operate as a sole trader.

1.2 Legal status of the sole trader

Whilst the business is a separate accounting entity the business is **not legally distinct** from the person who owns it. In law, the person and the business are viewed as the same entity.

The **advantages** of being a sole trader are as follows.

- **No formal procedures** are required to set up in business. However, for certain classes of business a licence may be required (eg retailing wines and spirits), and VAT registration is often necessary.
- **Independence** and **self-accountability**. A sole trader need consult nobody about business decisions and is not required to reveal the state of the business to anyone (other than the tax authorities each year).
- **Personal supervision** of the business by the sole trader should ensure its effective operation. Personal contact with customers may enhance commercial flexibility.
- **All** the **profits** of the business **accrue** to the sole trader. This can be a powerful motivator, and satisfying to the individual whose ability/energy results in reward.

The **disadvantages** of being a sole trader include the following.

- If the business gets into debt, a sole trader's **personal wealth** (for example, private house) might be lost if the debts are called in, as they are the same legal entity.
- Expansion of the business is usually only possible by **ploughing back** the **profits** of the business as further capital, although loans or overdraft finance may be available.
- The business has a **high dependence** on the **individual** which can mean long working hours and difficulties during sickness or holidays.
- The **death** of the proprietor may make it **necessary** to **sell** the **business** in order to pay the resulting tax liabilities, or family members may not wish to continue the business anyway.
- The **individual** may **only have one skill**. A sole trader may be, say, a good technical engineer or craftsman but may lack the skills to market effectively or to maintain accounting records to control the business effectively.
- Other **disadvantages** associated with small size, lack of diversification, absence of economies of scale and problems of raising finance.

2 Partnerships

FAST FORWARD

Partnership is defined as 'the relation which subsists between persons carrying on a business in common with a view of profit'. A partnership is *not* a separate legal person distinct from its members, it is merely a 'relation' between persons. Each partner (there must be at least two) is usually **personally liable** for all the debts of the firm.

Partnership is a common form of business association. It is **flexible**, because it can either be a **formal** or **informal** arrangement, so can be used for large organisations or a small husband and wife operation.

Partnership is normal practice in the **professions** as most professions prohibit their members from carrying on practice through limited companies, though some professions permit their members to trade as limited liability partnerships which have many of the characteristics of companies. Business people are not so restricted and generally prefer to trade through a limited company for the advantages this can bring.

Exam focus point

Your syllabus requires you to demonstrate knowledge of the legislation governing both limited and unlimited liability partnerships. You should therefore make careful note of the rules regarding the Partnership Act 1890, the Limited Partnership Act 1907 and the Limited Liability Partnership Act 2000.

2.1 Definition of partnership

Key term

'**Partnership** is the relation which subsists between persons carrying on a business in common with a view of profit.' S1 Partnership Act 1890.

We shall look at some points raised by this definition now.

2.1.1 The relation which subsists between persons

'**Person**' includes a corporation such as a **registered company** as well as an **individual** living person.

There must be at least **two** partners. If, therefore, two people are in partnership, one dies and the survivor carries on the business, that person is a sole trader. There is no longer a partnership.

2.1.2 Carrying on a business

Business can include every trade, occupation or profession. But three points should be noted.

(a) A business is a **form of activity**. If two or more persons are merely the passive joint owners of revenue-producing property, such as rented houses, that fact does not make them partners.

(b) A business can consist of a **single transaction**. These situations are often described as 'joint ventures'.

(c) Carrying on a business must have a **beginning and an end**. A partnership begins when the partners agree to conduct their **business activity** together. This can be before the business actually begins to trade, such as when premises are leased and a bank account opened: *Khan v Miah 2001*.

2.1.3 In common

Broadly this phrase means that the partners must be associated in the business as **joint proprietors**. The evidence that this is so is found in their taking a share of the profits, especially **net profit**.

2.1.4 A view of profit

If persons enter into a partnership with a **view of making profits** but they actually suffer losses, it is still a partnership. The test to be applied is one of **intention**. If the intention of trading together is just to gain experience, for example, there is no partnership: *Davies v Newman 2000*.

2.2 Consequences of the definition

In most cases there is no doubt about the existence of a partnership. The partners declare their intention by such steps as signing a **written partnership agreement** and adopting a **firm name**. These outward and visible signs of the existence of a partnership are not essential however – a partnership can exist without them.

2.2.1 Terminology

The word 'firm' is correctly used to denote a partnership. It is **not** correct to apply it to a registered company (though the newspapers often do so).

The word 'company' may form part of the name of a partnership, for example, 'Smith and Company'. But 'limited company' or 'registered company' is **only** applied to a properly registered company.

2.3 Liability of the partners

We shall see later that every partner is liable **without limit** for the debts of the partnership. It is possible to register a limited partnership in which one or more individual partners have limited liability, but the limited partners may not take part in the management of the business: Limited Partnerships Act 1907.

The limited partnership is useful where one partner wishes to invest in the activities of the partnership without being involved in its day-to-day operation. Such partners are entitled to inspect the accounts of the partnership.

Under the Limited Liability Partnership Act 2000 it is possible to register a partnership with limited liability (an LLP). LLPs are discussed in Section 3.

2.4 Forming a partnership

Partnerships can be **formed** very informally, but there may be complex formalities to ensure clarity.

A partnership can be a very **informal arrangement**. This is reflected in the procedure to form a partnership.

A partnership is **formed when two or more people agree to run a business together**. Partnerships can be formed in any trade or occupation or profession.

In order to be a partnership, the business must be **'carried on in common'**, meaning that all parties must have **responsibility** for the business. In other words, there is **more than one proprietor**.

A husband and wife who run a shop together are partners, but a shop owner and their employee are not.

In law then, the formation of a partnership is essentially straightforward. People **make an agreement** together to run a business, and **carry that agreement out**.

Question

Formation of partnership

Imagine that two large firms of accountants wanted to merge. The partners agreed on 1 June 20X7 that they would merge and become a new partnership, known as the Biggest Accountancy Partnership. In law, this is straightforward.

What problems do you think they might encounter?

Answer

In law, when the partners of the two firms agree to merge, then they have a new partnership.

In practice, however, if two massive businesses such as two large firms decided to merge, the details of the formation of the new partnership would be far more complex than that. Here is a list of just some of the things that they would have to consider.

- Profit share
- Employees
- Partnership property
- Partner hierarchy

- Recruitment policy
- Future partners' policy
- Standard partners' authority to act in the new firm's name
- Fair trading and monopoly issues

In practice, the formation of such a new partnership would be an enormous operation.

2.4.1 Common formation formalities

In practice, the formalities of setting up a partnership may be more **complex** than simple agreement. Many professional people use partnerships. These business associations can be vast organisations with substantial revenue and expenditure, such as the larger accountancy firms and many law firms.

Such organisations have so many partners that the relationships between them has to be **regulated**. Thus forming some partnerships can involve creating **detailed partnership agreements** which lay out terms and conditions of partnership.

2.4.2 The partnership agreement

A written partnership agreement is *not* legally required. In practice there are advantages in setting down in writing the terms of their association.

(a)   It **fills** in the **details** which the law would not imply – the nature of the firm's business, its name, and the bank at which the firm will maintain its account for instance.

(b) A written agreement serves to **override terms** otherwise implied by the Partnership Act 1890 which are inappropriate to the partnership. The Act for example implies that partners share profits equally.

(c) Additional clauses can be developed. **Expulsion clauses** are an example and they provide a mechanism to expel a partner where there would be no ability to do so otherwise.

2.5 Termination of partnership

Partnerships may be **terminated** by passing of time, termination of the underlying venture, death or bankruptcy of a partner, illegality, notice, agreement or by order of the court.

Termination is when the partnership comes to an end. In this context, 'partnership' means the existing partners.

Illustration

Alison, Ben, Caroline and David are in partnership as accountants. Caroline decides to change career and become an interior designer. In her place, Alison, Ben and David invite Emily to join the partnership.

As far as third parties are concerned, a partnership offering accountancy services still exists. In fact, however, the old partnership (ABCD) has been dissolved, and a new partnership (ABDE) has replaced it.

2.5.1 Events causing termination

The Partnership Act 1890 states that partnership is terminated in the following instances.

- **Passing of time**, if the partnership was entered into for a fixed term
- **Termination of the venture**, if entered into for a single venture
- The **death or bankruptcy** of a partner (partnership agreement may vary this)
- **Subsequent illegality**
- **Notice** given by a partner if it is a partnership of indefinite duration
- **Order of the court** granted to a partner
- **Agreement** between the partners

In the event of the **termination** of a partnership, the partnership's **assets are realised** and the proceeds applied in this order.
- Paying off external debts
- Repaying to the **partners** any **loans** or **advances**
- Repaying the partners' **capital contribution**
- Anything left over is then **repaid** to the **partners** in the **profit sharing ratio**.

The partnership agreement can exclude some of these provisions and can **avoid dissolution** in the following circumstances.

- Death of a partner
- Bankruptcy of a partner

It is wise to make such provisions to give **stability** to the partnership.

2.6 Authority of partners

The **authority** of partners to bind each other in contract is based on the principles of agency.

In simple terms, a partner is the **agent of the partnership and their co-partners**. This means that some of their acts bind the other partners, either because they have, or because they appear to have, authority. The **Partnership Act 1890 defines** the **authority** of a partner to make contracts as follows.

Authority of a partner

Every partner is an **agent** of the firm and his other partners for the purpose of the business of the partnership, and the acts of every partner who does any act for carrying on the **usual way** of business if the kind carried on by the firm of which he is a member **bind the firm** and his partners, **unless** the partner so acting has **in fact no authority** to act for the firm in the particular matter, **and the person with whom he is dealing** either **knows that he has no authority**, or **does not know or believe him to be a partner.**

Where a partner pledges the credit of the firm for a **purpose apparently not connected** with the firm's ordinary course of business, the **firm is not bound, unless** he is in fact **specially authorised** by the other partners: but this section does not affect any personal liability incurred by an individual.

If it has been **agreed between the partners** that any **restriction** shall be placed on the power of any one or more of them to bind the firm, **no act** done in contravention of the agreement is **binding** on the firm with respect to **persons having notice of the agreement.**

The key point to note about authority of partners is that, other than when the partner has actual authority, the authority often **depends on the perception of the third party**. If the third party genuinely believes that the partner has authority, the partner is likely to bind the firm.

Partners are also **jointly liable** for **crimes** and **torts** committed by one of their number in the course of business.

2.7 Liability of partners in an unlimited liability partnership

FAST FORWARD

Partners are **jointly liable** for all partnership debts that result from contracts that the partners have made which bind the firm.

Partners are **jointly liable** for all partnership debts that result from contracts made by other partners which bind the firm. The link between authority and liability can be seen in the following diagram.

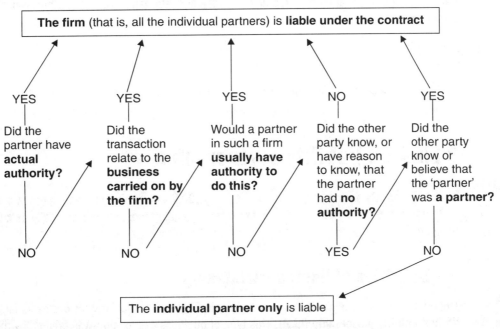

There are particular rules on liability for new and retiring partners.

Partner	Partner liability
New partners	A new partner admitted to an existing firm is liable for **debts incurred** only **after** they become a partner. They are not liable for debts incurred before they were a partner unless they agree to become liable.

Partner	Partner liability
Retiring partners	A partner who retires is still **liable** for any **outstanding debts** incurred while they were a partner, unless the creditor has agreed to release them from liability. They are also **liable** for debts of the firm **incurred after their retirement** if the creditor knew them to be a partner (before retirement) and has not had **notice** of their retirement.
	Therefore, it is **vital** on retirement that a partner **gives notice** to all the creditors of the firm. The retiring partner may have an indemnity from the remaining partners with respect to this issue.

2.8 Supervision and regulation

There is no formal statutory supervision or regulation of partnerships. Their accounts need not be in prescribed form nor is an audit necessary. The public has no means or legal right of inspection of the firm's accounts or other information such as companies must provide.

If, however, the partners carry on business under a firm name which is not the surnames of them all, say, 'Smith, Jones & Co', they are required to disclose the **names** of the **partners** on their letterheads and at their places of business. They are required to make a **return** of their **profits** for income tax and **usually** to **register** for VAT.

2.9 Property

Partnerships **can** grant a **mortgage** or **fixed charge** over property, but **cannot** grant **floating changes** (see Chapter 17).

Question	Partnership

Partners in a traditional partnership have an agency relationship with each other. What is the effect of this arrangement?

Answer

Each partner acts as an agent of the partnership and all partners are jointly liable for a partner's actions.

3 Limited liability partnerships

FAST FORWARD

A **limited liability partnership** formed under the 2000 Act, combines the features of a traditional partnership with the limited liability and creation of legal personality more usually associated with limited companies.

3.1 Definition of limited partnership

The other form of partnership commonly used in England, particularly for professional partnerships, is the **limited liability partnership (LLP)**. This type of business association was created by the Limited Liability Partnership Act 2000.

LPPs are similar to limited companies in that they have separate legal identity and unlimited liability for debts, but the liability of the individual partners is **limited to the amount of their capital contribution**.

LLPs have similar requirements for governance and accountability as limited companies. They are generally set up by firms of professionals such as accountants and lawyers, who are required by the rules of their professions to operate as partnerships but who seek to have the protection of limited liability.

Key term

> A **limited liability partnership (LLP)** is a corporate body which has separate legal personality from its members and therefore some of the advantages and disadvantages of a company.

The main advantage of an LLP over a traditional partnership is that the LLP will be liable for its own debts rather than the partners. All contracts with third parties will be with the LLP.

3.2 Formation

A limited liability partnership may be formed by persons associating to carry on lawful business with a view to profit, but it **must be incorporated** to be recognised. LLPs can have an unlimited number of partners. To be incorporated, the subscribers must send an **incorporation document** and a **statement of compliance** to the Registrar of Companies.

The document must be signed and state the following:

- The **name** of the LLP
- The **location** of its **registered office** (England and Wales/Wales/Scotland)
- The **address** of the registered office
- The name and address of all the **members** of the LLP
- Which of the members are to be **designated members** (see below)

There is also a registration fee of £95.

3.3 Internal regulation

LLPs are more flexible than companies as they provide similar protection for the owners, but with less statutory rules on areas such as meetings and management. No board of directors is needed. As can be seen in the incorporation procedures, LLPs come under the supervision of the **Registrar of Companies** (the Registrar).

The members of the LLP are those who subscribe to the original incorporation document, and those admitted afterwards in accordance with the terms of the partnership agreement.

The rights and duties of the partners will usually be set out in a **partnership agreement**. In the absence of a partnership agreement, the rights and duties are set out in regulations under the Act.

LLPs must have **two designated members**, who must take responsibility for the publicity requirements of the LLP.

With regard to publicity, the LLP's designated members must:

- **File** certain notices with the Registrar, such as when a member leaves
- Sign and file **accounts**
- Appoint **auditors** if appropriate

The Registrar will maintain a file containing the publicised documents of the LLP at Companies House.

3.4 External relationships

Every member is an **agent** of the LLP. As such, where the member has authority, the LLP will be bound by the acts of the member.

The **LLP will not be bound by the acts of the member where:**

- They have no authority and the third party is aware of that fact
- They have ceased to be a member, and the third party is aware of that fact

3.5 Dissolution

An LLP **does not dissolve on a member leaving** it, in the same way that a traditional partnership does. Where a member has died or (for a corporate member) been wound up, that member ceases to be a member, but the LLP continues in existence.

An **LLP must therefore be wound up** when the time has come for it to be dissolved. This is achieved under provisions **similar to company winding up** provisions (see Chapter 21).

3.6 Limited partnership

The other form of partnership that is seen, rarely, in the UK is the **limited partnership**. Under the Limited Partnership Act 1907, a partnership may be formed in which at least one partner (the general partner) must have **full, unlimited liability**. The other partners have **limited liability** for the debts of the partnership beyond the extent of the capital they have contributed. The rules are as follows:

- Limited partners may not withdraw their capital
- Limited partners may not take part in the management of the partnership
- Limited partners cannot bind the partnership in a contract with a third party without losing the benefit of limited liability
- The partnership must be registered with Companies House

Question

LLPs

Explain the publicity requirements that LLPs must meet.

Answer

The designated members must:

- File certain notices with the Registrar
- Sign and file accounts
- Appoint auditors if appropriate

4 A company's legal identity

FAST FORWARD

A company has a **legal personality** separate from its owners (known as members). It is a formal arrangement, surrounded by formality and publicity, but its chief advantage is that members' **liability** for the company's debts is typically **limited**.

A company is the most popular form of business association.

By its nature, a company is more **formal** than a partnership or a sole trader. There is often substantially **more legislation** on the formation and procedures of companies than any other business association, hence the weighting towards company law of most of the rest of this Study Text.

The key reason why the company is a popular form of business association is that the **liability of its members to contribute to the debts of the entity is significantly limited**. This will be explained more later in this chapter. For many people, this benefit outweighs the disadvantage of the formality surrounding companies, and encourages them not to trade as sole traders or (unlimited) partnerships.

4.1 Definition of a company

Key terms

For the purposes of this Study Text, a **company** is an entity registered as such under the Companies Act 2006.

The key feature of a company is that it has a **legal personality** (existence) distinct from its members and directors.

4.2 Legal personality

A person possesses legal rights and is subject to legal obligations. In law, the term 'person' is used to denote two categories of legal person.

- An individual human being is a **natural person**. A sole trader is a natural person, and there is legally no distinction between the individual and the business entity in sole tradership
- The law also recognises **artificial persons** in the form of companies and limited partnerships. Unlimited partnerships are not artificial persons.

Key term

> **Corporate personality** is a common law principle that grants a company a legal identity, separate from the members who comprise it. It follows that the property of a company belongs to that company, debts of the company must be satisfied from the assets of that company, and the company has perpetual succession until wound up.

A corporation is a **legal entity** separate from the natural persons connected with it, for example as members or directors. We shall come back to this later.

5 Limited liability of members

FAST FORWARD

> The fact that a company's members – not the company itself – have **limited liability** for its debts **protects** the **members** from the company's creditors and ultimately from the full risk of business failure.

A key consequence of the fact that the company is distinct from its members is that its members have **limited liability**.

Key term

> **Limited liability** is a protection offered to members of certain types of company. In the event of business failure, the members will only be asked to contribute identifiable amounts to the assets of the business.

5.1 Protection for members against creditors

The **company** itself is **liable without limit for its own debts.** If the company buys plastic from another company, for example, it owes the other company money.

Limited liability is a benefit to members. They own the business, so might be the people whom the creditors logically asked to pay the debts of the company if the company is unable to pay them itself.

Limited liability prevents this by stipulating the **creditors** of a limited company **cannot demand payment of the company's debts** from members of the company.

5.2 Protection from business failure

As the company is liable for all its own debts, limited liability only becomes an issue in the event of a business failure when the **company is unable to pay its own debts**.

This will result in the **winding up** of the company which will enable the creditors to be paid from the proceeds of any assets remaining in the company. It is at winding up that limited liability becomes most relevant.

5.3 Members asked to contribute identifiable amounts

Although the creditors of the company cannot ask the members of the company to pay the debts of the company, there are some amounts that **members are required to pay, in the event of a winding up**.

Type of company	Amount owed by member at winding up
Company limited by shares	Any **outstanding amount** from when they originally purchased their shares from the company. If the member's shares are fully paid, they **do not have to contribute anything in the event of a winding up**.
Company limited by guarantee	The **amount they guaranteed** to pay in the event of a winding up

Question

Limitations of liability

Hattie and two friends wish to set up a small business. Hattie is concerned that, following her initial investment, she will have no access to additional funds, and is worried what might happen if anything goes wrong. Advise her on the relative merits of a company and an unlimited partnership.

Answer

The question of liability appears to be important to Hattie. As a member of a limited company, her liability would be limited – as a member at least – to any outstanding amount payable for her shares. If the three friends decide to form an unlimited partnership, they should be advised that they will have **unlimited** liability for the debts of the partnership. (An unlimited partnership does **not** have a legal personality distinct from the partners.)

5.4 Liability of the company for tort and crime

As a company has a separate legal identity, it may also have liabilities in **tort** and **crime**. Criminal liability of companies in particular is a topical area but, is outside the scope of your syllabus.

6 Types of company

FAST FORWARD

Most companies are those **incorporated** under the **Companies Act**. However there are other types of company such as **corporations sole**, **chartered corporations**, **statutory corporations** and **community interest companies**.

Corporations are classified in one of the following categories.

Categories	Description
Corporations sole	A corporation sole is an **official position** which is filled by one person who is replaced from time to time. The Public Trustee and the Treasury Solicitor are corporations sole.
Chartered corporations	These are usually **charities** or bodies such as the Association of Chartered Certified Accountants, formed by Royal Charter.
Statutory corporations	Statutory corporations are formed by special Acts of Parliament. This method is little used now, as it is slow and expensive. It was used in the nineteenth century to form railway and canal companies.
Registered companies	Registration under the Companies Act is the normal method of incorporating a commercial concern. Any body of this type is properly called a company.
Community Interest Companies (CICs)	A special form of company for use by 'social' enterprises pursuing purposes that are beneficial to the community, rather than the maximisation of profit for the benefit of owners, created by the Companies (Audit, Investigation and Community Enterprise) Act 2004.

6.1 Limited companies

The meaning of limited liability has already been explained. It is the **member**, not the company, whose liability for the company's debts may be limited.

6.1.1 Liability limited by shares

Liability is usually **limited by shares.** This is the position when a company which has share capital states in its constitution that 'the liability of members is limited'.

6.1.2 Liability limited by guarantee

Alternatively a company may be **limited by guarantee.** Its constitution states the amount which each member **undertakes** to **contribute** in a winding up (also known as a liquidation). A creditor has no direct claim against a member under his guarantee, nor can the company require a member to pay up under his guarantee until the company goes into liquidation.

Companies limited by guarantee are appropriate to **non-commercial activities**, such as a charity or a trade association which is non-profit making but wish to have a form of reserve capital if it becomes insolvent. They do not have **share capital**.

6.2 Unlimited liability companies

Key term

> An **unlimited liability company** is a company in which members do not have limited liability. In the event of business failure, the liquidator can require members to contribute as much as may be required to pay the company's debts in full.

An unlimited company **can only be a private company**, as by definition, a **public company is always limited.**

An unlimited company need not **file** a copy of its **annual accounts** and reports with the Registrar, unless during the relevant accounting reference period:

(a)   It is (to its knowledge) a **subsidiary** of a limited company.
(b)   **Two** or more **limited companies** have **exercised rights** over the **company**, which (had they been exercised by only one of them) would have **made** the **company** a **subsidiary** of that one company.
(c)   It is the **parent company** of a limited liability company.

Attention!

> Some of these requirements and terms will seem unfamiliar to you, but we will look at them in more detail in the following chapters.

The unlimited company certainly has its uses. It provides a **corporate body** (a separate legal entity) which can conveniently hold assets to which liabilities do not attach.

Question

Limited liability

Explain the liability of members of companies limited by guarantee.

Answer

Members of companies limited by guarantee are required to pay the amount they guaranteed if required when the company is wound up.

6.3 Public and private companies

FAST FORWARD

A company may be **private** or **public**. Only the latter may offer its share to the public.

Key terms

A **public company** is a company whose constitution states that it is public and that it has complied with the registration procedures for such a company.

A **private company** is a company which has not been registered as a public company under the Companies Act. The major practical distinction between a private and public company is that the former may not offer its securities to the public.

A **public** company is a company registered as such under the Companies Act with the Registrar. **Any company not registered as public is a private company**.

A public company may be one which was **originally incorporated** as a public company or one which re-registered as a public company having been previously a private company.

6.4 Conditions for being a public company

FAST FORWARD

To trade, a public company must hold a **Registrar's trading certificate** having met the requirements, including **minimum capital** of £50,000.

6.4.1 Registrar's trading certificate

Before it can trade a company originally incorporated as a public company must have a trading certificate issued by the Registrar. The conditions for this are:

- The **name** of the company identifies it as a public company by ending with the words 'public limited company' or 'plc' or their Welsh equivalents, 'ccc', for a Welsh company.
- The **constitution** of the company states that 'the company is a public company' or words to that effect.
- The **allotted share capital** of the company is not less than the authorised minimum which is currently £50,000.
- It is a **company** limited by shares.

With regard to the minimum share capital of £50,000.

- A company originally incorporated as a public company will not be permitted to trade until its **allotted** share capital is at least £50,000.
- A private company which re-registers as a public company will not be permitted to trade until it has **allotted** share capital of at least £50,000; this needs only be paid up to one quarter of its nominal value (plus the whole of any premium).
- A private company which has share capital of £50,000 or more may of course continue as a private company; it is always **optional** to become a public company.

A company limited by guarantee which has no share capital, and an unlimited company, **cannot** be public companies.

6.4.2 Minimum membership and directors

A public company must have a minimum of **one member**. This is the same as a private company. However, unlike a private company it must have at least **two directors**. A private company must have just one. Directors do not usually have liability for the company's debts.

6.5 Private companies

A private company is the residual category and so does not need to satisfy any special conditions.

Private companies are generally small enterprises in which some if not all shareholders are also directors and **vice versa**. Ownership and management are combined in the same individuals. Therefore, it is unnecessary to impose on the directors complicated restrictions to safeguard the interests of members and so the number of rules that apply to public companies are reduced for private companies.

6.6 Differences between private and public companies

FAST FORWARD

The main differences between public and private companies relate to: **capital**, **dealings** in **shares**, **accounts**, **commencement of business**, **general meetings**, **names**, **identification**, and **disclosure requirements**.

The more important differences between public and private companies imposed by law relate to the following factors.

6.6.1 Capital

The main differences are:

(a) There is a minimum amount of **£50,000** for a **public** company, but **no minimum** for a **private** company.

(b) A public company may **raise capital** by **offering** its **shares** or debentures to the public; a **private** company is **prohibited** from doing so.

(c) Both **public** and **private companies** must generally **offer** to **existing members first** any ordinary shares to be allotted for cash. However a **private** company **may permanently disapply** this rule.

6.6.2 Dealings in shares

Only a **public company** can obtain a listing for its shares on the **Stock Exchange** or other investment exchange. To obtain the advantages of listing the company must agree to elaborate conditions contained in particulars in a **listing agreement** with The Stock Exchange. However, not all public companies are listed.

6.6.3 Accounts

(a) A **public** company has **six** months from the end of its accounting reference period in which to produce its statutory audited accounts. The period for a **private** company is **nine** months.

(b) A **private** company, if qualified by its size, may have **partial exemption** from various **accounting provisions** (discussed later in this text). These exemptions are not available to a public company or to its subsidiaries (even if they are private companies).

(c) A **listed public company** must publish its full accounts and reports on its **website**.

(d) Public companies must lay their **accounts** and reports before a general meeting annually. Private companies have no such requirement.

6.6.4 Commencement of business

A **private** company can commence business **as soon** as it is **incorporated**. A **public** company if incorporated as such must first **obtain a trading certificate from the Registrar**.

6.6.5 General meetings

Private companies are not required to hold annual general meetings, (AGMs). **Public companies** must hold one within six months of their financial year end.

6.6.6 Names and Identification

The rules on identification as public or private are as follows.

- The word **'limited'** or **'Ltd'** in the name denotes a private company; **'public limited company'** or **'plc'** must appear at the end of the name of a public company.

- The **constitution** of a **public** company must state that it is a public company. A **private company** should be identified as private.

6.6.7 Disclosure requirements

There are **special disclosure and publicity requirements** for public companies.

The main advantage of carrying on business through a public rather than a private company is that a public company, by the issue of listing particulars, may obtain a **listing** on The Stock Exchange and so mobilise capital from the investing public generally.

Attention!

> There is an important distinction between public companies and **listed public companies**. Listed (or quoted) companies are those which trade their shares (and other securities) on stock exchanges. Not all public companies sell their shares on stock exchanges (although, in law, they are entitled to sell their shares to the public). **Private** companies are not entitled to sell shares to the public in this way.
>
> In practice, only public companies meeting certain criteria would be allowed to obtain such a listing by the Stock Exchange.

Private companies may be broadly classified into two groups: independent (also called **free-standing**) private companies and **subsidiaries** of other companies.

7 Additional classifications

FAST FORWARD

> There are a number of other ways in which companies can be **classified**.

7.1 Parent (holding) and subsidiary companies

The Companies Act draws a distinction between an 'accounting' definition, and a 'legal' definition in, s 1162. A company will be the **parent** (or **holding**) **company** of another company, its **subsidiary company**, according to the following rules.

Key term

> **Parent company**
>
> (a) It holds a **majority of the voting rights** in the subsidiary.
>
> (b) It **is a member of the subsidiary and has the right to appoint or remove a majority of its board of directors.**
>
> (c) It **has the right to exercise a dominant influence over the subsidiary**:
>
>   (i) By virtue of provisions contained in the subsidiary's articles.
>
>   (ii) By virtue of a control contract.
>
> (d) It **is a member of the subsidiary and controls alone**, under an agreement with other members, **a majority of the voting rights in the company.**
>
> (e) **A company is also a parent if:**
>
>   (i) It has the power to exercise, or actually exercises, a dominant influence or control over the subsidiary
>
>   (ii) It and the subsidiary are managed on a unified basis
>
> (f) **A company is also treated as the parent of the subsidiaries of its subsidiaries.**

A company (A Ltd) is a **wholly owned subsidiary** of another company (B Ltd) if it has no other members except B Ltd and its wholly owned subsidiaries, or persons acting on B Ltd's or its subsidiaries' behalf.

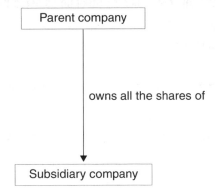

The diagram illustrates a **simple group**. In practice, such groups might be much larger and much more complex.

The importance of the parent and subsidiary company relationship is recognised in company law in a number of rules.

(a) A parent company must generally prepare **group accounts** in which the financial situation of parent and subsidiary companies is consolidated as if they were one person.

(b) A subsidiary may **not ordinarily be a member** of its parent company.

(c) Since directors of a parent company can **control** its **subsidiary**, some rules designed to regulate the dealings of companies with directors also apply to its subsidiaries, particularly loans to directors.

7.2 Quoted companies

As we have seen public companies may seek a listing on a public exchange. This option is not open to private companies, who are not allowed to offer their shares for sale to the public. Listed companies are sometimes referred to as quoted companies (because their shares are quoted publicly).

7.3 Small companies regime

Small companies benefit from the small companies regime's reduced legal requirements in terms of filing accounts with the Registrar and obtaining an audit. The definitions of a small company for the purposes of accounting and auditing are almost identical.

In **accounting terms**, a company is small if it meets two of the following applicable criteria:

(a) Balance sheet total of not more than £2.8 million
(b) Turnover of not more than £5.6 million
(c) 50 employees or fewer

For **audit purposes**, a company is classed as small if it qualifies on the above criteria, but must **meet both** of conditions (a) and (b).

7.4 Multinational companies

The vast majority of companies will simply operate in one country. However, some of the larger companies in the world will operate in more than one country. Such companies are **multinational**.

Key term

A **multinational company** is a company that produces and markets its products in more than one country.

7.4.1 Examples: multinational companies

The top three multinational companies by revenue as listed by Fortune Global 500 in 2007 were:

- Wal-mart Stores
- Royal Dutch Shell
- Exxon Mobil

Such companies sell their shares on stock exchanges around the world.

| Question | Small companies |

State the criteria that a company must meet to be classified as small.

| Answer |

A small company must meet two of the following criteria:

- Its balance sheet total must not exceed £2.8 million.
- Turnover must be no more than £5.6 million.
- It must employ fewer than 50 employees.

8 Effect of legal personality

FAST FORWARD

The case of *Salomon v Salomon & Co Ltd 1897* clearly demonstrates the **separate legal personality** of companies and is of great significance to any study of company law.

Salomon v Salomon & Co Ltd 1897

The facts: The claimant, S, had carried on business for 30 years. He decided to form a limited company to purchase the business so he and six members of his family each subscribed for one share.

The company then purchased the business from S for £38,782, the purchase price being payable to the claimant by way of the issue of 20,000 £1 shares, the issue of debentures, £10,000 of debentures and £8,782 in cash.

The company did not prosper and was wound up a year later, at which point its liabilities exceeded its assets. The liquidator, representing unsecured trade creditors of the company, claimed that the company's business was in effect still the claimant's (he owned 20,001 of 20,007 shares). Therefore he should bear liability for its debts and that payment of the debenture debt to him should be postponed until the company's trade creditors were paid.

Decision: The House of Lords held that the business was owned by, and its debts were liabilities of, the company. The claimant was under no liability to the company or its creditors, his debentures were validly issued and the security created by them over the company's assets was effective. This was because the company was a legal entity separate and distinct from S.

The principle of separate legal personality was confirmed in the following case.

Lee v Lee's Air Farming Ltd 1960

The facts: Mr Lee, who owned the majority of the shares of an aerial crop-spraying business, and was the sole working director of the company, was killed while piloting the aircraft.

Decision: Although he was the majority shareholder and sole working director of the company, he and the company were separate legal persons. Therefore he could also be an employee with rights against it when killed in an accident in the course of his employment.

8.1 Veil of incorporation

Incorporation 'veils' members from outsiders' view but this veil may be lifted in **some circumstances**, so creditors and others can seek redress directly from members. The veil may be lifted: by statute to enforce the law; to prevent the evasion of obligations; and in certain situations where companies trade as a group.

Because a company has separate legal personality from the people who own or run it (the members/shareholders/directors), people can look at a company and not know who or what owns or runs it.

The fact that members are 'hidden' in this way is sometimes referred to as the '**veil of incorporation**'. Literally, the members are 'veiled' from view.

9 Ignoring separate personality

It is sometimes necessary by law to look at who the owners of a company are. This is referred to as '**lifting the veil**'.

Separate personality can be ignored to:

- **Identify** the **company** with its **members** and/or directors.
- Treat a **group of companies** as a **single commercial entity** (if a company is owned by another company).

The more important of these two reasons is the first one, although the second reason can sometimes be more complex. The main instances for lifting the veil are given below.

9.1 Lifting the veil by statute to enforce the law

Lifting of the veil is permitted under a number of statutes to enforce the law.

9.1.1 Liability for trading without trading certificate

A public company must obtain a trading certificate from the Registrar before it may commence to trade. Failure to do so leads to **personal liability** of the directors for any loss or damage suffered by a third party resulting from a transaction made in contravention of the trading certificate requirement. They are also viable for a fine.

9.1.2 Fraudulent and wrongful trading

When a company is wound up, it may appear that its business has been carried on with **intent** to **defraud creditors** or others. In this case the court may decide that the persons (usually the directors) who were knowingly parties to the **fraudulent trading** shall be **personally responsible** under civil law for debts and other liabilities of the company: s 213 Insolvency Act 1986.

Fraudulent trading is also a criminal offence; under s 993 of the Companies Act 2006 any person guilty of the offence, even if the company has not been or is not being wound up, is liable for a fine or imprisonment for up to 10 years.

If a company in insolvency proceedings is found to have traded when there is no reasonable prospect of avoiding insolvent liquidation, its directors may be liable under civil law for **wrongful trading**. Again a court may order such directors to make a contribution to the company's assets: s 213 Insolvency Act 1986.

9.1.3 Disqualified directors

Directors who participate in the management of a company in contravention of an order under the Company Directors Disqualification Act 1986 will be **jointly** or **severally liable** along with the company for the company's debts.

9.1.4 Abuse of company names

In the past there were a number of instances where directors of companies which went into **insolvent liquidation** formed another company with an identical or similar name. This new company bought the original company's business and assets from its liquidator.

The Insolvency Act 1986 (s 217) makes it a criminal offence and the directors personally liable where; they are a director of a company that goes into insolvent liquidation and; they become involved with the directing, managing or promoting of a business which has an **identical name** to the original company, or a **name similar** enough to suggest a connection.

Exam focus point

It is very important to know the statutory ways of lifting the veil.

9.2 Lifting the veil to prevent evasion of obligations

A company may be identified with those who control it, for instance to determine its residence for tax purposes. The courts may also ignore the distinction between a company and its members and managers if the latter use that distinction to **evade** their **existing legal obligations**.

Gilford Motor Co Ltd v Home 1933

The facts: The defendant had been employed by the claimant company under a contract which forbade him to solicit its customers after leaving its service. After the termination of his employment he formed a company of which his wife and an employee were the sole directors and shareholders. However he managed the company and through it evaded the covenant that prevented him from soliciting customers of his former employer.

Decision: An injunction requiring observance of the covenant would be made both against the defendant and the company which he had formed as a 'a mere cloak or sham'.

9.2.1 Public interest

In time of war a company is not permitted to trade with '**enemy aliens**'. The courts may draw aside the veil if, despite a company being registered in the UK, it is suspected that it is controlled by aliens.

The question of nationality may also arise in peacetime, where it is convenient for a foreign entity to have a British **facade** on its operations.

Re F G Films Ltd 1953

The facts: An English company was formed by an American company to 'make' a film which would obtain certain marketing and other advantages from being called a British film. Staff and finance were American and there were neither premises nor employees in England. The film was produced in India.

Decision: The British company was the American company's agent and so the film did not qualify as British. Effectively, the corporate entity of the British company was swept away and it was exposed as a 'sham' company.

9.2.2 Evasion of liabilities

The veil of may also be lifted where directors **ignore** the separate legal personality of two companies and transfer assets from one to the other in disregard of their duties in order to avoid an existing liability.

Re H and Others 1996

The facts: The court was asked to rule that various companies within a group, together with the minority shareholders, should be treated as one entity in order to restrain assets prior to trial.

> *Decision:* The order was granted. The court thought there was evidence that the companies had been used for the fraudulent evasion of excise duty.

9.2.3 Evasion of taxation

The court may lift the veil of incorporation where it is being used to **conceal** the nationality of the company.

> *Unit Construction Co Ltd v Bullock 1960*
>
> *The facts:* Three companies, wholly owned by a UK company, were registered in Kenya. Although the companies' constitutions required board meetings to be held in Kenya, all three were in fact managed entirely by the holding company.
>
> *Decision:* The companies were resident in the UK and liable to UK tax. The Kenyan connection was a sham, the question being not where they ought to have been managed, but where they were actually managed.

9.2.4 Quasi-partnership

An application to wind up a company on the 'just and equitable' ground under the Insolvency Act 1986 may involve the court lifting the veil to reveal the company as a **quasi-partnership.** This may happen where the company only has a few members, all of whom are actively involved in its affairs. Typically the individuals have operated contentedly as a company for years but then fall out, and one or more of them seeks to remove the others.

The courts are willing in such cases to treat the central relationship between the directors as being that of partners, and rule that it would be unfair therefore to allow the company to continue with only some of its original members. This is illustrated by the case of *Ebrahimi v Westbourne Galleries Ltd 1973* (see Chapter 21).

Question
Quasi-partnership

Sandy and Pat have carried on business together for twenty years, most recently through a limited company in which each holds 500 shares. They share the profits equally in the form of directors' remuneration. Pat's son Craig joins the business, buying 100 shares from each of Sandy and Pat. Disputes arise and Pat and Craig use their voting majority to remove Sandy from the board. Advise Sandy.

Answer

Sandy cannot prevent her removal from her directorship. However, a court may find that, on the basis of the past relationship, it is unjust and inequitable to determine the case solely on legal rights. It could, on equitable principles, order liquidation of the company.

The veil of the company may be lifted to reveal a quasi-partnership.

9.3 Lifting the veil in group situations

The principle of the veil of incorporation extends to the holding (parent) company/subsidiary relationship. Although holding companies and subsidiaries are part of a group under company law, they retain their **separate legal personalities**.

In *Adams v Cape Industries 1990*, three reasons were put forward for identifying the companies as one, and lifting the veil of incorporation. They are:

- The subsidiary is acting as **agent** for the holding company.
- The group is to be treated as a **single economic entity** because of statutory provision.
- The **corporate structure** is being used as a **facade** (or sham) to conceal the truth.

> *Adams v Cape Industries plc 1990*
>
> *The facts:* Cape, an English company, headed a group which included many wholly-owned subsidiaries. Some of these mined asbestos in South Africa, and others marketed the asbestos in various countries including the USA.
>
> Several hundred claimants had been awarded damages by a Texas court for personal injuries suffered as a result of exposure to asbestos dust. The defendants in Texas included one of Cape's subsidiaries, NAAC. The courts also considered the position of AMC, another subsidiary, and CPC, a company linked to Cape Industries.
>
> *Decision:* The judgement would not be enforced against the English holding company, either on the basis that Cape had been 'present' in the US through its local subsidiaries or because it had carried on business in the US through the agency of NAAC. Slade LJ commented in giving the judgement that English law 'for better or worse recognises the creation of subsidiary companies ... which would fall to be treated as separate legal entities, with all the rights and liabilities which would normally be attached to separate legal entities'.
>
> Whether desirable or not, English law allowed a group structure to be used so that legal liability fell on an individual member of a group rather than the group as a whole.

Exam focus point

> Lifting the veil in group situations is easily forgotten. Ensure you know the *Cape Industries* case and the three reasons for lifting the veil in groups which it sets out.

9.4 Summary of situations in which the veil can be lifted

The instances in which the veil will be lifted are as follows.

Lifting the veil by statute to enforce the law	• Liability for trading without a trading certificate • Fraudulent and wrongful trading • Disqualified directors • Abuse of company names
Evasion of obligations	• Evasion of legal obligations • Public interest • Evasion of liabilities • Evasion of taxation • Quasi-partnership
Group situations	• Subsidiary acting as agent for the holding company • The group is to be treated as a single economic entity • The corporate structure is being used as a sham

9.5 Lifting the veil and limited liability

The above examples of lifting the veil include examples of where, if they have broken the law, **directors** can be made **personally liable** for a company's debts. This is very rare.

If those directors are also members, then limited liability **does not apply**. This is the only time that limited liability is overridden and that the **member** becomes **personally liable** for the company's debts **due to their actions as a director.**

Attention!

> Another consequence of the legal personality of a company being distinct from its members, is that the company is managed by people other than its owners. We shall look at issues relating to corporate governance in Chapter 22.

10 Comparison of companies and partnerships

> Because it is a separate legal entity, a company has a number of features which are different from a partnership. The most important difference between a company and a traditional partnership is that a company has a **separate legal personality** from its members, while a traditional partnership does not.

10.1 The differences

The separate legal personality of a company gives rise to a number of characteristics which mark it out from a traditional partnership. These are outlined below. The other key differences relate to the **formality** of a company as opposed to a partnership and the **regulations** it has to adhere to.

Factor	Company	Traditional partnership
Entity	Is a legal entity separate from its members.	Has no existence outside of its members.
Liability	Members' liability can be limited	Partner's liability is usually unlimited
Size	May have any number of members (at least one)	Some partnerships are limited to twenty members (professional partnerships excluded)
Succession	Perpetual succession – change in ownership does not affect existence	Partnerships are dissolved when any of the partners leaves it
Owners' interests	Members own transferable shares	Partners cannot assign their interests in a partnership
Assets	Company owns the assets	Partners own assets jointly
Management	Company must have at least one director (two for a public company)	All partners can participate in management
Constitution	Company must have a written constitution	A partnership may have a written partnership agreement, but also may not
Accounts	A company must usually deliver accounts to the Registrar	Partners do not have to send their accounts to the Registrar
Security	A company may offer a floating charge over its assets	A partnership may not usually give a floating charge on assets
Withdrawal of capital	Strict rules concerning repayment of subscribed capital	More straightforward for a partner to withdraw capital
Taxation	Company pays tax on its profit. Directors are taxed through PAYE system. Shareholders receive dividends which are taxed 10 months after the tax year	Partners extract 'drawings' weekly or monthly. No tax is deducted. Income tax is payable on their share of the final profit for the year.
Management	Members elect directors to manage the company	All partners have a right to be involved in management

Revise this table above when you have studied the rest of the book and know more of the details concerning the distinctive factors of companies.

Chapter Roundup

- In a **sole tradership**, there is no legal distinction between the individual and the business.

- **Partnership** is defined as 'the relation which subsists between persons carrying on a business in common with a view of profit'. A partnership is *not* a separate legal person distinct from its members, it is merely a 'relation' between persons. Each partner (there must be at least two) is **personally liable** for all the debts of the firm.

- Partnerships can be **formed** very informally, but there may be complex formalities to ensure clarity.

- Partnerships may be **terminated** by passing of time, termination of the underlying venture, death or bankruptcy of a partner, illegality, notice, agreement or by order of the court.

- The **authority** of partners to bind each other in contract is based on the principles of agency.

- Partners are **jointly liable** for all partnership debts that result from contracts that the partners have made which bind the firm.

- **A limited liability partnership** formed under the 2000 Act, combines the features of a traditional partnership with the limited liability and creation of a legal personality more usually associated with limited companies.

- A company has a **legal personality** separate from its owners (known as members). It is a formal arrangement, surrounded by formality and publicity, but its chief advantage is that members' **liability** for the company's debts is typically **limited**.

- The fact that a company's members – not the company itself – have **limited liability** for its debts **protects** the **members** from the company's creditors and ultimately from the full risk of business failure.

- Most companies are those **incorporated** under the **Companies Act**. However there are other types of company such as **corporations sole**, **chartered corporations**, **statutory corporations** and **community interest companies**.

- A company may be **private** or **public**. Only the latter may offer its shares to the public.

- To trade a public company must hold a **Registrar's trading certificate** having met the requirements, including **minimum capital** of **£50,000**.

- The main differences between public and private companies relate to: **capital**; **dealings** in shares, **accounts**; **commencement of business**; **general meetings**; **names**; **identification**; and **disclosure requirements**.

- There are a number of other ways in which companies can be **classified**.

- The case of *Salomon v Salomon & Co Ltd 1897* clearly demonstrates the **separate legal personality** of companies and is of great significance to any study of company law.

- Incorporation '**veils**' members from outsiders' view but this veil may be lifted in **some circumstances**, so creditors and others can seek redress directly from members. The veil may be lifted: by statute to enforce the law; to prevent the evasion of obligations; and in certain situations where companies trade as a group.

- It is sometimes necessary by law to look at who the owners of a company are. This is referred to as '**lifting the veil**'.

- Because it is a separate legal entity, a company has a number of features which are different from a partnership. The most important difference between a company and a traditional partnership is that a company has a **separate legal personality** from its members, while a traditional partnership does not.

1   Which of the following types of company can be incorporated under the Companies Act 2006?

   A   A private limited company
   B   A public limited company
   C   A company limited by guarantee with a share capital
   D   A company limited by guarantee with no share capital
   E   A private unlimited company
   F   A public unlimited company

2   Which one of the following statements about traditional partnerships is incorrect?

   A   In England a partnership has no existence distinct from the partners.
   B   A partnership must have a written partnership agreement.
   C   A partnership is subject to the Partnership Act.
   D   Each partner is an agent of the firm.

3   An LLP dissolves when a member leaves.

   True   ☐

   False   ☐

4   Which two of the following statements is true? A private company

   A   Is defined as any company that is not a public company

   B   Sells its shares on the junior stock market known as the Alternative Investment Market and on the Stock Exchange

   C   Must have at least one director with unlimited liability

   D   Is a significant form of business organisation in areas of the economy that do not require large amounts of capital

5   Under which circumstance would a member of a limited company have to contribute funds on winding up?

   A   Where there is not enough cash to pay the creditors
   B   Where they have an outstanding amount from when they originally purchased their shares
   C   To allow the company to repurchase debentures it issued
   D   Where the company is a community interest company and the funds are required to complete a community project

6   The minimum allotted and paid up share capital of a company incorporated as a public limited company is

   A   £12,500
   B   £50,000
   C   £100,000
   D   £500,000

7   **Fill in the blanks** in the statement below using the figures in the box.

   A small company formed under the Companies Act 2006 must meet two of the following criteria.

   Its balance sheet total must be less than £ … million and its turnover must be less than £ … million. The number of employees must be less than … people.

50	5.6
2.8	100

8 Which two of the following are correct? A public company or plc

A   Is defined as any company which is not a private company
B   Has a legal personality that is separate from its members or owners
C   Must have at least one director with unlimited liability
D   Can own property and make contracts in its own name

9 State the main advantage of forming an unlimited company.

10 What was the name of the case that originally demonstrated the principle of separate legal personality?

11 Businesses in the form of sole traders are legally distinct from their owners.

True   ☐

False ☐

12 Put the examples given below in the correct category box.

WHEN THE VEIL OF INCORPORATION IS LIFTED		
To enforce law	To enforce obligations	To expose groups

- Wrong use of company name
- Legal obligations
- Quasi-partnership
- Disqualified directors
- Fraudulent and wrongful trading
- Single economic entity
- Corporate structure a sham
- Public interest

Answers to Quick Quiz

1   A, B, D and E are correct. It is not possible to incorporate a company limited by guarantee with a share capital, so C is incorrect. A public limited company is by definition limited, so F is wrong.

2   B. A written agreement is not needed.

3   False. LLPs are only dissolved when they cease to trade.

4   A and D are correct. A private company cannot sell its shares to the public on any stock market, so B is incorrect. Directors need not have unlimited liability, so C is incorrect.

5   B   Members only have a liability for any outstanding amounts of share capital partly paid for.

6   B   £50,000. Where the company was incorporated as a private one found subsequently re-registered on a public one, only a quarter of the authorised minimum must be paid up (£12,500).

7   Balance sheet total £2.8 million
    Turnover £5.6 million
    Employees less than 50

8   B and D are correct. A public company has to be defined as such in its constitution so A is incorrect. No directors *need* have unlimited liability, so C is incorrect.

9   An unlimited company need not usually file annual accounts.

10 Salomon v Salomon Ltd 1897.

11 False. Sole trader businesses are not legally distinct from their owners.

12

WHEN THE VEIL OF INCORPORATION IS LIFTED		
To enforce law	**To enforce obligations**	**To expose groups**
Wrong use of company name Disqualified directors Fraudulent and wrongful trading Trading without a trading certificate	Legal obligations Quasi-partnership Public interest	Single economic entity Corporate structure a sham

Now try the questions below from the Exam Question Bank

Number	Level	Marks	Time
Q17	Examination	10	18 mins
Q18	Examination	10	18 mins

13: Organisations and legal personality | Part D The formation and constitution of business organisations

Company formation

Topic list	Syllabus reference
1 Promoters and pre-incorporation contracts	D4(a)
2 Pre-incorporation expenses and contracts	D4(a)
3 Registration procedures	D4(b)
4 Statutory books and records	D4(c)
5 Statutory returns	D4(c)

Introduction

In Chapter 13 of this Study Text you were introduced to the idea of the separate legal personality of a company.

Sections 1 to 3 of this chapter concentrate on the **procedural aspects** of **company formation**. Important topics in these sections include the **formalities** that a company must observe in order to be formed, and the liability of **promoters for pre-incorporation contracts**.

Sections 4 and 5 of this chapter consider the concept of the **public accountability** of **limited companies**. Later on in your coverage of the syllabus you will meet references to a company's obligation to publicise certain decisions, so it is important to understand at this stage how and why this should be done.

Study guide

Exam guide

These topics can easily be examined in a knowledge question, but this does not preclude them from forming part of a scenario question. Questions could be set that require you to explain the procedures that need to be followed in order to set up a private or public limited company. You may need to advise a promoter on a potential liability they could encounter.

1 Promoters and pre-incorporation contracts

FAST FORWARD

> A promoter **forms** a company. They must act with **reasonable skill** and **care**, and if shares are to be allotted they are the agent of the company, with an agent's fiduciary duties.

A company cannot form itself. The person who forms it is called a '**promoter**'. A promoter is an example of an **agent**.

Key term

> A **promoter** is one who undertakes to form a company with reference to a given project and to set it going and who takes the necessary steps to accomplish that purpose: *Twycross v Grant 1877*.

In addition to the person who takes the procedural steps to get a company incorporated, the term 'promoter' includes anyone who makes **business preparations** for the company. **However** a person who acts **merely** in a **professional capacity** in company formation, such as a solicitor or an accountant, **is not** on that account a **promoter**.

1.1 Duties of promoters

Promoters have the general duty to exercise **reasonable skill and care.**

If the promoter is to be the owner of the company there is no conflict of interest and it does not matter if the promoter obtains some advantage from this position, for example, by selling their existing business to the company for 100% of its shares.

If, however, **some or all the shares** of the company when formed **are to be allotted to other people**, the promoter is as **agent** of the company. This means they have the customary **duties** of an agent (see Chapter 12) and the following fiduciary duties.

(a) A promoter must account for any **benefits obtained** through acting as a promoter.

(b) Promoters must not put themselves in a position where their own **interests conflict** with those of the company.

(c) A promoter must provide **full information** on their transactions and account for all monies arising from them. The promoter must therefore make **proper disclosure** of any personal advantage to **existing** and **prospective** company **members** or to an **independent board of directors**.

A promoter may make a **profit** as a result of their position.

(a) A **legitimate** profit is made by a promoter who acquires interest in property **before promoting** a company and then makes a profit when they sell the property to the promoted company, provided they disclose it.

(b) A **wrongful** profit is made by a promoter who enters into and makes a profit personally in a contract as a promoter. They are in breach of fiduciary duty.

A promoter of a public company makes their disclosure of legitimate profit through listing particulars or a prospectus. If they make proper disclosure of a legitimate profit, they may retain it.

1.1.1 Remedy for breach of promoter's fiduciary duty

If the promoter does not make a proper disclosure of legitimate profits or if they make wrongful profits the primary remedy of the company is to **rescind** the **contract** and **recover its money**.

However sometimes it is too late to rescind because the property can no longer be returned or the company prefers to keep it. In such a case the company can **only recover** from the promoter their **wrongful profit**, unless some special circumstances dictate otherwise.

Where shares are sold under a **prospectus offer**, promoters have a statutory liability to compensate any person who acquires securities to which the prospectus relates and suffered loss as a result of any untrue or misleading statement, or omission.

Statutory and listing regulations together with rigorous investigation by merchant banks have greatly lessened the problem of the dishonest promoter.

2 Pre-incorporation expenses and contracts

FAST FORWARD

A promoter has **no automatic right** to be reimbursed **pre-incorporation expenses** by the company, though this can be expressly agreed.

2.1 Pre-incorporation expenses

A promoter usually incurs **expenses** in preparations, such as drafting legal documents, made before the company is formed. They have **no automatic right to recover these 'pre-incorporation expenses'** from the company. However they can generally arrange that the first directors, of whom they may be one, **agree** that the company shall pay the bills or refund to them their expenditure. They could also include a special article in the company's constitution containing an indemnity for the promoter.

2.2 Pre-incorporation contracts

FAST FORWARD

Pre-incorporation contracts **cannot** be ratified by the company. A new contract on the same terms must be expressly created.

Key term

> A **pre-incorporation contract** is a contract purported to be made by a company or its agent at a time before the company has been formed.

In agency law a principal may ratify a contract made by an agent retrospectively. However, a company can **never ratify** a contract made on its behalf **before it was incorporated**. It did not exist when the pre-incorporation contract was made so one of the conditions for ratification fails.

A company may enter into a **new contract** on **similar terms** after it has been incorporated (**novation**). However there must be **sufficient evidence** that the company has made a new contract. Mere recognition of the pre-incorporation contract by performing it or accepting benefits under it is not the same as making a new contract.

2.3 Liability of promoters for pre-incorporation contracts

The company's **agent** is **liable** on a contract to which they are deemed to be a party. The agent may also be entitled to enforce the contract against the other party and so they could transfer the right to **enforce** the contract to the company. Liability is determined by s 51(1) of the Companies Act 2006.

> 'A contract that purports to be made by or on behalf of a company at a time when the company has not been formed has effect, subject to any agreement to the contrary, as one made with the person purporting to act for the company or as agent for it, and he is personally liable on the contract accordingly.'

2.4 Other ways of avoiding liability as a promoter for pre-incorporation contracts

There are various other ways for promoters to avoid liability for a pre-incorporation contract.

(a) The contract remains as a **draft** (so not binding) until the company is formed. The promoters are the directors, and the company has the power to enter the contract. Once the company is formed, the directors take office and the company enters into the contract.

(b) If the contract has to be finalised before incorporation it should contain a clause that the personal liability of promoters is to cease if the company, when formed, enters a **new contract** on identical terms. This is known as **novation**.

(c) A common way to avoid the problem concerning pre-incorporation contracts is to buy a company **'off the shelf'** (see Section 3 of this chapter). Even if a person contracts on behalf of the new company before it is bought the company should be able to ratify the contract since it existed 'on the shelf' at the time the contract was made.

Exam focus point

> A favourite question in law exams is the status of a pre-incorporation contract.

Question
Promoter

Fiona is the promoter of Enterprise Ltd. Before the company is incorporated, she enters into a contract purportedly on its behalf. After the certificate of incorporation is issued, the contract is breached. Who is liable?

Answer

Fiona is liable as promoters are liable for pre-incorporation contracts: s 51(1).

3 Registration procedures

FAST FORWARD

> A company is **formed** and registered under the Companies Act 2006 when it is issued with a **certificate of incorporation** by the Registrar, after submission to the Registrar of a number of documents and a fee.

Most companies are registered under the Companies Act 2006.

A company is formed under the Companies Act 2006 by one or more persons subscribing to a memorandum of association who comply with the requirements regarding registration. A company may not be formed for an unlawful purpose.

3.1 Documents to be delivered to the Registrar

To obtain registration of a company limited by shares, an application for registration, various documents and a fee must be sent to the Registrar (usually electronically). We shall look at two of them (the articles and the memorandum of association) in detail, later in this Study Text.

3.1.1 Application for registration

S 9 requires an **application for registration** must be made and submitted to the Registrar with the other documents described in the table below.

The application must contain:

- The company's **proposed name**
- The **location** of its **registered office** (England and Wales, Wales, Scotland or Northern Ireland)
- That the **liability of members** is to be **limited** by **shares** or **guarantee**
- Whether the company is to be **private** or **public**.
- A statement of the **intended address** of the **registered office**.

Documents to be delivered	Description
Memorandum of association	This is a **prescribed form** signed by the subscribers. The memorandum states that the subscribers wish to form a company and they agree to become members of it. If the company has share capital each subscriber agrees to subscribe for at least one share.
Articles of association (only required if the company does not adopt model articles)	Articles are signed by the same subscriber(s), dated and witnessed. **Model articles** are provided by statute and can be adopted by a new company if: • No other articles are registered, or • If the articles supplied do not exclude or modify the model articles.
Statement of proposed officers	The statement gives the particulars of the proposed **director(s)** and **company secretary** if applicable. The persons named as directors must consent to act in this capacity. When the company is incorporated they are deemed to be appointed.
Statement of compliance	The statement that the **requirements** of the **Companies Act** in respect of registration have been **complied** with.
Statement of capital and initial shareholdings (only required for companies limited by shares)	A statement of capital and initial shareholdings must be delivered by all companies with **share capital**. (See Chapter 16 for the contents of this statement.) Alternatively, a statement of guarantee is required by companies limited by guarantee.
Registration fee	A registration fee (currently **£20**) is also payable on registration.

Exam focus point

Questions on incorporation could require you to identify the documents which should be sent to the Registrar.

3.2 Certificate of incorporation

The Registrar considers whether the documents are formally in order. If satisfied, the company is given a 'registered number'. A **certificate of incorporation is** issued and notice of it is publicised.

A company is registered by the inclusion of the company in the register, and the issue of a **certificate of incorporation** by the Registrar. The certificate:

- Identifies the company by its **name** and **registered number**
- States that it is **limited** (if appropriate) and whether it is a **private** or **public** company
- States whether the **registered office** is in England and Wales, Wales, Scotland or Northern Ireland
- States the **date of incorporation**
- Is **signed** by the **Registrar**, or authenticated by the Registrar's official seal.

A **certificate of incorporation** is a certificate issued by the Registrar which denotes the date of incorporation, 'the subscribers, together with any persons who from time to time become members, become a body corporate capable of exercising all the functions of an incorporated company'.

The certificate of incorporation is conclusive evidence that:

- All the **requirements** of the **Companies Act** have been **followed.**
- The company is a **company authorised** to be **registered** and has been **duly registered.**
- If the certificate states that the company is a **public company** it is conclusive.

If irregularities in formation procedure or an error in the certificate itself are later discovered, the certificate is nonetheless **valid** and **conclusive:** *Jubilee Cotton Mills Ltd v Lewes 1924.*

Upon incorporation persons named as **directors** and **secretary** in the statement of proposed officers automatically become such officers.

3.3 Companies 'off the shelf'

Buying a company 'off the shelf' avoids the administrative burden of registering a company.

Because the registration of a new company can be a lengthy business, it is often easiest for people wishing to operate as a company to purchase an **'off the shelf' company**.

This is possible by contacting enterprises specialising in registering a stock of companies, ready for sale when a person comes along who needs the advantages of incorporation.

Normally the persons associated with the company formation enterprise are registered as the company's subscribers, and its first secretary and director. When the company is purchased, the **shares** are **transferred** to the **buyer**, and the Registrar is notified of the director's and the secretary's resignation.

The principal **advantages** for the purchaser of purchasing an off the shelf company are as follows.

(a)   The **following documents** will **not need** to be **filed** with the Registrar by the purchaser:

    (i)   Memorandum and articles (unless the articles are not model articles)
    (ii)   Application for registration
    (iii)   Statement of proposed officers
    (iv)   Statement of compliance
    (v)   Statement of capital and initial shareholdings
    (vi)   Fee

    This is because the specialist has already registered the company. It will therefore be a quicker, and very possibly cheaper, way of incorporating a business.

(b)   There will be **no risk** of **potential liability** arising from pre-incorporation contracts. The company can trade without needing to worry about waiting for the Registrar's certificate of incorporation.

The **disadvantages** relate to the changes that will be required to the off-the-shelf company to make it compatible with the members' needs.

(a)   The off-the-shelf company is likely to have **model articles**. The directors may wish to amend these.

(b)   The directors may want to **change** the **name** of the company.

(c)   The **subscriber shares** will need to be **transferred**, and the transfer recorded in the register of members. Stamp duty will be payable.

Documents required on formation of a company

What are the documents which must be delivered to the Registrar for registration of a company?

The memorandum of association (and articles if not in model form), application for registration, a statement of proposed officers, a statement of compliance, a statement of capital and initial shareholdings, and a fee.

3.4 Re-registration procedures

A **private company** with share capital may be able to re-register as a **public company** if the share capital requirement is met. A public company may re-register as a private one.

Note. For a private company to re-register as a public company it must fulfil the share capital requirement of a public company: Its allotted share capital must be at least £50,000 of which a quarter must be paid up, plus the whole of any premium.

	Re-registering as a public company	Re-registering as a private company
Resolution	The **shareholders must agree** to the company going public • Convene a general meeting • Pass a **special resolution** (75% majority) – Alters the constitution	The **shareholders must agree** to the company going private • Convene a general meeting • Pass a **special resolution** (75% majority of those present and voting) – Alters the constitution

Application	The **company must** then **apply** to the Registrar to go public
	
	• Send application to the Registrar
	
	• Send additional information to the Registrar, comprising
	
	  – Copy of the special resolution
	  – Copy of proposed new public company articles
	  – Statement of the company's proposed name on re-registration
	  – Statement of proposed company secretary
	  – Balance sheet and related auditors' statement which states that at the balance sheet date the company's net assets are not less than its called-up share capital and undistributable reserves.
	  – Statement of compliance
	  – Valuation report regarding allotment of shares for non-cash consideration since the balance sheet date
		The **company must** then **apply** to the Registrar to go private
		
		• Send the application to the Registrar
		
		• Send additional information to the Registrar, comprising
		
		  – Copy of the special resolution
		  – Copy of altered new private company articles
		  – Statement of Compliance
		  – Statement of the company's proposed name on re-registration

	Re-registering as a public company	Re-registering as a private company
Approval	The Registrar must accept the statement of compliance as sufficient evidence that the company is entitled to be re-registered as public. A certificate of incorporation on re-registration is issued.	The Registrar issues a certificate of incorporation on re-registration.
Compulsory re-registration	If the **share capital** of a public company **falls below £50,000**, it must re-register as a private company.	There is **no such compulsion** for a private company.

3.5 Commencement of business rules

FAST FORWARD

To **trade** or **borrow**, a public company needs a **trading certificate**. Private companies may commence business on **registration**.

3.5.1 Public companies

A **public company** incorporated as such may not do business or exercise any borrowing powers unless it has obtained a **trading certificate** from the Registrar: s 761. This is obtained by sending an application to the Registrar. A private company which is re-registered as a public company is not subject to this rule.

The application:

- States the nominal value of the allotted share capital is not less than £50,000
- States the particulars of preliminary expenses and payments or benefits to promoters
- Must be accompanied by a statement of compliance.

If a public company does business or borrows before obtaining a certificate the other party is protected since the **transaction is valid**. However the company and any officer in default have committed an offence **punishable** by a **fine**. They may also have to indemnify the third party.

Under s 122 of the Insolvency Act 1986 a court may **wind-up** a public company which does not obtain a trading certificate within **one year** of incorporation.

3.5.2 Private company

A **private company** may do business and exercise its borrowing powers from the date of its incorporation. After registration the following procedures are important.

(a)   A **first meeting** of the directors should be held at which the chairman, secretary and sometimes the auditors are appointed, shares are allotted to raise capital, authority is given to open a bank account and other commercial arrangements are made.

(b)   A **return of allotments** should be made to the Registrar.

(c)   The company may give notice to the Registrar of the **accounting reference date** on which its annual accounts will be made up. If no such notice is given within the prescribed period, companies are deemed to have an accounting reference date of the **last day of the month** in which the **anniversary of incorporation** falls.

4 Statutory books and records

4.1 The requirement for public accountability

FAST FORWARD

The price of limited liability is greater **public accountability** via the Companies Registry, registers, the *London Gazette* and company letterheads.

Under company law the privileges of trading through a separate corporate body are matched by the duty to provide information which is available to the public about the company.

Basic sources of information on UK companies
The Registrar keeps a file at **Companies House** which holds all documents delivered by the company for filing. Any member of the public, for example someone who intends to do business with the company, may inspect the file (usually electronically).
The **registers and other documents** which the company is required to hold at its registered office (or in some cases at a different address). These are looked at later in this chapter.
The *London Gazette*, a specialist publication, in which the company itself or the Registrar is required to publish certain notices or publicise the receipt of certain documents.
The **company's letterheads** and other forms which must give particulars of the company's place of registration, its identifying number and the address of its office.

4.2 The Registrar of Companies

The Registrar of Companies (the Registrar) and the Registrar's department within the Government is usually called Companies House (in full it is 'the Companies Registration Office').

For **English** and **Welsh** companies the Registrar is located at the Companies House in **Cardiff**; for **Scottish** companies the Registrar is in **Edinburgh**.

The company is identified by its **name** and **serial number** which must be stated on every document sent to Companies House for filing.

On first incorporation the company's file includes a copy of its **certificate of incorporation** and the **original documents** presented to secure its incorporation.

Once a company has been in existence for some time the file is likely to include the following.

- Certificate of incorporation
- Public company trading certificate
- Each year's annual accounts and return
- Copies of special and some ordinary resolutions
- A copy of the altered articles of association if relevant
- Notices of various events such as a change of directors or secretary
- If a company issues a prospectus, a signed copy with all annexed documents

4.3 Statutory books

FAST FORWARD

A company must keep **registers** of certain aspects of its constitution, including the registers of members, charges and directors.

Various people are entitled to have access to **registers** and copies of records that the company must keep, so the company must keep them at its registered office or another location permitted by the secretary of state if the Registrar is notified.

Register/copies of records	Relevant CA2006 section
Register of **members**	s 113
Register of **charges**	s 876
Records of **directors (and secretaries)**	s 162 and s 275
Records of **directors' service contracts and indemnities**	s 228 and s 237
Records of **resolutions and meetings** of the company	s 355
Register of **debentureholders**	s 743
Register of disclosed **interests** in shares (public company ONLY)	s 808

Attention!

> We will learn more about the **registered office** in Chapter 15. Some of the registers below contain details of shares and classes of shares. We will learn more about types of share in Chapter 16. Similarly, others refer to charges, directors and debentures. We shall learn about all of these later. For now you must just learn the content of each register.

4.4 Register of members

Every company must keep a register of members. It must contain:

(a)   The **name** and **address** of **each member**

(b)   **The shareholder class** (if more than one) to which they belong unless this is indicated in the particulars of their shareholding

(c)   If the company has a share capital, the **number of shares** held by each member. In addition:

    (i)   If the shares have **distinguishing numbers**, the member's shares must be identified in the register by those numbers

    (ii)   If the company has more than one class of share the member's shares must be **distinguished** by their **class**, such as preference, ordinary, or non-voting shares

(d)   The date on which each member **became** and eventually the date on which they **ceased** to be a member

The company may choose where it keeps the register of members available for inspection from:

- The registered office
- Another office of the company
- The office of a professional registrar

Any member of the company can inspect the register of members of a company without charge. A member of the public must pay but has the right of inspection.

A company with more than 50 members must keep a separate index of those members, unless the register itself functions as an index.

4.5 Register of charges

The register of charges must contain:

- **Details of fixed or floating charges** affecting the company property or undertaking
- **Brief descriptions** of property charged
- The **amount** of the charge
- The **name** of the person entitled to the charge

A company must also keep copies of every instrument creating a charge at its registered office or some other designated place notified to the Registrar. Any person may inspect the instruments and the charges register; members and creditors may inspect free of charge.

4.6 Register of directors

The register of directors must contain the following details in respect of a director who is an individual (that is, not a company).

- **Present** and **former** forenames and surnames
- A **service address** (may be the company's registered address rather than the director's home address)
- **Residency** and **nationality**
- **Business occupation** (if any)
- **Date of birth**

The register does not include shadow directors (discussed in a later chapter). It must be open to inspection by a member (free of charge), or by any other person (for a fee).

Note the company must keep a separate **register** of **directors' residential addresses** but this is not available to members or the general public.

4.6.1 Corporate directors

Where a legal person (such as a company) is a director, the register of directors must contain:

- The corporate or firm name
- Its registered or principal office

4.7 Records of directors' service contracts

The company should keep **copies** or written memoranda of all **service contracts** for its directors, including contracts for services which are not performed in the capacity of director. Members are entitled to view these copies for free, or request a copy on payment of a set fee.

Key term

> Under s 227 a director's **service contract**, means a contract under which:
>
> (a) A director of the company undertakes personally to perform services (as director or otherwise) for a company, or for a subsidiary of the company, or
>
> (b) Services (as director or otherwise) that a director of the company undertakes personally to perform are made available by a third party to the company, or to a subsidiary of the company.

4.8 Register of debentureholders

Companies with debentures issued nearly always keep a **register of debentureholders**, but there is no statutory compulsion to do so. If a register of debentureholders is maintained, it should be held at the **registered office** or another location permitted by the Secretary of State and notified to the Registrar.

4.9 Accounting records

FAST FORWARD

Companies must keep **sufficient accounting records** to explain the company's transactions and its financial position, in other words so a profit and loss account and balance sheet can be prepared.

A company is required to keep accounting records sufficient to **show and explain** the company's transactions. At any time, it should be possible:

- To **disclose** with reasonable accuracy the **company's financial position** at intervals of not more than six months
- For the directors to ensure that any accounts required to be prepared **comply** with the **Act** and **International Accounting Standards**

Certain specific records are required by the Act.

(a) Daily entries of **sums paid** and **received**, with details of the source and nature of the transactions

(b) A **record** of **assets** and **liabilities**

(c) **Statements of stock** held by the company at the end of each financial year

(d) **Statements of stocktaking** to back up the records in (c)

(e) **Statements of goods bought and sold** (except retail sales), together with details of buyers and sellers sufficient to identify them

The requirements (c) to (e) above apply only to businesses involved in dealing in goods.

Accounting records must be kept for **three** years (in the case of a **private** company), and **six** years in that of a **public** one.

Accounting records should be kept at the company's **registered office** or at some other place thought fit by the directors. Accounting records should be open to **inspection** by the **company's officers**. Shareholders have **no statutory rights** to inspect the records, although they may be granted the right by the articles.

Failure in respect of these duties is an offence by the officers in default.

4.10 Annual accounts

FAST FORWARD

A registered company must prepare **annual accounts** showing a true and fair view, lay them and various reports before members, and file them with the Registrar following directors' approval.

For each **accounting reference period** (usually 12 months) of the company the directors must prepare accounts. Where they are prepared in Companies Act format they must include a **balance sheet** and **profit and loss account** which give a **true and fair view** of the individual company's and the group's

- Assets
- Liabilities
- Financial position
- Profit or loss

The accounts can either be in **Companies Act format** or prepared in accordance with **International Accounting Standards**. Where international accounting standards are followed a note to this effect must be included in the notes to the accounts.

Most private companies are permitted to file abbreviated accounts.

The company's board of directors must **approve** the **annual accounts** and they must be signed by a director on behalf of the board. When directors approve annual accounts that do not comply with the Act or IAS they are **guilty** of an **offence.**

A public company is required to **lay its accounts**, and the **directors' report**, before **members** in **general meeting**. A quoted company must also lay the directors' remuneration report before the general meeting.

A company must file its annual accounts and its report with the **Registrar** within a maximum period reckoned from the date to which the accounts are made up. The standard permitted interval between the end of the accounting period and the filing of accounts is **six months** for a **public** and **nine months** for a **private company.**

The accounts must be **audited** (if the company exceeds any of the three Companies Act criteria already mentioned). The **auditors' report** must be attached to the copies issued to members, filed with the Registrar or published. Exemptions apply to **small and dormant companies,** though members may require an audit. The accounts must also be accompanied by a **directors' report** giving information on a number of prescribed matters. These include (where an audit was necessary) a statement that there is no relevant information of which the auditors are unaware, and another statement from the directors that they exercised due skill and care in the period. Quoted companies must submit the **directors' remuneration report.**

Each **member** and **debentureholder** is entitled to be sent a copy of the **annual accounts**, together with the directors' and auditor's reports. In the case of public companies, they should be sent at least 21 days before the meeting at which they shall be laid. In the case of private companies they should be sent at the same time as the document are filed, if not earlier.

Anyone else entitled to **receive** notice of a general meeting, including the company's auditor, should **also be sent** a copy. At any other time any member or debentureholder is entitled to a copy free of charge within **seven days** of requesting it.

All companies may prepare a summary financial statement to be circulated to members instead of the full accounts, subject to various requirements as to form and content being met. However, members have the right to receive full accounts should they wish to.

Quoted companies must make their annual accounts and reports available on a website which is maintained on the company's behalf and which identifies it. The documents must be made available as soon as reasonably practicable and access should not be conditional on the payment of a fee or subject to other restrictions.

Where the company or its directors **fail to comply** with the requirements of the Act, they may be subject to a **fine**.

5 Statutory returns

FAST FORWARD Every company must make an **annual return** to the Registrar.

Every company must make an annual return each year to the Registrar which is made up to a 'return date'. This date is either the **anniversary of incorporation** or the **anniversary of the date** of the previous return (if this differs). The return must be delivered to the Registrar within **28 days** of the return date.

The **return** must be **signed** by a director or a secretary, and **accompanied** by a fee of £30 or £15 if sent electronically.

The form of the annual return prescribed for a company which has share capital is:

- The address of the **registered office** of the company
- The address (if different) at which the **register of members** or **debentureholders** is kept
- The type of company and its principal **business activities**
- The total number of **issued shares,** their **aggregate nominal value** and the amounts paid and unpaid on each share
- For each **class of shares**, the **right** of those shares, the **total number** of shares in that class and their **total nominal value**
- Particulars of **members** of the company
- Particulars of those who have **ceased** to be members since the last return
- The number of shares of each **class** held by members at the return date, and transferred by members since incorporation or the last return date
- The particulars of **directors,** and **secretary (if applicable)**

Question   Records and returns

Which of the following must be filed with the Registrar each year?

1   Accounts
2   Register of members
3   Copies of directors' service contracts
4   The annual return

Only the accounts and annual return would be filed. The register of members and copies of directors' service contracts are held by the company and are not required by the Registrar.

Chapter Roundup

- A promoter **forms** a company. They must act with **reasonable skill** and **care**, and if shares are allotted they are the agent of the company, with an agent's fiduciary duties.

- A promoter has **no automatic right** to be reimbursed pre-incorporation expenses by the company, though this can be expressly agreed.

- Pre-incorporation contracts **cannot** be ratified by the company. A new contract on the same terms must be expressly created.

- A company is **formed and registered** under the Companies Act 2006 when it is issued with a **certificate of incorporation** by the Registrar, after submission to the Registrar of a number of documents and a fee.

- Buying a company **'off the shelf'** avoids the administrative burden of registering a company.

- A **private company** with share capital may be able to re-register as a **public company** if the share capital requirement is met. A public company may re-register as a private one.

- To **trade** or **borrow**, a public company needs a **trading certificate**. Private companies may commence business on **registration**.

- The price of limited liability is greater **public accountability** is via the Companies Registry, registers, the *London Gazette* and company letterheads.

- A company must keep **registers** of certain aspects of its constitution, including the registers of members, charges and directors.

- Companies must keep **sufficient accounting records** to explain the company's transactions and its financial position, in other words so a profit and loss account and balance sheet can be prepared.

- A registered company must prepare **annual accounts** showing a true and fair view, lay them and various reports before members, and file them with the Registrar following directors' approval.

- Every company must make an **annual return** to the Registrar.

1   A company can confirm a pre-incorporation contract by performing it or obtaining benefits from it.

True   ☐

False   ☐

2   If a public company does business or borrows before obtaining a trading certificate from the Registrar, the transaction is:

A   Invalid, and the third party cannot recover any loss
B   Invalid, but the third party may recover any loss from the directors
C   Valid, and the directors are punishable by a fine
D   Valid, but the third party can sue the directors for further damages

3   A company must keep a register of directors. What details must be revealed?

A   Full name
B   Service address
C   Nationality
D   Date of birth
E   Business occupation

4   An accountant or solicitor acting in their professional capacity during the registration of a company may be deemed a promoter.

True   ☐

False   ☐

5   If a certificate of incorporation is dated 6 March, but is not signed and issued until 8 March, when is the company deemed to have come into existence?

1   False. The company must make a new contract on similar terms

2   C. The directors are punished for allowing the company to trade before it is allowed to.

3   All of them.

4   False. A person acting in a professional capacity will not be deemed a promoter.

5   6 March. The date on the certificate is conclusive.

Now try the questions below from the Exam Question Bank

Number	Level	Marks	Time
Q19	Examination	10	18 mins

15

Constitution of a company

Topic list	Syllabus reference
1 Memorandum of association	D4(e)
2 A company's constitution	D4(d), D4(e), D4(f)
3 Company objects and capacity	D4(e)
4 The constitution as a contract	D4(e)
5 Company name and registered office	D4(e)

Introduction

In the previous chapter the **articles of association** was mentioned briefly as one of the documents that may be required to be submitted to the Registrar when applying for registration. The articles, together with any resolutions and agreements which may affect them, form the company's **constitution**.

The constitution sets out what the company does; if there are no restrictions specified then the company may do anything provided it is legal. Clearly this includes the capacity to contract, an important aspect of legal personality. Also significant is the concept of **ultra vires**, a term used to describe transactions that are outside the scope of the company's capacity.

Study guide

		Intellectual level
(D)	**The formation and constitution of business organisations**	
4	Company formations	
(d)	Describe the contents of model articles of association	1
(e)	Analyse the effect of a company's constitutional documents	2
(f)	Explain how articles of association can be changed	2

Exam guide

A company's constitution could easily be examined in either a knowledge or an application question. You may be asked to explain any of the constitutional documents and how they may be altered.

1 Memorandum of association

> **FAST FORWARD**
>
> The memorandum is a **simple document** which states that the subscribers wish to form a company and become members of it.

Before the Companies Act 2006, the **memorandum of association** was an extremely important document containing information concerning the relationship between the company and the outside world – for example its aims and purpose (its objects).

The position changed with the 2006 Act and much of the information contained in the old memorandum is now to be found in the Articles of Association, which we will come to shortly. The **essence** of the memorandum has been retained, although it is now a very simple historical document which states that the **subscribers** (the initial shareholders):

(a) Wish to **form a company** under the Act, and

(b) Agree to **become members** of the company and, to take at least one share each if the company is to have share capital.

The memorandum must be in the **prescribed form** and must be **signed** by each subscriber.

It has been deemed by the Companies Act 2006 that companies which were incorporated under a **previous** Act and whose memorandum contains provisions now found in the articles, shall have these provisions interpreted as if they are part of the articles.

2 A company's constitution

> **FAST FORWARD**
>
> A **company's constitution** comprises the **Articles of Association** and any **resolutions and agreements** it makes which affect the constitution.

According to s 17 of the Companies Act 2006, the constitution of a company consists of:

- The **Articles of Association**
- **Resolutions and agreements** that it makes that affects the constitution

We shall consider resolutions and agreements first as an understanding of what they are is required to understand how the Articles of Association are amended.

2.1 Resolutions and agreements

In addition to the main **constitutional document** (the Articles of Association), **resolutions** and **agreements** also form part of a company's constitution. Resolutions are covered in Chapter 20 of this Study Text so you may find it beneficial to study Section 3 of that chapter now so that you understand the various types of resolution that a company may pass.

Resolutions directly affect the constitution of a company as they are used to **introduce** new provisions, or to **amend** or **remove** existing ones. **Agreements** made, for example between the company and members of specific classes of share (see Chapter 16) are also deemed as amending the constitution.

Copies of resolutions or agreements that amend the constitution must be sent to the Registrar within **15 days** of being passed or agreed. If a company fails to do this then every officer who is in default commits an offence punishable by fine. Where a **resolution** or **agreement** which affects a company's constitution is **not in writing**, the company is required to send the registrar a **written memorandum** that sets out the terms of the resolution or agreement in question.

2.2 Articles of Association

Key term

> The **articles of association** consist of the internal rules that relate to the management and administration of the company.

The articles contain detailed **rules** and **regulations** setting out how the company is to be **managed** and **administered**. The Act states that the registered articles should be contained in a **single document** which is divided into **consecutively numbered paragraphs**. Articles should contain rules on a number of areas, the most important being summarised in the table below.

CONTENTS OF ARTICLES	
Appointment and dismissal of directors	Communication with members
Powers, responsibilities and liabilities of directors	Class meetings
Directors' meetings	Issue of shares
General meetings; calling, conduct and voting	Transfer of shares
Members' rights	Documents and records
Dividends	Company secretary

2.2.1 Model articles

Rather than each company having to draft their own articles, and to allow companies to be set up **quickly** and **easily**, the Act allows the Secretary of State to provide **model** (or standard) **articles** that companies can adopt. Different models are available for different types of company; most companies would adopt model **private** or **public company** articles.

Companies are free to use **any** of the model articles that they wish to by registering them on incorporation. If **no articles** are registered then the company will be **automatically incorporated** with the **default model articles** which are relevant to the type of company being formed. Model articles can be **amended** by the members and therefore tailored to the specific needs of the company.

Model articles are effectively a **'safety net'** which allow directors and members to take decisions if the company has failed to include suitable provisions in its registered articles or registered no articles at all.

The following summarises the draft model articles for a private limited company as provided by the **Department for Business, Enterprise and Regulatory Reform** (BERR). Do not try to learn the contents but use it to understand the type of information contained in them. We shall cover a number of the draft articles later in this Study Text.

Draft model articles for private companies limited by shares

Index to the articles

Part 1 Definitions and interpretation

1. Defined terms

Part 2 Directors

Directors' powers and responsibilities

2. Directors' general authority
3. Shareholders' reserve power
4. Directors may delegate
5. Committees

Decision-making by directors

6. Directors to take decisions collectively
7. Unanimous decisions
8. Majority decisions without directors' meeting
9. Calling a directors' meeting
10. Participation in directors' meetings
11. Quorum for majority decisions
12. Chairing of majority decision-making processes
13. Casting vote
14. Conflicts of interest
15. Records of decisions to be kept
16. Directors' discretion to make further rules

Appointment of directors

17. Methods of appointing directors
18. Termination of director's appointment
19. Directors' remuneration
20. Directors' expenses

Part 3 Shares and distributions

Shares

21. All shares to be fully paid up
22. Powers to issue different classes of share
23. Company not bound by less than absolute interests
24. Share certificates
25. Replacement share certificates
26. Share transfers
27. Transmission of shares
28. Exercise of transmittees' rights
29. Transmittees bound by prior notices

Dividends and other distributions

30. Procedure for declaring dividends
31. Payment of dividends and other distributions
32. No interest on distributions
33. Unclaimed distributions
34. Non-cash distributions
35. Waiver of distributions

Capitalisation of profits

36. Authority to capitalise and appropriation of capitalised sums

Part 4 Decision-making by shareholders

Organisation of general meetings

37. Attendance and speaking at general meetings
38. Quorum for general meetings
39. Chairing of general meetings
40. Attendance and speaking by directors and non-shareholders
41. Adjournment

Voting at general meetings

42. Voting: general
43. Errors and disputes
44. Poll votes
45. Content of proxy notices
46. Delivery of proxy notices
47. Amendments to resolutions

Part 5 Administrative arrangements

48. Means of communication to be used
49. Addresses and other contact details
50. Company seals
51. No right to inspect accounts and other records
52. Provision for employees on cessation of business

Directors' indemnity and insurance

53. Indemnity
54. Insurance

2.2.2 Alteration of the articles

FAST FORWARD

The articles may be altered by a **special resolution**. The basic test is whether the alteration is for the **benefit of the company as a whole.**

Any company has a statutory power to alter its articles by **special resolution**: s 21. A private company may pass a **written resolution** with a **75% majority.** The alteration will be valid and binding on **all** members of the company. **Copies** of the amended articles must be sent to the **Registrar**, within 15 days of the amendment, taking effect.

2.2.3 Making the company's constitution unalterable

There are devices by which some provisions of the company's constitution can be made **unalterable** unless the member who wishes to prevent any alteration consents.

(a) The articles may give to a member **additional votes** so that he can block a resolution to alter articles on particular points (including the removal of his weighted voting rights from the articles): *Bushell v Faith 1970*. However, to be effective, the articles must also limit the powers of members to alter the articles that give extra votes.

(b) The articles may provide that when a meeting is held to vote on a proposed alteration of the articles the **quorum present must include** the **member concerned**. They can then deny the meeting a quorum by absenting themselves (see Chapter 20).

(c) Section 22 of the Act permits companies to **'entrench' provisions** in its articles. This means specific provisions may only be **amended** or **removed** if certain **conditions** are met which are more restrictive than a special resolution such as agreement of all the members. However, such 'entrenched provisions' **cannot** be drafted so that the articles can never be amended or removed.

2.2.4 Restrictions on alteration

Even when it is possible to hold a meeting and pass a special resolution, alteration of the articles is **restricted** by the following principles.

(a)   The alteration is **void** if it **conflicts with the Companies Act** or with general law.

(b)   In various circumstances, such as to protect a minority (s 994), the **court may order** that an alteration be made or, alternatively, that an existing article shall not be altered.

(c)   An existing **member may not be compelled** by alteration of the articles to **subscribe for additional shares** or to accept increased liability for the shares which they hold unless they have given their consent: s 25.

(d)   An alteration of the articles which varies the rights attached to a class of shares may only be made if the **correct rights variation procedure** has been followed to obtain the consent of the class: s 630. A 15 per cent minority may apply to the court to cancel the variation under s 633.

(e)   A person whose **contract** is contained in the articles cannot obtain an injunction to prevent the articles being altered, **but** they may be entitled to **damages** for breach of contract: *Southern Foundries 1926 Ltd v Shirlaw 1940* in Chapter 19. Alteration cannot take away rights already acquired by performing the contract.

(f)   An alteration may be **void** if the **majority** who approve it are **not acting *bona fide* in what they deem to be the interests of the company as a whole** (see below).

The case law on the **bona fide test** is an effort to hold the balance between two principles:

(a)   The **majority** is **entitled** to **alter articles** even though a minority considers that the alteration is prejudicial to its interests.

(b)   A minority is entitled to protection against an alteration which is intended to **benefit** the **majority** rather than the company and which is **unjustified discrimination** against the minority.

Principle (b) tends to be **restricted** to cases where the majority seeks to expel the minority from the company.

The most elaborate analysis of this subject was made by the Court of Appeal in the case of *Greenhalgh v Arderne Cinemas Ltd 1950* Two main propositions were laid down by Evershed MR.

(a)   **'Bona fide for the benefit of the company as a whole'** is a **single test** and also a **subjective test** (what did the majority believe?). The court will not substitute its own view.

(b)   'The company as a whole' means, in this context, **the general body of shareholders.** The test is whether every 'individual hypothetical member' would in the honest opinion of the majority benefit from the alteration.

If the purpose is to benefit the company as a whole the alteration is valid even though it can be shown that the minority does in fact suffer special detriment and that other members escape loss. In *Allen v Gold Reefs of West Africa Ltd 1900* the articles were altered to extend the company's lien from just partly paid shares to all shares. In fact only one member held fully paid shares. The court overruled his objections on the grounds that:

*   The alteration was for the benefit of the company as a whole and applied to any member who held fully paid shares.

*   The members held their shares subject to the constitution, and hence were subject to any changes to those documents.

2.2.5 Expulsion of minorities

Expulsion cases are concerned with:

*   Alteration of the articles for the purpose of **removing** a **director from office**

*   Alteration of the articles to permit a majority of members to **enforce** a **transfer** to themselves of the shareholding of a minority

The action of the majority in altering the articles to achieve 'expulsion' will generally be treated as **valid** even though it is discriminatory, if the majority were concerned to **benefit the company** or to remove some detriment to its interests.

If on the other hand the majority was **blatantly seeking** to secure an **advantage** to themselves by their discrimination, the alteration made to the articles by their voting control of the company will be invalid. The cases below illustrate how the distinctions are applied in practice.

Shuttleworth v Cox Bros & Co (Maidenhead) Ltd 1927

The facts: Expulsion of director appointed by the articles who had failed to account for funds was held to be valid.

Sidebottom v Kershaw, Leese & Co Ltd 1920

The facts: The articles were altered to enable the directors to purchase at a fair price the shareholding of any member who competed with the company in its business. The minority against whom the new article was aimed did carry on a competing business. They challenged the validity of the alteration on the ground that it was an abuse of majority power to 'expel' a member.

Decision: There was no objection to a power of 'expulsion' by this means. It was a justifiable alteration if made *bona fide* in the interests of the company as a whole. On the facts this was justifiable.

Brown v British Abrasive Wheel Co 1919

The facts: The company needed further capital. The majority who held 98 per cent of the existing shares were willing to provide more capital but only if they could buy up the 2 per cent minority. As the minority refused to sell, the majority proposed to alter the articles to provide for compulsory acquisition on a fair value basis. The minority objected to the alteration.

Decision: The alteration was invalid since it was merely for the benefit of the majority. It was not an alteration 'directly concerned with the provision of further capital' and therefore not for the benefit of the company.

Dafen Tinplate Co Ltd v Llanelly Steel Co (1907) Ltd 1920

The facts: The claimant was a minority shareholder which had transferred its custom from the defendant company to another supplier. The majority shareholders of the defendant company sought to protect their interests by altering the articles to provide for compulsory acquisition of the claimant's shares.

The new article was not restricted (as it was in *Sidebottom's* case above) to acquisition of shares on specific grounds where benefit to the company would result. It was simply expressed as a power to acquire the shares of a member. The claimant objected that the alteration was invalid since it was not for the benefit of the company.

Decision: The alteration was invalid because it 'enables the majority of the shareholders to compel any shareholder to transfer his shares'. This wide power could not 'properly be said to be for the benefit of the company'. The mere unexpressed intention to use the power in a particular way was not enough.

Therefore if the majority intend that the power to acquire the shares of a minority is to be restricted to specific circumstances for the benefit of the company, they should ensure that this restriction is included in the new article.

 Question   Articles of Association

Explain the nature of the model articles of association under the Companies Act 2006.

The model articles are a single document containing model rules and regulations concerning the management and administration of a company. They can be amended by the company but do not need to be to have effect.

2.2.6 Filing of alteration

Whenever any alteration is made to the articles a copy of the altered articles must be delivered to the Registrar within **15 days**, together with a signed copy of the special resolution making the alteration.

2.2.7 Interaction of statute and articles

There are two aspects to consider.

(a) The Companies Act may permit companies to do something **if** their **articles** also authorise it. For example a company may reduce its capital if its articles give power to do this. If, however, they do not, then the company must **alter** the articles to include the **necessary power** before it may exercise the statutory power.

(b) The Companies Act will **override** the articles:

　(i) If the Companies Act **prohibits something**

　(ii) If something is permitted by the Companies Act **only** by a **special procedure** (such as passing a special resolution in general meeting)

3 Company objects and capacity

 FAST FORWARD

A **company's objects** are its aims and purposes. If a company enters into a contract which is outside its objects, that contract is said to be **ultra vires.** However the rights of third parties to the contract are protected.

3.1 The objects

The objects are the **'aims'** and **'purposes'** of a company. Under previous companies legislation they were held in a specific clause within the memorandum of association. This clause set out everything the company could do, including being a 'general commercial company' which meant it could pretty much do anything.

The 2006 Act changed matters. The objects could now be found in the **articles** but most articles will **not** mention any objects. This is because under the Act a company's objects are **completely unrestricted** (ie it can carry out any lawful activity). Only where the company wishes to restrict its activities is there an inclusion of those **restrictions** in the articles: s 31.

3.1.1 Alteration of the objects

As a company's objects are located in its articles it may, under s 21, alter its objects by **special resolution** for any reason. The procedure is the same as for any other type of alteration.

3.2 Contractual capacity and *ultra vires*

FAST FORWARD

Companies may only act in accordance with their **objects**. If the directors permit an act which is restricted by the company's objects then the act is *ultra vires.*

Ultra vires is where a company exceeds its objects and acts outside its capacity.

Companies which have **unrestricted objects** are highly unlikely to act *ultra vires* since their constitution permits them to do anything. Where a company has restrictions placed on its objects and it breaches these restrictions then it would be acting *ultra vires*.

Ashbury Railway Carriage & Iron Co Ltd v Riche 1875

The facts: The company had an objects clause which stated that its objects were to make and sell, or lend on hire, railway carriages and wagons and all kinds of railway plant, fittings, machinery and rolling stock; and to carry on business as mechanical engineers. The company bought a concession to build a railway in Belgium, subcontracting the work to the defendant. Later the company repudiated the contract.

Decision: Constructing a railway was not within the company's objects so the company did not have capacity to enter into either the concession contract or the sub-contract. The contract was void for *ultra vires* and so the defendant had no right to damages for breach. The members could not ratify it and the company could neither enforce the contract nor be forced into performing its obligations.

The approach taken by the Companies Act 2006 is to give **security** to commercial transactions for **third parties**, whilst preserving the rights of shareholders to restrain directors from entering an *ultra vires* action.

S 39 provides as follows:

'the validity of an act done by a company shall not be called into question on the ground of lack of capacity by reason of anything in the company's constitution.'

S 40 provides as follows:

'in favour of a person dealing with a company in good faith, the power of the directors to bind the company, or authorise others to do so, shall be deemed to be free of any limitation under the company's constitution.'

There are a number of points to note about s 40.

(a)   The section applies in favour of the **person dealing with the company**, it does not apply to the members.

(b)   In contrast with s 39 **good faith** is required on the part of the third party. The company has, however, to prove lack of good faith in the third party and this may turn out to be quite difficult: s 40(2).

(c)   The **third party** is not required to **enquire** whether or not there are any **restrictions** placed on the power of directors: s 40(2). They are free to assume the directors have any power they profess to have.

(d)   The section covers not only acts beyond the capacity of the company, but acts beyond **'any limitation under the company's constitution'**.

Whilst sections 39 and 40 deal with the company's transactions with **third parties**, the **members** may take action against the directors for permitting *ultra vires* acts. Their action will be based on the fact that the **objects specifically restricted** the particular act and under section 171, the **directors** must **abide** by the **company's constitution**.

The main problem for **members** is that they are most likely to be **aware** of the *ultra vires* act only **after** it has occurred. Therefore they are not normally in a position to prevent it, although in theory they could seek an **injunction** if they found out about the potential *ultra vires* act before it took place.

Describe how a company's capacity to contract can be regulated and what third parties may assume when entering into a contract with the company.

Answer

A company's capacity to contract is regulated by its members passing resolutions which restrict its objects. Under section 40(2) of the Act, third parties can assume the directors have the necessary power to authorise the act.

Exam focus point

Make sure you understand how s 39 and s 40 protect third parties.

3.3 Transactions with directors

S 41 of the Companies Act 2006 applies when the company enters into a contract with one of its **directors**, or its holding company, or any **person connected** with such a director. Any contract made between the company and these parties are **voidable** by the company.

Whether or not the contract is avoided, the party and any authorising director is liable to repay any profit they made or make good any losses that result from such a contract.

4 The constitution as a contract

FAST FORWARD

The articles **constitute a contract** between:

- Company and members
- Members and the company
- Members and members

The articles **do not constitute** a contract between the **company** and **third parties**, or members in a **capacity** other than as **members** (the *Eley* case).

4.1 Effect

A company's constitution bind, under s 33:

- Members to company
- Company to members (but see below)
- Members to members

The company's constitution does **not** bind the company to third parties.

This principle applies only to rights and obligations which affect members **in their capacity as members**.

Hickman v Kent or Romney Marsh Sheepbreeders Association 1915

The facts: The claimant (H) was in dispute with the company which had threatened to expel him from membership. The articles provided that disputes between the company and its members should be submitted to arbitration. H, in breach of that article, began an action in court against the company.

Decision: The proceedings would be stayed since the dispute (which related to matters affecting H as a member) must, in conformity with the articles, be submitted to arbitration.

The principle that only rights and obligations of members are covered by s 33 applies when an outsider who is also a member seeks to rely on the articles in support of a claim made as an **outsider**.

Eley v Positive Government Security Life Assurance Co 1876

The facts: E, a solicitor, drafted the original articles and included a provision that the company must always employ him as its solicitor. E became a member of the company some months after its incorporation. He later sued the company for breach of contract in not employing him as its solicitor.

Decision: E could not rely on the article since it was a contract between the company and its members and he was not asserting any claim as a member.

4.2 Constitution as a contract between members

S 33 gives to the **constitution** the effect of a contract made between (a) the **company** and (b) its **members individually**. It can also impose a contract on the members in their dealings with each other.

Rayfield v Hands 1958

The facts: The articles required that (a) every director should be a shareholder and (b) the directors must purchase the shares of any member who gave them notice of his wish to dispose of them. The directors, however, denied that a member could enforce the obligation on them to acquire his shares.

Decision: There was 'a contract ... between a member and member-directors in relation to their holdings of the company's shares in its articles' and the directors were bound by it.

Articles and resolutions are usually **drafted** so that each stage is a dealing between the company and the members, to which s 33 clearly applies, so that:

(a)   A member who intends to transfer his shares must, if the articles so require, give notice of his intention to the company.

(b)   The company must then give notice to other members that they have an option to take up his shares.

4.3 Constitution as a supplement to contracts

FAST FORWARD

The constitution can be used to **establish the terms** of a contract existing elsewhere.

If an outsider makes a separate contract with the company and that contract contains no specific term on a particular point but the constitution does, then the contract is deemed to incorporate the constitution to that extent. One example is when services, say as a director, are provided under contract without agreement as to remuneration: *Re New British Iron Co, ex parte Beckwith 1898*.

If a contract incorporates terms of the articles it is subject to the company's **right** to **alter** its articles: *Shuttleworth v Cox Bros & Co (Maidenhead) Ltd 1927*. However a company's articles cannot be altered to deprive another person of a right already earned, say for services rendered **prior** to the alteration.

Point to note

Remember the articles only create contractual rights/obligations in relation to rights **as a member**.

4.4 Shareholder agreements

FAST FORWARD

Shareholders' agreements sometimes supplement a company's constitution.

Shareholder agreements are concerned with the **running of the company**; in particular they often contain terms by which the shareholders agree how they will vote on various issues.

They offer more protection to the interests of shareholders than do the articles of association. Individuals have a **power of veto** over any proposal which is contrary to the terms of the agreement. This enables a minority shareholder to protect his interests against unfavourable decisions of the majority.

Question   Constitution

State the parties who are bound by a company's articles.

Answer

The company is bound to the members, the members to the company and the members to the other members in their capacity as members.

5 Company name and registered office

FAST FORWARD

Except in **certain circumstances** a company's name must end with the words limited (Ltd), public limited company (plc) or the Welsh equivalents.

A company's name is its **identity**. There are a number of rules which restrict the choice of name that a company may adopt.

5.1 Statutory rules on the choice of company name

FAST FORWARD

No company may use a name which is:

- The **same** as an existing company on the Registrar's index of company names
- A **criminal offence, offensive,** or **'sensitive'**
- Suggest a **connection** with the **government or local authority** (unless approved)

The choice of name of a limited company must conform to the following rules.

(a) The name must **end** with the word(s):

   (i) **Public limited company** (abbreviated **plc**) if it is a public company

   (ii) **Limited** (or Ltd) if it is a private limited company, unless permitted to omit 'limited' from its name

   (iii) The **Welsh equivalents** of either (i) or (ii) may be used by a Welsh company

(b) No company may have a name which is the **same** as any other company appearing in the statutory index at Companies House. For this purpose two names are treated as 'the same' in spite of minor or non-essential differences. For instance the word 'the' as the first word in the name is ignored. 'John Smith Limited' is treated the same as 'John Smith' (an unlimited company) or 'John Smith & Company Ltd'. Where a company has a name which is the same or too similar to another, the Secretary of State may direct the company to **change its name**.

(c) No company may have a name the use of which would be a **criminal** offence or which is considered **offensive** or **'sensitive'** (as defined by the Secretary of State).

(d) Official approval is required for a name which in the Registrar's opinion suggests a **connection** with the **government** or a **local authority** or which is subject to **control**.

   A name which suggests some professional expertise such as 'optician' will only be permitted if the appropriate representative association has been consulted and raises no objection.

The general purpose of the rule is to **prevent** a company **misleading** the public as to its real circumstances or activities. Certain names may be approved by the Secretary of State on written application.

5.2 Omission of the word 'limited'

A private company which is a charity and a company limited by shares or guarantee and licensed to do so before 25 February 1982 may omit the word 'limited' from its name if the following conditions are satisfied.

(a) The objects of the company must be the **promotion** of either commerce, art, science, education, religion, charity or any profession (or anything incidental or conducive to such objects).

(b) The memorandum or articles must require that the **profits** or other income of the company are to be **applied to promoting** its objects and no dividends or return of capital may be paid to its members. Also on liquidation the **assets** (otherwise distributable to members) are to be **transferred** to another body with similar objects. The articles must not then be altered so that the company's status to omit 'Limited' is lost.

5.3 Change of name

A company may decide to change its name by:

(a) Passing a **special resolution**

(b) By **any other means** provided for in the **articles** (in other words the company can specify its own procedure for changing its name).

Where a **special resolution** has been passed, the **Registrar** should be notified and a copy of the resolution sent. If the change was made by **any other procedure** covered by (b), the Registrar should be notified and a statement provided which states that the change has been made in accordance with the articles.

The change is effective from when a new **incorporation certificate is issued**, although the company is still treated as the same legal entity as before. The same limitations as above apply to adoption of a name by change of name as by incorporation of a new company.

5.4 Passing-off action

A person who considers that their rights have been infringed can apply for an injunction to restrain a company from using a name (**even if** the name has been duly registered). It can do this if the name suggests that the latter company is carrying on the business of the complainant or is otherwise connected with it.

A company can be **prevented** by an **injunction** issued by the court in a **passing-off action** from **using** its **registered name**, if in doing so it causes its goods to be confused with those of the claimant.

Ewing v Buttercup Margarine Co Ltd 1917

The facts: The claimant had since 1904 run a chain of 150 shops in Scotland and the north of England through which he sold margarine and tea. He traded as 'The Buttercup Dairy Co'. The defendant was a registered company formed in 1916 with the name above. It sold margarine as a wholesaler in the London area. The defendant contended that there was unlikely to be confusion between the goods sold by the two concerns.

Decision: An injunction would be granted to restrain the defendants from the use of its name since the claimant had the established connection under the Buttercup name. He planned to open shops in the south of England and if the defendants sold margarine retail, there could be confusion between the two businesses.

If, however, the two companies' businesses are different, confusion is unlikely to occur, and hence the courts will refuse to grant an injunction: *Dunlop Pneumatic Tyre Co Ltd v Dunlop Motor Co Ltd 1907*

The complaint will not succeed if the claimant lays claim to the exclusive use of a word which has a general use: *Aerators Ltd v Tollit 1902*.

5.5 Appeal to the Company Names Adjudicators

A company which feels that another company's name which is **too similar** to its own may object to the Company Names Adjudicator under the Companies Act. The Adjudicator will review the case and, within **90 days**, make their decision and provide their reasons for it in public. In most cases the Adjudicator will require the offending company to **change its name** to one which does not breach the rules. In some cases the **Adjudicator may determine** the new name.

An appeal against the decision may be made in Court. The Court may **reverse** the Adjudicator's decision, **affirm** it and may even **determine** a new name.

Question

Company name

Do It Yourself Ltd was incorporated on 1 September 20X7. On 1 October 20X7 the directors received a letter from DIY Ltd stating that it was incorporated in 19X4, that its business was being adversely affected by the use of the new company's name, and demanding that Do It Yourself Ltd change its name.

Advise Do It Yourself Ltd.

Answer

DIY Ltd may seek to bring a 'passing-off action'. This is a common law action which applies when one company believes that another's conduct (which may be the use of a company name) is causing confusion in the minds of the public over the goods which each company sells. DIY Ltd would apply to the court for an injunction to prevent Do It Yourself Ltd from using its name.

However, in order to be successful, DIY Ltd will need to satisfy the court that confusion has arisen because of Do It Yourself Ltd's use of its registered name and that it lays claim to something exclusive and distinctive and not something in general use: *Aerators Ltd v Tollit 1902*.

Appeal to Company Names Adjudicator

Alternatively DIY Ltd might object to the Company Names Adjudicator that the name Do It Yourself Ltd is too like its own name and is causing confusion, thus appealing to compel a change of name. In these circumstances, the Adjudicator would hear the case and make a decision. If they compel a name change Do It Yourself Ltd may appeal to the court.

5.6 Publication of the company's name

The company's name must appear legibly and conspicuously:

- **Outside** the **registered office** and all **places of business**.
- On all **business letters, order forms**, **notices** and **official publications**.
- On all **receipts** and **invoices** issued on the company's behalf.
- On all **bills of exchange, letters of credit, promissory notes, cheques** and **orders** for money or goods purporting to be signed by, or on behalf, of the company
- On its **website**

5.7 Business names other than the corporate name

Key term

> A **business name** is a name used by a company which is different from the company's corporate name or by a firm which is different from the name(s) of the proprietor or the partners.

Most companies trade under their own registered names. However a company may prefer to use some other name. If it does so it becomes subject to the **Business Names Act 1985** (to be repealed by Schedule 16 of the Companies Act 2006 in October 2008).

The rules require any person (company, partnership or sole trader) who carries on business under a different name from his own:

(a) To **state** its **name**, registered **number** and registered **address** on all **business letters (including emails)**, invoices, receipts, written orders for goods or services and written demands for payment of debts.

(b) To **display** its **name** and **address** in a **prominent position** in any **business premises** to which its customers and suppliers have access.

(c) On **request** from any **person** with whom it does business to give **notice** of its name and address.

5.8 Registered office

Section 86 of the Companies Act 2006 provides that a company must at all times have a **registered office** to which all communications and notices can be sent. It may **change its registered office** under section 87 by notifying the Registrar, but for a period of 14 days after notice is served any person may validly present documents to the previous address.

Chapter Roundup

- The memorandum is a **simple document** which states that the subscribers wish to form a company and become members of it.

- A **company's constitution** comprises the **Articles of Association** and any **resolutions and agreements** it makes which affect the constitution.

- The articles may be altered by a **special resolution**. The basic test is whether the alteration is for the **benefit of the company as a whole**.

- A **company's objects** are its aims and purposes. If a company enters into a contract which is outside its objects, that contract is said to be **ultra vires**. However the rights of third parties to the contract are protected.

- Companies may only act in accordance with their **objects**. If the directors permit an act which is restricted by the company's objects then the act is *ultra vires*.

- The articles **constitute** a **contract** between:

  – Company and members
  – Members and the company
  – Members and members

  The articles **do not constitute** a contract between the **company** and **third parties**, or members in a **capacity** other than as **members** (the *Eley* case).

- The constitution can be used to **establish the terms** of a contract existing elsewhere.

- **Shareholders' agreements** sometimes supplement a company's constitution.

- Except in **certain circumstances** the name must end with the words limited (Ltd), public limited company (plc) or the Welsh equivalents.

- No company may use a name which is:

  – The **same** as an existing company on the Registrar's index of company names
  – A **criminal offence, offensive** or **'sensitive'**
  – Suggest a **connection** with the **government** or **local authority** (unless approved)

1 Percy Limited has recently formed a contract with a third party which is restricted by the objects in the company's constitution.

Which of the following statements is incorrect?

A   The validity of the act cannot be questioned on the grounds of lack of capacity by reason of anything in the company's constitution.

B   The act may be restrained by the members of Percy Ltd.

C   The act may be enforced by the company and the third party.

D   The directors have a duty to observe any limitation on their powers flowing from the company's constitution.

2 If a company wishes to restrict its objects, what kind of resolution is required?

A   Special resolution

B   Special resolution with special notice

C   Ordinary resolution with special notice

D   Ordinary resolution

3 A company has been formed within the last six months. Another long-established company considers that because of similarity there may be confusion between it and the new company. The only action the long-established company can take is to bring a passing-off action if it is to prevent the new company using its name.

True ☐

False ☐

4 Which of the following persons are not bound to one another by the constitution?

A   Members to company

B   Company to members

C   Members to members

D   Company to third parties

5 How long does a company have to file amended articles with the Registrar if they have been altered?

A   14 days

B   15 days

C   21 days

D   28 days

1   A, C and D are true. Members can only act before the contract is signed, so B is incorrect.

2   A. A special resolution is required to restrict the objects as with any alteration to the articles in general.

3   False. The long-established company can also complain to the Company Names Adjudicator.

4   A, B and C are correct: s 33. D is incorrect, illustrated by *Eley v Positive Government Security Life Assurance Co Ltd 1876*.

5   B. A company has 15 days to file amended articles with the Registrar.

Now try the questions below from the Exam Question Bank			
Number	**Level**	**Marks**	**Time**
Q20	Examination	10	18 mins
21	Examination	10	18 mins

Capital and the financing of companies

16

Share capital

Topic list	Syllabus reference
1 Members	E1(a)
2 The nature of shares and capital	E1(a)
3 Types of share	E1(b), E1(c)
4 Allotment of shares	E1(a)

Introduction

In this chapter the nature of share capital is explained. You should note (and **not** confuse) the different types of capital that are important for company law purposes.

The rest of the chapter discusses procedural matters relating to the **issue** and **transfer** of shares. You will see that there are built-in safeguards to protect members' rights, **pre-emption rights** and the necessity for directors to be authorised to **allot** shares. There are also safeguards that ensure that a company receives **sufficient consideration** for its shares. This is an aspect of **capital maintenance**, which we discuss further in Chapter 18.

Study guide

		Intellectual level
(E)	**Capital and the financing of companies**	
1	Share capital	
(a)	Examine the different meanings of capital	2
(b)	Illustrate the difference between various classes of shares	2
(c)	Explain the procedure for altering class rights	2

Exam guide

Share capital is an important syllabus area that lends itself well to different types of question. You may be required to distinguish between different types of share and explain what class rights are and how they can be altered.

1 Members

FAST FORWARD

> A member of a company is a person who has **agreed to become a member**, and whose name has been **entered** in the **register of members**. This may occur by: subscription to the memorandum; applying for shares; the presentation to the company of a transfer of shares to the prospective member applying as personal representative of a deceased member or a trustee of a bankrupt.

1.1 Becoming a member

Key term

> A **member** of a company is a person who has agreed to be a member and whose name has been entered in the register of members.

Entry in the register is **essential**. Mere delivery to the company of a transfer does not make the transferor a member – until the transfer is entered in the register.

1.2 Subscriber shares

Subscribers to the memorandum are deemed to have agreed to become members of the company. As soon as the company is formed their names should be entered in the register of members.

Other persons may acquire shares and become members:

- By **applying** and being allotted shares
- By presenting to the company for registration a **transfer** of shares to them
- By applying as **personal representative** or **trustee** of a
  - Deceased member
  - Bankrupt member

1.3 Ceasing to be a member

FAST FORWARD

> There are **eight** ways in which a member ceases to be so.

A member ceases to be a member in any of the following circumstances.

- He **transfers** all his shares to another person and the transfer is registered.
- The member **dies**.
- The **shares** of a bankrupt member are **registered** in the name of his trustee.

- A **member who is a minor repudiates his shares**.
- The **trustee** of a **bankrupt member disclaims** his shares.
- The **company forfeits** or **accepts** the **surrender of shares.**
- The **company** sells them in exercise of a lien.
- The **company is dissolved** and **ceases to exist**.

1.4 The number of members

Public and private companies must have a minimum of **one** member (s 7). There is **no maximum** number.

Public and private companies must have a minimum **of one member** (s 7). There is **no maximum** number. Where a company has a sole member, the following rules will apply.

(a) The **register of members** must contain a statement that there is **only one member** and give his address.

(b) **Quorum**. The Act **automatically permits** a **quorum of one** for general meetings.

2 The nature of shares and capital

A **share** is a transferable form of property, carrying rights and obligations, by which the interest of a member of a company limited by shares is measured.

2.1 Shares

Key term

> A **share** is 'the interest of a shareholder in the company measured by a sum of money, for the purpose of a liability in the first place, and of interest in the second, but also consisting of a series of mutual covenants entered into by all the shareholders *inter se*': *Borland's Trustee v Steel Bros & Co Ltd 1901*.

The key points in this definition are:

- The share must be **paid for** ('liability'). The nominal value of the share fixes this liability, it is the base price of the share eg a £1 ordinary share.
- It gives a **proportionate entitlement** to dividends, votes and any return of capital ('interest').
- It is a form of **bargain** ('mutual covenants') between shareholders which underlies such principles as majority control and minority protection.

Key term

> A share's **nominal value** is its face value. So a £1 ordinary share for instance, has a nominal value of £1. No share can be issued at a value below its nominal value.

A share is a form of personal property, carrying rights and obligations. It is by its nature **transferable**.

A member who holds one or more shares is a **shareholder**. However some companies (such as most companies limited by guarantee) do not have a share capital. So they have members who are not also shareholders.

Information about any special rights attached to shares is obtainable from one of the following documents which are on the file at Companies House:

- The **articles**, which are the normal context in which share rights are defined.
- A **resolution** or agreement incidental to the creation of a new class of shares (copies must be delivered to the Registrar).
- A **statement of capital** given to the Registrar within one month of **allotment**, together with the return of allotment.

2.2 Types of capital

FAST FORWARD

> The term **'capital'** is used in several senses in company legislation, to mean issued, allotted or called up share capital or loan capital.

2.2.1 Authorised share capital

Under previous company legislation, companies had to specify a **maximum authorised share capital** that it could issue. Under the 2006 Act, the concept of authorised share capital was removed.

2.2.2 Issued and allotted share capital

Key terms

> **Issued** and **allotted share capital** is the type, class, number and amount of the shares issued and allotted to specific shareholders, including shares taken on formation by the subscribers to the memorandum

A company need not issue all its share capital at once. If it retains part this is unissued share capital. We shall come back to the distinction between 'issued' and 'allotted' in Section 4.

2.2.3 Called up and paid up share capital

Key terms

> **Called up share capital** is the amount which the company has required shareholders to pay now or in the future on the shares issued.
>
> **Paid up share capital** is the amount which shareholders have actually paid on the shares issued and called up.

For example, a company has issued and allotted 70 £1 (nominal value) shares, has received 25p per share on application and has called on members for a second 25p. Therefore its issued and allotted share capital is £70 and its **called up** share capital is £35 (50p per share). When the members pay the call, the **'paid up'** share capital is then £35 also. Capital not yet called is **'uncalled capital'**. Called capital which is not yet paid is termed **'partly paid'**; the company therefore has an outstanding claim against its shareholders and this debt is transferred to the new shareholder if the share is transferred.

As we saw earlier, on allotment public companies must receive at least one quarter of the nominal value of the shares paid up, plus the whole of any premium.

2.2.4 Loan capital

Key term

> **Loan capital** comprises debentures and other long-term loans to a business.

Loan capital, in contrast with the above, is the term used to describe **borrowed money** obtained usually by the issue of debentures. **It is nothing to do with shares**.

Attention!

> We shall look at loan capital in detail in Chapter 17.

2.3 Market value

Shares of a public company are freely transferable (providing the appropriate procedures are followed) and therefore may be subsequently sold by some or all of the shareholders. The sale price will not necessarily be the nominal value, rather it will reflect the prospects of the company and therefore may be greater or less than the nominal value.

3 Types of share

FAST FORWARD

If the constitution of a company states no differences between shares, it is assumed that they are all **ordinary** shares with parallel rights and obligations. There may, however, be other types, notably **preference shares** and **redeemable shares**.

3.1 Ordinary shares (equity)

If no differences between shares are expressed then all shares are equity shares with the **same rights**, known as ordinary shares.

Key terms

Equity is the residual interest in the assets of the company after deducting all its liabilities. It comprises issued share capital excluding any part of that does not carry any right to participate beyond a specified amount in a distribution.

Equity share capital is a company's issued share capital less capital which carries preferential rights.

Ordinary shares are shares which entitle the holders to the remaining divisible profits (and, in a liquidation, the assets) after prior interests, eg creditors and prior charge capital, have been satisfied.

3.2 Class rights

Key term

Class rights are rights which are attached to particular types of shares by the company's constitution.

A company may at its option attach special rights to different shares regarding:

- Dividends
- Return of capital
- Voting
- The right to appoint or remove a director

Any share which has different rights from others is grouped with the other shares carrying identical rights to form a **class**.

The most common types of share capital with different rights are **preference shares** and **ordinary shares**. There may also be ordinary shares with voting rights and ordinary shares without voting rights.

3.3 Preference shares

FAST FORWARD

The most common right of preference shareholders is a **prior right** to receive a fixed dividend. This right is not a right to **compel payment** of a dividend, but it is **cumulative** unless otherwise stated. Usually, preference shareholders **cannot participate** in a dividend over and above their fixed dividend and **cease to be entitled to arrears of undeclared dividends** when the company goes into liquidation.

Key term

Preference shares are shares carrying one or more rights such as a fixed rate of dividend or preferential claim to any company profits available for distribution.

A preference share may and generally will carry a **prior right** to receive an annual dividend of fixed amount, say a dividend of 6% of the share's nominal value.

Ordinary and preference shares are deemed to have identical rights. However, a company's articles or resolutions may create differences between them.

As regards the priority dividend entitlement, four points should be noted.

(a) **The right is merely to receive a dividend at the specified rate before any other dividend may be paid or declared**. It is **not** a right to compel the company to pay the dividend, *(Bond v Barrow Haematite Steel Co 1902)*. The company can decline to pay the dividend if it decides to transfer available profits to reserves instead of using the profits to pay the preference dividend.

(b) **The right to receive a preference dividend is deemed to be cumulative unless the contrary is stated.** If, therefore, a 6% dividend is not paid in Year 1, the priority entitlement is normally carried forward to Year 2, increasing the priority right for that year to 12% – and so on.

When arrears of cumulative dividend are paid, the holders of the shares at **the time when the dividend is declared** are entitled to the whole of it even though they did not hold the shares in the year to which the arrears relate.

An intention that preference shares should not carry forward an entitlement to arrears is usually expressed by the word **'non-cumulative'**.

(c) **If a company which has arrears of unpaid cumulative preference dividends goes into liquidation, the preference shareholders cease to be entitled to the arrears unless:**

(i) A **dividend** has been **declared** though **not yet paid** when liquidation commences.

(ii) The **articles** (or other terms of issue) **expressly provide** that in a liquidation arrears are to be paid in priority to return of capital to members.

(d) **Holders of preference shares have no entitlement to participate in any additional dividend over and above their specified rate.** If, for example, a 6% dividend is paid on 6% preference shares, the entire balance of available profit may then be distributed to the holders of ordinary shares.

This rule also may be expressly overridden by the terms of issue. For example, the articles may provide that the preference shares are to receive a priority 6% dividend and are also to participate equally in any dividends payable after the ordinary shares have received a 6% dividend. Preference shares with these rights are called **participating preference shares**.

In all other respects preference shares carry the **same** rights as ordinary shares **unless otherwise stated**. If they do rank equally they carry the same rights, no more and no less, to return of capital, distribution of surplus assets and voting.

In practice, it is unusual to issue preference shares on this basis. More usually, it is expressly provided that:

(a) The preference shares are to carry a **priority right** to **return of capital**.

(b) They are **not to carry a right to vote, or voting is permitted in specified circumstances**. For example failure to pay the preference dividend, variation of their rights or a resolution to wind up.

When preference shares carry a **priority right** to **return** of **capital** the result is that:

(a) The amount paid up on the preference shares, say £1 on each £1 share, is to be repaid in liquidation before anything is repaid to ordinary shareholders.

(b) Unless otherwise stated, the holders of the preference shares are **not** entitled to share in surplus assets when the ordinary share capital has been repaid.

3.3.1 Advantages and disadvantages of preference shares

The advantages of preference shares are **greater security of income** and (if they carry priority in repayment of capital) **greater security of capital**. However in a period of persistent inflation, the benefit of entitlement to fixed income and to capital fixed in money terms is an illusion.

A number of other drawbacks and pitfalls, such as loss of arrears, winding up and enforced payment, have been indicated above. Preference shares may be said to fall between the two stools of risk and reward (as seen in ordinary shares) and security (debentures).

3.4 Variation of class rights

FAST FORWARD

> The holders of **issued** shares have **vested rights** which can only be varied by using a strict procedure. The standard procedure is by **special resolution** passed by at least **three quarters** of the votes cast at a **separate class meeting** or by written consent.

Key term

> A **variation of class rights** is an alteration in the position of shareholders with regard to those rights or duties which they have by virtue of their shares.

The holders of issued shares have **vested rights** which can only be varied by the company with the consent of all the holders or with such consent of a majority as is specified (usually) in the articles.

The standard procedure for variation of class rights requires that a **special resolution** shall be passed by a **three quarters majority** cast either at a **separate meeting** of the class, or by **written consent**: s 630.

If any other requirements are imposed by the company's articles then these must also be followed.

3.4.1 When variation rules apply

FAST FORWARD

> It is **not** a variation of class rights to issue shares to new members, to subdivide shares of another class, to return capital to preference shareholders, or to create a new class of preference shareholders.

It is only necessary to follow the variation of class rights procedure **if what is proposed amounts to a variation of class rights**. There are many types of transaction that do not actually constitute a variation of class rights.

3.4.2 Examples: Not a variation of class rights

(a)   **To issue shares of the same class to allottees who are not already members of the class** (unless the defined class rights prohibit this).

> *White v Bristol Aeroplane Co Ltd 1953*
>
> *The facts:* The company made a bonus issue of new ordinary and preference shares to the existing ordinary shareholders who alone were entitled under the articles to participate in bonus issues. The existing preference shareholders objected. They stated that reducing their proportion of the class of preference shares (by issuing the bonus of preference shares) was a variation of class rights to which they had not consented.
>
> *Decision:* This was not a variation of class rights since the existing preference shareholders had the same number of shares (and votes at a class meeting) as before.

(b)   **To subdivide shares of another class with the incidental effect of increasing the voting strength of that other class.**

> *Greenhalgh v Arderne Cinemas Ltd 1946*
>
> *The facts:* The company had two classes of ordinary shares, 50p shares and 10p shares. Every share carried one vote. A resolution was passed to subdivide each 50p share into five 10p shares, thus multiplying the votes of that class by five.
>
> *Decision:* The rights of the original 10p shares had not been varied since they still had one vote per share as before.

(c)   **To return capital to the holders of preference shares**: *House of Fraser plc v ACGE Investments Ltd 1987.*

(d)   **To create and issue a new class of preference shares with priority over an existing class of ordinary shares**: *Re John Smith's Tadcaster Brewery Co Ltd 1953.*

The cases cited in the preceding paragraph illustrate the principle that without a '**literal variation**' of class rights there is no alteration of rights to which the safeguards of proper procedure and appeal to the court apply. The fact that the **value** of existing rights may be affected will not concern the court if the rights are unchanged.

Exam focus point

Knowledge of what does **not** constitute a variation of class rights is vital in this area.

3.4.3 Special situations

To deal with unusual special situations which in the past caused some difficulty, the following rules apply.

(a)   If the class rights are set **by the articles and** they **provide** a **variation procedure**, that procedure must be followed for any variation even if it is less onerous than the statutory procedure.

(b)   If class **rights** are **defined otherwise than by the articles** and there is **no variation procedure**, consent of a **three quarters majority** of the class is both necessary and sufficient.

The rules on notice, voting, polls, circulation of resolutions and quorum relating to general meetings relate also to class meetings when voting on alteration of class rights. We shall come back to these in Chapter 20.

3.4.4 Minority appeals to the court for unfair prejudice

FAST FORWARD

A **dissenting minority** holding 15% or more of the issued shares may apply to the court within 21 days of class consent to have the variation cancelled as 'unfairly prejudicial'.

Whenever class rights are varied under a procedure contained in the constitution, a minority of holders of shares of the class may apply to the court to have the variation cancelled. The objectors together must:

• Hold **not less** than **15%** of the **issued shares** of the class in question
• **Not** themselves have **consented** to or voted in favour of the variation
• **Apply** to the court within **21 days** of the consent being given by the class s 633.

The court can either approve the variation as made or cancel it as 'unfairly prejudicial'. It cannot, however, modify the terms of the variation.

To establish that a variation is 'unfairly prejudicial' to the class, the minority must show that the majority was seeking **some advantage** to themselves as **members** of a **different class** instead of considering the interests of the class in which they were then voting.

3.5 Redeemable shares

Redeemable shares, which are shares issued on terms that they may be bought back by a company either at a future specific date or at the shareholder's or company's option, are discussed further in Chapter 18.

Question   Types of share

Give brief definitions of the following types of share.

(a)   Equity share
(b)   Ordinary share
(c)   Preference share

Answer

(a) An equity share is a share which gives the holder the right to participate in the company's surplus profit and capital. In a winding up the holder is entitled to a repayment of the nominal value plus a share of surplus assets. The term equity share embraces ordinary shares but also includes preference shares when the terms of issue include either the right to an additional dividend or the right to surplus assets in a winding up.

(b) An ordinary share is the more common type of equity share, as discussed in (a) above. The dividend is payable only when preference dividends, including arrears, have been paid.

(c) Preference shares carry a prior right to receive an annual dividend of a fixed amount, usually as a percentage of the share's nominal value. There are no other implied differences between preference and ordinary shares, although there may be express differences between them. For example, preference shares may carry a priority right to return of capital. Generally preference shares do not carry voting rights in the company other than those relating to their own class. Unless otherwise stated, dividends allocated to preference shares are assumed to be cumulative. This means that, if the company does not make sufficient profits to pay a dividend in one year, the arrears are carried forward to future years.

3.6 Statement of capital

We have already seen, in Chapter 14 Section 3 (registration of the company) and above in Section 2 (rights of shares), that a return known as a **statement of capital** is required to be made to the **Registrar** in certain circumstances, including the registration of the company.

The statement of capital must give the following details in respect of the **share capital** of the company and be **up to date** as of the statement date.

(a) The **total number of shares** of the company

(b) The **aggregate nominal value of the shares**

(c) For **each class** of share:
  (i) The **prescribed particulars** of any rights attached
  (ii) The **total number of shares** in the class
  (iii) The **aggregate nominal value** of shares in the class

(d) The **amount paid up** and the **amount (if any) unpaid** on each share, either on account of the nominal value of the share or by way of premium.

4 Allotment of shares

Directors exercise the **delegated power** to allot shares, either by virtue of the articles or a resolution in general meeting.

4.1 Definition

Key term

> **Allotment of shares** is the issue and allocation to a person of a certain number of shares under a contract of allotment. Once the shares are allotted and the holder is entered in the register of members, the holder becomes a member of the company. The member is issued with a share certificate.

The allotment of shares is a **form of contract**. The intending shareholder applies to the company for shares, and the company accepts the offer.

The terms 'allotment' and 'issue' have slightly different meanings.

(a) A share is **allotted** when the person to whom it is allotted acquires an unconditional right to be entered in the register of members as the holder of that share. That stage is reached when the board of directors (to whom the power to allot shares is usually given) considers the application and formally resolves to allot the shares.

However if the directors imposed a condition, for instance that the shares should be allotted only on receipt of the subscription money, the allotment would only take effect when payment was made.

(b) The **issue** of shares is not a defined term but is usually taken to be a later stage at which the allottee **receives** a **letter of allotment** or share certificate issued by the company.

The allotment of shares of a private company is a simple and immediate matter. The name of the allottee is usually entered in the register of members soon after the allotment of shares to him. They then become a member.

4.2 Public company allotment of shares

There are various methods of selling shares to the public.

Key terms

> **Public offer:** where members of the public subscribe for shares directly to the company.
>
> **Offer for sale:** an offer to members of the public to apply for shares based on information contained in a prospectus
>
> **Placing:** a method of raising share capital where shares are offered in a small number of large 'blocks', to persons or institutions who have previously agreed to purchase the shares at a predetermined price.

In order to encourage the public to buy shares in a public company, it may issue a prospectus, or in the case of a company listed on the Stock Exchange, listing particulars. Listing particulars are subject to rules set down by the UK Listing Authority (part of the Financial Services Authority).

4.3 Private company allotment of shares

The allotment of shares in a private company is more straightforward. The rule to remember is that private companies cannot sell shares to the public. An application must be made to the directors directly. After that shares are allotted and issued, and a return of allotment made to the Registrar, as for a public company.

4.4 Directors' powers to allot shares

Directors of **private companies** with **one class of share** have the **authority** to allot shares **unless restricted** by the articles.

Directors of **public companies** or **private companies with more than one class of share may not allot shares** (except to subscribers to the memorandum and to employees' share schemes) **without authority from the members.**

Authority may be given either by the **articles** or by **ordinary resolution** passed in general meeting in accordance with the following conditions.

Directors' power to allot shares	
Timescale	• Authority to allot must be given until a **specified date** • Authority to allot must be given for a **specified period** • Authority can be received by **ordinary resolution** in general meeting even if it would require the articles being amended • Extension cannot be for more than **five years**
Maximum	Must specify a maximum number of shares which may be allotted.
Additional conditions	May give additional conditions.
Resolution	An **ordinary** resolution is required. A copy must be sent to the Registrar within 15 days.

Directors' power to allot shares	
General authority	Directors may have been given general authority to allot by the articles without further reference to general meeting.
	A **general meeting** must be called if
	• **No authority** has been given in advance
	• Authority is subject to certain **conditions**
	• Authority has **lapsed** or been used up
Documents	Allotments of shares have to be **recorded in the register of members** within **two months**.
	A **return of allotment** containing prescribed particulars and a statement of capital to be sent within one month to the Registrar.

Exam focus point

Remember the basic distinction that (a) directors can only allot shares if they have the power to do so *and* (b) if they have the authority to *exercise* the power.

4.5 Pre-emption rights: s 561

FAST FORWARD

If the directors propose to allot 'equity securities' wholly for cash, there is a general requirement to offer these shares to **holders** of **similar shares** in proportion to their holdings.

Key term

Pre-emption rights are the rights of existing ordinary shareholders to be offered new shares issued by the company *pro rata* to their existing holding of that class of shares.

If a company proposes to allot ordinary shares wholly for cash, it has a **statutory obligation** to offer those shares first to holders of similar shares in **proportion to their holdings** and on the same or more favourable terms as the main allotment. This is known as a **rights issue**.

4.6 Rights issues

Key term

A **rights issue** is a right given to a shareholder to subscribe for further shares in the company, usually *pro rata* to their existing holding in the company's shares.

A rights issue must be made **in writing** (hard copy or electronic) in the same manner as a notice of a general meeting is sent to members. It must specify a period of **not less than 21 days** during which the offer may be accepted but may not be withdrawn. If not accepted or renounced in favour of another person within that period the offer is deemed to be declined.

Equity securities which have been offered to members in this way but are **not accepted** may then be allotted on the same (or less favourable) terms to non-members.

If equity securities are allotted in breach of these rules the members to whom the offer should have been made may within the ensuing two years recover **compensation** for their loss from those in default. The allotment will generally be valid.

4.6.1 Exclusion of pre-emption rights: s567

A **private** company may by its articles permanently exclude these rules so that there is no statutory right of first refusal.

4.6.2 Disapplication of pre-emption rights: s 570

Any company may, by special resolution resolve that the statutory right of first refusal shall not apply: s 570. Such a resolution to 'disapply' the right may either:

(a) Be combined with the grant to directors of authority to allot shares, or

(b) Simply permit an offer of shares to be made for cash to a non-member (without first offering the shares to members) on a particular occasion

In case (b) the directors, in inviting members to 'disapply' the right of first refusal, must issue a circular. This sets out their reasons, the price at which the shares are to be offered direct to a non-member and their justification of that price.

4.7 Bonus issues

Key term

> A **bonus issue** is the capitalisation of the reserves of a company by the issue of additional shares to existing shareholders, in proportion to their holdings. Such shares are normally fully paid-up with no cash called for from the shareholders.

A bonus issue is more correctly but less often called a '**capitalisation issue**' (also called a 'scrip' issue). The articles of a company usually give it power to apply its reserves to paying up unissued shares wholly or in part and then to allot these shares as a bonus issue to members.

Chapter Roundup

- A member of a company is a person who has **agreed to become a member**, and whose name has been **entered** in the **register of members**. This may occur by: subscription to the memorandum; applying for shares; the presentation to the company of a transfer of shares to the prospective member; applying as personal representative of a deceased member or a trustee of a bankrupt.

- There are **eight** ways in which a member ceases to be so.

- **Public** and **private companies** must have a minimum of **one** member (s 7). here is **no maximum** number.

- A **share** is a transferable form of property, carrying rights and obligations, by which the interest of a member of a company limited by shares is measured.

- The term **'capital'** is used in several senses in company legislation, to mean issued, allotted or called up share capital or loan capital.

- If the constitution of a company states no differences between shares, it is assumed that they are all **ordinary** shares with parallel rights and obligations. There may, however, be other types, notably **preference shares** and **redeemable shares**.

- The most common right of preference shareholders is a **prior right** to receive a fixed dividend. This right is not a right to **compel payment** of a dividend, but it is **cumulative** unless otherwise stated. Usually, preference shareholders **cannot participate** in a dividend over and above their fixed dividend and **cease to be entitled to arrears of undeclared dividends** when the company goes into liquidation.

- The holders of **issued** shares have **vested rights** which can only be varied by using a strict procedure. The standard procedure is by **special resolution** passed by at least **three quarters** of the votes cast at a **separate class meeting** or by written consent.

- It is **not** a variation of class rights to issue shares to new members, to subdivide shares of another class, to return capital to preference shareholders, or to create a new class of preference shareholders.

- A **dissenting minority** holding 15% or more of the issued shares may apply to the court within 21 days of class consent to have the variation cancelled as 'unfairly prejudicial'.

- Directors exercise the **delegated power** to allot shares, either by virtue of the articles or a resolution in general meeting.

- If the directors propose to allot 'equity securities' wholly for cash, there is a general requirement to offer these shares to **holders** of **similar shares** in proportion to their holdings.

1   If a company fails to pay preference shareholders their dividend, they can bring a court action to compel the company to pay it.

True   ☐

False   ☐

2   Which two of the following are implied rights of preference shareholders?

A   The right to receive a dividend is cumulative.

B   If the company goes into liquidation, preference shareholders are entitled to claim all arrears of dividend from the liquidator.

C   As well as rights to their preference dividends, preference shareholders can share equally in dividends payable to ordinary shareholders.

D   Preference shareholders have equal voting rights to ordinary shareholders.

3   If a company issues new ordinary shares for cash, the general rule is that:

A   The shares must first be offered to existing members in the case of a public but not a private company.

B   The shares must first be offered to existing members whether the company is public or private.

C   The shares must first be offered to existing members in the case of a private but not a public company.

D   The shares need not be issued to existing members.

4   **Fill in the blanks** in the statements below.

A .... issue is an allotment of additional shares to existing members in exchange for consideration payable by the members.

A .... issue is an allotment of additional shares to existing members where the consideration is paid by using the company's reserves.

5   **Fill in the blanks** in the statements below.

If there has been a variation of class rights, a minority of holders of shares of the class (who have not consented or voted in favour of the variation) may apply to the court to have the variation cancelled. The objectors must hold not less than .... of the issued shares of that class, and apply to the court within .... days of the giving of consent by that class.

6   What is the minimum number of members that a plc must have?

A   One
B   Two
C   Three
D   Four

7   Match the definitions to the correct type of capital

(a)   Issued share capital
(b)   Called up share capital
(c)   Paid up share capital

(i)   The amount which the company has required shareholders to pay on shares issued.
(ii)   The type, class, number and amount of the shares held by the shareholders.
(iii)   The amount which shareholders have actually paid on the shares issued and called up.

1   False. The company may decide not to pay any dividend, or may be unable to because it does not have any distributable profits. What the preference shareholders have is a right to receive their dividends before other dividends are paid or declared.

2   A and D are implied rights; the others have to be stated explicitly.

3   B. The shares must be first offered to existing members whether the company is public or private.

4   A **rights issue** is an allotment of additional shares to existing members in exchange for consideration payable by the members.

     A **bonus issue** is an allotment of additional shares to existing members where the consideration is effectively paid by using the company's reserves.

5   If there has been a variation of class rights, a minority of holders of shares of the class (who have not consented or voted in favour of the variation) may apply to the court to have the variation cancelled. The objectors must hold not less than **15%** of the issued shares of that class, and apply to the court within **21** days of the giving of consent by that class.

6   A. All companies must have a minimum of one member (s 7).

7   (a)   (ii)
     (b)   (i)
     (c)   (iii)

Now try the questions below from the Exam Question Bank

Number	Level	Marks	Time
Q22	Examination	10	18 mins

17

Borrowing and loan capital

Topic list	Syllabus reference
1 Borrowing	E2(a)
2 Debentures and loan capital	E2(b), E2(c)
3 Charges	E2(d)
4 Registration of charges	E2(e)
5 Debentureholders' remedies	E2(b)

Introduction

The last chapter was concerned with share capital. In this chapter on borrowing and **loan capital**, you should note that the interests and position of a lender is very different from that of a shareholder.

This chapter covers how loan capital holders protect themselves, specifically through taking out **fixed or floating charges**.

You need to understand the differences between fixed and floating charges, and also how they can protect loan creditors, for example by giving chargeholders the ability to appoint a **receiver**.

Study guide

Exam guide

Loan capital is most likely to crop up in a knowledge question. Together with insolvency and corporate finance in general, however, it is a topic that could also be examined in a scenario question.

You may be required to identify instances where a company has exceeded its borrowing powers or to explain the differences between types of charges.

1 Borrowing

FAST FORWARD

Companies have an **implied power** to borrow for purposes incidental to their trade or business.

All companies registered under the Companies Act 2006 have an **implied power to borrow** for purposes **incidental to their trade or business**. A company formed under earlier Acts will have an implied power to borrow if its object is to carry on a trade or business.

In delegating the company's power to borrow to the directors it is usual, and essential in the case of a company whose shares are quoted on the Stock Exchange, to impose a **maximum limit** on the **borrowing** arranged by directors.

A contract to repay borrowed money may in principle be unenforceable if either:

- It is money borrowed for an **ultra vires** (or restricted) purpose, and this is known to the lender.
- The directors **exceed their borrowing powers** or have no powers to borrow.

However:

- In both cases the lender will probably be **able** to **enforce** the contract.
- If the contract is within the capacity of the company but beyond the delegated powers of the directors the company may **ratify** the **loan contract**.

Case law has determined that if a company has power to borrow, it also has power to **create charges** over the company's assets as **security** for the loan. *Re Patent File Co 1870*.

2 Debentures and loan capital

2.1 Loan capital

FAST FORWARD

Loan capital comprises all the longer term borrowing of a company. It is distinguished from share capital by the fact that, at some point, borrowing must be repaid. Share capital on the other hand is only returned to shareholders when the company is wound up.

A company's **loan capital** comprises all amounts which it borrows for the long-term, such as:

(a) Permanent overdrafts at the bank
(b) Unsecured loans, from a bank or other party
(c) Loans secured on assets, from a bank or other party

Companies often issue long-term loans as capital in the form of **debentures**.

2.2 Debentures

FAST FORWARD

> A **debenture** is a document stating the terms on which a company has borrowed money. There are three main types.
>
> - A **single debenture**
> - **Debentures issued as a series** and usually registered
> - **Debenture stock** subscribed to by a large number of lenders. Only this form requires a **debenture trust deed**, although the others may often incorporate one

Key term

> A **debenture** is the written acknowledgement of a debt by a company, normally containing provisions as to payment of interest and the terms of repayment of principal. A debenture may be secured on some or all of the assets of the company or its subsidiaries.

A debenture may create a **charge** over the company's assets as security for the loan (see Section 3). However a document relating to an unsecured loan is also a debenture in company law.

2.3 Types of debenture

A debenture is usually a formal legal document, often in printed form. Broadly, there are three main types.

(a) **A single debenture**

If, for example, a company obtains a secured loan or overdraft facility from its bank, the latter is likely to insist that the company seals the bank's standard form of debenture creating the charge and giving the bank various safeguards and powers.

(b) **Debentures issued as a series and usually registered**

Different lenders may provide different amounts on different dates. Although each transaction is a separate loan, the intention is that the lenders should rank equally *(pari passu)* in their right to repayment and in any security given to them. Each lender therefore receives a debenture in identical form in respect of his loan.

The debentures are transferable securities.

(c) **The issue of debenture stock subscribed to by a large number of lenders**

Only a public company may use this method to offer its debentures to the public and any such offer is a prospectus; if it seeks a listing on The Stock Exchange then the rules on listing particulars must be followed.

Each lender has a right to be **repaid** his **capital** at the **due time** (unless they are perpetual) and to receive **interest** on it until **repayment**. This form of borrowing is treated as a single loan 'stock' in which each debenture stockholder has a specified fraction (in money terms) which they or some previous holder contributed when the stock was issued. Debenture stock is transferable in multiples of, say, £1 or £10.

A company must maintain a **register of all debenture holders** and register an allotment within 2 months.

One advantage of debenture stock over debentures issued as single and indivisible loan transactions is that the holder of debenture stock can sell part of his holding, say £1,000 (nominal), out of a larger amount.

Debenture stock must be created using a **debenture trust deed** though single and series debenture's may also use a debenture trust deed.

2.4 Debenture trust deed

Major elements of a debenture trust deed for debenture stock
The appointment usually of a trustee for prospective debenture stockholders. The trustee is usually a bank, insurance company or other institution but may be an individual.
The nominal amount of the debenture stock is defined, which is the maximum amount which may be raised then or later. The date or period of repayment is specified, as is the rate of interest and half-yearly interest payment dates.
If the debenture stock is secured **the deed creates a charge or charges** over the assets of the company.
The trustee is authorised to **enforce the security** in case of default and, in particular, to appoint a receiver with suitable powers of management.
The company enters into **various covenants**, for instance to keep its assets fully insured or to limit its total borrowings; breach is a default by the company.
There may be elaborate provisions for **transfer of stock** and **meetings** of debenture stockholders.

Advantages of a debenture trust deed for debenture stock
The **trustee** with appropriate powers can **intervene promptly** in case of default.
Security for the debenture stock in the form of charges over property can be **given to a single trustee**.
The **company** can **contact a representative of the debentureholders** with whom it can negotiate.
By calling a **meeting of debentureholders**, the trustee can consult them and obtain a decision binding on them all.
The **debentureholders** will be able to **enjoy the benefit of a legal mortgage** over the company's land.

2.5 Register of debentureholders

Company law does not specifically require a register of debentureholders be maintained. However, a company is normally required to maintain a register by the debenture or debenture trust deed when debentures are issued as a series or when debenture stock is issued.

When there is a register of debentureholders, the following regulations apply.

(a)   The company is required by law to keep the **register** at its registered office, or at an **address** notified to the registrar: s 743.

(b)   The register must be open to **inspection** by **any person** unless the constitution or trust deed provide otherwise. Any person may obtain a copy of the register or part of it for a fee. A holder of debentures issued under a trust deed may require the company (on payment) to supply them with a copy of the deed: s 749.

        Under s 745 a company has **five days** to respond to an inspection request or seek exemption to do so from the court.

(c)   The register should be **properly kept** in accordance with the requirements of the Companies Act.

2.6 Rights of debentureholders

The position of debentureholders is best described by comparison with that of shareholders. At first sight the two appear to have a great deal in common.

- Both **own transferable company securities** which are usually long-term investments in the company.
- The **issue procedure** is much the same. An offer of either shares or debentures to the public is a prospectus as defined by the Act.
- The **procedure** for **transfer** of registered shares and debentures is the same.

But there are significant differences.

Differences	Shareholder	Debentureholder
Role	Is a proprietor or owner of the company	Is a creditor of the company
Voting rights	May vote at general meetings	May not vote
Cost of investment	Shares may not be issued at a discount to nominal value	Debentures may be offered at a discount to nominal value
Return	Dividends are only paid • Out of distributable profits • When directors declare them	Interest must be paid when it is due
Redemption	Statutory restrictions on redeeming shares	No restriction on redeeming debentures
Liquidation	Shareholders are the last people to be paid in a winding up	Debentures must be paid back before shareholders are paid

From the investor's standpoint debenture stock is often **preferable to preference shares**. Although both yield a fixed income, debenture stock offers greater security.

2.6.1 Advantages and disadvantages of debentures (for the company)

Advantages	Disadvantages
Easily traded	May have to pay high interest to make them attractive
Terms clear and specific	Interest payments mandatory
Assets subject to a floating charge may be traded	Interest payments may upset shareholders if dividends fall
Popular due to guaranteed income	Debentureholder's remedies of liquidators or receivers may be disastrous for the company
Interest tax-deductible	Crystallisation of a floating charge can cause trading difficulties for a company
No restrictions on issue or purchase by a company	

Question | Rights of shareholders and debentureholders

Explain how the rights of the shareholders of a company differ from the rights of its debentureholders.

Rights of shareholders and debentureholders

Shareholders are members of the company. Debentureholders are creditors but not members of the company. Their relationships with the company differ in the following principal respects.

What governs the relationship

A company's relationship with its shareholders is governed by

(a) Its articles which operate as a contract between them and between the shareholders and each other, and

(b) The Companies Act

The relationship between a company and its debentureholders is regulated by:

(a) The terms of the trust deed or other formal document, and

(b) (Different) provisions of the Companies Act

The major practical differences are set out below.

Voting

As members of the company, shareholders have the right to attend and vote at meetings. Debentureholders have no such automatic rights; they may however have votes if the articles and deed allow.

Income

A shareholder, even if he holds preference shares on which fixed dividends are due on specific days, can only receive dividends out of distributable profits. In addition he cannot force the company to pay dividends: *Bond v Barrow Haematite Steel Co 1902.*

By contrast interest at the agreed rate must be paid on debentures even if that interest has to be paid out of capital.

Rights on securities

The Companies Act confers pre-emption rights on shareholders, entitling them to first call on any new shares which are to be issued.

Debentureholders have no right of objection to further loans and debentures being taken out, unless the trust deed sets out restrictions. However there is no statutory restriction on debentureholders having debentures redeemed or purchased by the company. By contrast there are detailed rules regulating redemption or purchase of a company's own shares.

Rights if aggrieved

Shareholders have the right to complain to the court if directors are allowing *ultra vires* transactions or acting in a manner unfairly prejudicial to their interests. Shareholders can, by simple majority, remove directors from the board.

Debentureholders may have rights under the trust deed if the company breaches the agreement. These include:

(a) The right to appoint a receiver, or

(b) The right to enforce charges and sell the property under the charge to realise their debts.

Their consent may also be required before the company deals with certain of its assets, when the debentureholders have secured their loan by means of a fixed charge over those assets.

Rights on liquidation

In liquidation debentureholders must be repaid in full before anything is distributed to shareholders.

3 Charges

A charge over the assets of a company gives a creditor a **prior claim** over other creditors to payment of their debt out of these assets.

Charges may be either **fixed**, which attach to the relevant asset on creation, or **floating**, which attach on 'crystallisation'. For this reason it is not possible to identify the assets to which a **floating** charge relates (until **crystallisation**).

3.1 Definition

Key term

A **charge** is an encumbrance upon real or personal property granting the holder certain rights over that property. They are often used as security for a debt owed to the charge holder. The most common form of charge is by way of legal mortgage, used to secure the indebtedness of borrowers in house purchase transactions. In the case of companies, charges over assets are most frequently granted to persons who provide loan capital to the business.

A charge **secured** over a company's assets gives to the creditor (called the 'chargee') a prior claim (over other creditors) to payment of their debt out of those assets. Charges are of two kinds, fixed and floating.

3.2 Fixed charges

Key term

A **fixed charge** is a form of protection given to secured creditors relating to specific assets of a company. The charge grants the holder the right of enforcement against the identified asset (in the event of default in repayment or some other matter) so that the creditor may realise the asset to meet the debt owed. Fixed charges rank first in order of priority in liquidation.

Fixed (or specific) charges attach to the relevant asset as soon as the charge is created. By its nature a fixed charge is best suited to assets which the company is likely to retain for a long period. A mortgage is an example of a fixed charge.

If the company disposes of the charged asset it will either **repay the secured debt** out of the proceeds of sale so that the charge is discharged at the time of sale, or **pass the asset over to** the purchaser still subject to the charge.

3.3 Floating charges

Key term

A **floating charge** has been defined, in *Re Yorkshire Woolcombers Association Ltd 1903*, as:

(a) A charge on a class of assets of a company, present and future ...

(b) Which class is, in the ordinary course of the company's business, changing from time to time and ...

(c) Until the holders enforce the charge the company may carry on business and deal with the assets charged.

Floating charges do not attach to the relevant assets until the charge crystallises.

A floating charge is **not restricted** to assets such as **receivables** or **inventory**. A floating charge over 'the undertaking and assets' of a company (the most common type) applies to future as well as to current assets.

3.4 Identification of charges as fixed or floating

It is not always immediately apparent whether a charge is fixed or floating. Chargees often do not wish to identify a charge as being as it may get paid later than preferential debts in insolvency proceedings.

A charge contract may declare the charge as fixed, or fixed and floating, whether it is or not. **The label attached** by parties in this way is **not a conclusive statement of the charge's legal nature**.

The general rule is that a **charge over assets will not be registered as fixed if it envisages that the company will still be able to deal with the charged assets without reference to the chargee**.

> *R in Right of British Columbia v Federal Business Development Bank 1988*
>
> *The facts:* In this Canadian case the Bank had a charge over the company's entire property expressed as 'a fixed and specific mortgage and charge'. Another term allowed the company to continue making sales from stock in the ordinary course of business until notified in writing by the bank to stop doing so.
>
> *Decision:* The charge was created as a floating, not a fixed, charge.

However, the courts have found **exceptions** to the general rule concerning permission to deal.

(a)   In *Re GE Tunbridge Ltd 1995* it was held that as the three criteria stated in the *Yorkshire Woolcombers* case applied. The charge over certain fixed assets was a floating charge even though the company was required to obtain the chargee's permission before dealing with the assets.

(b)   In *Re Cimex Ltd 1994* the court decided that the charge in dispute was a fixed charge. The assets did not in the ordinary course of business change from time to time. This was despite the company being able to deal with the assets without the chargee's permission.

3.4.1 Charges over receivables

Charges expressed to be fixed which cover **present and future receivables** (book debts) are particularly tricky.

Again the general rule applies. If the company is allowed to deal with money collected from customers without notifying the charge, the courts have decided that the charge is floating. If the money collected must be paid to the chargee, say in reduction of an overdraft, the courts have determined that the charge is fixed: *Siebe Gorman & Co Ltd v Barclays Bank Ltd 1979*.

In 2005 the House of Lords held in *Re Spectrum Plus* that there can be no fixed charge over a company's book debts.

3.5 Creating a floating charge

A **floating charge** is **often created by express words**. However no special form of words is essential. If a **company** gives to a chargee rights over its assets while **retaining freedom to deal with them in the ordinary course of business** until the charge crystallises, that will be a charge which 'floats'. The particular assets subject to a floating charge cannot be identified until the charge attaches by crystallisation.

3.6 Crystallisation of a floating charge

FAST FORWARD

Floating charges **crystallise** or harden (convert into a fixed charge) on the happening of certain relevant events.

Key term

Crystallisation of a floating charge occurs when it is converted into a fixed charge: that is, a fixed charge on the assets owned by the company at the time of crystallisation.

Events causing crystallisation
The **liquidation** of the company
Cessation of the company's **business**
Active intervention by the chargee, generally by way of appointing a receiver
If the **charge contract so provides**, when notice is given by the chargee that the charge is converted into a fixed charge (on whatever assets of the relevant class are owned by the company at the time of the giving of notice)
The **crystallisation** of **another floating charge** if it causes the company to cease business.

Floating charge contracts sometimes make provision for 'automatic crystallisation'. This is where the charge is to crystallise when a **specified event** – such as a breach of some term by the company – occurs, regardless of whether:

- The chargee learns of the event.
- The chargee wants to enforce the charge as a result of the event.

Such clauses have been accepted by the courts if they state that, on the event happening, the floating charge is converted to a fixed one. Clauses which provide only that a company is to cease to deal with charged assets on the occurrence of a particular event have been rejected.

3.7 Comparison of fixed and floating charges

FAST FORWARD

Floating charges rank **behind** a number of other creditors on liquidation, in particular preferential creditors such as employees.

A **fixed charge** is normally the more satisfactory form of security since it **confers immediate rights** over identified assets. A **floating charge** has some advantage in being applicable to **current assets which may be easier to realise** than long term assets subject to a fixed charge. If for example a company becomes insolvent it may be easier to sell its inventory than its empty factory.

The principal disadvantages of floating charges
The **holder** of a floating charge **cannot be certain** until the charge crystallises which assets will form his security.
Even when a floating charge has crystallised over an identified pool of assets the **chargeholder** may find themself **postponed** to the claim of **other creditors** as follows. (a) A **judgement creditor or landlord** who has seized goods and sold them may retain the proceeds if received before the appointment of the debentureholder's receiver: s 183 IA. (b) **Preferential debts** such as wages may be paid out of assets subject to a floating charge unless there are other uncharged assets available for this purpose: ss 40 and 175 IA. (c) The **holder** of a **fixed charge** over the same assets will usually have priority over a floating charge on those assets even if that charge was created before the fixed charge (see below). (d) A creditor may have sold goods and delivered them to the company on condition that he is to retain legal ownership until he has been paid (a **Romalpa** clause).
A **floating charge** may become **invalid automatically** if the company creates the charge to secure an existing debt and goes into liquidation within a year thereafter (s 245 IA). The period is only six months with a fixed charge.

3.8 Priority of charges

FAST FORWARD

If more than one charge exists over the **same class of property** then legal rules must be applied to see which takes priority in the event the company goes into liquidation.

Different charges over the **same** property may be given to different creditors. It will be necessary in such cases to determine which party's claim has **priority**.

Illustration

If charges are created over the same property to secure a debt of £5,000 to X and £7,000 to Y and the property is sold yielding only £10,000, either X or Y is paid in full and the other receives only the balance remaining out of £10,000 realised from the security.

Priority of charges
Fixed charges rank according to the **order of their creation**. If two successive fixed charges over the same factory are created on 1 January and 1 February the earlier takes priority over the later one.
A floating charge created before a fixed charge will only take priority if, when the latter was created, the **fixed chargee** had **notice** of a clause in the floating charge that prevents a later prior charge.
A **fixed charge created before** a **floating one** has **priority**.
Two floating charges take priority according to the **time of creation**.

If a floating charge is existing and a fixed charge over the same property is created later the fixed charge has priority. This is unless the fixed chargeholder knew of the floating charge. The **fixed** charge ranks **first** since it attached to the property at the time of **creation** but the **floating** charge attaches at the time of **crystallisation**. Once a floating charge has crystallised it becomes a fixed charge and a fixed charge created subsequently ranks after it.

A floating chargeholder may seek to protect himself against losing his priority by including in the terms of his floating charge a prohibition against the company creating a fixed charge over the same property (sometimes called a **'negative pledge clause'**).

If the company **breaks that prohibition** the creditor to whom the fixed charge is given nonetheless obtains priority, unless at the time when his charge is created he has **actual** knowledge of the prohibition.

If a company sells a charged asset to a **third party** the following rules apply.

- A chargee with a fixed charge still has recourse to the property in the hands of the third party – the **charge** is **automatically** transferred with the property.
- Property only remains charged by a floating charge if the **third party** had **notice** of it when he acquired the property.

Exam focus point

> You should be aware of what fixed and floating charges are and what the implications are of the differences between them.

Question

Registering charges

A floating charge is created on 1 January 20X1. A fixed charge over the same property is created on 1 April 20X1. Assuming both are registered within the prescribed time limits, which ranks first?

Answer

The fixed charge attaches to the asset on creation; the floating charge only attaches on crystallisation, and the effect of crystallisation is not retrospective. Therefore the fixed charge ranks first.

4 Registration of charges

To be valid and enforceable, charges must be **registered** within **21 days** of creation by the Registrar.

Certain types of **charge** created by a company **should be registered** within **21 days** with the Registrar by either the company or a person interested in it (eg the debenture trustee). Charges securing a **debenture issue** and **floating charges** are **specifically registrable**.

Other charges that are registrable include charges on:

- Uncalled share capital or calls made but not paid
- Land or any interest in land, other than a charge for rent
- Receivables (book debts)
- Goodwill or any intellectual property
- Ships or aircraft or any share in a ship

4.1 The registration process

The **company is responsible for registering the charge** but the charge **may** also **be registered** as a result of an application **by another person** interested in the charge.

The Registrar should be sent **the instrument** by which the charge is created or evidenced. The Registrar also has to be sent **prescribed particulars of the charge**.

- The date when the charge was created
- The amount of the debt which it secures
- Short particulars of the property to which the charge applies
- The person entitled to it

The Registrar files the particulars in the companies 'charges' register and notes the date of delivery. They also issue a **certificate** which is **conclusive evidence** that the **charge had been duly registered**.

The 21 day period for registration runs from the **creation** of the **charge**, or the acquisition of property charged, and not from the making of the loan for which the charge is security. Creation of a charge is usually effected by **execution of a document**.

4.2 Rectification of register of changes

A mistake or omission in registered particulars can only be rectified by the court ordering an extension of the period for registration, and with the subsequent rectification of the register. The court will only make the order if the error or omission was accidental or if it is just equitable to do so.

4.3 Failure to deliver particulars

The duty to deliver particulars falls upon the **company** creating the charge and if no one delivers particulars within 21 days, the **company and its officers are liable to a fine**: s 860.

Non-delivery in the time period results in the **charge** being **void** against an administrator, liquidator or any creditor of a company: s 874.

Non-delivery of a charge means that the sum secured by it is **payable forthwith on demand**: s 874.

4.3.1 Late delivery of particulars

The rules governing late delivery are the **same** as governing registration of **further particulars**, that is, a **court order** is required for registration.

A charge can only be registered late if it does not prejudice the creditors or shareholders of the company. Therefore a correctly registered fixed charge has priority over a fixed charge created earlier but registered after it, if that charge is registered late. s 873.

4.4 Register of charges

As you already know, every company is under an obligation to keep a copy of documents creating charges, and a register of charges, at its registered office or any other location permitted by the Secretary of State.

Question | **Registering more charges**

A company creates a charge over a property in favour of Margaret on 1 May 20X7. It creates a further charge of the same type in favour of Chris over the same property on 13 May 20X7. The company has Chris's charge registered on 25 May 20X7, and Margaret's charge on 29 May 20X7.

Whose charge ranks first, and why?

Answer

Margaret's charge would have taken precedence because it was created first, had it been registered within the allowed period of 21 days, up to 22 May. However it was not registered until 29 May, and Chris's charge was legitimately registered in the period between 22 and 29 May when Margaret's charge was void. The court would probably have allowed late registration of Margaret's charge but not at the expense of Chris's rights per s 873.

5 Debentureholders' remedies

5.1 Rights of unsecured debentureholders

FAST FORWARD ▶ A debentureholder **without security** has the same rights as any other creditor.

Any debentureholder is a creditor of the company with the normal remedies of an unsecured creditor. He could:

- **Sue** the company for debt and seize its property if his judgement for debt is unsatisfied
- Present a petition to the court for the **compulsory liquidation** of the company
- Apply to the court for an **administration order**, that is, a temporary reprieve to try and rescue a company

Point to note | We shall look at liquidation and administration in Chapter 21.

5.2 Rights of secured debentureholders

FAST FORWARD ▶ A **secured** debentureholder may enforce the security if the company defaults on payment of interest or repayment of capital. They may take possession of the asset subject to the charge and sell it or apply to the court for its transfer to their ownership by a foreclosure order. They may also appoint a receiver or administrator of it. A floating charge holder may place the company into administration.

A **secured** debentureholder (or the trustee of a debenture trust deed) may enforce the security. They may:

- Take **possession of the asset** subject to the charge if they have a fixed charge (if they have a floating charge they may only take possession if the contract allows)
- **Sell it** (provided the debenture is executed as a deed)
- Apply to the court for its **transfer** to their ownership by foreclosure order (rarely used and only available to a legal chargee)
- Appoint a **receiver** of it, provided an **administration order** is not in effect or (in the case of floating charge holders), appoint an administrator without needing to apply to the court, (see Chapter 21).

Exam focus point | The last part of a question on charges may well ask what debentureholders can do if a company defaults.

- Companies have an **implied power** to borrow for purposes incidental to their trade or business.

- **Loan capital** comprises all the longer term borrowing of a company. It is distinguished from share capital by the fact that, at some point, borrowing must be repaid. Share capital on the other hand is only returned to shareholders when the company is wound up.

- A **debenture** is a document stating the terms on which a company has borrowed money. There are three main types.

    - A **single debenture**
    - **Debentures issued as a series** and usually registered
    - **Debenture stock** subscribed to by a large number of lenders. Only this form requires a **debenture trust deed**, although the others may often incorporate one

- A charge over the assets of a company gives a creditor a **prior claim** over other creditors to payment of their debt out of these assets.

- Charges may be either **fixed**, which attach to the relevant asset on creation, or **floating**, which attach on 'crystallisation'. For this reason it is not possible to identify the assets to which a **floating** charge relates (until **crystallisation**).

- Floating charges **crystallise** or harden (convert into a fixed charge) on the happening of certain relevant events.

- Floating charges rank **behind** a number of other creditors on liquidation, in particular preferential creditors such as employees.

- If more than one charge exists over the **same class of property** then legal rules must be applied to see which takes priority in the event the company goes into liquidation.

- To be valid and enforceable, charges must be **registered** within **21 days** of creation by the Registrar.

- A debentureholder **without security** has the same rights as any other creditor.

- A **secured** debentureholder may enforce the security if the company defaults on payment of interest or repayment of capital. They may take possession of the asset subject to the charge and sell it or apply to the court for its transfer to their ownership by a foreclosure order. They may also appoint a receiver or administrator of it. A floating charge holder may place the company into administration.

1   Which of the following are correct statements about the relationship between a company's ordinary shares and its debentures?

    A   Debentures do not confer voting rights, whilst ordinary shares do.
    B   The company's duty is to pay interest on debentures, and to pay dividends on ordinary shares.
    C   Interest paid on debentures is deducted from pre-tax profits, dividends are paid from net profits.
    D   A debentureholder takes priority over a member in liquidation.

2   A fixed charge

    A   Cannot be an informal mortgage
    B   Can be a legal mortgage
    C   Can only attach to land, shares or book debts
    D   Cannot attach to land

3   What are the elements of the definition of a floating charge?

4　Company law requires a company to maintain a register of charges, but not a register of debentureholders.

True ☐

False ☐

5　In which of the following situations will crystallisation of a floating charge occur?

A　Liquidation of the company
B　Disposal by the company of the charged asset
C　Cessation of the company's business
D　After the giving of notice by the chargee if the contract so provides

6　Certain types of charges need to be registered within 28 days of creation.

True ☐

False ☐

7　What steps can a fixed debentureholder take to enforce their security? (Max 30 words)

Answers to Quick Quiz

1　A, C and D are correct. Whilst the company has a contractual duty to pay interest on debentures, there is no duty on it to pay dividends on shares. B is therefore incorrect.

2　B. A mortgage is an example of a fixed charge. It can extend to, for instance, plant and machinery as well as land.

3　The charge is:

(a)　A charge on a class of assets, present and future
(b)　Which class is in the ordinary course of the company's business changing from time to time
(c)　Until the holders enforce the charge, the company may carry on business and deal with the assets charged

4　True. A register of charges must be kept, a register of debentureholders is not required to be kept by the Act.

5　A, C and D are true. As the charge does not attach to the asset until crystallisation, B is untrue.

6　False. Certain charges such as charges securing a debenture issue and floating charges need to be registered within 21 days.

7　Take possession of the asset subject to the charge
Sell it
Apply to the court for a transfer to his ownership
Appoint a receiver of it

Now try the question below from the Exam Question Bank

Number	Level	Marks	Time
Q23	Examination	10	18 mins

Capital maintenance and dividend law

Topic list	Syllabus reference
1 Capital maintenance	E3(a)
2 Reduction of share capital	E3(a)
3 Issuing shares at a premium or at a discount	E3(b)
4 Distributing dividends	E3(c)

Introduction

The capital which a limited company obtains from its members as consideration for their shares is sometimes called **'the creditors' buffer'**. No one can prevent an unsuccessful company from losing its capital by trading at a loss. However, whatever capital the company does have must be held for the payment of the company's debts and may not be returned to members except under procedures which safeguard the interest of creditors. That is the price which members of a limited company are required to pay for the protection of limited liability. This principle has been developed in a number of detailed applications.

- Capital may only be distributed to members under the formal procedure of a **reduction** of **share capital** or a **winding up** of the company.
- A **premium** obtained on the allotment of shares and profits used to redeem or purchase shares of the company are statutory reserves subject to the basic rules on capital.
- **Dividends** may only be paid out of distributable profits.

Study guide

		Intellectual level
(E)	**Capital and the financing of companies**	
3	Capital maintenance and dividend law	
(a)	Explain the doctrine of capital maintenance and capital reduction	2
(b)	Examine the effect of issuing shares at either a discount, or at a premium	2
(c)	Explain the rules governing the distribution of dividends in both private and public companies	2

Exam guide

Capital maintenance can be a difficult area. The different components of this chapter could all be examined separately in a knowledge question, or as an application question on the liability of a shareholder who took shares at a discount to nominal value, as in the Pilot Paper.

1 Capital maintenance

FAST FORWARD

The rules which dictate how a company is to manage and maintain its capital exist to maintain the delicate balance between the **members' enjoyment of limited liability** and the **creditors' requirements that the company shall remain able to pay its debts**.

Key term

Capital maintenance is a fundamental principle of company law, that limited companies should not be allowed to make payments out of capital to the detriment of company creditors. Therefore the Companies Act contains many examples of control upon capital payments. These include provisions restricting dividend payments, and capital reduction schemes.

Exam focus point

The rules affecting the possible threats to capital are complicated in certain areas. However, provided you know the rules, questions on capital maintenance tend to be straightforward.

2 Reduction of share capital

FAST FORWARD

Reduction of capital can be achieved by: **extinguishing/reducing liability on partly-paid shares**; **cancelling paid-up share capital**; or **paying off part of paid-up share capital**. Court confirmation is required for public companies. The court considers the interests of creditors and different classes of shareholder. There must be power in the articles and a special resolution.

A limited company is permitted without restriction to cancel **unissued shares** as that change does not alter its financial position.

If a limited company with a share capital wishes to **reduce** its **issued share capital** it may do if:

- It has **power** to do so in its articles. (if it does not have power in the articles, these may be amended by a **special resolution).**
- It passes a **special resolution**. (If the articles have been amended, this is another special resolution)
- It obtains **confirmation** of the reduction **from the court**

2.1 Solvency statement

A private company need not apply to the court if it supports its special resolution with a solvency statement. A **solvency statement** is a **declaration** by the directors, provided **15 days** in advance of the meeting where the special resolution is to be voted on. It states there is **no ground** to suspect the company is currently **unable** or will be **unlikely to be able** to pay its debts for the next **twelve months**. All possible liabilities must be taken into account and the statement should be in the prescribed form, naming all the directors.

2.2 Why reduce share capital?

A company may wish to reduce its capital for one or more of the following reasons.

- The company has suffered a **loss** in the **value** of its **assets** and it reduces its capital to reflect that fact.
- The company wishes to **extinguish** the **interests** of some members entirely.
- The capital reduction is part of a **complicated arrangement** of capital which may involve, for instance, replacing share capital with loan capital.

There are three basic methods of reducing share capital specified in s 641 of the Act.

Method	What happens	Effects
Extinguish or reduce liability on partly paid shares	Eg Company has nominal value £1 shares 75p paid up. Either (a) reduce nominal value to 75p; or (b) reduce nominal value to a figure between 75p and £1.	Company gives up claim for amount not paid up (nothing is **returned** to shareholders).
Pay off part of paid-up share capital out of surplus assets	Eg Company reduces nominal value of fully paid shares from £1 to 70p and repays this amount to shareholders	Assets of company are reduced by 30p in £.
Cancel paid-up share capital which has been lost or which is no longer represented by available assets.	Eg Company has £1 nominal fully paid shares but net assets only worth 50p per share. Difference is a debit balance on reserves. Company reduces nominal value to 50p, and applies amount to write off debit balance	Company can resume dividend payments out of future profits without having to make good past losses.

2.3 Role of the court in reduction of share capital

When the court receives an application for reduction of capital its **first concern** is the effect of the reduction on the company's ability to pay its debts, that is, that the creditors are protected.

If the reduction is by extinguishing liability or paying off part of paid-up share capital, the court requires that **creditors** shall be **invited** by advertisement to state their objections (if any) to the reduction. Where paid-up share capital is cancelled, the court **may** require an invitation to creditors.

Normally the company persuades the court to dispense with advertising for creditors' objections (which can be commercially damaging to the company).

Two possible approaches are:

- To **pay off** all **creditors** before application is made to the court; or, if that is not practicable
- To produce to the court a **guarantee**, say from the company's bank, that its existing debts will be paid in full

The **second** concern of the court, where there is more than one class of share, is whether the reduction is fair in its effect on different classes of shareholder.

If the reduction is, **in the circumstances**, a **variation of class rights** the **consent** of the class must be obtained under the variation of class rights procedure.

Within each class of share it is usual to make a uniform reduction of every share by the same amount per share, though this is **not** obligatory.

The court may also be concerned that the **reduction should not confuse or mislead people who may deal with the company in future**. It may insist that the company add 'and reduced' to its name or publish explanations of the reduction.

2.3.1 Confirmation by the court

If the court is satisfied that the reduction is in order, it confirms the reduction by making an order to that effect. A **copy of the court order** and a **statement of capital**, approved by the court, to show the altered share capital is delivered to the Registrar who issues a certificate of registration.

Question

Reduction of share capital

What are the main methods for a public company to reduce its share capital? What procedures must it follow?

Answer

If a public company wishes to reduce its **issued** share capital it may do so provided that:

(a)   It has power to do so in its articles.
(b)   It passes a special resolution.
(c)   It obtains confirmation of the reduction from the court: s 641.

Requirement (a) is simply a matter of procedure. Articles usually contain the necessary power. If not, the company in general meeting would first pass a special resolution to alter the articles appropriately. They would then proceed to pass a special resolution to reduce the capital.

There are three basic methods of reducing share capital under s 641:

(a)   Extinguish or reduce liability on partly-paid shares
(b)   Cancel paid-up share capital which has been lost or which is no longer represented by available assets
(c)   Pay off part of the paid-up share capital out of surplus assets

Although these are the methods specified in s 641, they are not the only possibilities.

If method (a) or (b) is used (or is part of a more complex scheme to reduce capital) creditors must be invited to object, and their consent must be granted. An alternative is that they are paid off, which will allow the court to confirm the reduction.

It should be remembered that public companies are subject to a minimum capital requirement, currently of £50,000. This means that any public company wishing to reduce its capital below this figure will only be allowed to do so by the court if it re-registers as a private company, which is not subject to the minimum capital requirement. This situation is, relatively rare.

3 Issuing shares at a premium or at a discount

FAST FORWARD

In issuing shares, a company must fix a **price** which is **equal** to or **more than** the **nominal value of the shares**. It may not allot shares at a discount to the nominal value.

Every share has a **nominal value** and **may not be allotted at a discount** to that: s 580.

In allotting shares every company is required to obtain in money or money's worth, consideration of a value at least equal to the nominal value of the shares plus the whole of any premium. To issue shares **'at par'** is to obtain equal value, say, £1 for a £1 share.

> *Ooregum Gold Mining Co of India v Roper, 1892*
>
> *The facts:* Shares in the company, although nominally £1, were trading, at a market price 12.5p. In an honest attempt to refinance the company, new £1 preference shares were issued and credited with 75p already paid, so the purchasers of the shares were actually paying twice the market value of the ordinary shares. When, however, the company subsequently went into insolvent liquidation the holders of the new shares were required to pay a further 75p.

If shares are allotted at a discount on their nominal value the allottee (and subsequent owners of the shares) must nonetheless pay the **full nominal value** with **interest** at the appropriate rate. Any subsequent holder of such a share who knew of the underpayment must make good the shortfall: s 588.

Consideration for shares	
Partly-paid shares	The no-discount rule only requires that, in allotting its shares, a company shall not fix a price which is less than the nominal value of the shares. It may leave part of that price to be paid at some later time. Thus £1 shares may be issued partly-paid – 75p on allotment and 25p when called for or by instalment. The unpaid capital passes with the shares. If transferred, they are a debt payable by the holder at the time when payment is demanded.
Underwriting fees	A company may pay underwriting or other commission in respect of an issue of shares if so permitted by its Articles. This means that, if shares are issued at par the net amount received will be below par value. This is not a contravention of s 580 (prohibiting allotment of shares at a discount).
Bonus issue	The allotment of shares as a 'bonus issue' is for full consideration since reserves, which are shareholders' funds, are converted into fixed capital and are used to pay for the shares.
Money's worth	The price for the shares may be paid in **money** or **'money's worth'**, including goodwill and know-how: s 582. It need not be paid in cash and the company may agree to accept a **'non-cash'** consideration of sufficient value. For instance, a company may issue shares in payment of the price agreed in the purchase of a property.

3.1 Private companies

FAST FORWARD

Private companies may issue shares for **inadequate consideration** provided the directors are behaving reasonably and honestly.

A private company may allot shares for **inadequate consideration** by acceptance of goods or services at an over-value. This loophole has been allowed to exist because in some cases it is very much a matter of opinion whether an asset is or is not of a stated value.

The **courts** therefore have **refused** to overrule directors in their valuation of an asset acquired for shares if it appears **reasonable** and **honest**: *Re Wragg 1897*. However a blatant and unjustified overvaluation will be declared **invalid**.

3.2 Public companies

FAST FORWARD

There are **stringent rules** on consideration for shares in public companies.

More stringent rules apply to public companies.

(a) The company must, at the time of allotment, receive **at least one quarter of the nominal value** of the shares and the **whole** of any premium: s 586.

(b) Any **non-cash consideration** accepted must be **independently valued** (see below).

(c) **Non-cash consideration** may **not** be accepted as payment for shares if an undertaking contained in such consideration is to be, or may be, **performed more than five years after the allotment.** This relates to, say, a property or business in return for shares. To enforce the five year rule the law requires that:

    (i) At the time of the allotment the **allottee** must **undertake** to **perform** his side of the agreement within a specified period which must not exceed five years. If no such undertaking is given the **allottee** becomes **immediately liable** to pay cash for his shares as soon as they are allotted

    (ii) If the **allottee later fails** to **perform** his undertaking to transfer property at the due time he becomes liable to pay **cash** for his shares when he defaults

(d) An **undertaking to do work or perform services is not to be accepted as consideration**. A public company may, however, allot shares to discharge a debt in respect of services already rendered.

    If a public company does accept future services as consideration the holder must pay the company their **nominal value** plus any **premium** treated as paid-up, and **interest** at 5% on any such amount.

(e) Within **two years of receiving its trading certificate**, a public company **may not receive a transfer of non-cash assets from a subscriber** to the memorandum. This is unless its value is less than 10% of the issued nominal share capital and it has been independently valued and agreed by an ordinary resolution.

3.2.1 Valuation of non-cash assets

When a public company allots shares for a non-cash consideration the company must usually obtain a **report on its value** from an independent valuer.

The valuation report must be made to the company within the six months before the allotment. On receiving the report the company must send a copy to the proposed allottee and later to the Registrar.

The independent valuation rule does not apply to an allotment of shares made in the course of a takeover bid.

3.3 Allotment of shares at a premium

FAST FORWARD

If shares are issued at a premium, the **excess** must be credited to a **share premium** account.

Key term

> **Share premium** is the excess received, either in cash or other consideration, over the nominal value of the shares issued.

An established company may be able to obtain consideration for new shares in excess of their nominal value. The excess, called 'share premium', must be credited to a **share premium account**.

Exam focus point

> The prohibition on offer of shares at a discount on **nominal** value is often confused with a company issuing shares at a price below **market** value (which is not, provided there is no discount below nominal value, prohibited).

If a company obtains non-cash consideration for its shares which exceeds the nominal value of the shares the excess should also be credited to the **share premium account.**

3.3.1 Example: Using a share premium account

If a company allots its £1 (nominal) shares for £1.50 in cash, £1 per share is credited to the share capital account, and 50p to the share premium account.

Illustration

We will use the above example to illustrate the effects of the transaction on the balance sheet. The company has issued 100 shares.

	Before share issue £	After share issue £
Cash	100	250
Share capital	100	200
Share premium	–	50
	100	250

The general rule is that reduction of the share premium account is subject to the **same** restrictions as reduction of share capital. You should learn the fact that **a company cannot distribute any part of its share premium account as dividend**.

3.4 Uses of the share premium account

FAST FORWARD

Use of the share premium account is limited. It is most often used for **bonus issues**.

The permitted uses of share premium are to pay:

- **Fully paid shares under a bonus issue** since this operation merely converts one form of fixed capital into another
- **Issue expenses** and **commission** in respect of a **new share issue**

Question

Increasing a company's share capital

Explain the rule concerning issuing shares at a discount to their nominal value.

Answer

Shares may not be issued at a discount to their nominal value: s 580. However shares may be issued 'partly paid' with, for example, 75p of a £1 share paid up. The 25p balance remains a liability that the shareholder must pay when demanded.

4 Distributing dividends

FAST FORWARD

Various rules have been created to ensure that dividends are only paid out of **available profits**.

Key term

A **dividend** is an amount payable to shareholders from profits or other distributable reserves.

4.1 Power to declare dividends

A company may only pay dividends out of **profits available for the purpose**.

The power to declare a dividend is given by the articles which often include the following rules.

Rules related to the power to declare a dividend
The **company** in **general meeting** may declare dividends.
No dividend may exceed the **amount recommended** by the directors who have an implied power in their discretion to set aside profits as reserves.
The directors may declare such **interim dividends** as they consider justified.
Dividends are normally declared payable on the **paid up amount** of **share capital**. For example a £1 share which is fully paid will carry entitlement to twice as much dividend as a £1 share 50p paid.
A dividend may be paid **otherwise than in cash**.
Dividends may be paid by **cheque** or **warrant** sent through the post to the shareholder at his registered address. If shares are held jointly, payment of dividend is made to the first-named joint holder on the register.

Listed companies generally pay two dividends a year; an **interim dividend** based on interim profit figures, and a **final dividend** based on the annual accounts and approved at the AGM.

A **dividend becomes a debt** when it is **declared** and **due for payment**. A shareholder is not entitled to a dividend unless it is declared in accordance with the procedure prescribed by the articles and the declared date for payment has arrived.

This is so even if the member holds **preference shares** carrying a priority entitlement to receive a specified amount of dividend on a specified date in the year. The directors may decide to withhold profits and cannot be compelled to recommend a dividend.

If the articles refer to 'payment' of dividends this means **payment in cash**. A power to pay dividends **in specie** (otherwise than in cash) is not implied but may be expressly created. **Scrip dividends** are dividends paid by the issue of additional shares.

Any provision of the articles for the declaration and payment of dividends is subject to the overriding rule that **no dividend may be paid except out of profits distributable by law**.

4.2 Distributable profit

FAST FORWARD

Distributable profits may be defined as 'accumulated realised profits ... less accumulated realised losses'. **'Accumulated'** means that any losses of previous years must be included in reckoning the current distributable surplus. **'Realised'** profits are determined in accordance with generally accepted accounting principles.

Key term

Profits available for distribution are accumulated realised profits (which have not been distributed or capitalised) less accumulated realised losses (which have not been previously written off in a reduction or reorganisation of capital).

The word **'accumulated'** requires that any **losses** of **previous years** must be included in reckoning the current distributable surplus.

A profit or loss is deemed to be **realised** if it is treated as realised in accordance with generally accepted accounting principles. Hence, financial reporting and accounting standards in issue, plus generally accepted accounting principles (GAAP), should be taken into account when determining realised profits and losses.

Depreciation must be treated as a **realised loss**, and debited against profit, in determining the amount of distributable profit remaining.

However, a **revalued asset** will have deprecation charged on its historical cost and the increase in the value in the asset. The Companies Act allows the depreciation provision on the valuation increase to be treated also as a realised profit.

Effectively there is a cancelling out, and at the end **only depreciation that relates to historical cost will affect dividends**.

 Illustration

Suppose that an asset purchased for £20,000 has a 10 year life. Provision is made for depreciation on a straight line basis. This means the annual depreciation charge of £2,000 must be deducted in reckoning the company's realised profit less realised loss.

Suppose now that after five years the asset is revalued to £50,000 and in consequence the annual depreciation charge is raised to £10,000 (over each of the five remaining years of the asset's life).

The effect of the act is that £8,000 of this amount may be reclassified as a realised profit. The net effect is that realised profits are reduced by only £2,000 in respect of depreciation, as before.

If, on a general revaluation of all fixed assets, it appears that there is a diminution in value of any one or more assets, then any related provision(s) need **not** be treated as a realised loss.

The Act states that if a company shows development expenditure as an asset in its accounts it must usually be treated as a realised loss in the year it occurs. However it can be carried forward in special circumstances (generally taken to mean in accordance with accounting standards).

4.3 Dividends of public companies

FAST FORWARD

A public company may only make a distribution if its **net assets** are, at the time, **not less than the aggregate of its called-up share capital and undistributable reserves**. It may only pay a dividend which will leave its net assets at not less than that aggregate amount.

A public company may only make a distribution if its **net assets are**, at the time, **not less than the aggregate of its called-up share capital and undistributable reserves**. The dividend which it may pay is limited to such amount as will leave its net assets at not less than that aggregate amount: s 831.

Undistributable reserves in s 831 are defined as:

(a) **Share premium account**

(b) **Capital redemption reserve**

(c) Any **surplus** of **accumulated unrealised profits** over **accumulated unrealised losses** (known as a revaluation reserve). However a deficit of accumulated unrealised profits compared with accumulated unrealised losses must be treated as a realised loss

(d) Any **reserve** which the company is **prohibited** from **distributing** by **statute** or by its constitution or any law.

 Illustration

Suppose that a public company has an issued share capital (fully paid) of £800,000 and £200,000 on share premium account (which is an undistributable reserve). If its assets less liabilities are less than £1 million it may not pay a dividend. If however its net assets are say £1,250,000 it may pay a dividend but only of such amount as will leave net assets of £1 million or more, so its maximum permissible dividend is £250,000.

The dividend rules apply to every form of distribution of assets of the company to its members except the following

- The **issue of bonus shares** whether fully or partly paid
- The **redemption** or **purchase** of the company's **shares** out of **capital** or **profits**
- A **reduction** of **share capital**
- A **distribution** of **assets** to members in a **winding up**

<table>
<tr><td>**Exam focus point**</td><td>You must appreciate how the rules relating to public companies in this area are more stringent than the rules for private companies.</td></tr>
</table>

Question

Distribution of profit

What are the main rules affecting a company's ability to distribute its profits as dividends?

Answer

Dividends may only be paid by a company out of profits available for the purpose. There is a detailed code of statutory rules which determines what are distributable profits. The profits which may be distributed as dividend are accumulated realised profits, so far as not previously utilised by distribution or capitalisation, less accumulated realised losses, so far as not previously written off in a reduction or reorganisation of capital duly made.

The word 'accumulated' requires that any losses of previous years must be included in reckoning the current distributable surplus.

The word 'realised' presents more difficulties. It clearly prevents the distribution of an increase in the value of a retained asset resulting from revaluation. However, it does not prevent a company from transferring to profit and loss account profit earned on an uncompleted contract, if it is in accordance with generally accepted accounting principles.

There is no mention here of realised profits and so it would seem that there is no statutory guidance on this point. Nevertheless, in view of the authority of accounting standards, it is unlikely that profits determined in accordance with accounting standards would be considered unrealised. A realised capital loss will reduce realised profits.

The above rules on distributable profits apply to all companies, private or public. A public company is subject to an additional rule which may diminish but cannot increase its distributable profit as determined under the above rules.

A public company may only make a distribution if its net assets are, at the time, not less than the aggregate of its called-up share capital and undistributable reserves. The dividend which it may pay is limited to such amount as will leave its net assets at not less than that aggregate amount.

4.4 Relevant accounts

<table>
<tr><td>FAST FORWARD</td><td>The profits available for distribution are generally determined from the **last annual accounts** to be prepared.</td></tr>
</table>

Whether a company has profits from which to pay a dividend is determined by reference to its **'relevant accounts'**, which are generally the last annual accounts to be prepared: s 836.

If the auditor has qualified their report on the accounts they must also state in writing whether, in their opinion, the subject matter of his qualification is **material** in determining whether the dividend may be paid. This statement must have been circulated to the members (for a private company) or considered at a general meeting (for a public company).

A company may produce **interim accounts** if the latest annual accounts do not disclose a sufficient distributable profit to cover the proposed dividend. It may also produce **initial accounts** if it proposes to pay a dividend during its first accounting reference period or before its first accounts are laid before the company in general meeting. These accounts may be unaudited, but they must suffice to permit a proper judgement to be made of amounts of any of the relevant items.

If a **public** company has to produce initial or interim accounts, which is unusual, they must be full accounts such as the company is required to produce as final accounts at the end of the year. They need not be audited. However the auditors must, in the case of initial accounts, satisfy themselves that the accounts have been 'properly prepared' to comply with the Act. A copy of any such accounts of a public company (with any auditors' statement) must be delivered to the Registrar for filing.

4.5 Infringement of dividend rules

FAST FORWARD

> In certain situations the **directors** and **members** may be liable to make good to the company the amount of an **unlawful dividend**.

If a dividend is paid otherwise than out of distributable profits the company, the **directors and** the **shareholders** may be involved in making good the unlawful distribution.

The directors are held **responsible** since they either recommend to members in general meeting that a dividend should be declared or they declare interim dividends.

(a)   **The directors are liable if they recommend or declare a dividend which they know is paid out of capital.**

(b)   **The directors are liable if, without preparing any accounts, they declare or recommend a dividend which proves to be paid out of capital.** It is their duty to satisfy themselves that profits are available.

(c)   **The directors are liable if they make some mistake of law or interpretation of the constitution which leads them to recommend or declare an unlawful dividend.** However in such cases the directors may well be entitled to relief as their acts were performed 'honestly and reasonably'.

The directors may however **honestly** rely on proper accounts which disclose an apparent distributable profit out of which the dividend can properly be paid. They are not liable if it later appears that the assumptions or estimates used in preparing the accounts, although reasonable at the time, were in fact unsound.

The position of members is as follows.

- A member may obtain an **injunction** to restrain a company from paying an unlawful dividend.
- Members voting in general meeting **cannot authorise** the payment of an unlawful dividend nor release the directors from their liability to pay it back.
- The company can **recover from members** an **unlawful dividend** if the **members knew** or had **reasonable grounds** to believe that it was unlawful, s847.
- If the directors have to make good to the company an unlawful dividend they may claim **indemnity from members** who at the time of receipt knew of the irregularity.
- Members knowingly receiving an unlawful dividend may **not bring an action** against the directors.

If an unlawful dividend is paid by **reason of error** in the **accounts** the company may be unable to claim against either the directors or the members. The company might then have a claim against its **auditors** if the undiscovered mistake was due to negligence on their part.

> **Re London & General Bank (No 2) 1895**
>
> *The facts:* The auditor had drawn the attention of the directors to the fact that certain loans to associated companies were likely to prove irrecoverable. The directors refused to make any provision for these potential losses. They persuaded the auditor to confine his comments in his audit report to the uninformative statement that the value of assets shown in the balance sheet 'is dependent on realisation'. A dividend was paid in reliance on the apparent profits shown in the accounts. The company went into liquidation and the liquidator claimed from the auditor compensation for loss of capital due to his failure to report clearly to members what he well knew affecting the reliability of the accounts.
>
> *Decision:* The auditor has a duty to report what he knows of the true financial position: otherwise his audit is 'an idle farce'. He had failed in this duty and was liable.

Chapter Roundup

- The rules which dictate how a company is to manage and maintain its capital exist to maintain the delicate balance between the **members' enjoyment of limited liability** and the **creditors' requirements that the company shall remain able to pay its debts**.

- Reduction of capital can be achieved by: **extinguishing/reducing liability on partly-paid shares; cancelling paid-up share capital**; or **paying off part of paid up share capital**. Court confirmation is required for public companies. The court considers the interests of creditors and different classes of shareholder. There must be power in the articles and a special resolution.

- In issuing shares, a company must fix a **price** which is **equal** to or **more than** the **nominal value of the shares**. It may not allot shares at a discount to the nominal value.

- Private companies may issue shares for **inadequate consideration** provided the directors are behaving reasonably and honestly.

- There are **stringent rules** on consideration for shares in public companies.

- If shares are issued at a premium, the **excess** must be credited to a **share premium** account.

- Use of the share premium account is limited. It is most often used for **bonus issues**.

- Various rules have been created to ensure that dividends are only paid out of **available profits**.

- Distributable profits may be defined as 'accumulated realised profits ... less accumulated realised losses'. **'Accumulated'** means that any losses of previous years must be included in reckoning the current distributable surplus. **'Realised'** profits are determined in accordance with generally accepted accounting principles.

- A public company may only make a distribution if its **net assets** are, at the time, **not less than the aggregate of its called-up share capital and undistributable reserves**. It may only pay a dividend which will leave its net assets at not less than that aggregate amount.

- The profits available for distribution are generally determined from the **last annual accounts** to be prepared.

- In certain situations the **directors** and **members** may be liable to make good to the company the amount of an **unlawful dividend**.

1   Where application is made to the court for confirmation of a reduction in capital, the court may require that creditors should be invited by advertisement to state their objections. In which of the following ways can the need to advertise be avoided?

    A   Paying off all creditors before application to the court
    B   Producing a document signed by the directors stating the company's ability to pay its debts
    C   Producing a guarantee from the company's bank that its existing debts will be paid in full
    D   Renouncement by existing shareholders of their limited liability in relation to existing debts

2   A share premium account can be used for bonus issues of shares or issue costs for new share issues.

    True   ☐

    False   ☐

3   **Fill in the blanks** in the statements below.

    Distributable profits may be defined as ……………….. ……..…. profits less ……………….. ………….. losses.

4   If a company makes an unlawful dividend, who may be involved in making good the distribution?

    A   The company
    B   The directors
    C   The shareholders

5   Give four examples of undistributable reserves.

6   What normally are a company's relevant accounts in the context of payments of dividends?

Answers to Quick Quiz

1   A and C. The only guarantee that the courts will accept is from the company's bank.

2   True. Both are acceptable uses for the share premium account.

3   Distributable profits may be defined as **accumulated realised** profits less **accumulated realised** losses.

4   All three may be liable.

5   Share premium account

    Capital redemption reserve

    A surplus of accumulated unrealised profits over accumulated unrealised losses (revaluation reserve)

    Any reserve which the company is prohibited from distributing by statute or by its constitution or any law.

6   The relevant accounts are the last accounts to have been prepared and laid in general meeting.

Now try the question below from the Exam Question Bank

Number	Level	Marks	Time
Q24	Examination	10	18 mins

Management, administration
and regulation of companies

19

Company directors and other company officers

Topic list	Syllabus reference
1 The role of directors	F1(a)
2 Appointment of directors	F1(b)
3 Remuneration of directors	F1(b)
4 Vacation of office	F1(b)
5 Disqualification of directors	F1(b)
6 Powers of directors	F1(c)
7 Powers of the managing director	F1(c)
8 Powers of an individual director	F1(c)
9 Duties of directors	F1(d), F1(e)
10 The company secretary	F2(a)
11 The company auditor	F2(b)

Introduction

In this chapter we turn our attention to the **appointment** and **removal**, and the **powers and duties, of the directors**.

The important principle to grasp is that the **extent of directors' powers is defined by the articles**.

If **shareholders** do not approve of the directors' acts they must either **remove them** under s 168 or **alter the articles** to regulate their future conduct. However, they **cannot** simply **take over** the functions of the directors.

In essence, the directors act as **agents of the company**. This ties in with the **agency** part of your law studies also discussed in connection with partnerships. The different types of authority a director can have (implied and actual) are important in this area.

We also consider the **duties** of directors under statute and **remedies for the breach of such duties**.

Statute also imposes some duties on directors, specifically concerning openness when transacting with the company.

Finally we look at the duties and powers of the **company secretary** and **auditor**.

Study guide

		Intellectual level
(F)	**Management, administration and regulation of companies**	
1	Company directors	
(a)	Explain the role of directors in the operation of a company	2
(b)	Discuss the ways in which directors are appointed, can lose their office or be subject to a disqualification order	2
(c)	Distinguish between the powers of the board of directors, the managing director and individual directors to bind their company	2
(d)	Explain the duties that directors owe to their companies	2
(e)	Demonstrate an understanding of the way in which statute law has attempted to control directors	2
2	Other company officers	
(a)	Discuss the appointment procedure relating to, and the duties and powers of, a company secretary	2
(b)	Discuss the appointment procedure relating to, and the duties and powers of, company auditors	2

Exam guide

The relationship between members of a company and their directors could be examined in a knowledge based or scenario question. The detailed rules regarding directors and other company officers are all highly examinable.

1 The role of directors

FAST FORWARD

Any person who occupies the position of director is treated as such, the test being one of **function**.

Key term

A **director** is a person who is responsible for the overall direction of the company's affairs. In company law, director means any person occupying the position of director, by whatever name called.

Any person who occupies the position of director is treated as such. The test is one of **function**. The directors' function is to take part in **making decisions** by **attending meetings** of the board of directors. Anyone who does that is a director whatever they may be called.

A person who is given the title of director, such as 'sales director' or 'director of research', to give them status in the company structure is not a director in company law. This is unless by virtue of their appointment they are a **member** of the **board** of **directors**, or they carry out functions that would be properly discharged only by a director. Anyone who is held out by a company as a director, and who acts as a director although not validly appointed as one, is known as a **de facto** director.

1.1 Shadow directors

A person might seek to **avoid the legal responsibilities of being a director** by avoiding appointment as such but using his power, say as a major shareholder, to manipulate the acknowledged board of directors.

Company law seeks to prevent this abuse by extending several statutory rules to **shadow directors**. Shadow directors are directors for legal purposes if the board of directors are accustomed to act in **accordance with their directions** and **instructions**.

This rule does not apply to professional advisers merely acting in that capacity.

1.2 Alternate directors

A director may, if the articles permit, appoint an **alternate director** to attend and vote for them at board meetings which they are unable to attend. Such an alternate may be another director, in which case they have the vote of the absentee as well as their own. More usually they are an outsider. Company articles could make specific provisions for this situation.

1.3 Executive directors

Key term

An **executive director** is a director who performs a specific role in a company under a **service contract** which requires a regular, possibly daily, involvement in management.

A director may also be an **employee** of his company. Since the company is also his **employer** there is a potential conflict of interest which in principle a director is required to avoid.

To allow an individual to be **both a director and employee** the articles usually make express provision for it, but prohibit the director from voting at a board meeting on the terms of their own employment.

Directors who have additional management duties as employees may be distinguished by **special titles**, such as 'Finance Director'. However (except in the case of a managing director) **any such title does not affect their personal legal position**. They have two distinct positions as:

- A member of the board of directors; and
- A manager with management responsibilities as an **employee**

1.4 Non-executive directors

Key term

A **non-executive director** does not have a function to perform in a company's management but is involved in its governance.

In **listed companies**, corporate governance codes state that boards of directors are more likely to be fully effective if they comprise both **executive directors** and strong, independent **non-executive directors**. We shall look at this further in Chapter 22.

The main tasks of the NEDs are as follows:

- **Contribute** an **independent view** to the board's deliberations
- **Help the board provide** the company with **effective leadership**
- **Ensure** the **continuing effectiveness** of the **executive directors** and management
- **Ensure high standards** of **financial probity** on the part of the company

Non-executive and shadow directors are subject to the same duties as executive directors. Duties are discussed in Section 9.

1.5 The managing director

Key term

A **managing director** is one of the directors of the company appointed to carry out overall day-to-day management functions.

If the articles provide for it the board may appoint one or more directors to be **managing directors**. A managing director ('MD') does have a special position and has wider apparent powers than any director who is not appointed an MD.

Part F Management, administration and regulation of companies | **19: Company directors and other company officers**   **301**

1.6 Number of directors

Every company must have at least **one** director and for a **public** company the minimum is **two**. There is no statutory maximum in the UK but the articles usually impose a limit. At least one director must be a **natural person**, not a body corporate.

A **company** may be a director. In that case the director company sends an individual to attend board meetings as its representative.

1.7 The board of directors

Companies are run by the directors collectively, in a **board of directors**.

> The **board of directors** is the elected representative of the shareholders acting collectively in the .
> management of a company's affairs.

One of the basic principles of company law is that the **powers** which are delegated to the directors under the articles are given to them as a **collective body.**

The **board meeting** is the **proper place for the exercise of the powers,** unless they have been validly passed on, or 'sub-delegated', to committees or individual directors.

2 Appointment of directors

FAST FORWARD

The method of appointing directors, along with their rotation and co-option is **controlled** by the **articles.**

A director may be **appointed expressly**, in which case they are known as a *de jure* director.

Where a person acts as a director without actually being appointed as such (a *de facto* or **shadow director**) they incur the obligations and have some of the powers of a proper director. In addition, a shadow director is subject to many of the duties imposed on directors.

2.1 Appointment of first directors

The application for registration delivered to the Registrar to form a company includes particulars of the first directors, with their consents. On the formation of the company those persons become the first directors.

2.2 Appointment of subsequent directors

Once a company has been formed further directors can be appointed, either to **replace** existing directors or as **additional** directors.

Appointment of further directors is carried out **as the articles provide**. Most company articles allow for the appointment of directors:

- By **ordinary resolution** of the shareholders, and
- By a **decision** of the directors.

However the articles do not have to follow these provisions and may impose **different methods** on the company.

When the appointment of directors is proposed at a general meeting of a public company a **separate** resolution should be proposed for the election of **each director**. However the rule may be waived if a resolution to that effect is first carried without any vote being given against it.

2.3 Publicity

In addition to giving notice of the first directors, every company must within **14 days** give **notice** to the **Registrar** of any change among its directors. This includes any changes to the register of directors' residential addresses.

2.4 Age limit

The **minimum age** limit for a director is **16** and, unless the articles provide otherwise, there is no upper limit.

3 Remuneration of directors

FAST FORWARD

Directors are entitled to **fees** and **expenses** as directors as per the articles, and **emoluments** (and compensation for loss of office) as per their service contracts (which can be inspected by members). Some details are published in the directors' remuneration report along with accounts.

Details of directors' remuneration is usually contained within their service contract (see Section 4 Chapter 14). This is a contract where the director agrees to personally perform services for the company.

3.1 Directors' expenses

Most articles state that directors are entitled to **reimbursement** of **reasonable expenses** incurred whilst carrying out their duties or functions as directors.

In addition, most directors have **written service contracts** setting out their entitlement to emoluments and expenses. Where service contracts **guarantee employment** for longer than **two years** then an **ordinary resolution** must be passed by the members of the company that the contract is with.

3.2 Compensation for loss of office

Any director may receive **non-contractual** compensation for loss of office paid to him voluntarily. Any such compensation is lawful **only if** approved by members of the company in general meeting after proper disclosure has been made to all members, whether voting or not.

This only applies to uncovenanted payments; approval is not required where the company is contractually bound to make the payment.

Compensation paid to directors for loss of office is distinguished from any payments made to directors **as employees**. For example to settle claims arising from the premature termination of the service agreements. These are contractual payments which do not require approval in general meeting.

3.3 Directors' remuneration report

Quoted companies are required to include a **directors' remuneration report** as part of their annual report, part of which is subject to audit. The report must cover:

- The details of each **individual directors' remuneration package**
- The company's **remuneration policy**
- The **role** of the **board** and **remuneration committee** in deciding the **remuneration of directors**

Under s 421(3), it is the duty of the directors (including those who were a director in the preceding five years) to provide any information about themselves that is necessary to produce this report.

Quoted companies are required to allow a vote by members on the directors' remuneration report. The vote is purely advisory and does not mean the remuneration should change if the resolution is not passed. A negative vote would be a strong signal to the directors that the members are unhappy with remuneration levels.

Items not subject to audit

- Consideration by the directors (remuneration committee) of matters relating to directors' remuneration
- Statement of company's policy on directors' remuneration
- Performance graph (share performance)
- Directors' service contracts (dates, unexpired length, compensation payable for early termination)

Items subject to audit

- Salary/fees payable to each director
- Bonuses paid/to be paid
- Expenses
- Compensation for loss of office paid
- Any benefits received
- Share options and long term incentive schemes – performance criteria and conditions
- Pensions
- Excess retirement benefits
- Compensation to past directors
- Sums paid to third parties in respect of a director's services

3.4 Inspection of directors' service agreements

A company must make available for inspection by members a copy or particulars of **contracts of employment** between the company or a subsidiary with a director of the company. Such contracts must cover all services that a director may provide, including services outside the role of a director, and those made by a third party in respect of services that a director is contracted to perform.

Contracts must be **retained** for **one year** after expiry and must be available either at the **registered office**, or any other location permitted by the Secretary of State.

Prescribed particulars of **directors' emoluments** must be given in the accounts and also particulars of any **compensation for loss of office** and directors' **pensions**.

4 Vacation of office

A director may vacate office as director due to: **resignation**; **not going** for **re-election**; **death**; **dissolution** of the company; **removal**; **disqualification**.

A director may leave office in the following ways.

- **Resignation**
- Not **offering themselves for re-election** when their term of office ends
- **Death**
- **Dissolution of the company**
- Being **removed** from office
- Being **disqualified**

A form should be filed with the Registrar whenever and however a director vacates office.

4.1 Retirement and re-election of directors

The model articles for public companies provide the following rules for the retirement and re-election of all directors except the managing director ('rotation').

(a) Every year **half** (or the number nearest to half) shall **retire**; at the first AGM of the company they all retire.

(b) **Retiring directors** are **eligible** for **re-election**.

(c)   Those retiring shall be those **in office longest** since their last election.

(d)   When calculating which directors are required to retire by rotation, directors who were **appointed to the board** during the year (and therefore are obliged to stand for re-election) and those **retiring** and **not seeking re-election** are **not included** in the calculation.

The board of Teddy plc has the following directors at the start of its AGM on 31 December 20X7.

	Age	*When last re-elected*
Mrs Clare	42	31 December 20X4
Mr Paul	64	31 December 20X5
Mr Bob	27	31 December 20X5
Miss Alison	70	31 December 20X6
Mr Maurice	38	31 December 20X6
Mrs Pippa	34	31 December 20X6
Mr Gordon	43	2 May 20X7
Mrs Helen	41	2 May 20X7

At the board meeting on 2 May 20X7 Mr Gordon and Mrs Helen were appointed to fill casual vacancies and Mrs Clare was appointed managing director. The company has adopted model articles but also requires the re-election of directors who reach age 70.

Which directors would be due for re-election at the AGM on 31 December 20X7?

Answer

Mr Gordon and Mrs Helen must stand for re-election since they have been appointed during the year. Miss Alison must stand for re-election as she has reached the age of 70 and the articles require re-election when a director reaches that age.

Calculation of who is to retire by rotation excludes Mr Gordon, Mrs Helen, Miss Alison and Mrs Clare (as Managing Director), thus leaving four directors. Two of those must therefore retire, and as Mr Paul and Mr Bob have been in office the longest, it must be them.

4.2 Removal of directors

In addition to provisions in the articles for removal of directors, a director may be removed from office by **ordinary** resolution at a meeting of which **special notice** to the company has been given by the person proposing it: s 168.

On receipt of the special notice the company must send a copy to the director who may require that a **memorandum of reasonable length** shall be issued to members. They also have the **right to address the meeting** at which the resolution is considered.

The articles and the service contract of the director **cannot override the statutory power**. However, the articles can **permit dismissal without the statutory formalities** being observed, for example dismissal by a resolution of the board of directors.

The power to remove a director is **limited** in its effect in four ways.

Restrictions on power to remove directors	
Shareholding qualification to call a meeting	In order to propose a resolution to remove a director, the shareholder(s) involved must call a general meeting. To do this they must hold: • Either, 10% of the paid up share capital • Or, 10% of the voting rights where the company does not have shares

Restrictions on power to remove directors	
Shareholding to request a resolution	Where a meeting is already convened, 100 members holding an average £100 of share capital each may request a resolution to remove a director: s 338.
Weighted voting rights	A director who is also a member may have weighted voting rights given to them under the constitution for such an eventuality, so that they can automatically defeat any motion to remove them as a director: *Bushell v Faith 1970*
Class right agreement	It is possible to draft a shareholder agreement stating that a member holding each class of share must be present at a general meeting to constitute quorum. If so, a member holding shares of a certain class could prevent a director being removed by not attending the meeting.

Exam focus point

The courts have stressed that the s 168 power of members to remove directors is an important right, but you should remember the ways in which members' intentions might be frustrated.

The dismissal of a director may also entail payment of a **substantial sum** to settle their claim for breach of contract if they have a service contract. Under s 168(5), no resolution may deprive a removed director of any compensation or damages related to their termination to which they are entitled to.

Southern Foundries (1926) Ltd v Shirlaw 1940

The facts: In 1933 S entered into a written agreement to serve the company as managing director for ten years. In 1936 F Co gained control of the company and used their votes to alter its articles to confer on F Co power to remove any director from office. In 1937 F Co exercised the power by removing S from his directorship and thereby terminated his appointment as managing director (which he could only hold so long as he was a director).

Decision: The alteration of the articles was not a breach of the service agreement but the exercise of the power was a breach of the service agreement for which the company was liable.

Question
Resolution for removal of director

A company has three members who are also directors. Each holds 100 shares. Normally the shares carry one vote each, but the articles state that on a resolution for a director's removal, the director to be removed should have 3 votes per share. On a resolution for the removal of Jeremy, a director, Jeremy casts 300 votes against the resolution and the other members cast 200 votes for the resolution. Has Jeremy validly defeated the resolution?

Answer

Yes. This was confirmed in a case called *Bushell v Faith 1970*.

---

5 Disqualification of directors

FAST FORWARD

Directors may be required to vacate office because they have been disqualified on grounds dictated by the articles. Directors **may** be disqualified from a wider range of company involvements under the Company Directors Disqualification Act 1986 (CDDA).

A person cannot be appointed a director or continue in office if he is or becomes **disqualified** under the articles or statutory rules as explained below.

The articles often embody the statutory grounds of disqualification and add some optional extra grounds. Public company model articles provide that a director must vacate office if:

(a)   They are **disqualified** by the **Act** or any rule of law.

(b)   They become **bankrupt** or enter into an arrangement with creditors.

(c)   They become of **unsound mind**.

(d)   They **resign** by notice in writing.

(e)   They are **absent** for a period of **three consecutive months** from board meetings held during that period, without obtaining leave of absence **and** the other directors resolve that they shall on that account vacate office.

Unless the court approves it, an **undischarged bankrupt** cannot act as a director nor be concerned directly or indirectly in the management of a company. If they do continue to act, they become personally liable for the company's relevant debts.

5.1 Disqualification under statute

The **Company Directors Disqualification Act 1986** (CDDA 1986) provides that a **court may** formally **disqualify a person from being a director** or in any way directly or indirectly being concerned or taking part in the promotion, formation or management of a company: s1.

Therefore the terms of the disqualification order are very wide, and include acting as a consultant to a company. The Act, despite its title, is not limited to the disqualification of people who have been directors. **Any person** may be disqualified if they fall within the appropriate grounds. These are discussed later in the chapter, in the context of directors' duties.

In addition to the grounds of disqualification described above, the articles may provide that **a director shall automatically vacate office** if they are **absent** from **board meetings** (without obtaining the leave of the board) for a **specified period** (three months is usual). The effect of this disqualification depends on the words used.

- If the articles refer merely to 'absence' this includes involuntary absence due to illness.
- The words 'if they shall absent himself' restrict the disqualification to periods of voluntary absence.

The period of **three months** is reckoned to begin from the **last meeting** which the absent director did attend. The normal procedure is that a director who foresees a period of absence, applies for leave of absence at the last board meeting which they attend; the leave granted is duly minuted. They are not then absent 'without leave' during the period.

If they fail to obtain leave but later offer a reasonable explanation the other directors may let the matter drop by simply not resolving that they shall vacate office. The general intention of the rule is to **impose a sanction against slackness**; a director has a duty to attend board meetings when they are able to do so.

Question	Disqualification of directors

Which of the following are grounds provided for a director being compelled to leave office?

A   Becoming bankrupt

B   Entering into an arrangement with personal creditors

C   Becoming of unsound mind

D   Resigning by notice in writing

E   Being absent from board meetings for six consecutive months without obtaining leave of absence

Answer

All of them.

Question	Vacation of office

The articles of Robert Ltd provide that if a director should 'absent himself' for a period exceeding three months from board meetings, the director shall automatically vacate office. Miles, a director, obtains a

Part F Management, administration and regulation of companies | **19: Company directors and other company officers**   **307**

twelve month leave of absence to go abroad. Whilst abroad, he contracts a rare illness; on his return he is rushed to hospital and remains there for nine months. On the day of his release, there is a board meeting which he does not attend, and he resolves not to attend board meetings again. After a further two months he has a relapse and dies a fortnight later. At what point does he cease to be a director?

A   After three months of his holiday
B   After three months of hospitalisation
C   At the point where he decides not to attend board meetings again
D   When he dies

Answer

D   The board can grant leave of absence, and 'absenting himself' does not include forced hospitalisation. The period of three months **begins** on his release from hospital, and has not been completed when he dies.

5.2 Grounds for disqualification of directors

Directors may be **disqualified** from acting as directors or being involved in the management of companies in a number of circumstances. They must be disqualified if the company is insolvent, and the director is found to be unfit to be concerned with management of a company.

Under the CDDA 1986 the court **may** make a disqualification order on any of the following grounds.

(a)   **Where a person is convicted of an indictable offence in connection with the promotion, formation, management or liquidation of a company or with the receivership or management of a company's property** (s 2).

      An indictable offence is an offence which may be tried at a crown court; it is therefore a serious offence. It need not actually have been tried on indictment but if it was the maximum period for which the court can disqualify is 15 years, compared with only 5 years if the offence was dealt with summarily (at the magistrates court).

(b)   **Where it appears that a person has been persistently in default in relation to provisions of company legislation.**

      This legislation requires any return, account or other document to be filed with, delivered or sent or notice of any matter to be given to the Registrar (s 3). Three defaults in five years are conclusive evidence of persistent default.

      The maximum period of disqualification under this section is five years.

(c)   **Where it appears that a person has been guilty of fraudulent trading**. This means carrying on business with intent to defraud creditors or for any fraudulent purpose whether or not the company has been, or is in the course of being, wound-up (see Chapter 21).

      The person does not actually have to have been convicted of fraudulent trading. The legislation also applies to anyone who has otherwise been guilty, of any fraud in relation to the company or of any breach of their duty as an officer (s 4).

      The maximum period of disqualification under this section is 15 years.

(d)   **Where the Secretary of State acting on a report made by the inspectors or from information or documents obtained under the Companies Act, applies to the court for an order believing it to be expedient in the public interest.**

      If the court is satisfied that the person's conduct in relation to the company makes that person unfit to be concerned in the management of a company, then it may make a disqualification order (s 8). Again the maximum is 15 years.

(e)   **Where a director was involved in certain competition violations**. Maximum – 15 years.

(f) **Where a director of an insolvent company has participated in wrongful trading (s 10)** (see Chapter 21). Maximum – 15 years.

The court **must** make an order where it is satisfied that the following apply:

(a) A person has been a director of a company which has at any time become **insolvent** (whether while they were a director or subsequently).

(b) Their conduct as a director of that company makes them **unfit** to be **concerned** in the **management** of a company. The courts may also take into account their conduct as a director of other companies, whether or not these other companies are insolvent. Directors can be disqualified under this section even if they take no active part in the running of the business.

In such cases the **minimum** period of disqualification is two years.

Illustration

Offences for which directors have been disqualified include the following.

(a) **Insider dealing**: *R v Goodman 1993*
(b) **Failure** to **keep proper accounting records**: *Re Firedart Ltd, Official Receiver v Fairall 1994*
(c) **Failure to read the company's accounts**: *Re Continental Assurance Co of London plc 1996*
(d) **Loans** to another company for the purposes of purchasing its own shares with **no grounds for believing the money would be repaid**: *Re Continental Assurance Co of London plc 1996*
(e) **Loans** to associated companies on **uncommercial terms** to the detriment of creditors: *Re Greymoat Ltd 1997*

5.3 Disqualification periods

In *Re Sevenoaks Stationers (Retail) Ltd 1991* the Court of Appeal laid down certain 'disqualification brackets'. The appropriate period of disqualification which should be imposed was a **minimum of two to five years** if the conduct was not very serious, **six to ten years** if the conduct was serious but did not merit the maximum penalty, and **over ten years** only in particularly serious cases.

Disqualification as a director need not mean disqualification from all involvement in management: (*Re Griffiths 1997*), and it may mean that the director can continue to act as an **unpaid director** (*Re Barings plc 1998*), but only if the court gives leave to act.

5.3.1 Mitigation of disqualification

Examples of circumstances which have led the court to imposing a lower period of disqualification include the following.

- **Lack of dishonesty**: *Re Burnham Marketing Services Ltd 1993*
- **Loss of director's own money** in the company: *Re GSAR Realisations Ltd 1993*
- **Absence of personal gain**, for example excessive remuneration: *Re GSAR Realisations Ltd 1993*
- **Efforts to mitigate** the situation: *Re Burnham Marketing Services Ltd 1993*
- **Likelihood of re-offending**: *Re Grayan Building Services Ltd 1995*
- **Proceedings hanging over director** for a long time: *Re Aldermanbury Trust 1993*

5.4 Procedures for disqualification

Company administrators, receivers and liquidators all have a statutory duty to report directors to the Government where they believe the conditions for a disqualification order have been satisfied.

The Secretary of State then decides whether to apply to the court for an order, but if they do decide to apply they must do so within two years of the date on which the company became insolvent.

Question

In what circumstances can a court make a disqualification order against a director of a company?

Answer

The provisions for disqualification of directors are contained in the Company Directors Disqualification Act 1986. A court may, by order, disqualify a person from being a director, liquidator, administrator, receiver or manager of a company, and from being concerned in the promotion or management of any company.

The order may be made in any one of the following circumstances.

(a)   The director concerned is convicted of an indictable offence in connection with a company.

(b)   The director concerned has been persistently in default in relation to company law requirements requiring the delivery to the Registrar of annual accounts, the annual return and other documents. A previous decision of a court on three previous occasions in five years that the person concerned has been in default in compliance with these requirements is conclusive evidence of 'persistent' default.

(c)   The director concerned has been guilty of fraudulent trading.

(d)   The Secretary of State applies for disqualification in the public interest. This would arise from an investigation by Government inspectors or documents obtained under the Companies Act.

(e)   The director has been found to be in breach of certain aspects of competition law.

(f)   The director has participated in wrongful trading in insolvency.

In general, disqualification may be ordered for up to 15 years. But the maximum is 5 years in case (b) above or when the order is made by a magistrates' court. A person subject to disqualification may apply to the court for remission of the order.

Bankruptcy

An undischarged bankrupt may not, without leave of the court, act as a director of a company or be concerned in the management or promotion of a company.

Here the disqualification is the automatic result of the bankruptcy order made against him by the court.

6 Powers of directors

FAST FORWARD

> The **powers** of the directors are **defined** by the **articles**.

The powers of the directors are **defined by the articles**. The directors are usually authorised 'to manage the company's business' and 'to exercise all the powers of the company for any purpose connected with the company's business'.

Therefore they may take **any decision which is within the capacity** of the company **unless** either **the Act** or **the articles** themselves **require** that the **decision shall be taken by the members in general meeting**.

6.1 Restrictions on directors' powers

FAST FORWARD

> Directors' powers may be restricted by statute or by the articles. The directors have a duty to exercise their powers in what they honestly believe to be the **best interests** of the company and for the **purposes** for which the powers are given.

6.1.1 Statutory restrictions

Many transactions, such as an alteration of the articles or a reduction of capital, must by law be effected by passing a **special resolution**. If the directors propose such changes they must secure the passing of the appropriate resolution by shareholders in a general meeting.

6.1.2 Restrictions imposed by articles

As an example, the articles often set a maximum amount which the directors may borrow. If the directors wish to exceed that limit, they should **seek authority** from a **general meeting**.

When the directors clearly have the necessary power, their decision may be challenged if they exercise the power in the wrong way. They must exercise their powers:

- In what they **honestly believe to be the interests of the company:** *Re Smith v Fawcett Ltd 1942*
- For a **proper purpose**, being the purpose for which the power is given: *Bamford v Bamford 1969*.

We shall come back to these points when we consider directors' duties.

6.1.3 Members' control of directors

There is a **division of power** between the board of directors who manage the business and the members who as owners take the major policy decisions at general meetings. How, then, do the owners seek to 'control' the people in charge of their property?

- The members **appoint** the directors and may **remove** them from office under s 168, or by other means.
- The members can, by **altering the articles** (special resolution needed), re-allocate powers between the board and the general meeting.
- Articles may allow the members to pass a **special resolution ordering** the **directors to act** (or **refrain from acting**) in a **particular way**. Such special resolutions cannot invalidate anything the directors have already done.

Remember that **directors are not agents of the members.** They cannot be instructed by the members in general meeting as to how they should exercise their powers. **The directors' powers are derived from the company as a whole** and are to be exercised by the directors as they think best in the **interests of the company**.

6.1.4 Control by the law

Certain powers must be exercised **'for the proper purpose'** and all powers must be exercised *bona fide* **for the benefit of the company**. Failure by the directors to comply with these rules will result in the **court setting aside their powers** unless the shareholders **ratify** the directors' actions by **ordinary resolution** (50 % majority).

7 Powers of the managing director

> One or more directors may be appointed by the board as **managing director**. The managing director has **apparent** authority to make business contracts on behalf of the company. The managing director's **actual** authority is whatever the board gives them.

If the articles provide for it the **board** may appoint one or more directors to be **managing directors**.

In their dealings with outsiders the managing director has **apparent authority** as agent of the company to **make business contracts**. No other director, even if they work full time, has that **apparent** authority as a director, though if they are employed as a manager they may have apparent authority at a slightly lower level.

The managing director's **actual authority** is whatever the board gives them.

Part F Management, administration and regulation of companies | **19: Company directors and other company officers** 311

Although a managing director (MD) has this special status, their appointment as MD may be **terminated** like that of any other director (or employee); they then revert to the position of an ordinary director. Alternatively the company in general meeting may **remove them from their office of director** and they immediately cease to be MD since being a director is a necessary qualification for holding the post of MD.

7.1 Agency and the managing director

The directors are **agents of the company, not the members**. Where they have **actual or usual** authority they can **bind the company**. In addition a director may have **apparent authority** by virtue of **holding out**.

Holding out is a basic rule of the law of agency and we saw it in Chapter 12. This means, if the principal (the company) holds out a person as its authorised agent they are estopped from denying that they are its **authorised agent**. They are bound by a contract entered into by them on the company's behalf.

> **Apparent authority** is the authority which an agent appears to have to a third party. A contract made within the scope of such authority will bind the principal even though the agent was not following their instructions.

Therefore if the board of directors **permits a director** to behave as if he were a **managing director** duly appointed when in fact they are not, the company may be bound by their actions.

A managing director has, by virtue of their position, **apparent authority** to make commercial contracts for the company. Moreover if the board allows a director to enter into contracts, being aware of their dealings and taking no steps to disown them, the company will usually be bound.

> *Freeman & Lockyer v Buckhurst Park Properties (Mangal) Ltd 1964*
>
> *The facts:* A company carried on a business as property developers. The articles contained a power to appoint a managing director but this was never done. One of the directors of the company, to the knowledge but without the express authority of the remainder of the board, acted as if he were managing director. He found a purchaser for an estate and also engaged a firm of architects to make a planning application. The company later refused to pay the architect's fees on the grounds that the director had no actual or apparent authority.
>
> *Decision:* The company was liable since by its acquiescence it had represented that the director was a managing director with the authority to enter into contracts that were normal commercial arrangements, and which the board itself would have been able to enter.

> Situations where the facts are similar to the *Freeman & Lockyer* case often occur in law exams so be prepared to spot them.

In the *Freeman & Lockyer* case, Diplock L J laid down four conditions which must be satisfied in claiming under the principle of **holding out**. The claimant must show that:

(a) A **representation** was made to them that the **agent had** the **authority** to enter on behalf of the company into the contract of the kind sought to be enforced.

(b) Such **representation** was **made by a person** who had **'actual' authority** to **manage** the **business** of the company.

   The board of directors would certainly have actual authority to manage the company. Some commentators have also argued that the managing director has actual or apparent authority to make representations about the extent of the actual authority of other company agents. (However a third party cannot rely on the representations a managing director makes about their own actual authority).

(c) They were **induced** by the **representation** to enter into the contract; they had in fact relied on it.

(d) There must be **nothing** in the **articles** which would prevent the company from giving valid authority to its agent to enter into the contract.

Under the articles of association of Recycle Ltd the directors of the company need the consent of the general meeting by ordinary resolution to borrow sums of money in excess of £50,000. The other articles are all standard model articles.

Mary has been appointed managing director of the company and she holds 1% of the issued shares of the company. Early in May 20X5 Mary entered into two transactions for the benefit of Recycle Ltd. First, she arranged to borrow £100,000 from Conifer Bank Ltd, secured by a floating charge on the company's assets. She had not sought the approval of the members as required by the articles. Secondly, she placed a contract worth £10,000 with Saw Ltd to buy some agricultural machinery.

Advise the directors of Recycle Ltd whether they are bound by the agreements with Conifer Bank Ltd and Saw Ltd.

Answer

The enforceability of the loan agreement and floating charge by Conifer Bank Ltd against Recycle Ltd is determined by reference to s 40. The transaction is *intra vires* the company, but beyond the authority of the managing director. Mary failed to obtain an ordinary resolution of the company as required by its articles of association.

S 40 provides that, in favour of a person dealing in good faith with a company, the power of the board of directors to bind the company or (importantly in this case) to authorise others to do so, shall be deemed to be free of any limitation under the company's constitution.

There is no suggestion that Conifer Bank Ltd has not acted in good faith and it will be presumed that it has in fact acted in good faith unless the contrary is proved by the company.

The articles allow the board to appoint a managing director. In that position, Mary has apparent authority as agent of the company to make business contracts including the type of transaction entered into with Saw Ltd.

Under the Act, the restriction placed on her actual authority (by the article requiring an ordinary resolution) shall be deemed not to exist in favour of the third party, Conifer Bank Ltd. The power of the board to authorise Mary to bind the company is deemed to be free of any constitutional limitation.

In conclusion, Recycle Ltd will be bound to the contracts with both Conifer Bank Ltd and Saw Ltd.

8 Powers of an individual director

The position of any other individual director (not an MD) who is also an employee is that:

(a)   They **do not have the apparent authority to make general contracts** which attaches to the position of MD, but they have **whatever apparent authority attaches** to their **management position**.

(b)   **Removal** from the office of director may be a **breach** of their **service contract** if that agreement stipulates that they are to have the status of director as part of the conditions of employment.

9 Duties of directors

 FAST FORWARD

The Company's Act 2006 sets out the **seven principal duties** of **directors**

 BPP
LEARNING MEDIA

Part F Management, administration and regulation of companies | **19: Company directors and other company officers**   313

The Company's Act 2006 sets out the **principal duties** that directors owe to their company. Many of these duties developed over time through the operation of **common law** and **equity,** or are **fiduciary duties** which have now been codified to make the law clearer and more accessible.

Point to note

> When deciding whether a duty has been broken, the courts will consider the Companies Act primarily. All case law explained in this section applied before the 2006 Act and is included here to help you understand the types of situation that arise and how the law will be interpreted and applied by the courts in the future.

Key term

> **Fiduciary duty** is a duty imposed upon certain persons because of the position of trust and confidence in which they stand in relation to another. The duty is more onerous than generally arises under a contractual or tort relationship. It requires full disclosure of information held by the fiduciary, a strict duty to account for any profits received as a result of the relationship, and a duty to avoid conflict of interest.

Broadly speaking directors must be **honest** and **not allow their personal interests to conflict with their duties as directors**. The directors are said to hold a **fiduciary position** since they make contracts as **agents** of the company and have control of its property.

The duties included in the Companies Act 2006 form a **code of conduct** for directors. They do not tell them what to do but rather create a framework that sets out how they are expected to **behave** generally. This code is important as it addresses situations where:

- A director may put their **own interests** ahead of the company's, and
- A director may be **negligent** and liable to an action under tort.

9.1 Who are the duties owed to?

Section 170 makes it clear that directors owe their duties to the company, **not** the members. This means that the **only company itself can take action against a director** who breaches them. However, it is possible for a member to bring a derivative claim against the director on behalf of the company.

The effect of the **duties are cumulative**, in other words, a director owes **every duty** to the company that could apply in any given situation. The Act provides guidance for this. Where a director is offered a bribe for instance they will be breaking the duty not to accept a benefit from a third party and they will also not be promoting the company for the benefit of the members.

When deciding whether or not a director has breached a duty, the court should consider their actions in the context of **each individual duty** in turn.

9.2 Who are the duties owed by?

Every person who is **classed as a director** under the Act owes the duties that are outlined below. Certain aspects of the duties regarding conflicts of interest and accepting benefits from third parties also apply to **past directors**. This is to prevent directors from exploiting a situation for their own benefit by simply resigning. The courts are directed to apply duties to **shadow directors** where they would have been applied to them previously under common law and equity.

Directors must at all times continue to **act in accordance with all other laws**; no authorisation is given by the duties for a director to breach any other law or regulation.

9.3 The duties and the articles

The articles may provide more onerous regulations than the Act, but they may not reduce the level of duty expected unless it is in the following circumstances:

- If a director has **acted in accordance with the articles** they cannot be in breach of the duty to exercise independent judgement.
- Some **conflicts of interest by independent directors** are permissible by the articles.

- Directors will not be in breach of duty concerning **conflicts of interest** if they follow any **provisions in the articles for dealing with them** as long as the provisions are lawful.
- The company may **authorise anything** that would otherwise be a breach of duty.

9.4 The duties of directors

FAST FORWARD

The **statutory duties** owed by directors are to:

- Act within their powers
- Promote the success of the company
- Exercise independent judgement
- Exercise reasonable skill, care and diligence
- Avoid conflicts of interest
- Not to accept benefits from third parties
- Declare an interest in a proposed transaction or arrangement

We shall now consider the duties placed on directors by the Act. Where cases are mentioned it is to **demonstrate** the previous common law or equitable principle that courts will follow when interpreting and applying the Act.

9.4.1 Duty to act within powers (s 171)

The directors owe a duty to act in accordance with the company's constitution, and only to exercise powers for the purposes for what they were conferred. They have a **fiduciary duty to the company to exercise their powers bona fide in what they honestly consider to be the interests of the company**: Re *Smith v Fawcett Ltd 1942*. This honest belief is effective even if, in fact, the interests of the company were not served.

This duty is owed **to the company** and **not generally to individual shareholders**. The directors will not generally be liable to the members if, for instance, they purchase shares without disclosing information affecting the share price: *Percival v Wright 1902*.

In exercising the powers given to them by the articles the directors have a fiduciary duty not only to act *bona fide* **but also only to use their powers for a proper purpose.** *Bamford v Bamford 1969*

The powers are restricted to the **purposes** for **which they were given**. If the directors infringe this rule by exercising their powers for a collateral purpose the transaction will be invalid **unless** the **company** in **general meeting authorises it, or subsequently ratifies it**.

Most of the directors' powers are found in the **articles,** so this duty means that the directors must not act outside their power or the capacity of the company (in other words *ultra vires*).

If the irregular use of directors' powers is in the **allotment of shares** the votes attached to the new shares may not be used in reaching a decision in general meeting to sanction it.

> *Howard Smith Ltd v Ampol Petroleum Ltd 1974*
>
> *The facts:* Shareholders who held 55% of the issued shares intended to reject a takeover bid for the company. The directors honestly believed that it was in the company's interest that the bid should succeed. The directors therefore allotted new shares to the prospective bidder so that the shareholders opposed to the bid would then have less than 50% of the enlarged capital and the bid would succeed.
>
> *Decision:* The allotment was invalid. 'It must be unconstitutional for directors to use their fiduciary powers over the shares in the company purely for the purpose of destroying an existing majority or creating a new majority which did not previously exist'.

Any **shareholder** may **apply to the court** to declare that a transaction in breach of s 171 should be set aside. However the practice of the courts is generally to **remit the issue** to the **members in general meeting** to see if the members wish to confirm the transaction. If the majority approve what has been done (or have authorised it in advance) that decision is treated as a proper case of **majority control** to which the minority must normally submit.

Hogg v Cramphorn 1966

The facts: The directors of a company issued shares to trustees of a pension fund for employees to prevent a takeover bid which they honestly thought would be bad for the company. The shares were paid for with money belonging to the company provided from an employees' benevolent and pension fund account. The shares carried 10 votes each and as a result the trustees and directors together had control of the company. The directors had power to issue shares but not to attach more than one vote to each. A minority shareholder brought the action on behalf of all the other shareholders.

Decision: If the directors act honestly in the best interests of the company, the company in general meeting can ratify the use of their powers for an improper purpose, so the allotment of the shares would be valid. But only one vote could be attached to each of the shares because that is what the articles provided.

Bamford v Bamford 1969

The facts: The directors of Bamford Ltd allotted 500,000 unissued shares to a third party to thwart a takeover bid. A month after the allotment a general meeting was called and an ordinary resolution was passed ratifying the allotment. The holders of the newly-issued shares did not vote. The claimants (minority shareholders) alleged that the allotment was not made for a proper purpose.

Decision: The ratification was valid and the allotment was good. There had been a breach of fiduciary duty but the act had been validated by an ordinary resolution passed in general meeting.

These cases can be distinguished from the *Howard Smith* case (where the allotment was invalid) in that in the *Howard Smith* case the original majority would not have sanctioned the use of directors' powers. In the *Bamford* case the decision could have been sanctioned by a vote which excluded the new shareholders.

Ratification is not effective when it attempts to validate a transaction when

- It constitutes **fraud on a minority**.
- It involves **misappropriation of assets**.
- The transaction **prejudices creditors' interests** at a time when the company is insolvent.

Under s 239, any resolution which proposes to ratify the acts of a director which are negligent in default or in breach of duty or trust regarding the company must exclude the director or any members connected with them from the vote.

Most of the cases discussed above concern the **duty of directors** to exercise their power to allot shares. This is only one of the powers given to directors that are subject to this **fiduciary duty**. Others include:

- Power to borrow
- Power to give security
- Power to refuse to register a transfer of shares
- Power to call general meetings
- Power to circulate information to shareholders

9.4.2 Duty to promote the success of the company (s 172)

An overriding theme of the Companies Act 2006 is the principle that the **purpose of the legal framework** surrounding companies should be **to help companies do business**. Their main purpose is to create wealth for the shareholders.

This theme is evident in the **duty of directors to promote the success of a company**. During the development of the Act, the independent Company Law Review recommended that company law should consider the interests of those who companies are run for. It decided that the new Act should embrace the principle of **'enlightened shareholder value'**.

In essence, this principle means that the law should encourage **longtermism** and **regard for all stakeholders** by directors and that **stakeholder interests** should be **pursued** in an **enlightened** and **inclusive** way.

To achieve this, a duty of directors to act in a way, which, in **good faith**, promotes the success of the company for the benefit of the members as a whole, was created.

The requirements of this duty are difficult to define and possibly problematic to apply, so the Act provides directors with a **non-exhaustive list** of issues to keep in mind.

When exercising this duty directors should consider:

- The **consequences of decisions** in the long term.
- The **interests of** their **employees**.
- The need to **develop good relationships** with **customers** and **suppliers**.
- The **impact of the company** on the **local community** and the **environment**.
- The desirability of **maintaining high standards of business conduct** and a **good reputation**.
- The need to **act fairly as between all members** of the company.

The list identifies areas of **particular importance** and **modern day expectations** of **responsible business behaviour**. For example the interests of the company's employees and the impact of the company's operations on the community and the environment.

The **Act does not define** what should be regarded as the **success of a company**. This is down to a director's judgement in good faith. This is important as it ensures that business decisions are for the directors rather than the courts.

No guidance is given for what the **correct course of action** would be where the various s172 **duties are in conflict**. For example a decision to shut down an office may be in the long term best interests of the company but it is certainly not in the interests of the employees affected, nor the local community in which they live. Conflicts such as this are inevitable and could potentially leave directors open to breach of duty claims by a wide range of stakeholders if they do not deal with them carefully.

9.4.3 Duty to exercise independent judgement (s 173)

This is a simple duty that states directors must **exercise independent judgement.** They should **not delegate** their powers of decision-making or be **swayed by the influence of others**. Directors may delegate their functions to others, but they must continue to make independent decisions.

This duty is not infringed by acting in accordance with any agreement by the company that restricts the exercise of discretion by directors, or by acting in a way authorised by the company's constitution.

9.4.4 Duty to exercise reasonable skill, care and diligence (s 174)

Directors have a **duty of care** to show **reasonable skill, care and diligence**.

Section 174 provides that a director 'owes a duty to his company to exercise the same standard of 'care, skill and diligence that would be exercised by a reasonably diligent person with:

(a) *The general knowledge, skill and experience that may reasonably be expected of a person carrying out the functions carried out by the director in relation to the company; and*

(b) *The general knowledge, skill and experience that the director has.*

There is therefore a **reasonableness test** consisting of two parts:

(a) An **objective test**

Did the director act in a manner reasonably expected of a person performing the same role?

A director, when carrying out his functions, must show such **care** as could **reasonably** be expected from a **competent person** in that role. If a 'reasonable' director could be expected to act in a certain way, it is no defence for a director to claim, for example, lack of expertise.

(b)   A **subjective test**

Did the director act in accordance with the skill, knowledge and experience that they actually have?

In the case of *Re City Equitable Fire and Insurance Co Ltd 1925* it was held that a director is expected to show the **degree of skill** which may **reasonably be expected** from a person of his knowledge and experience. The standard set is personal to the person in each case. An accountant who is a director of a mining company is not required to have the expertise of a mining engineer, but they should show the expertise of an accountant.

The duty to be competent extends to **non-executive directors**, who may be liable if they fail in their duty.

Dorchester Finance Co Ltd v Stebbing 1977

The facts: Of all the company's three directors S, P and H, only S worked full-time. P and H signed blank cheques at S's request who used them to make loans which became irrecoverable. The company sued all three; P and H, who were experienced accountants, claimed that as non-executive directors they had no liability.

Decision: All three were liable, P's and H's acts in signing blank cheques being negligent and not showing the necessary objective or subjective skill and care.

In other words, the **standard of care** is an objective 'competent' standard, plus a higher 'personal' standard of application. If the director actually had particular expertise that leads to a higher standard of competence being reasonably expected.

9.4.5 Duty to avoid conflicts of interest (s 175)

Directors have a **duty to avoid circumstances** where their **personal interests conflict**, or may possibly conflict, **with the company's interests**. It may occur when a director makes personal use of information, property or opportunities belonging to the company, whether or not the company was able to take advantage of them at the time.

Therefore directors must be careful not to breach this duty when they **enter into a contract** with their company or if they **make a profit in the course of being a director**.

This duty does not apply to a conflict of interest in relation to a transaction or arrangement with the company, provided the director declared an interest (see Section 9.4.7 below).

As **agents**, directors have a **duty to avoid a conflict of interest**. In particular:

- The directors must **retain their freedom of action** and **not fetter their discretion** by agreeing to vote as some other person may direct.
- The directors owe a fiduciary duty to **avoid a conflict of duty and personal interest.**
- The directors **must not obtain any personal advantage** from their position as directors **without the consent of the company** for whatever gain or profit they have obtained.

The following cases are important in the area of conflict of interest.

Regal (Hastings) Ltd v Gulliver 1942

The facts: The company owned a cinema. It had the opportunity of acquiring two more cinemas through a subsidiary to be formed with an issued capital of £5,000. However the company could not proceed with this scheme since it only had £2,000 available for investment in the subsidiary.

The directors and their friends therefore subscribed £3,000 for shares of the new company to make up the required £5,000. The chairman acquired his shares not for himself but as nominee of other persons. The company's solicitor also subscribed for shares. The share capital of the two companies (which then owned three cinemas) was sold at a price which yielded a profit of £2.80 per share of the new company in which the directors had invested. The new controlling shareholder of the company caused it to sue the directors to recover the profit which they had made.

Decision:

(a)   The directors were **accountable** to the company for their profit since they had obtained it from an opportunity which came to them as directors.

(b)   It was **immaterial** that the **company** had **lost nothing** since it had been unable to make the investment itself.

(c)   The directors might have kept their profit if the company had **agreed** by resolution passed in general meeting that they should do so. The directors might have used their votes to approve their action since it was not fraudulent (there was no misappropriation of the company's property).

(d)   The chairman was not accountable for the profit on his shares since he did not obtain it for himself. The solicitor was not accountable for his profit since he was **not a director** and so was not subject to the rule of accountability as a director for personal profits obtained in that capacity.

Industrial Development Consultants Ltd v Cooley 1972

The facts: C was managing director of the company which provided consultancy services to gas companies. A gas company was unlikely to award a particular contract to the company but C realised that, acting personally, he might be able to obtain it. He told the board of his company that he was ill and persuaded them to release him from his service agreement. On ceasing to be a director of the company C obtained the contract on his own behalf. The company sued him to recover the profits of the contract.

Decision: C was accountable to his old company for his profit.

Directors will not be liable for a breach of this duty if:

- The **members** of the company **authorised** their actions
- The **situation cannot reasonably be regarded** as likely to give rise to a conflict of interest
- The **actions have been authorised by the other directors**. This only applies if they are genuinely independent from the transaction and:
    - If the company is private - the articles do not restrict such authorisation, or
    - If it is public - the articles expressly permit it.

9.4.6 Duty not to accept benefits from third parties (s 176)

This duty **prohibits the acceptance of benefits** (including bribes) from third parties conferred by reason of them being director, or doing, (or omitting to do) something as a director. Where a director accepts a benefit that may also create or potentially create a conflict of interest, they will also be in breach of their s 175 duty (see above).

Unlike s 175, an act which would potentially be in breach of this duty **cannot be authorised** by the **directors**, but **members do have the right to authorise it**.

Directors will not be in breach of this duty if the acceptance of the benefit **cannot reasonably** be regarded as likely to give rise to a conflict of interest.

9.4.7 Duty to declare interest in proposed transaction or arrangement (s 177)

Directors are required to disclose to the other directors the nature and extent of any interest, direct or indirect, that they have in relation to a **proposed transaction** or **arrangement** with the **company**. Even if the director is not a party to the transaction, the duty may apply if they are aware, or ought reasonably to be aware, of the interest. For example, the interest of another person in a contract with the company may require disclosure under this duty if that other person's interest is a direct or indirect interest on the part of the director.

Directors are required to disclose their interest in any transaction **before** the company enters into the transaction. Disclosure can be made by:

- Written notice
- General notice
- Verbally at a board meeting

Disclosure to the **members** is **not** sufficient to discharge the duty. Directors must declare the **nature** and **extent** of their interest to the **other directors** as well.

If the declaration becomes **void** or **inaccurate**, a **further declaration** should be made.

No declaration of interest is required if the director's interest in the transaction **cannot reasonably** be regarded as likely to give rise to a conflict of interest.

9.5 Consequences of breach of duty

Breach of duty comes under the **civil law** rather than criminal law and, as mentioned earlier, the company itself must take up the action. This usually means the other directors starting proceedings.

Consequences for breach include:

- **Damages** payable to the company where it has suffered loss.
- **Restoration** of company property
- **Repayment of any profits** made by the director
- **Rescission of contract** (where the director did not disclose an interest)

9.6 Declaration of an interest in an existing transaction or arrangement (s 182)

Directors have a statutory obligation to declare any direct or indirect interest in an existing transaction entered into by the company. This obligation is almost identical to the duty to disclose an interest in a proposed transaction or arrangement under s 177 (see above). However, this section is relevant to transactions or arrangements that have already occurred.

A declaration under s 182 is **not** required if:

- It has **already been disclosed** as a proposed transaction under s 177
- The director is **not aware** of either
    - **The interest** they have in the transaction, or
    - In **the transaction** itself
- The director's interest in the transaction **cannot reasonably** be regarded as likely to give rise to a conflict of interest
- The **other directors are aware** (or reasonably should be aware) of the situation
- It concerns the **director's service contract** and it has been considered by a board meeting or special board committee

Where a declaration is required it should be made as soon as **reasonably practicable** either:

- By written notice
- By general notice
- Verbally at a board meeting

If the declaration becomes **void** or **inaccurate**, a **further declaration** should be made.

9.7 Other controls over directors

The table below summarises other statutory controls over directors included in the Companies Act 2006.

CA06 Ref	Control
188	Directors' service contracts lasting more than two years must be approved by the members.
190	Directors or any person connected to them may not acquire a non-cash asset from the company without approval of the members. This does not apply where the asset's value is less than £5,000, or less than 10% of the company's asset value. All sales of assets with a value exceeding £100,000 must be approved.
197	Any loans given to directors, or guarantees provided as security for loans provided to directors, must be approved by members.
198	Expands section 197 to prevent unapproved quasi-loans to directors (public companies only).
201	Expands section 197 to prevent unapproved credit transactions by the company for the benefit of a director (public companies only).
217	Non-contractual payments to directors for loss of office must be approved by the members.

9.8 Examples of remedies against directors

Remedies against directors for breach of duties include accounting to the company for a **personal gain**, **indemnifying the company**, and **rescission of contracts** made with the company.

The type of remedy varies with the breach of duty.

(a) The director may have to **account for a personal gain:** *Regal (Hastings) Ltd v Gulliver 1942*.

(b) They may have to **indemnify the company** against loss caused by their negligence such as an unlawful transaction which they approved.

(c) If they contract with the company in a conflict of interest the **contract may be rescinded by the company**. However under common law rules the company cannot both affirm the contract and recover the director's profit: *Burland v Earle 1902*.

(d) The court may declare that a transaction is *ultra vires* or unlawful: *Re Lee Behrens & Co 1932*.

A company may, either by its **articles** or by **passing a resolution** in general meeting, **authorise or ratify** the conduct of directors in breach of duty. There are some limits on the power of members in general meeting to **sanction a breach of duty** by directors or to release them from their strict obligations.

(a) If the directors **defraud** the company and vote in general meeting to approve their own fraud, their votes are invalid (*Cook v Deeks 1916*).

(b) If the directors **allot shares** to alter the balance of votes in a general meeting the votes attached to those shares may not be cast to support a resolution approving the issue (see *Bamford's* case above).

9.9 Directors' liability for acts of other directors

A director is **not liable** for acts of fellow directors. However if they become aware of serious breaches of duty by other directors, they may have a duty to inform members of them or to take control of assets of the company without having proper delegated authority to do so.

In such cases the director is **liable for their own negligence** in what they allow to happen and not directly for the misconduct of the other directors.

9.10 Directors' personal liability

As a general rule a director has no personal liability for the debts of the company. But there are certain exceptions.

- Personal liability **may arise** by **lifting the veil** of incorporation.
- A **limited company** may by its articles or by **special resolution** provide that its directors shall have unlimited liability for its debts
- A director may be **liable** to the **company's creditors** in certain circumstances.

Can a director be held personally liable for **negligent advice** given by his company? The case below shows that they can, but only when they assume responsibility in a personal capacity for advice given, rather than simply giving advice in their capacity as a director.

Williams and Another v Natural Life Health Foods Ltd 1998

The facts: The director was sued personally by claimants who claimed they were misled by the company's brochure. The director helped prepare the brochure, and the brochure described him as the source of the company's expertise. The claimants did not however deal with the director but with other employees.

Decision: The House of Lords overruled the Court of Appeal, and ruled that the director was not personally liable. In order to have been liable, there would have had to have been evidence that the director had assumed personal responsibility. Merely acting as a director and advertising his earlier experience did not amount to assumption of personal liability.

9.11 Negligence

FAST FORWARD Directors have a duty to show **reasonable competence**.

The company may recover damages from its directors for loss caused by their negligence. However something more than imprudence or want of care must be shown. It must be shown to be a case of **gross negligence**. This was defined in *Overend Gurney & Co v Gibb 1872* as conduct such that 'no men with any degree of prudence, acting on their own behalf, would have entered into such a transaction as they entered into'.

Therefore, in the absence of fraud it was difficult to control careless directors effectively. The statutory provisions on disqualification of directors of insolvent companies and on liability for wrongful trading therefore both set out how to judge a director's competence, and provide more effective enforcement (discussed below).

The company by decision of its members in general meeting decides whether to sue the directors for their negligence. Even if it is a case in which they could be liable **the court has discretion under s 1157 to relieve directors of liability** if it appears to the court that:

- The directors acted **honestly** and **reasonably**
- They **ought**, having regard to the circumstances of the case, **fairly to be excused**.

Re D' Jan of London Ltd 1993

The facts: D, a director of the company, signed an insurance proposal form without reading it. The form was filled in by D's broker. An answer given to one of the questions on the form was incorrect and the insurance company rightly repudiated liability for a fire at the company's premises in which stock worth some £174,000 was lost. The company became insolvent and the liquidator brought this action under s 212 of the Insolvency Act 1986 alleging D was negligent.

Decision: In failing to read the form D was negligent. However, he had acted honestly and reasonably and ought therefore to be partly relieved from liability by the Court under s 727 of the Companies Act 1985, (now s 1157 under the Companies Act 2006).

In the absence of **fraud**, **bad faith** or **ultra vires** the members may vote unanimously to forgive the director's negligence, even if it is those negligent directors who control the voting and exercise such forgiveness: *Multinational Gas & Petrochemical Co v Multinational Gas and Petrochemical Services Ltd 1983*. Where there is no fraud on the minority, a majority decision is sufficient: *Pavlides v Jensen 1956*.

9.12 Fraudulent and wrongful trading

In cases of **fraudulent or wrongful trading** liquidators can apply to the court for an order that those responsible (usually the directors) are liable to repay all or some specified part of the **company's debts**.

The liquidator should also report the facts to the Director of Public Prosecutions so that the DPP may **institute criminal proceedings**. We shall come back to these points in Chapter 21.

10 The company secretary

Every public company must have a **company secretary**, who is one of the officers of a company and may be a director. Private companies are not required to have a secretary.

Every public company must have a **company secretary**, who is one of the officers of a company and may be a director. Private companies are not required to have a secretary. In this case the roles normally done by the company secretary may be done by one of the directors, or an approved person. The secretary of state may require a public company to appoint a secretary where it has failed to do so.

10.1 Appointment of a company secretary

To be appointed as a company secretary to a plc, the directors must ensure that the candidate should be qualified (s 273) by virtue of:

- **Employment** as a plc's secretary for **three out of the five years** preceding appointment
- **Membership** of one of a list of **qualifying bodies**: the ACCA, CIMA, ICAEW, ICAS, ICAI or CIPFA
- **Qualification** as a **solicitor**, **barrister** or **advocate** within the UK
- **Employment** in a position or **membership** of a professional body that, in the opinion of the directors, **appears to qualify that person** to act as company secretary

They should also have the *'necessary knowledge and experience'* as deemed by the directors.

A **sole director** of a private company cannot also be the company secretary, but a company can have **two** or more joint secretaries. A **corporation** can fulfil the role of company secretary. A register of secretaries must be kept.

Under the **Combined Code** on **Corporate Governance** (See Chapter 22), the appointment of the company secretary is a matter for the board as a whole.

10.2 Duties of a company secretary

The specific **duties** of each company secretary are **determined by the directors** of the company. As a company officer, the company secretary is responsible for ensuring that the company complies with its statutory obligations. In particular, this means:

- **Establishing** and **maintaining** the company's **statutory registers**
- **Filing accurate returns** with the Registrar on time
- **Organising** and **minuting** company and **board meetings**
- **Ensuring** that **accounting records** meet **statutory requirements**
- **Ensuring** that **annual accounts** are **prepared** and **filed** in accordance with **statutory requirements**
- **Monitoring statutory requirements** of the company
- **Signing company documents** as may be required by law

Under the Combined Code on Corporate Governance, the company secretary must:

- **Ensure good information flows** within the board and its committees
- **Facilitate induction of board members** and assist with professional development
- **Advise** the **chairman** and the **board** on all **governance issues**

10.3 Powers and authority of a company secretary

The powers of the company secretary have historically been very limited. However, the common law increasingly recognises that they may be able to act as agents to exercise apparent or **ostensible authority**, therefore, they may enter the company into contracts connected with the administrative side of the company.

Panorama Developments (Guildford) Ltd v Fidelis Furnishing Fabrics Ltd 1971

The facts: B, the secretary of a company, ordered cars from a car hire firm, representing that they were required to meet the company's customers at London Airport. Instead he used the cars for his own purposes. The bill was not paid, so the car hire firm claimed payment from B's company.

Decision: B's company was liable, for he had apparent authority to make contracts such as the present one, which were concerned with the administrative side of its business. The decision recognises the general nature of a company secretary's duties.

---

11 The company auditor

FAST FORWARD

Every company (apart from certain small companies) must appoint appropriately qualified **auditors**. An audit is a check on the stewardship of the directors.

Every company (except a dormant private company and certain small companies) must **appoint auditors** for each financial year: s 475.

11.1 Appointment

The **first auditors** may be appointed by the directors, to hold office until the **first general meeting** at which their appointment is considered.

Subsequent auditors may not take office until the previous auditor has ceased to hold office. They will hold office until the end of the next financial period (private companies) or the next accounts meeting (public companies) unless re-appointed.

Appointment of auditors	
Members	• Usually appoint auditor in general meeting by ordinary resolution.
	• Auditors hold office from 28 days after the meeting in which the accounts are laid until the end of the corresponding period the next year. This is the case even if the auditors are appointed at the meeting where the accounts are laid.
	• May appoint in general meeting to fill a casual vacancy.
Directors	• Appoint the first ever auditors. They hold office until the end of the first meeting at which the accounts are considered.
	• May appoint to fill a casual vacancy.
Secretary of State	• May appoint auditors if members fail to.
	• Company must notify Secretary of State within 28 days of the general meeting where the accounts were laid.

11.1.1 Eligibility as auditor

Membership of a **Recognised Supervisory Body** is the main prerequisite for eligibility as an auditor. An audit firm may be either a body corporate, a partnership or a sole practitioner.

The Act requires an auditor to hold an **'appropriate qualification'**. A person holds an 'appropriate qualification' if they:

- Have satisfied **existing criteria** for appointment as an auditor
- Hold a **recognised qualification** obtained in the UK
- Hold an **approved overseas qualification**

11.1.2 Ineligibility as auditor

Under the Companies Act 2006, a person may be ineligible on the grounds of **'lack of independence'**.

A person is ineligible for appointment as a company auditor if they are:

- An **officer** or **employee** of the company being audited
- A **partner** or **employee** of such a person
- A **partnership** in which such a person is a partner
- **Ineligible** by virtue of the above for appointment as auditor of any parent or subsidiary undertaking where there exists a **connection** of any description as may be specified in regulations laid down by Secretary of State.

11.1.3 Effect of lack of independence or ineligibility

No person may act as auditor if they lack independence or become ineligible. If during their term of office an auditor loses their independence or eligibility they must **resign** with immediate effect, and **notify** their client of their resignation giving the reason.

A person continuing to act as auditor despite losing their independence or becoming ineligible is **liable to a fine**. However it is a defence if they can prove they were not aware that they lost independence or became ineligible.

The legislation does **not** disqualify the following from being an auditor of a limited company:

- A shareholder of the company
- A debtor or creditor of the company
- A close relative of an officer or employee of the company

However, the **regulations** of the **accountancy bodies** applying to their own members are **stricter than statute in this respect**.

11.2 Reappointing an auditor of a private company

The above rules on appointment make reference to a **meeting** where the accounts are laid. This is not always relevant for private companies as under the Act they are not required to hold an AGM or lay the accounts before the members. Therefore **auditors of private companies are deemed automatically reappointed** unless one of the following circumstances apply.

- The auditor was **appointed by the directors** (most likely when the first auditor was appointed).
- The **articles require formal reappointment**.
- **Members holding 5% of the voting rights** serve notice that the auditor should not be reappointed s 488.
- A **resolution** (written or otherwise) has been passed that prevents reappointment.
- The **directors have resolved that auditors should not be appointed** for the forthcoming year as the company is likely to be exempt from audit.

11.3 Auditor remuneration

Whoever appoints the auditors has power to **fix their remuneration** for the period of their appointment. It is usual when the auditors are appointed by the general meeting to leave it to the directors to fix their remuneration (by agreement at a later stage). The auditors' remuneration must be **disclosed** in a **note to the accounts**.

11.4 Exemption from audit

Certain **companies** are exempt from audit provided the following conditions are fulfilled.

(a) A company is totally exempt from the annual audit requirement in a financial year if its turnover for that year is **not more** than **£5,600,000**, and its **balance sheet total** is **not more than £2.8 million**.

(b) The exemptions do not apply to **public companies**, **banking** or **insurance companies** or those subject to a **statute-based regulatory regime**.

(c) The company is **non-commercial**, **non-profit making public sector body** which is subject to audit by a **public sector auditor**.

(d) **Members** holding **10%** or more of the capital of any company can veto the exemption.

(e) **Dormant companies** which qualify for exemption from an audit as a dormant company.

11.5 Duties of auditors

The **statutory duty** of auditors is to report to the members whether the accounts give a **true and fair view** and have been properly prepared in accordance with the Companies Act.

They must also:

- **State** whether or not the **directors' report** is **consistent** with the **accounts**.
- For **quoted companies**, **report** to the members on the **auditable** part of the **directors' remuneration report** including whether or not it has been properly prepared in accordance with the Act.
- Be **signed** by the **auditor**, stating their **name**, and **date**. Where the auditor is a firm, the **senior auditor** must sign in their **own name** for, and on behalf, of the auditor.

To fulfil their statutory duties, the auditors **must carry out such investigations as are necessary** to form an opinion as to whether:

(a) **Proper accounting records** have been kept and proper returns adequate for the audit have been received from branches.

(b) The **accounts** are in **agreement** with the **accounting records**.

(c) The **information** in the **directors' remuneration report** is consistent with the **accounts**.

The auditors' report must be **read** before any general meeting at which the accounts are considered and must be open to inspection by members. Auditors have to make disclosure of other services rendered to the company and the remuneration received.

Where an auditor **knowingly** or **recklessly** causes their report to be **materially misleading**, **false** or **deceptive**, they commit a criminal offence and may be liable to a **fine**: s 507.

11.6 Rights of auditors

FAST FORWARD

> The Companies Act provide **statutory rights** for auditors to enable them to carry out their duties.

The **principal rights** of auditors, excepting those dealing with resignation or removal, are set out in the table below, and the following are notes on more detailed points.

Access to records	A right of access at all times to the books, accounts and vouchers of the company: S 499 (1)
Information and explanations	A right to require from the company's officers, employees or any other relevant person, such information and explanations as they think necessary for the performance of their duties as auditors: S 499 (1)
Attendance at/notices of general meetings	A right to attend any general meetings of the company and to receive all notices of and communications relating to such meetings which any member of the company is entitled to receive: s 502 (2)

Right to speak at general meetings	A right to be heard at general meetings which they attend on any part of the business that concerns them as auditors: s 502 (2)
Rights in relation to written resolutions	A right to receive a copy of any written resolution proposed: s 502 (1)

If auditors have **not received** all the information and explanations they consider necessary, they should state this fact in their audit report.

The Act makes it an **offence** for a company's officer knowingly or recklessly to make a statement in any form to an auditor which:

- Conveys or purports to convey any information or explanation required by the auditor and
- Is materially misleading, false or deceptive

The **penalty** is a maximum of two years' imprisonment, a fine or both.

11.7 Auditors' liability

Under s 532 any **agreement** between an auditor and a company that seeks to **indemnify the auditor** for their own negligence, default, or breach of duty or trust is **void**. However under s 534, an agreement can be made which **limits the auditor's liability** to the company. Such **liability limitation agreements** can only stand for **one financial year** and must therefore be replaced annually.

Liability can only be **limited** to what is **fair and reasonable** having regard to the auditor's responsibilities, their contractual obligations and the professional standards expected of them. Such agreements must be approved by the members and **publicly disclosed** in the **accounts** or **directors' report**.

11.8 Termination of auditors' appointment

FAST FORWARD

Auditors may leave office in the following ways: **resignation**; **removal from office** by an ordinary resolution with special notice passed before the end of their term; **failing** to **offer themselves** for re-**election**; and **not being re-elected** at the general meeting at which their term expires.

Departure of auditors from office can occur in the following ways.

(a) Auditors may **resign** their appointment by giving notice in writing to the company delivered to the registered office.

(b) Auditors may **decline reappointment**.

(c) Auditors may be **removed** from office before the expiry of their appointment by the passing of an ordinary resolution in general meeting. Special notice is required and members and auditors must be notified. **Private companies cannot remove an auditor by written resolution;** a meeting must be held.

(d) Auditors **do not have to be reappointed** when their term of office expires, although in most cases they are. Special notice must be given of any resolution to appoint auditors who were not appointed on the last occasion of the resolution, and the members and auditor must be notified.

Where a private company resolves to **appoint** a replacement auditor by **written resolution**, copies of the resolution must be sent to the proposed and outgoing auditor. The outgoing auditor may circulate a **statement of reasonable length** to the members if they notify the company within 14 days of receiving the copy of the written resolution.

11.8.1 Resignation of auditors

FAST FORWARD

However auditors leave office they must either: state there are **no circumstances** which should be brought to **members' and creditors' attention**; or list **those circumstances**. Auditors who are resigning can also: **circulate a statement** about their resignation to members; **requisition a general meeting'**, **or speak** at a general meeting.

Procedures for resignation of auditors	
Statement of circumstances	Auditors must deposit a statement at the registered office with their resignation stating: • For quoted companies – the circumstances around their departure. • For non-quoted public companies and all private companies – there are no circumstances that the auditor believes should be brought to the attention of the members or creditors. • If there are such circumstances the statement should describe them. • Statements should also be submitted to the appropriate audit authority.
Company action	• The company must send notice of the resignation to the Registrar. • The company must **send** a copy of the statement of circumstances to **every person entitled to receive a copy of the accounts.**
Auditor rights	If the auditors have deposited a statement of circumstances, they may: • Circulate a statement of reasonable length to the members • Requisition a general meeting to explain their reasons: s 518 • Attend and speak at any meeting where appointment of successors is to be discussed.

If the auditors decline to seek reappointment at an AGM, they must nevertheless fulfil the requirements of a **statement of the circumstances** just as if they had resigned.

The reason for this provision is to prevent auditors who are unhappy with the company's affairs keeping their suspicions secret. The statement must be deposited not less than **14 days** before the time allowed for next appointing auditors.

11.8.2 Removal of the auditor from office

Procedures for removal from office	
Auditor representations	If a resolution is proposed either to: • Remove the auditors before their term of office expires or • Change the auditors when their term of office is complete the auditors have the right to make representations of reasonable length to the company
Company action	The company must: • Notify members in the notice of the meeting of the representations • Send a copy of the representations in the notice • If it is not sent out, the auditors can require it is read at the meeting
Attendance at meeting	Auditors removed before expiry of their office may: • Attend the meeting at which their office would have expired • Attend any meeting at which the appointment of their successors is discussed
Statement of circumstances	If auditors are removed at a general meeting they must: • Make a statement of circumstances for members and creditors as above.

- Any person who occupies the position of director is treated as such, the test being one of **function**.

- The method of appointing directors, along with their rotation and co-option is **controlled** by the **articles.**

- Directors are entitled to **fees** and **expenses** as directors as per the articles, and **emoluments** (and compensation for loss of office) as per their service contracts (which can be inspected by members). Some details are published in the directors' remuneration report along with the accounts.

- A director may vacate office as director due to: **resignation**; **not going** for **re-election**; **death**; **dissolution** of the company; **removal**; **disqualification**.

- Directors may be required to vacate office because they have been disqualified on grounds dictated by the articles. Directors **may** be disqualified from a wider range of company involvements under the Company Directors Disqualification Act 1986 (CDDA).

- Directors may be **disqualified** from acting as directors or being involved in the management of companies in a number of circumstances. They must be disqualified if the company is insolvent, and the director is found to be unfit to be concerned with management of a company.

- The **powers** of the directors are **defined** by the **articles**.

- Directors' powers may be restricted by statute or by the articles. The directors have a duty to exercise their powers in what they honestly believe to be the **best interests** of the company and for the **purposes** for which the powers are given.

- One or more directors may be appointed by the board as **managing director**. The managing director has **apparent** authority to make business contracts on behalf of the company. The managing director's **actual** authority is whatever the board gives them.

- The Company's Act 2006 sets out the **seven principal duties** of **directors**.

- The **statutory duties** owed by directors are to:

  - Act within their powers
  - Promote the success of the company
  - Exercise independent judgement
  - Exercise reasonable skill, care and diligence
  - Avoid conflicts of interest
  - Not accept benefits from third parties
  - Declare an interest in a proposed transaction or arrangement

- Directors have a duty to show **reasonable competence**.

- Every public company must have a **company secretary**, who is one of the officers of a company and may be a director. Private companies are not required to have a secretary.

- Every company (apart from certain small companies) must appoint appropriately qualified **auditors**. An audit is a check on the stewardship of the directors.

- The Companies Act provide **statutory rights** for auditors to enable them to carry out their duties.

- Auditors may leave office in the following ways: **resignation**; **removal from office** by an ordinary resolution with special notice passed before the end of their term; **failing** to **offer themselves** for **re-election**; and **not being re-elected** at the general meeting at which their term expires.

- However auditors leave office they must either: state there are **no circumstances** which should be brought to **members' and creditors' attention**; or list **those circumstances**. Auditors who are resigning can also: **circulate a statement** about their resignation to members; **requisition a general meeting**; **or speak** at a general meeting.

1   Model articles provide a number of rules on retirement and re-election of directors. These include which of the following?

    A   Every year one third of the directors (or the nearest number thereto) shall retire.

    B   The managing director and any other director holding executive office are not subject to retirement by rotation and are excluded from the reckoning of the one third figure.

    C   Those retiring will be those in service longest since their last election.

    D   Directors appointed to the board during the year are not included in the calculation.

2   **Fill in the blanks** in the statements below.

    Under model articles directors are authorised to m................... the b................... of the company, and e................... the p...................of the company.

3   Under which of the following grounds may a director be disqualified if he is guilty, and under which must a director be disqualified?

    A   Conviction of an indictable offence in connection with a company

    B   Persistent default with the provisions of company legislation

    C   Wrongful trading

    D   Director of an insolvent company whose conduct makes him unfit to be concerned in the management of the company

4   What is the extent of a managing director's actual authority?

5   What are the two principal ways by which members can control the activities of directors?

6   A public company must have two directors, a private company only needs one.

    True   ☐

    False   ☐

7   The directors of a company are in breach of the rule requiring them to act for a proper purpose. A general meeting can

    A   Do nothing that will authorise the transaction
    B   Authorise the transaction by ordinary resolution
    C   Authorise the transaction by special resolution only
    D   Relieve the directors of any liability under the transaction by special resolution only

8   Describe the level of skill that directors have a duty to demonstrate.

9   A private company with a sole director is not legally required to have a company secretary, but if it does, the sole director cannot also be the company secretary.

    True   ☐

    False   ☐

10   Name two reasons a person would be ineligible to be an auditor under Companies Act 2006.

    (1)   ....

    (2)   ....

1   C and D are correct. One half of the directors shall retire each year. Executive directors excluding the MD are subject to retirement by rotation.

2   Under model articles directors are authorised to **manage** the **business** of the company, and **exercise all** the **powers** of the company.

3   A to C are grounds under which a director may be disqualified; D is grounds under which a director must be disqualified.

4   The actual authority is whatever the board gives them.

5   Appointing and removing directors in general meeting

    Reallocating powers by altering the articles

6   True. Private companies only need one director.

7   B. This was the decision in *Bamford v Bamford 1969*.

8   A director is expected to show the degree of skill which may reasonably be expected from a person of his knowledge or experience.

9   True. Sole directors cannot be company secretaries. Private companies are not legally required to have a company secretary.

10 Any of:

    (1)   Is an officer/employee of the company being audited
    (2)   A partner or employee of a person in (1)
    (3)   A partnership in which (1) is a partner
    (4)   Ineligible by (1), (2) and (3) to be auditor of any of the entity's subsidiaries

Now try the question below from the Exam Question Bank

Number	Level	Marks	Time
Q25	Examination	10	18 mins

Company meetings and resolutions

Introduction

In this chapter we consider the **procedures** by which companies are controlled by the shareholders, namely general meetings and resolutions. These afford members a measure of protection of their investment in the company. There are many transactions which, under the Act, cannot be entered into without a **resolution** of the company.

Moreover, a general meeting at which the annual accounts and the auditors' and directors' reports will be laid must normally be held by public companies annually. This affords the members an opportunity of questioning the directors on their **stewardship**.

Study guide

		Intellectual level
(F)	**Management, administration and regulation of companies**	
3	Company meetings and resolutions	
(a)	Distinguish between types of meetings: ordinary general meetings and annual general meetings	1
(b)	Explain the procedure for calling such meetings	2
(c)	Detail the procedure for conducting company meetings	1
(d)	Distinguish between types of resolutions: ordinary, special and written	2

Exam guide

For the exam you must be quite clear about the different types of resolution, when each type is used, and the percentage vote needed for each type to be passed. This topic lends itself to knowledge questions. However, resolutions in particular are important in many areas of the corporate part of the syllabus and meetings of members are an important control on the acts of the directors. Therefore, this topic could easily be incorporated into an application question.

1 The importance of meetings

FAST FORWARD

> Although the management of a company, is in the hands of the directors, the **decisions which affect the existence of the company**, its structure and scope are **reserved to the members** in general meeting.

The decision of a general meeting is only valid and binding if the meeting is **properly convened** by notice and if the **business** of the meeting is **fairly** and **properly conducted**. Most of the rules on company meetings are concerned with the issue of notices and the casting of votes at meetings to carry resolutions of specified types.

1.1 Control over directors

The members in general meeting can exercise control over the directors, though only to a limited extent.

(a) Under normal procedure **one half** of the **directors retire** at each annual general meeting though they may offer themselves for re-election. The company may remove directors from office by **ordinary resolution**: s 168.

(b) Member approval in general meeting is required if the directors wish to:
   (i) **Exceed their delegated power** or to use it for other than its given purpose
   (ii) **Allot shares** (unless private company with one class of shares)
   (iii) **Make a substantial contract** of sale or purchase with a director
   (iv) Grant a director a **long-service agreement**

(c) The **appointment and removal of auditors** is normally done in general meeting.

1.2 Resolution of differences

In addition, general meetings are the means by which **members resolve differences** between themselves by voting on resolutions.

2 General meetings

FAST FORWARD

There are two kinds of general meeting of members of a company:

- **Annual general meeting (AGM)**
- **General meetings at other times**

2.1 Annual general meeting (AGM)

The **AGM** plays a major role in the life of a public company although often the business carried out seems fairly routine. It is a statutorily protected way for members to have a regular assessment and discussion of their company and its management.

Private companies are **not required** to have an **AGM** each year and therefore their business is usually conducted through **written resolutions**. However, members holding sufficient shares or votes can request a general meeting or written resolution.

Rules for directors calling an AGM	
Timing s 336	• Public companies must hold an AGM within **six months** of their year end • Not more than **fifteen months** may elapse between meetings
Notice s 337	• Must be in **writing** and in **accordance** with the **articles** • May be in **hard** or **electronic form** and may also by means of a **website** (s 308) • At least **21 days notice** should be given; a longer period may be specified in the articles • Shorter notice is only **valid** if all members agree • The notice must specify the **time**, **date** and **place** of the meeting and that the meeting is an AGM • Where notice is given on a **website** it must be available from the **date of notification** until the **conclusion of the meeting** (s 309)

The business of an annual general meeting usually includes:

- Considering the accounts
- Receiving the directors' report, the directors' remuneration report and the auditors' report
- Dividends
- Electing directors
- Appointing auditors

2.2 General meetings at other times

2.2.1 Directors

The **directors** may have power under the articles to convene a general meeting whenever they see fit.

2.2.2 Members

The directors of **public and private** companies may be required to convene a general meeting by **requisition of the members:** s 303.

Rules for members requisitioning a general meeting (s 303)	
Shareholding	• The requisitioning members of public companies must hold at least **10%** of the **paid up share capital** holding **voting rights**. In private companies they need either **5%** or **10%**, depending on when there was last a meeting at which the members had a right to vote. Over 12 months ago = 5%; under 12 months = 10%

Rules for members requisitioning a general meeting (s 303)	
Requisition	• They must deposit a **signed requisition** at the registered office or make the request in electronic form • This must state the 'objects of the meeting': the **resolutions proposed** (s 303(5))
Date	• A notice conveying the meeting must be set out within **21 days** of the requisition • It must be held within **28 days** of the notice calling to a meeting being sent out. • If the directors have not called the meeting within 21 days of the requisition, the **members may convene** the meeting for a date within 3 months of the deposit of the requisition
Quorum	• If **no quorum** is present, the meeting is **adjourned**.

2.2.3 Court order

The court, on the application of a director or a member entitled to vote, may order that a meeting shall be held and may give instructions for that purpose including fixing a quorum of one: s 306.

This is a method of last resort to resolve a deadlock such as the refusal of one member out of two to attend (and provide a quorum) at a general meeting.

2.2.4 Auditor requisition

An auditor who gives a statement of circumstances for their resignation or other loss of office in their written notice may also requisition a meeting to receive and consider their explanation: s 518.

2.2.5 Loss of capital by public company

The directors of a public company must convene a general meeting if the net assets fall to half or less of the amount of its called-up share capital: s 656.

3 Types of resolution

FAST FORWARD

A meeting can pass two types of resolution. **Ordinary resolutions** are carried by a simple majority (more than 50%) of votes cast and requiring 14 days notice. **Special resolutions** require a 75% majority of votes cast and also 14 days notice.

A meeting reaches a decision by passing a resolution (either by a show of hands or a poll). There are **two major kinds** of resolution, and an additional one for **private** companies.

Types of resolution	
Ordinary	For most business Requires simple (50%+) majority of the votes cast 14 days notice
Special	For major changes Requires 75% majority of the votes cast 14 days notice
Written (for private companies)	Can be used for all general meeting resolutions except for removing a director or auditor before their term of office expires. Either a simple (50%+) or 75% majority is required depending on the business being passed.

3.1 Differences between ordinary and special resolutions

Apart from the required size of the majority and period of notice, the main differences between the types of resolution are as follows.

(a) The **text** of **special resolutions** must be **set out** in **full** in the notice convening the meeting, and it must be described as a special resolution. This is not necessary for an ordinary resolution if it is routine business.

(b) A **signed copy** of every **special resolution** must be **delivered** to the **Registrar** for filing. **Some ordinary resolutions**, particularly those relating to share capital, have to be **delivered** for filing but many do not.

3.2 Special resolutions

A special resolution is required for **major changes** in the company such as the following.

- A change of name
- Restriction of the objects or other alteration of the articles
- Reduction of share capital
- Winding up the company
- Presenting a petition by the company for an order for a compulsory winding up

Question — Notice period

The period of notice for a general meeting at which a special resolution is proposed is:

A   14 days
B   21 days
C   28 days
D   42 days

Answer

A   A general meeting at which a special resolution is proposed requires 14 days notice.

3.3 Written resolutions

FAST FORWARD A private company can pass any decision needed by a **written resolution**, except for removing a director or auditor before their term of office has expired.

As we saw earlier, a private company is **not** required to hold an **AGM**. Therefore the Act provides a mechanism for directors and members to conduct business solely by **written resolution**.

3.3.1 Written resolutions proposed by directors

Copies of the resolution proposed by directors must be sent to **each member** eligible to vote by hard copy, electronically or by a website. Alternatively, the same copy may be sent to each member in turn.

The resolution should be accompanied by a statement informing the member:

- How to **signify their agreement** to the resolution
- The **date** the resolution must be passed by

3.3.2 Written resolutions proposed by members

Members holding 5% (or lower if authorised by the articles) of the **voting rights** may request a written resolution providing it:

- **Would be effective** (not prevented by the articles or law)
- Is **not defamatory, frivolous** or **vexatious**

A **statement** containing no more than **1,000 words** on the subject of the resolution may accompany it.

Copies of the resolution, and statements containing information on the subject matter, how to agree to it and the date of the resolution must be sent to each member within **21 days** of the request for resolution.

Expenses for circulating the resolution **should be met by the members** who requested it unless the company resolves otherwise.

The company may **appeal to the court** not to circulate the 1,000 word statement by the members if the rights provided to the members are being abused by them.

3.3.3 Agreement

The members may indicate their agreement to the resolution in **hard copy** or **electronically**.

If no **period for agreement** is specified by the articles, then the default period is **28 days** from the date the resolution was circulated. Agreement after this period is ineffective.

Once agreed, a member **may not revoke** their decision.

Either a **simple** (50% plus one) or **75% majority** is required to pass a written resolution depending on the nature of the business being decided.

Three further points should be noted concerning written resolutions.

(a) Written resolutions can be used **notwithstanding any provisions** in the company's **articles**.

(b) A written resolution **cannot** be **used to remove a director or auditor** from office, since such persons have a right to **speak** at a **meeting**.

(c) **Copies of written resolutions** should be **sent to auditors** at or before the time they are sent to shareholders. Auditors do not have the right to object to written resolutions. If the auditors are not sent a copy, the resolution remains valid; however the directors and secretary will be liable to a fine. The purpose of this provision is to ensure auditors are kept informed about what is happening in the company.

Question
Resolutions

Briefly explain the main features of the following types of resolution which may be passed at a general meeting of a company:

(a) An ordinary resolution
(b) A special resolution

Answer

(a) Ordinary resolutions require a simple majority of votes cast (ie over 50%). 14 days notice is sufficient. Ordinary resolutions of a routine nature need not be set out in full in the notice of an annual general meeting, and most ordinary resolutions need not be filed with the Registrar.

(b) Special resolutions also require a 75% majority of votes cast and also require 14 days notice of the intention to propose such a resolution. The full text of the resolution should be set out in the notice.

4 Calling a meeting

A meeting cannot make valid and binding decisions until it has been properly convened. Notice of general meetings must be given **14 days** in advance of the meeting. The notice should contain **adequate information** about the meeting.

Meetings must be called by a **competent person** or authority.

A meeting cannot make valid and binding decisions until it has been properly convened according to the company's articles, though there are also statutory rules.

(a)   The meeting must generally be **called by** the **board of directors** or other competent person or authority.

(b)   The notice must be issued to members in advance of the meeting so as to give them **14 days** 'clear notice' of the meeting. The members may agree to waive this requirement (see below).

(c)   The **notice** must be sent to every member (or other person) entitled to receive the notice.

(d)   The notice must include any information **reasonably necessary** to enable shareholders to know in advance what is to be done.

(e)   As we saw earlier members may require the directors to call a meeting if:

   (i)   They hold at least **10% of the voting rights** (5% for a private company if 12 months have elapsed since the last meeting)

   (ii)   They provide a **statement of the general business** to be conducted and the text of any proposed resolution

   The directors must within **21 days call a meeting** to be held no later than **28 days from the date of the notice** they send calling the meeting.

In most cases the notice need **not** be sent to a member whose only shares do not give him a right to attend and vote (as is often the position of **preference shareholders**)

4.1 Electronic communication

We have already seen that **notice** may be given by means of a **website** and in **electronic form** (s 308). Section 333 extends this by deeming that where a company gives an **electronic address** in a notice calling a meeting, any information or document relating to the meeting may be sent to that address.

4.2 Timing of notices

Clear notice must be given to members. **Notice** must be **sent to all members** entitled to receive it.

Members may – and in small private companies often do – waive the required notice. For **short notice** to be effective:

(a)   All **members** of a public company must consent in respect of an **AGM**.

(b)   In **any other case** a **majority of members** who hold at least **90 per cent** of the **issued shares** or voting rights must consent. 95% is required by a public company.

The following specific rules by way of exception should be remembered.

- When **special notice** of a resolution is given to the company in the two circumstances mentioned in Section 4.3 below, it must be given **28 days** in advance as prescribed.

- In a **creditors' voluntary winding up** there must be at least **7 days notice** of the **creditors' meeting** (to protect the interests of creditors). The members may shorten the period of notice down to 7 days but that is all: s 98 IA.

The **clear days rule** in s 360 provides that the day of the meeting and the day the notice was given are **excluded** from the required notice period.

4.3 Special notice of a resolution

Special notice of 28 days of intention to propose certain resolutions (removal of directors/auditors) must be given.

Key term

Special notice is notice of 28 days which must be given to a company of the intention to put certain types of resolution at a company meeting.

Special notice must be given **to the company** of the intention to propose a resolution for any of the following purposes.

- To **remove** an **auditor** or to **appoint** an **auditor other** than the **auditor** who was **appointed** at the **previous year's meeting**
- To **remove a director from office** or to appoint a substitute in their place after removal

A member may request a resolution to be passed at a particular meeting. In this case, the **member must give special notice** of their intention **to the company** at **least 28 days** before the date of the meeting. If, however, the company calls the meeting for a date less than 28 days after receiving the special notice that notice is deemed to have been **properly given**.

On receiving special notice a **public company may be obliged** to **include the resolution** in the **AGM notice** which it issues.

If the company gives notice to members of the resolution it does so by a **21 day notice** to them that special notice has been received and what it contains. If it is not practicable to include the matter in the notice of meeting, the company may give notice to members by newspaper advertisement or any other means permitted by the articles.

Where special notice is received of intention to propose a resolution for the removal of a director or to change the auditor, the company must send a copy to the **director** or **auditor**. This is to allow them to exercise their statutory right to defend themself by issuing a memorandum and/or addressing the meeting in person.

The essential point is that a **special notice is given to the company**; it is **not a notice from the company to members** although it will be followed (usually) by such notice.

4.4 Members requisitioning a resolution

Members rather than directors may be able to requisition resolutions. This may be achieved by requesting the directors call a meeting, or proposing a resolution to be voted on at a meeting already arranged.

The directors normally have the **right to decide** what resolutions shall be included in the notice of a meeting. However, apart from the requisition to call a general meeting, members can also take the initiative to requisition certain resolutions be considered at the AGM.

Rules for members requisitioning a resolution at the AGM	
Qualifying holding s 338	• The members must represent 5% of the voting rights, or • Be at least 100 members holding shares with an average paid up of £100, per member
Request s 338	• Must be in hard copy or electronic form, identify the resolution and be delivered at least 6 weeks in advance of an AGM or other general meeting
Statement s 314	• Members may request a statement (<1,000 words) be circulated to all members by delivering a **requisition**. Members with a qualifying holding may request a statement regarding their own resolution or any resolution proposed at the meeting • The company must send the statement with the notice of the meeting or as soon as practicable after

In either instance, the **requisitionists** must bear the incidental costs unless the company resolves otherwise.

Exam focus point

> The right of members to have resolutions included on the agenda of AGM or other meetings is asked frequently in law assessments. It is an **important consideration if some of the members disagree with the directors.**

4.5 Content of notices

FAST FORWARD

> The **notice** convening the meeting must give certain details. The **date**, **time** and **place** of the meeting, and identification of AGM and special resolutions. Sufficient information about the business to be discussed at the meeting should be provided to enable shareholders to know what is to be done.

The notice of a general meeting must contain adequate information on the following points.

(a)   The **date**, **time** and **place** of the meeting must be given.

(b)   An **AGM** or a **special resolution** must be described as such.

(c)   Information must be given of the business of the meeting **sufficient** to enable members (in deciding whether to attend or to appoint proxies) to **understand what will be done** at the meeting.

4.5.1 Routine business

In issuing the notice of an AGM it is standard practice merely to list the **items of ordinary or routine business** to be transacted, such as the following.

- Declaration of dividends (if any)
- Election of directors
- Appointment of auditors and fixing of their remuneration

The articles usually include a requirement that members shall be informed of any intention to **propose** the **election** of a director, other than an existing director who retires by rotation and merely stands for re-election.

Question   Removal of a director

How can members remove a director from office? What is the significance of special notice in this context?

Answer

A company may by ordinary resolution remove any director from office, notwithstanding any provision to the contrary in the articles or in a contract such as a director's service agreement.

However, this procedure requires that special notice shall be given to the company at least 28 days before the meeting of the intention to propose such a resolution. Moreover, the directors are not required to include the resolution in the notice of the meeting unless the person who intends to propose it has a sufficient shareholding.

If a company receives special notice it must send a copy to the director concerned who has the right to have written representations of reasonable length circulated to members. They may also speak before the resolution is put to the vote at the meeting.

Question   General meeting

When is a public company compelled to call a general meeting?

Members of a company who hold not less than one tenth of the company's paid up share capital carrying voting rights, or members representing one tenth of the voting rights, may requisition the holding of a general meeting. The directors are then required within 21 days to issue a notice convening the meeting to transact the business specified in the requisition. This must be within 28 days.

An auditor who resigns giving reasons for his resignation may requisition a general meeting so that he may explain to members the circumstances of his resignation.

If the net assets of a public company are reduced to less than half in value of its called-up share capital, the directors must convene a general meeting to consider what, if any, steps should be taken.

The court has statutory power in certain circumstances to direct that a meeting shall be held.

5 Proceedings at meetings

5.1 How a meeting proceeds

FAST FORWARD

Company meetings need to be properly run if they are to be **effective** and within the **law**.

A meeting can only reach binding decisions if:

- It has been properly **convened** by notice
- A **quorum is present.**
- A **chairman presides**.
- The **business** is **properly transacted** and **resolutions** are **put to the vote.**

There is no obligation to allow a member to be present if their shares do not carry the right to attend and vote. However **full general meetings** and **class meetings** can be held when shareholders not entitled to vote are present.

Each **item of business** comprised in the notice should be taken separately, discussed and **put to the vote**.

Members may propose **amendments** to any resolutions proposed. The chairman should reject any amendment which is outside the limits set by the notice convening the meeting.

If the relevant business is an **ordinary resolution** it may be possible to amend the resolution's wording so as to **reduce its effect** to something less (provided that the change does not entirely alter its character). For example an ordinary resolution authorising the directors to borrow £100,000 might be amended to substitute a limit of £50,000 (but not to increase it to £150,000 as £100,000 would have been stated in the notice).

5.2 The chairman

FAST FORWARD

The meeting should usually be chaired by the **chairman** of the board of directors. They do not necessarily have a casting vote.

The articles usually provide that the **chairman** of the board of directors **is to preside** at general meetings; in their absence another director chosen by the directors shall preside instead. In the last resort a member chosen by the members present can preside.

The chairman derives their authority from the articles and they have **no casting vote unless** the **articles give them one**. Their duties are to **maintain order** and to **deal** with the **agenda** in a methodical way so that the business of the meeting may be properly transacted.

The chairman:

- **May dissolve** or **adjourn** the **meeting** if it has become disorderly or if the members present agree.
- Must **adjourn** if the meeting **instructs** them to do so.

5.3 Quorum

FAST FORWARD

The **quorum** for meetings may be two or more (except for single member private companies). **Proxies** can attend, speak and vote on behalf of members.

Key term

A **quorum** is the minimum number of persons required to be present at a particular type of (company) meeting. In the case of shareholders' meetings, the figure is usually two, in person or by proxy, but the articles may make other provisions.

There is a legal principle that a 'meeting means a coming together of more than one person'. Hence it follows that as a matter of law **one person generally cannot be a meeting.**

The rule that at least two persons must be present to constitute a 'meeting' does not require that both persons must be members. Every member has a **statutory right to appoint a proxy** to attend as their representative.

In theory, **ultimate control** over a company's business lies with the **members** in a **general meeting**. One would obviously conclude that a meeting involved more than one person, and indeed there is authority to that effect in *Sharp v Dawes 1876*. In this case a meeting between a lone member and the company secretary was held not to be validly constituted. It is possible, however, for a meeting of only one person to take place and we shall consider this shortly.

5.3.1 Proxies

Key term

A **proxy** is a person appointed by a shareholder to vote on behalf of that shareholder at company meetings.

Any member of a company which has a share capital, provided they are entitled to attend and vote at a general or class meeting of the company, has a statutory right (s 324) to appoint an **agent**, called a **'proxy'**, to attend and vote for them.

Rules for appointing proxies	
Basic rule	<ul><li>Any **member** may appoint a proxy</li><li>The proxy **does not** have to be a member</li><li>Proxies **may speak** at the meeting</li><li>A member may **appoint more than one proxy** provided each proxy is appointed in respect of a different class of share held by the member.</li></ul>
Voting	<ul><li>Proxies **may vote** on **poll** and on a **show of hands**</li><li>Proxies may **demand a poll** at a meeting</li><li>Most companies provide **two-way proxy cards** that the member can use to instruct a proxy how to vote, either for or against a resolution.</li></ul>
Notice	<ul><li>Every notice of a meeting must **state** the member's right to a proxy</li><li>**Notice** of a proxy appointment should be given to the company at least 48 hours before the meeting (excluding weekends and bank holidays)</li></ul>

Hence one member and another member's proxy may together provide the quorum (if it is fixed, as is usual, at 'two members present in person or by proxy'). However one member who is also the proxy appointed by another member cannot by themselves be a meeting, since a **minimum of two individuals** present is required.

There may, however, be a meeting attended by one person only, if:

(a)   It is a **class meeting** and all the **shares** of that class are **held** by **one member.**

(b)   The **court**, in exercising a power to order a general meeting to be held, **fixes** the **quorum** at one. This means that in a two-member company, a meeting can be held with one person if the other deliberately absents themself to frustrate business.

(c)   The company is a **single member private company**.

The articles usually fix a **quorum** for general meetings which may be as low as two (the minimum for a meeting) but may be more – though this is unusual.

If the articles do fix a quorum of two or more persons present, the meeting lacks a quorum (it is said to be an 'inquorate' meeting) if either:

•   The **required number** is **not present** within a **stipulated time** (usually half an hour) of the appointed time for commencing a meeting.

•   The **meeting begins** with a **quorum** but the **number present dwindles** to less than the quorum – unless the articles provide for this possibility.

The articles usually provide for automatic and compulsory **adjournment of an inquorate meeting**.

The articles can provide that a meeting which begins with a quorum may continue despite a reduction in numbers present to less than the quorum level. However, there must still be **two or more persons present**.

5.4 Voting and polls

FAST FORWARD

Voting at general meetings may be on a **show of hands** or a **poll**.

The **rights of members** to **vote** and the **number of votes** to which they are entitled in respect of their shares are fixed by the **articles**.

One vote per share is normal but some shares, for instance preference shares, may carry no voting rights in normal circumstances. To shorten the proceedings at meetings the procedure is as follows.

5.4.1 Voting on a show of hands

Key term

A **show of hands** is a method of voting for or against a resolution by raising hands. Under this method each member has one vote irrespective of the number of shares held, in contrast to a poll vote.

On putting a resolution to the vote the chairman calls for a show of hands. One vote may be given by each member present in person, including proxies.

Unless a poll is then demanded, the chairman's declaration of the result is **conclusive**. However it is still possible to challenge the chairman's declaration on the grounds that it was fraudulent or manifestly wrong.

5.4.2 Voting on a poll

Key term

A **poll** is a method of voting at company meetings which allows a member to use as many votes as their shareholding grants them.

If a **real test of voting strength** is required a poll may be demanded. The result of the previous show of hands is then disregarded. On a poll every member and also proxies representing absent members may cast the full number of votes to which they are entitled. A poll need not be held at the time but may be postponed so that arrangements to hold it can be made.

A poll may be **demanded** by:

- Not **less than five members**
- Member(s) **representing** not less than **one tenth** of the **total voting rights**
- Member(s) **holding shares** which **represent** not less than **one tenth** of the **paid-up capital**

Any provision in the articles is **void** if it seeks to prevent such members demanding a poll or to exclude the right to demand a poll on any question other than the election of a chairman by the meeting or an adjournment.

When a poll is held it is usual to appoint **'scrutineers'** and to ask members and proxies to sign voting cards or lists. The votes cast are checked against the register of members and the chairman declares the result.

Members of a quoted company may require the directors to obtain an **independent report** in respect of a poll taken, or to be taken, at a general meeting if:

- They represent at least 5% of the voting rights, or
- Are at least 100 in number holding at least £100 of paid up capital.

5.4.3 Result of a vote

In voting, either by show of hands or on a poll, the **number of votes cast determines the result**. Votes which are not cast, whether the member who does not use them is present or absent, are simply disregarded. Hence the majority vote may be much less than half (or three quarters) of the total votes which could be cast.

Results of quoted company polls of must be made available on a **website**. The following information should be made available as soon as **reasonably practicable**, and should remain on the website for at least **two years**.

- Meeting date
- Text of the resolution or description of the poll's subject matter
- Number of votes for and against the resolution

5.5 Minutes of company meetings

> **Minutes** must be kept of all **general, directors'** and **management meetings**, and members can inspect those of general meetings.

Key term

> **Minutes** are a record of the proceedings of meetings. Company law requires minutes to be kept of all company meetings including general, directors' and managers' meetings.

Every company is **required to keep minutes** which are a formal written record of the proceedings of its general meetings for ten years: s 355. These minutes are usually kept in **book form**. If a loose-leaf book is used to facilitate typing there should be safeguards against falsification, such as sequential prenumbering.

The chairman **normally signs** the minutes. If he does so, the signed minutes are admissible evidence of the proceedings, though evidence may be given to contradict or supplement the minutes or to show that no meeting at all took place.

Members of the company have the **right to inspect** minutes of general meetings. The minutes of general meetings must be held at the registered office (or other permitted location) available for inspection by members, who are also entitled to demand copies.

5.6 The assent principle

A unanimous decision of the members is often treated as a substitute for a formal decision in general meeting properly convened and held, and is equally binding.

6 Class meetings

FAST FORWARD

Class meetings are held where the interests of different groups of shareholders may be affected in different ways.

6.1 Types of class meeting

Class meetings are of two kinds.

(a)   If the company has more than one class of share, for example if it has 'preference' and 'ordinary' shares, it may be necessary to call a meeting of the holders of one class of shares, to approve a proposed **variation** of the **rights** attached to their shares.

(b)   Under a **compromise** or **arrangements with creditors** (s 895), the holders of shares of the same class may nonetheless be divided into **separate** classes if the scheme proposed will affect each group differently.

When separate meetings of a class of members are held, the same procedural rules as for general meetings apply (but there is a different rule on quorum).

6.2 Quorum for a class meeting

The standard general meeting rules, on issuing notices and on voting, apply to a class meeting.

However the **quorum** for a class meeting is fixed at two persons who hold, or represent by proxy, at least **one third** in nominal value of the issued shares of the class (unless the class only consists of a single member).

If no quorum is present, the meeting is **adjourned** (under the standard adjournment procedure for general meetings). When the meeting resumes, the quorum is **one** person (who must still hold at least one third of the shares).

7 Single member private companies

FAST FORWARD

There are **special rules** for **private companies** with only **one shareholder.**

If the sole member takes any decision that could have been taken in general meeting, that member shall (unless it is a written resolution) provide the company with a **written record** of it. This allows the sole member to conduct members' business informally without notice or minutes.

Filing requirements still apply, for example, in the case of alteration of articles.

Written resolutions **cannot** be used to remove a director or auditor from office as these resolutions require special notice.

Chapter Roundup

- Although the management of a company is in the hands of the directors, the **decisions which affect the existence of the company**, its structure and scope are **reserved to the members** in general meeting.

- There are two kinds of general meeting of members of a company:
    - **Annual general meeting (AGM)**
    - **General meetings at other times**

- A meeting can pass two types of resolution. **Ordinary resolutions** are carried by a simple majority (more than 50%) of votes cast and requiring 14 days notice. **Special resolution**s require a 75% majority of votes cast and also 14 days notice.

- A private company can pass any decision needed by a **written resolution**, except for removing a director or auditor before their term of office has expired.

- A meeting cannot make valid and binding decisions until it has been properly convened. Notice of general meetings must be given **14 days** in advance of the meeting. The notice should contain adequate information about the meeting.

- Meetings must be called by a **competent person** or authority.

- **Clear notice** must be given to members. **Notice** must be **sent to all members** entitled to receive it.

- **Special notice of 28 days** of intention to propose certain resolutions (removal of directors/auditors) must be given.

- **Members** rather than directors may be able to requisition resolutions. This may be achieved by requesting the directors call a meeting, or proposing a resolution to be voted on at a meeting already arranged.

- The **notice** convening the meeting must give certain details. The **date**, **time** and **place** of the meeting, and identification of AGM and special resolutions. Sufficient information about the business to be discussed at the meeting should be provided to enable shareholders to know what is to be done.

- Company meetings need to be properly run if they are to be **effective** and within the **law**.

- The meeting should usually be chaired by the **chairman** of the board of directors. They do not necessarily have a casting vote.

- The **quorum** for meetings may be two or more (except for single member private companies). **Proxies** can attend, speak and vote on behalf of members.

- Voting at general meetings may be on a **show of hands** or a **poll**.

- **Minutes** must be kept of all **general, directors'** and **management meetings**, and members can inspect those of general meetings.

- **Class meetings** are held where the interests of different groups of shareholders may be affected in different ways.

- There are **special rules** for **private companies** with only **one shareholder.**

1　Which of the following decisions can only be taken by the members in general meeting?

    A   Alteration of articles
    B   Change of name
    C   Reduction of capital
    D   Appointment of a managing director

2　Before a private company can hold a general meeting on short notice, members holding a certain percentage of the company's shares must agree. Which one of the following percentages is correct?

51%	90%
75%	95%

3　No more than fifteen months must pass between a public company's AGMs.

True   ☐

False ☐

4　Which of the following matters is a quoted company not legally required to make available on a website?

    A   Notice of all its general meetings
    B   Text of resolutions voted on in a poll
    C   The number of proxies voting for and against a resolution
    D   The number of votes cast for and against a resolution

5　A member of a public company may only appoint one proxy, but the proxy has a statutory right to speak at the meeting.

True   ☐

False ☐

Answers to Quick Quiz

1　A, B and C. The board can appoint someone to be managing director, so D is incorrect.

2　90%

3　True. No more than fifteen months should pass.

4　C. The number of proxies voting for and against a resolution is not legally required to be made available on a website. Notice of meetings, text of resolutions and the total number of votes cast for and against the resolution are required.

5　False. Public company members can appoint more than one proxy. They have a statutory right to speak.

Now try the questions below from the Exam Question Bank

Number	Level	Marks	Time
Q26	Examination	10	18 mins

Legal implications of companies in difficulty or in crisis

Insolvency and administration

Topic list	Syllabus reference
1 What is liquidation?	G1(a), G1(b)
2 Voluntary liquidation	G1(a)
3 Compulsory liquidation	G1(b)
4 Differences between compulsory and voluntary liquidation	G1(a), G1(b)
5 Saving a company: administration	G1(c)

Introduction

A **company in difficulty** or **in crisis** (an **insolvent** company) basically has a choice of two alternatives:

(1)   To carry on with the business, using statutory methods to help remedy the situation

(2)   To stop

A company which is heading towards insolvency can often be **saved**, using a variety of **legal protections** from creditors until the problem is sorted out. As we shall see in Chapter 23, the **directors** of a company can get into a lot of trouble if they carry on trading through a company in serious financial difficulties, and their actions result in **creditors** being **defrauded**.

However, alternative 1 does not have to mean carrying on as if everything is normal. It can mean **seeking help** from the **court** or a **qualified insolvency practitioner** to put a plan together to **save the company** and get it out of its bad financial position.

Unfortunately, many companies cannot be saved, and the members and directors are forced to take alternative 2, **to stop** operating the business through the company. Liquidation, sometimes called 'winding up', is **when a company is formally dissolved** and ceases to exist.

Various methods of achieving liquidation are covered in the first three sections of this chapter. Note though that a company **does not have to be in financial difficulty to be liquidated.**

Study guide

		Intellectual level
(G)	**Legal implications relating to companies in difficulty or in crisis**	
1	Insolvency	
(a)	Explain the meaning of and procedure involved in voluntary liquidation	2
(b)	Explain the meaning of and procedure involved in compulsory liquidation	2
(c)	Explain administration as an alternative to winding up	2

Exam guide

As well as being examined in knowledge questions, you may find that elements of insolvency creep into scenario questions on company finances and directors. Be prepared to explain the various methods of closing a business down and how they are investigated.

> **Statutory references in this chapter are to the Insolvency Act 1986 (as amended by the Insolvency Act 1994 and the Insolvency Act 2000) unless stated otherwise.**

1 What is liquidation?

FAST FORWARD

Liquidation is the **dissolution** or **'winding up'** of a company.

Key terms

Liquidation means that the company must be dissolved and its affairs 'wound up', or brought to an end.

The assets are realised, debts are paid out of the proceeds, and any surplus amounts are returned to members. Liquidation leads on to **dissolution** of the company. It is sometimes referred to as **winding up**.

1.1 Who decides to liquidate?

FAST FORWARD

There are three different methods of **liquidation; compulsory**, **members' voluntary** and **creditors' voluntary**. Compulsory liquidation and creditors' voluntary liquidation are proceedings for insolvent companies, and members' voluntary liquidation is for solvent companies.

The parties most likely to be involved in the decision to liquidate are:

- The directors
- The creditors
- The members

The **directors** are best placed to know the financial position and difficulty that the company is in. The **creditors** may become aware that the company is in financial difficulty when their invoices do not get paid on a timely basis, or at all.

The **members** are likely to be the last people to know that the company is in financial difficulty, as they rely on the directors to tell them. In public companies, there is a rule that the directors must call a general meeting of members if the net assets of the company fall to half or less of the amount of its called-up share capital. There is no such rule for private companies.

As we shall see in the next two sections, there are three methods of winding up. They depend on **who has instigated the proceedings**. Directors cannot formally instigate proceedings for winding up, they can only make recommendations to the members.

However, if the **members refuse** to put the company in liquidation and the directors feel that to continue to trade will prejudice creditors, they could resign their posts. This prevents them from committing the offences we shall see in Chapter 23.

In any case, if the company was in such serious financial difficulty for this to be an issue, it is likely that a **creditor** would have commenced proceedings against it.

1.1.1 Creditors

If a creditor has grounds (we shall discuss these in Section 2) they may **apply to the court** for the **compulsory winding up** of the company.

Creditors may also be closely involved in a **voluntary winding up**, if the company is **insolvent** when the **members** decide to wind the company up.

1.1.2 Members

The members may decide to wind the company up (probably on the advice of the directors). If they do so, the company is **voluntarily wound up**. This can lead to two different types of members' winding up:

- Members' voluntary winding up (if the company is solvent)
- Creditors' voluntary winding up (if the company is insolvent)

1.2 Role of the liquidator

A **liquidator** must be an authorised, qualified insolvency practitioner.

Once the decision to liquidate has been taken, the company goes under the **control of a liquidator** who must be a **qualified** and **authorised** insolvency practitioner.

We shall look at the procedures that the liquidator carries out in the next two sections. However, the liquidator also has a statutory duty to **report** to the Secretary of State where he feels that any **director** of the insolvent company is **unfit** to be involved in the management of a company.

1.3 Common features of liquidations

Once **insolvency procedures** have commenced, share trading must cease, the company documents must state that the company is in liquidation and the directors' power to manage ceases.

Regardless of what method of liquidation is used, similar **legal problems** may arise in each of them. In addition, the following factors are true at the start of any liquidation:

- **No share dealings** or **changes in members** are allowed
- All company documents (eg invoices, letters, emails) and the website must **state the company is in liquidation**
- The **directors' power to manage ceases**

2 Voluntary liquidation

A **winding up** is **voluntary** where the decision to wind up is taken by the company's members, although if the company is insolvent, the creditors will be heavily involved in the proceedings.

As we discussed in Section 1, there are two types of voluntary liquidation:

- A **members' voluntary winding up**, where the company is **solvent** and the members merely decide to 'kill it off'
- A **creditors' voluntary winding up**, where the company is **insolvent** and the members resolve to wind up in consultation with creditors

The main differences between a members' and a creditors' voluntary winding up are set out below.

Function	Winding up	
	Members' voluntary	Creditors' voluntary
(1) Appointment of liquidator	By members	Normally by creditors though responsible to both members and creditors
(2) Approval for liquidator's actions	General meeting of members	Liquidation committee
(3) Liquidation committee	None	Up to 5 representatives of creditors and 5 representatives of members

The effect of the voluntary winding up being a creditors' one is that the **creditors** have a **decisive influence** on the conduct of the liquidation.

Meetings in a creditors' voluntary winding up are held in the same sequence as in a members' voluntary winding up, but meetings of creditors are called at the same intervals as the meetings of members and for similar purposes.

In both kinds of voluntary winding up, the **court has the power to appoint a liquidator** (if for some reason there is none acting) or to remove one liquidator and appoint another: s 108.

2.1 Members' voluntary liquidation

FAST FORWARD

In order to be a members' winding up, the directors must make a **declaration of solvency**. It is a criminal offence to make a declaration of solvency without reasonable grounds.

Type of resolution to be passed	
Ordinary	This is **rare, but** if the **articles** specify liquidation at a certain point, only an ordinary resolution is required
Special	A company may resolve to be **wound up** by special resolution

The winding up **commences** on the passing of the resolution. A signed copy of the resolution must be delivered to the Registrar within 15 days. A **liquidator** is usually appointed by the same resolution (or a second resolution passed at the same time).

2.1.1 Declaration of solvency

A voluntary winding up is a members' voluntary winding up **only** if the directors make and deliver to the Registrar a **declaration of solvency**: s 89.

This is a **statutory declaration** that the directors have made full enquiry into the affairs of the company and are of the opinion that it will be able to pay its debts, within a specified period not exceeding 12 months.

(a) The declaration is made by all the directors or, if there are more than two directors, by a **majority** of them.

(b) The declaration includes a statement of the company's assets and liabilities as at the latest practicable date before the declaration is made.

(c) The declaration must be:

(i) Made not more than five weeks before the resolution to wind up is passed, and

(ii) Delivered to the Registrar within 15 days after the meeting.

If the liquidator later concludes that the company will be unable to pay its debts they must call a meeting of creditors and lay before them a **statement of assets and liabilities**: s 95.

It is a **criminal offence** punishable by fine or imprisonment for a director to make a declaration of solvency without having **reasonable grounds** for it. If the company proves to be insolvent they will have to justify their previous declaration or be punished.

In a members' voluntary winding up the **creditors play no part** since the assumption is that their debts will be paid in full. The liquidator calls special and annual general meetings of contributories (members) to whom they report:

(a)   Within three months after each anniversary of the commencement of the winding up the liquidator must call a meeting and lay before it an account of his transactions during the year.

(b)   When the liquidation is complete the liquidator calls a meeting to lay before it his final accounts.

After holding the final meeting the liquidator sends a **copy of his accounts** to the Registrar who dissolves the company three months later by removing its name from the register: s 201.

2.2 Creditors' voluntary liquidation

FAST FORWARD

When there is no declaration of solvency there is a **creditors' voluntary winding** up.

If no declaration of solvency is made and delivered to the Registrar the liquidation proceeds as a creditors' voluntary winding up **even if** in the end the company pays its debts in full.

To commence a creditors' voluntary winding up the directors convene a general meeting of members to pass a **special resolution** (private companies may pass a written resolution with a 75% majority). They must also convene a meeting of creditors, giving at least seven days notice of this meeting. The notice must be advertised in the **Gazette** and two local newspapers. The notice must either:

*   Give the name and address of a **qualified insolvency practitioner** to whom the creditors can apply before the meeting for information about the company, **or**

*   State a place in the locality of the company's principal place of business where, on the two business days before the meeting, a **list of creditors** can be inspected.

The **meeting of members** is held first and its business is as follows:

*   To resolve to wind up
*   To appoint a liquidator, and
*   To nominate up to five representatives to be members of the liquidation committee.

The **creditors' meeting** should preferably be convened on the same day but at a later time than the members' meeting, or on the next day, but in any event within 14 days of it.

One of the **directors** presides at the creditors' meeting and lays before it a full statement of the company's affairs and a list of creditors with the amounts owing to them. The meeting may nominate a liquidator and up to five representatives to be members of the liquidation committee.

If the creditors nominate a different person to be liquidator, **their choice prevails** over the nomination by the members.

Of course, the creditors may decide **not to appoint a liquidator** at all. They cannot be compelled to appoint a liquidator, and if they do fail to appoint one it will be the members' nominee who will take office.

However even if creditors do appoint a liquidator there is a period of up to two weeks before the creditors' meeting takes place at which they will actually make the **appointment**. In the interim it will be the members' nominee who takes office as liquidator.

In either case the presence of the members' nominee as liquidator has been exploited in the past for the purpose known as **'centrebinding'**.

> **Re Centrebind Ltd 1966**
>
> *The facts:* The directors convened a general meeting, without making a statutory declaration of solvency, but failed to call a creditors' meeting for the same or the next day. The penalty for this was merely a small default fine. The liquidator chosen by the members had disposed of the assets before the creditors could appoint a liquidator. The creditors' liquidator challenged the sale of the assets (at a low price) as invalid.
>
> *Decision:* The first liquidator had been in office when he made the sale and so it was a valid exercise of the normal power of sale.

In a 'centrebinding' transaction the assets are sold by an **obliging liquidator** to a new company formed by the members of the insolvent company. The purpose is to defeat the claims of the creditors at minimum cost and enable the same people to continue in business until the next insolvency supervenes.

The Government has sought to limit the abuses during the period between the members' and creditors' meetings. The **powers of the members' nominee as liquidator are now restricted** to:

- Taking control of the company's property,
- Disposing of perishable or other goods which might diminish in value if not disposed of immediately, and
- Doing all other things necessary for the protection of the company's assets.

If the members' liquidator wishes to perform any act other than those listed above, he will have to **apply to the court for leave**.

Question
Voluntary liquidation

What are the key differences between a creditors' voluntary liquidation and a members' voluntary liquidation?

Answer

Creditors' voluntary liquidation	Members' voluntary liquidation
Company is insolvent	Company is solvent
Creditors (usually) appoint liquidator	Members appoint liquidator
Liquidation committee approve liquidator's action	Members approve liquidator's actions in general meeting

3 Compulsory liquidation

FAST FORWARD

A creditor may apply to the court to wind up the company, primarily if the company is **unable to pay its debts**. There are statutory tests to prove that a company is unable to pay its debts.

A **creditor** may apply to the court for a compulsory winding up. There are seven statutory reasons he can give, which can all be found in s122. We shall consider the two most important here.

	Statutory reasons for compulsory liquidation
s122(1)(f)	Company is unable to pay its debts
s122(1)(g)	It is just and equitable to wind up the company

The **Government** may petition for the compulsory winding up of a company:

- If a public company has not obtained a, **trading certificate** within one year of incorporation
- Following a report by Government inspectors that it is in the **public interest** and **just and equitable** for the company to be wound up

3.1 Company unable to pay its debts

A creditor who petitions on the grounds of the company's insolvency must show that the company is unable to pay its debts. There are three permitted ways to do that: s 123.

(a) A **creditor owed more than £750 serves** the company at its registered office a **written demand** for payment and the **company neglects** either to **pay the debt** or to offer reasonable security for it within **21 days**.

   If the company denies it owes the amount demanded on apparently reasonable grounds, the court will dismiss the petition and leave the creditor to take legal proceedings for debt.

(b) A creditor obtains **judgement** against the company for debt, and attempts to enforce the judgement. However they are **unable to obtain payment** because no assets of the company have been found and seized.

(c) A creditor satisfies the court that, taking into account the contingent and prospective liabilities of the company, it is **unable to pay its debts**. The creditor may be able to show this in one of two ways:

   (i) By proof that the company is not able to pay its debts as they fall due – the **commercial insolvency test**

   (ii) By proof that the company's assets are less than its liabilities – the **balance sheet test**

   This is a residual category. Any suitable evidence of actual or prospective insolvency may be produced.

Exam focus point

> In Chapter 18, we outlined that a secured creditor might appoint a receiver to control the secured asset for the purpose of realising the creditors' loan. If the receiver cannot find an asset to realise, the creditor might file a petition for compulsory liquidation under (b).

3.2 The just and equitable ground

FAST FORWARD

> A **dissatisfied member** may get the court to wind the company up on the **just and equitable ground**.

A member who is dissatisfied with the directors or controlling shareholders over the management of the company may petition the court for the company to be wound up on the **just and equitable ground**.

For such a petition to be successful, the member must show that **no** other remedy is available. It is not enough for a member to be **dissatisfied** to make it just and equitable that the company should be wound up, since winding up what may be an otherwise healthy company is a **drastic step**.

3.2.1 Examples: When companies have been wound up

(a) **The substratum of the company has gone – the only or main object(s) of the company (its underlying basis or substratum) cannot be or can no longer be achieved.**

> *Re German Date Coffee Co 1882*
>
> *The facts:* The objects clause specified very pointedly that the sole object was to manufacture coffee from dates under a German patent. The German government refused to grant a patent. The company manufactured coffee under a Swedish patent for sale in Germany. A member petitioned for compulsory winding up.
>
> *Decision:* The company existed only to 'work a particular patent' and as it could not do so it should be wound up.

(b) **The company was formed for an illegal or fraudulent purpose or there is a complete deadlock in the management of its affairs.**

Re Yenidje Tobacco Co Ltd 1916

The facts: Two sole traders merged their businesses in a company of which they were the only directors and shareholders. They quarrelled bitterly and one sued the other for fraud. Meanwhile they refused to speak to each other and conducted board meetings by passing notes through the hands of the secretary. The defendant in the fraud action petitioned for compulsory winding up.

Decision: 'In substance these two people are really partners' and by analogy with the law of partnership (which permits dissolution if the partners are really unable to work together) it was just and equitable to order liquidation.

(c) **The understandings between members or directors which were the basis of the association have been unfairly breached by lawful action.**

Ebrahimi v Westbourne Galleries Ltd 1973

The facts: E and N carried on business together for 25 years, originally as partners and for the last 10 years through a company in which each originally had 500 shares. E and N were the first directors and shared the profits as directors' remuneration; no dividends were paid. When N's son joined the business he became a third director and E and N each transferred 100 shares to N's son. Eventually there were disputes. N and his son used their voting control in general meeting (600 votes against 400) to remove E from his directorship under the power of removal given by what is now s 168 of the Companies Act 2006 (removal by ordinary resolution).

Decision: The company should be wound up. N and his son were within their legal rights in removing E from his directorship, but the past relationship made it 'unjust or inequitable' to insist on legal rights and the court could intervene on equitable principles to order liquidation.

Re A company 1983

The facts: The facts were similar in essentials to those in *Ebrahimi's case* but the majority offered and the petitioner agreed that they would settle the dispute by a sale of his shares to the majority. This settlement broke down however because they could not agree on the price. The petitioner then petitioned on the just and equitable ground.

Decision: An order for liquidation on this ground may only be made 'in the absence of any other remedy'. As the parties had agreed in principle that there was an alternative to liquidation the petition must be dismissed.

3.3 Proceedings for compulsory liquidation

When a petition is presented to the **court** a copy is delivered to the **company** in case it objects. It is advertised so that other creditors may intervene if they wish.

The petition **may** be presented by a member. If the petition is presented by **a member** he **must show** that:

(a) The company is **solvent** or alternatively refuses to supply information of its financial position, and

(b) He has been a **registered shareholder** for at least 6 of the 18 months up to the date of his petition. However this rule is not applied if the petitioner acquired his shares by allotment direct from the company or by inheritance from a deceased member or if the petition is based on the number of members having fallen below two.

Attention!

The court will not order compulsory liquidation on a member's petition if he has nothing to gain from it. If the company is insolvent he would receive nothing since the creditors will take all the assets.

Once the court has been petitioned, a **provisional liquidator** may be appointed by the **court**. The **official receiver** is usually appointed, and his powers are conferred by the court. These usually extend to taking control of the company's property and applying for a special manager to be appointed.

> The **official receiver** is an officer of the court. They are appointed as liquidator of any company ordered to be wound up by the court, although an insolvency practitioner may replace them.

3.4 Effects of an order for compulsory liquidation

The effects of an **order** for compulsory liquidation are:

(a)   The **official receiver** (an official of the Government whose duties relate mainly to bankruptcy of individuals) **becomes liquidator**: s 136.

(b)   The liquidation is **deemed to have commenced at the time** (possibly several months earlier) **when the petition was first presented**.

(c)   Any **disposition** of the **company's property** and any transfer of its shares subsequent to the commencement of liquidation is **void** unless the court orders otherwise: s 127.

(d)   Any **legal proceedings** in progress against the company are halted (and none may thereafter begin) unless the court gives leave. Any seizure of the company's assets after commencement of liquidation is void: ss 130 and 128.

(e)   The **employees** of the company are **automatically dismissed**. The liquidator assumes the powers of management previously held by the directors.

(f)   Any **floating charge crystallises**.

The assets of the company may remain the company's legal property but **under the liquidator's control** unless the court by order **vests** the assets in the liquidator. The business of the company may continue but it is the liquidator's duty to continue it with a view only to realisation, for instance by sale as a going concern.

Within 21 days of the making of the order for winding up a **statement of affairs** must be delivered to the liquidator verified by one or more directors and by the secretary (and possibly by other persons). The statement shows the assets and liabilities of the company and includes a list of creditors with particulars of any security: s 131.

The liquidator may require that any **officers or employees** concerned in the recent management of the company shall join in submitting the statement of affairs.

3.4.1 Investigations by the official receiver

The official receiver **must investigate** (s 132)

- The **causes of the failure** of the company, and
- Generally the **promotion, formation, business dealings** and **affairs** of the company.

The official receiver **may report** to the court on the results.

(a)   The official receiver may require the **public examination** in open court of those believed to be implicated (a much-feared sanction).

(b)   The official receiver may apply to the court for public examination where half the **creditors** or three-quarters of the **shareholders** (in value in either case) so request. Failure to attend, or reasonable suspicion that the examinees will abscond, may lead to arrest and detention in custody for contempt of court.

3.4.2 Meetings of contributories and creditors

> **Contributories** are **members** of a company.
>
> At winding up, the member may have to make payments to the company in respect of any unpaid share capital or guarantees (see Chapter 16).

The official receiver has 12 weeks to decide whether or not to convene **separate meetings** of creditors and contributories. The meetings provide the creditors and contributories with the opportunity to appoint their own nominee as permanent liquidator to replace the official receiver, and a **liquidation committee** to work with the liquidator.

If the official receiver believes there is little interest and that the creditors will be unlikely to appoint a liquidator he can **dispense with a meeting**, informing the court, the creditors and the contributories of the decision. He can always be required to call a meeting if at least 25 per cent in value of the creditors require him to do so: s 136.

If no meeting is held, or one is held but no liquidator is appointed, the official receiver continues to act as liquidator. If the creditors do hold a meeting and **appoint their own nominee** this person automatically becomes liquidator subject to a right of objection to the court. Any person appointed to act as liquidator must be a qualified insolvency practitioner.

At any time after a winding up order is made, **the official receiver may ask the Secretary of State to appoint a liquidator**. Similarly, he may request an appointment if the creditors and members fail to appoint a liquidator: s 137.

If separate meetings of creditors and contributories are held and different persons are nominated as liquidators, it is the **creditors' nominee** who **takes precedence**.

Notice of the order for compulsory liquidation and of the appointment of a liquidator is given to the Registrar and in the **Gazette**.

If, while the liquidation is in progress, the liquidator decides to call meetings of contributories or creditors he may arrange to do so under powers vested in the court.

3.5 Completion of compulsory liquidation

When the liquidator completes his task he reports to the Government, which **examines his accounts**. He may apply to the court for an order for dissolution of the company.

An official receiver may also apply to the Registrar for an **early dissolution** of the company if its realisable assets will not cover his expenses and further investigation is not required: s 202.

Question Compulsory liquidation order

What are the six effects of a compulsory liquidation order?

Answer

- Official receiver appointed as liquidator
- Liquidation deemed to have commenced at time when petition first presented
- Disposition of company property since commencement of liquidation deemed void
- Legal proceedings against the company are halted
- Employees are dismissed
- Any floating charge crystallises

4 Differences between compulsory and voluntary liquidation

FAST FORWARD
The differences between compulsory and voluntary liquidation are associated with **timing**, the **role** of the **official receiver**, **stay of legal proceedings** and the **dismissal of employees**.

The main differences in **legal consequences** between a compulsory and a voluntary liquidation up are as follows.

	Differences
Control	Under a members' voluntary liquidation the members control the liquidation process. Under a creditors' voluntary liquidation the creditors control the process. The court controls the process under a compulsory liquidation.
Timing	A voluntary winding up commences on the day when the **resolution to wind up is passed**. It is not retrospective. A compulsory winding up, once agreed to by the court, commences on the day the **petition was presented**.
Liquidator	The **official receiver** plays **no role** in a **voluntary winding up**. The members or creditors select and appoint the liquidator and he is not an officer of the court.
Legal proceedings	In a voluntary winding up there is no automatic **stay of legal proceedings** against the company, nor are previous dispositions or seizure of its assets void. However the liquidator has a general right to apply to the court to make any order which the court can make in a compulsory liquidation. He would do so, for instance, to prevent any creditor obtaining an unfair advantage over the other creditors.
Management and staff	In any **liquidation the liquidator replaces the directors** in the management of the company (unless he decides to retain them). However, the employees are **not automatically dismissed by commencement of voluntary liquidation**. Insolvent liquidation may amount to repudiation of their employment contracts (provisions of the statutory employment protection code apply).

5 Saving a company: administration

Administration is a method of **'saving' a company from liquidation**, under the Enterprise Act 2002.

5.1 What is administration?

FAST FORWARD
An **administrator** is appointed primarily to try to rescue the company as a going concern. A company may go into administration to carry out an established plan to save the company.

Key term

> **Administration** puts an **insolvency practitioner** in **control** of the company with a defined programme for **rescuing the company** from insolvency as a going concern.

Its purpose is to **insulate** the company **from its creditors while it seeks:**

- To save itself as a going concern, or failing that
- To achieve a better result for creditors than an immediate winding up would secure, or failing that
- To realise property so as to make a distribution to creditors.

Administration orders and liquidations are **mutually exclusive**. Once an administration order has been passed by the court, it is **no longer possible to petition the court** for a **winding up** order against the company. Similarly, however, once an order for winding up has been made, an administration order cannot be granted (except when appointed by a floating chargeholder, see Section 5.2).

Administration can be initiated with or without a court order.

5.2 Appointment without a court order

FAST FORWARD

Some parties – **secured creditors** and **directors** and the **members** by resolution – can appoint an administrator without a court order.

It is possible to appoint an administrator **without reference to the court**. There are three sets of people who might be able to do this:

- Floating chargeholders
- Directors
- Company

Attention!

> Floating chargeholders were introduced in Chapter 17. Revise them now if you are not sure.

5.2.1 Floating chargeholders

Floating chargeholders have the right to appoint an administrator without reference to the court even if there is no actual or impending insolvency. They may also **appoint an administrator even if the company is in compulsory liquidation**. This enables steps to be taken to save the company before its financial situation becomes irreversible.

In order to qualify for this right, the **floating charge must entitle the holder to appoint an administrator**. This would be in the terms of the charge. It must also be over all, or substantially all, the company's property.

Point to note

> In practice, such a floating chargeholder with a charge over all or substantially all the company's property is likely to be a **bank**.

However, the **floating chargeholder may only appoint an administrator** if:

- They have given **two days** written notice to the holder of any prior floating charge where that person has the right to appoint an administrator.
- Their floating charge is **enforceable**.

After any relevant two day notice period (see above), the floating chargeholder will file the following **documents** at court:

- A **notice of appointment** in the prescribed form identifying the administrator
- A **statement by the administrator** that he **consents to the appointment**
- A **statement by the administrator** that, in his **opinion**, the **purpose of the administration** is likely to be **achieved**
- A **statutory declaration** that he **qualifies** to make the appointment

Once these documents have been filed, the **appointment is valid**. The appointer must notify the administrator and other people prescribed by regulations of the appointment as soon as is reasonably practicable.

5.2.2 Company and directors

The process by which a company commences appointing an administrator will depend upon its **articles of association**. A company or its directors may appoint an administrator if:

- The company has not done so in the last 12 months or been subject to a **moratorium** as a result of a voluntary arrangement with its creditors in the last 12 months
- The company is, or is likely to be, **unable to pay its debts**
- **No petition for winding up** nor any **administration order** in respect of the company has been presented to the court and is outstanding
- The company is **not in liquidation**
- **No administrator** is already in office
- **No administrative receiver** is already in office

The company or its directors must give notice to any floating chargeholders entitled to appoint an administrator. This means that the **floating chargeholders may** appoint their own administrator within this time period, and so **block the company's choice of administrator**.

5.3 Appointment of an administrator by the court

FAST FORWARD

Various parties can apply for **administration** through the court.

There are four sets of parties that may apply to the court for an administration order:

- The **company** (that is, a majority of the members by (ordinary) resolution)
- The **directors** of the company
- One or more **creditors** of the company
- The **Justice** and **Chief Executive of the Magistrates' Court** following non-payment of a fine imposed on the company

Exam focus point

Individual members **cannot** apply to the court for an administration order.

The court will grant the administration order if it is satisfied that:

- The company is, or is likely to be, **unable to pay its debts**, and
- The administration order is reasonably likely to **achieve the purpose of administration**

The application will name the person whom the applicants want to be the **administrator**. Unless certain interested parties object, this person is appointed as administrator.

5.4 The effects of appointing an administrator

FAST FORWARD

The **effects** of administration depend on whether it is effected by the **court** or by a **floating chargeholder**, to some degree.

Effects of an administrator appointment
A **moratorium** over the company's debts commences (that is, no creditor can enforce their debt during the administration period without the court's permission). This is the advantageous aspect of being in administration.
The court must give its permission for: • **Security** over company property to be **enforced**   • Goods held under hire purchase to be **repossessed**   • A landlord to conduct **forfeiture** by peaceable entry   • Commencement/continuation of any **legal process** against the company
The **powers of management** are subjugated to the authority of the administrator and managers can only act with his consent.
All outstanding **petitions for winding-up** of the company are **dismissed.**
Any **administrative receiver** in place must **vacate office**. No appointments to this position can be made.

5.5 Duties of the administrator

FAST FORWARD

The administrator has **fiduciary duties** to the company as its agent, plus some legal duties.

The administrator is an **agent of the company** and the **creditors as a whole**. He therefore owes fiduciary duties to them and has the following legal duties:

Legal duties of the administrator
As soon as **reasonably practicable** after appointment he must:
• **Send notice** of appointment to the company
• **Publish notice** of appointment
• Obtain a list of **company creditors** and sent notice of appointment to each
• Within 7 days of appointment, send notice of appointment to **Registrar**
• Require certain relevant people to provide a **statement of affairs** of the company
• Ensure that every **business document** of the company **bears the identity** of the administrator and a statement that the affairs, business and property of the company are being managed by him.
• Consider the **statements of affairs** submitted to him and set out his **proposals** for achieving the aim of administration. The proposals must be **sent to the Registrar** and the company's **creditors,** and be made available to **every member of the company** as soon as is reasonably practicable, and **within eight weeks**.
• Whilst preparing their proposals, the administrator must **manage the affairs** of the company.

The **statement of affairs** must be provided by the people from whom it is requested within 11 days of it being requested. It is in a prescribed form, and contains:

* Details of the **company's property**
* The company's **debts** and **liabilities**
* The **names** and **addresses** of the **company's creditors**
* Details of any **security** held by any **creditor**

Failing to provide a statement of affairs, or providing a statement in which the writer has no reasonable belief of truth, is a **criminal offence** punishable by fine.

5.6 Administrator's proposals

FAST FORWARD

The administrator must either **propose a rescue plan**, or state that the **company cannot be rescued**.

Having considered all information the administrator must within 8 weeks (subject to possible extension) either:

* Set out his **proposals for achieving the aim of the administration**; or
* Set out why it is not **reasonable and practicable** that the company be rescued. In this case he will also set out why the creditors as a whole would benefit from winding up.

The proposal must be sent to all members and creditors he is aware of. It must not

* Affect the right of a **secured creditor** to enforce his security,
* Result in a non-preferential debt being paid in priority to a preferential debt
* Result in one preferential creditor being paid a smaller proportion of his debt than another.

5.6.1 Creditors' meeting

The administrator must call a **meeting of creditors** within **10 weeks** of their appointment to approve the proposals. The creditors may either accept or reject them. Once the proposals have been agreed, the administrator cannot make any substantial amendment without first gaining the creditors' consent.

5.7 Administrator's powers

The administrator takes on the **powers** of the directors.

The powers of the administrator are summed up as follows:

'The administrator of a company may do **anything necessarily expedient** for the management of the affairs, business and property of the company.'

The administrator **takes on the powers previously enjoyed by the directors** and the following specific powers to:

- Remove or appoint a **director**
- Call a **meeting of members or creditors**
- **Apply to court for directions** regarding the carrying out of his functions
- Make payments to **secured or preferential creditors**
- With the permission of the court, **make payments to unsecured creditors**

The administrator usually requires the permission of the court to make payments to unsecured creditors. However, this is not the case if the administrator feels that paying the unsecured creditor will assist the **achievement of the administration**. For example, if the company has been denied further supplies by a major supplier unless payment is tendered.

Any creditor or member of the company may **apply to the court** if they feel that the administrator has acted or will act in a way that has harmed or will harm his interest. The court may take various actions against the administrator.

5.8 End of administration

Administration can last up to **12 months**.

The administration period **ends** when:

- The administration has been successful
- Twelve months have elapsed from the date of the appointment of administrator
- The administrator applies to the court to end the appointment
- A creditor applies to the court to end the appointment
- An improper motive of the applicant for applying for the administration is discovered.

The administrator automatically vacates office after **12 months of his appointment**. This time period can be extended by court order or by consent from the appropriate creditors.

Alternatively, the administrator may **apply to the court** when he thinks:

- The purpose of administration cannot be achieved
- The company should not have entered into administration
- The administration has been successful (if appointed by the court)

He must also apply to the court if required to by the **creditors' meeting**.

Where the administrator was appointed by a chargeholder or the company/its directors, and he feels that the purposes of administration have been achieved, he must file a **notice** with the court and the Registrar.

5.9 Advantages of administration

FAST FORWARD

Administration has been found to have many advantages for the **company**, the **members** and the **creditors**.

Advantages of administration	
To the company	The company does not necessarily cease to exist at the end of the process, whereas liquidation will always result in the company being wound up.
	It provides temporary relief from creditors to allow breathing space to formulate rescue plans.
	It prevents any creditor applying for compulsory liquidation.
	It provides for past transactions to be challenged.
To the members	They will continue to have shares in the company which has not been wound up. If the administration is successful, regenerating the business should enhance share value and will restore any income from the business.
To the creditors	Creditors should obtain a return in relation to their past debts from an administration.
	Unsecured creditors will benefit from asset realisations.
	Any creditor may apply to the court for an administration order, while only certain creditors may apply for other forms of relief from debt. For example, the use of receivers or an application for winding up.
	Floating chargeholders may appoint an administrator without reference to the court.
	It may also be in the interests of the creditors to have a continued business relationship with the company once the business has been turned around.

Exam focus point

You may be asked to consider the advantages of administration as opposed to liquidation from the point of view of all the parties involved.

Chapter Roundup

- **Liquidation** is the **dissolution** or 'winding up' of a company.

- There are three different methods of **liquidation: compulsory**, **members' voluntary** and **creditors' voluntary**. Compulsory liquidation and creditors' voluntary liquidation are proceedings for insolvent companies, and members' voluntary liquidation is for solvent companies.

- A **liquidator** must be an authorised, qualified insolvency practitioner.

- Once **insolvency procedures** have commenced, share trading must cease, the company documents must state that the company is in liquidation and the directors' power to manage ceases.

- A **winding** up is **voluntary** where the decision to wind up is taken by the company members in general meeting, although if the company is insolvent, the creditors will be heavily involved in the proceedings.

- In order to be a members' winding up, the directors must make a **declaration of solvency**. It is a criminal offence to make a declaration of solvency without reasonable grounds.

- When there is no declaration of solvency there is a **creditors' voluntary winding** up.

- A creditor may apply to the court to wind up the company, primarily if the company is **unable to pay its debts**. There are statutory tests to prove that a company is unable to pay its debts

- A **dissatisfied member** may get the court to wind the company up on the **just and equitable ground**.

- The differences between compulsory and voluntary liquidation are associated with **timing**, the **role** of the **official receiver**, **stay of legal proceedings** and the **dismissal of employees**.

- An **administrator** is appointed primarily to try to rescue the company as a going concern. A company may go into administration to carry out an established plan to save the company.

- Some parties – **secured creditors** and **directors** and the **members** by resolution – can appoint an administrator without reference to the court.

- Various parties can apply for **administration** through the court.

- The **effects** of administration depend on whether it is effected by the **court** or by a **floating chargeholder**, to some degree.

- The administrator has **fiduciary duties** to the company as its agent, plus some legal duties.

- The administrator must either **propose a rescue plan**, or state that the **company cannot be rescued**.

- The administrator takes on the **powers** of the directors.

- Administration can last up to **12 months**.

- Administration has been found to have many advantages for the **company**, the **members** and the **creditors**.

1   Complete the following definition

Liquidation means that a company must be .... and its affairs wound up.

2   Name three common effects of liquidations.

(1)   ....

(2)   ....

(3)   ....

3   What are the two most important grounds for **compulsory liquidation**?

(1)   ....

(2)   ....

4   A members' voluntary winding up is where the members decide to dissolve a healthy company.

True   ☐

False   ☐

5   Rearrange the list in order of proceedings in a creditors' voluntary winding up

(a)   Creditors' meeting
(b)   Liquidator appointed
(c)   Directors' notice of meeting outlines situation
(d)   Members' meeting
(e)   Liquidation committee nominated

6   Complete the following definition, using the words given below.

An (1) .... is an arrangement which puts an (2).....................
(3)............................. in control of the business to attempt to save it.

| (1)   insolvency | (2)   practitioner | (3)   administration |

7   Name two advantages of administration.

(1)   ....

(2)   ....

1   Dissolved

2   (1)   No further changes in membership permitted
     (2)   All documents must state prominently that company is in liquidation
     (3)   Directors' power to manage ceases

3   (1)   Company is unable to pay its debts
     (2)   It is just and equitable to wind up the company

4   True. Members can decide to wind up a healthy company.

5   (c)
     (d)
     (a)
     (b)/(e). Both these steps occur at the creditors' meeting

6   Administration, insolvency, practioner

7   (1)   It does not necessarily result in the dissolution of the company
     (2)   It prevents creditors applying for compulsory liquidation

     Subsidiary advantages are

     (3)   All creditors can apply for an administration order
     (4)   The administrator may challenge past transactions of the company

Now try the question below from the Exam Question Bank

Number	Level	Marks	Time
Q27	Examination	10	18 mins

P
A
R
T

H

Governance and ethical issues relating to business

Corporate governance

Introduction

Corporate governance is about the direction and control of a company. In this chapter we shall start to look at the structures put in place to ensure that companies are managed well and in the best interests of the owners (the shareholders).

The law sets out basic principles. The **directors manage** the company, as we saw in Chapter 19. The **owners** are entitled to retain **ultimate control** over company strategy by exercising powers in **general meetings**, as we saw in Chapter 20.

In recent years, much attention has been focused on the issue of **corporate governance**. This is because **company failure** due to poor management or even fraud by management has had a significant impact on large numbers of people. The response to the need for better governance has been both extra-legal and statutory. We shall look in Section 3 at the UK's Combined Code on Corporate Governance (as 'extra-legal' approach) and at the US Sarbanes-Oxley Act (a statutory approach).

Study guide

		Intellectual level
(H)	**Governance and ethical issues relating to business**	
1	Corporate governance	
(a)	Explain the idea of corporate governance	2
(b)	Recognise the extra-legal codes of corporate governance	2
(c)	Identify and explain the legal regulation of corporate governance	2

Exam guide

There are many issues that have an impact on corporate governance, and it will feature in some form on every exam paper, either explicitly (such as in a question on the Combined Code) or implicitly (such as in a question on directors' duties).

1 What is corporate governance?

> **FAST FORWARD**
>
> Corporate governance is simply a term used for **the way that companies** (corporate) **are run and operated** (governed).

> **Key term**
>
> **Corporate governance** is the system by which companies are directed and controlled.   *Cadbury Report*

According to the OECD:

> 'Corporate governance is the system by which business corporations are directed and controlled. The corporate governance structure specifies the distribution of rights and responsibilities among different participants in the corporation, such as the board, managers, shareholders and other stakeholders, and spells out the rules and procedures for making decisions on corporate affairs. By doing this, it also provides the structure through which the company objectives are set, and the means of attaining those objectives and monitoring performance.'   *OECD*

1.1 A company's stakeholders

> **FAST FORWARD**
>
> There are many different **stakeholders** in most companies.

As is made clear in the quotation from the OECD above, a company has **various interested parties**, known as **stakeholders**. Examples include:

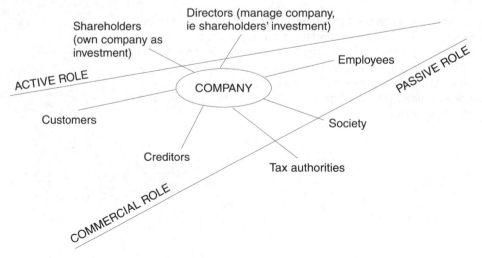

Each of the stakeholders has a **different role**, some of which are more passive than others. For example, **society** is a stakeholder in a company, but it is generally a **passive** participant. The tax authorities passively receive income from the company's profits. Customers, employees and creditors are more active, playing the 'commercial' role that keeps the company's operations going.

1.2 Shareholders and directors

> The stakeholders most closely involved in corporate governance are the **directors** (the managers of the company) and the **shareholders** (who have some ultimate controls in general meeting).

The key active stakeholders are **shareholders**, who **own the company**, and **directors**, who **manage the company**, and therefore, they manage the shareholders' investment.

Corporate governance is therefore all about **shareholders** (the owners) and **directors** (the management), as between them they direct and control the company. A UK government report on corporate governance in 1992, the **Cadbury report**, identified the role of directors:

'The directors are responsible for the corporate governance of the company.'

Sometimes, particularly in smaller businesses, companies are **owned and managed by the same people**. This is the situation where people form a company to carry out their own business, buy the shares and appoint themselves as directors. Such companies are known as 'owner-managed businesses'. The first diagram on the next page illustrates such a company.

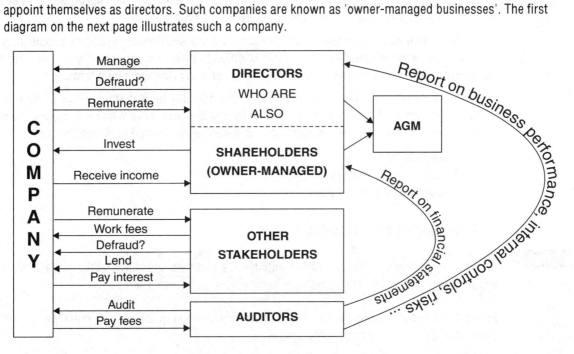

In other, often **bigger**, companies, the directors and shareholders are different sets of people. Often in larger companies quoted on stock exchanges, **shareholders** purchase shares as an investment and may have very little personal contact with the company. **Directors** are employed for their management expertise and have no other connection with the company. The diagram below illustrates such a company.

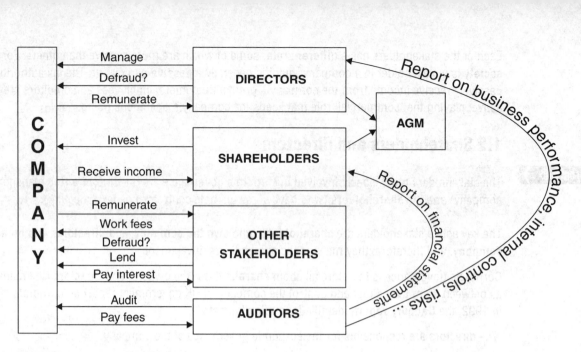

1.2.1 Knowledge gap

These two diagrams illustrate two positions between which there is a wide spectrum. They also illustrate a key difference between the two companies, which is a '**knowledge gap**'.

In the **owner-managed company**, as the directors and shareholders are the same people, they have **access to the same information** and are **in a position to direct company policy**. In the other company, the shareholders do not have access to day-to-day company management information.

This 'gap' in the shareholders' knowledge may cause difficulty for **investors**, who **will want to be assured that their investment is being managed correctly and in accordance with their wishes, as owners**. Company law and practice have adopted various measures to attempt to bridge the gap.

- Financial statements
- Annual general meetings
- Corporate governance codes

1.3 Financial statements

FAST FORWARD

Directors must prepare **financial statements** for shareholders annually, and these are independently audited to provide an objective check on the directors.

As we discussed in Chapter 19, the directors are required by law to **report to members** on the **financial position** of the company on an annual basis.

Company law requires that an independent professional **audits** these financial statements to ensure that they **give a true and fair view**. The Cadbury report on corporate governance (mentioned earlier) referred to the **audit** as a **cornerstone of good corporate governance**, as it gives an **objective check** on the stewardship of the directors.

1.4 Annual general meeting (AGM)

FAST FORWARD

At the AGM the shareholders can exercise their **ultimate control**.

The AGM is the **key shareholder meeting**. It gives **shareholders** an opportunity to **conduct dialogue with directors and to be heard by them**. There is also some **routine business** carried out at an AGM. For example, it is the meeting at which the financial statements are presented to the shareholders and the meeting at which directors and auditors are re-elected.

Although directors make day-to-day management decisions for the company, **shareholders retain control of the major company policy at company meetings**. Remember that, as we have observed in previous chapters, **certain key decisions and capabilities**, such as amending the object of the company or authorising additional share capital, are **retained by shareholders in general meetings**.

Despite the legal protection of the AGM for shareholders, they are often poorly attended by shareholders. Also, where shareholders invest in the largest of companies, there is often **apathy amongst shareholders** about decisions taken by management. This **reduces the effectiveness** of the statutory protection to shareholders given by the AGM and **can expose the company to poor management, and even fraud**.

1.5 Voluntary codes of corporate governance

FAST FORWARD

Following high-profile corporate failures, corporate governance codes set out **best practice**.

Although these interrelated issues have always been of concern in the way companies function, the recent increase in the attention placed on matters of corporate governance has been a result of the perceived **weaknesses** in company regulation. These have become apparent in some of the recent **scandals** involving large companies such as Enron and Worldcom in the US, and Marconi and Parmalat in Europe.

In order to ensure an **effective corporate governance framework** it has been deemed necessary to set out defined rules and regulations, including voluntary codes. The UK has the **Combined Code on Corporate Governance**, which is the result of the review of the role and effectiveness of non-executive directors conducted by Derek Higgs and a review of audit committees conducted by Sir Robert Smith. The revised combined code has applied to listed companies since June 2006. Companies have either to confirm that they **comply** with the Code's provisions or, where they do not, to **provide an explanation** of their non-compliance. Whilst listed companies are expected to comply with the Code's provisions most of the time, it is recognised that departure from its provisions may be justified in particular circumstances. Every company must review each provision carefully and give a considered explanation if it departs form the Code provisions.

1.5.1 Voluntary or prescriptive?

A feature of the **Combined Code** is that there is a voluntary 'extra-legal' code. The company is required to report if it has not complied with the Code, but it is not required to comply with the Code (unless it is a listed company and therefore required to do so under the Stock Exchange rules).

An alternative approach would be for governments to make such corporate governance requirements **mandatory** for companies. This approach is often shunned, arguments in favour of keeping codes voluntary include:

(a) The fact that all companies are different and the make up of their stakeholders is different means that statutory standards might be **inflexible**. The **additional costs** and regulatory burdens **might not be justified** in all cases.

(b) In such cases, the result might be **detrimental to shareholders** (in terms of cost) who are key stakeholders the regulation is seeking to protect.

(c) Statutory **monitoring** of compliance would be required, which again could add to the burden for the company.

(d) Some of the requirements of the codes are **subjective** (for example, in relation to non-executive directors) and it would be difficult to prescribe regulations in respect of them.

While codes are not mandatory, or legally required, they are **heavily encouraged**, particularly for listed companies, and **companies not complying with such requirements may find that they suffer in investment markets as a result**.

Question

Good corporate governance

Why is good corporate governance important?

Shareholders and managers are usually separate in a company and it is important that the management of a company deals fairly with the investment made by the owners.

2 Governance structures

Whether their status is down to **voluntary** or **statutory** rules, there are certain aspects of governance, or 'governance structures' which are generally acceptable.

2.1 The split between executive and non-executive directors

One of the best forms of internal control is the segregation of duties, separating the roles of directors into those who have **executive** powers (the power to **manage** the company) and those who have **non-executive** powers (the power to **direct** and **control** the company).

In Chapter 19 we looked briefly at the difference between executive and non-executive directors. We shall come back to them shortly when we cover the Combined Code.

2.2 Unitary board of directors

Many companies have a **unitary board** system, where there is one board to run a company.

The UK and many other countries, including the US, follow a **single**, sometimes called a **unitary**, **board** structure. This is where the company is **managed by a single board of directors**.

This board may be formed of executive directors only, or a mixture of executive and non-executive directors. The Combined Code, which we shall look at shortly, gives significant guidance about the **composition of unitary boards**.

We shall consider the **advantages and disadvantages** of a unitary board structure later, as it will be easier to see the advantages and disadvantages in comparison to the other major type of board structure, used internationally, the supervisory board structure.

2.2.1 Composition of the unitary board

There are **very few legal requirements** relating to the composition of a unitary board. As we have discussed above, there are requirements concerning the **number of directors** a company has and there are requirements concerning **quorum**. There are also requirements about **who is allowed to be a director** as we saw in Chapter 19. The law is otherwise silent on the composition of the board.

2.3 Supervisory board structure

In Germany and some other countries, a supervisory (or dual) board system is used. This means that there is a **management board to run the company** plus a **supervisory board to oversee** the management board.

Some countries, notably **Germany** and **Holland**, use a different board structure to the UK. The type of board structure used in Germany, is known as the **supervisory board structure**, sometimes called the **two-tier or dual system**.

The supervisory board system involves the use of two boards, **management** and **supervisory**. The management board is loosely comparable to the UK unitary board, and it has general responsibility to **manage** the company. The supervisory board is an **independent, separate board**.

2.3.1 Composition of the supervisory board

The supervisory board consists of **members elected by the shareholders and by employees of the company**. Usually, a third of the board is elected by the employees and the remainder by the shareholders. If the company has more than 2,000 employees, half the members of the board must be representatives of the employees of the company.

2.3.2 Role of the supervisory board

The **supervisory board** has an advisory role in relation to the business. It has the following key powers:

- Appoints members of the management board
- May request information from members of the management board
- Must be formally reported to about matters of policy
- Must be formally reported to about profit and loss
- Must be formally reported to about the state of the company's affairs
- Must be formally reported to in exceptional circumstances
- Approves the financial statements and dividends
- Inspects the books and accounts
- May set up committees and delegate jobs to them
- May initiate independent investigations
- May convene shareholder meetings
- May remove management board members (as a last resort and on legitimate grounds)

However, this power is limited in that it does not have power to manage the company, only to **supervise the managers**. It is not entitled to make **policy decisions** and cannot represent the company in **legal action**.

2.4 Unitary board and supervisory board compared

In practice, the principles of **independence** and **verification** behind both the **unitary** and the **dual systems** are increasingly growing closer. Both systems face **similar problems** in terms of finding **suitably qualified people** to undertake supervisory roles and to be an **independent** voice in a company.

2.4.1 Advantages of the unitary board structure

The fact that all participants in the management of the company are given responsibility for management of the company suggests a **more involved approach** by those directors who are non-executive directors and therefore act in an independent and 'supervisory' capacity.

If all the directors attend the same meetings, the **independent directors** are **less likely to be** effectively **excluded from decision-making and given restricted access to information**. The **presence of non-executive directors** to question the actions and decisions of executive directors as they are taking place **should lead to better decisions being made**.

2.4.2 Criticisms of the unitary board structure

Asking an 'external' or 'independent' director to be **both manager and supervisor** may be **too awkward and demanding a task**.

Criticism has also been made of the requirement to have as many **independent non-executive directors** as **executive directors** on the board. Who are these non-executive directors? Where are people with such expertise and time-availability to be found?

The criticism is intensified when the **independence requirement** is considered. It raises questions such as: How can people who fulfil the independence requirement be expected to have sufficient knowledge about the company to properly fulfil their management capacity?

The supervisory board system takes account of the needs of stakeholders other than shareholders, specifically **employees**, who are clearly important stakeholders in practice. The unitary board system makes no specific provision for employees to be represented on the management board, other than by the people who employ them.

The unitary board **emphasises the divide between the shareholders and the directors** as there is no crossover between them. It **puts pressure on the annual general meeting** as the only place where shareholder grievance or concern can be heard.

2.4.3 Advantages of the supervisory board structure

The formal supervisory role given to the members of this board has the **capacity** to be an **effective guard** against management inefficiency or worse. Indeed its very existence may be a **deterrent** to fraud or irregularity in a similar way to the independent audit.

The system actively **encourages transparency within the company**, between the boards and, through the supervisory board, to the employees and the shareholders. This is in sharp contrast to the closed doors policy of UK boards.

It also **actively involves the shareholders and employees** in the supervision and appointment of directors.

2.4.4 Criticisms of the supervisory board structure

The main criticism of the system centres around the fact that in practice, the supervisory board may not be as effective as it seems in theory:

- The **management board may restrict the information passed on** to the supervisory board
- In practice, the boards may only liaise **infrequently**

The supervisory board may not be as **independent** as would be wished, depending on how rigorous the appointment procedures are. In addition, members of the supervisory board can be shareholder representatives, and this could detract from the legal requirement that shareholders should not instruct directors how to manage.

2.5 Board committees

Whether a unitary or a supervisory board system is used, the effective operation of the board is often facilitated by the creation of **board committees**. Authority of the board as a whole is delegated to these committees with respect to certain defined areas, such as audit, directors' remuneration and nominations/appointments to the board.

3 The Combined Code on Corporate Governance

FAST FORWARD

Guidance on the composition of a board in the UK is given in the **Combined Code on Corporate Governance**. This sets out a series of principles about how boards should be composed: effective board collectively responsible for the success of the company; balance of non-executive and executive directors; division of responsibility between the chief executive and the chairman.

We shall now look at the requirements of the **Combined Code on Corporate Governance** in relation to the composition of boards. The Code was revised in 2006 and, in the form below, applies in full to companies listed on the **London Stock Exchange**. It is set out in terms of main and supporting principles, and code provisions.

You are unlikely to be tested on the detail of the Combined Code. Read the following information but only learn the principles behind the regulation.

3.1 Effective board

Principle

Every company should be headed by an **effective board**, which is **collectively responsible** for the success of the company.

A key point to be made about the single board is that on a unitary board, **every director has responsibility for the success of the company. Every director has an active role in managing the company**, not just in supervising the company. Contrast this to the supervisory board system.

3.1.1 Principles supporting an effective board

The board's role is to provide **entrepreneurial leadership** of the company within a framework of prudent and effective controls. The board should:

(a) Set the company's **strategic aims**,

(b) Ensure that the **necessary financial and human resources** are in place for the company to meet its objectives, and

(c) **Review management performance**.

The board should set the company's **values and standards** and ensure that its **obligations** to its shareholders and others are understood and met.

All directors must take decisions **objectively in the interests of the company**.

Non-executive directors should:

(a) Constructively challenge and help develop proposals on strategy

(b) Scrutinise the performance of management in meeting agreed goals and objectives

(c) Monitor the reporting of performance

(d) Satisfy themselves on the integrity of financial information and that financial controls and systems of risk management are robust and defensible

(e) Be responsible for determining appropriate levels of remuneration of executive directors

(f) Have prime roles in appointing, and where necessary removing, executive directors, and in succession planning.

3.1.2 Provisions supporting an effective board

1 The board should **meet regularly** with a **formal schedule** of matters specifically reserved for its decision.

2 The annual report should include a **statement** of how the **board operates**, including a high level statement of which types of decision are taken by the board and which are delegated to management.

3 The annual report should identify the **chairman**, the **deputy chairman** (where there is one), the **chief executive**, the **senior independent** (non-executive) **director** and the **chairmen** and **members** of the **nomination**, **audit** and **remuneration committees**. It should also set out the number of meetings of the board and those committees and individual attendance by directors.

4 The chairman should hold meetings with the non-executive directors **without** the executives present. Led by the senior independent director, the non-executive directors should meet without the chairman present at least annually to appraise the chairman's performance and on such other occasions as are deemed appropriate.

5 Where directors have concerns which cannot be resolved about the running of the company or a proposed action, they should ensure that their concerns are recorded in the **board minutes**.

6   On resignation, a non-executive director should provide a **written statement** to the chairman, for circulation to the board, if they have any such concerns.

7   The company should arrange appropriate **insurance cover** in respect of legal action against its directors.

3.2 Chairman and chief executive

Principle

There should be a clear division of responsibilities at the head of the company between the running of the board and the executive with responsibility for the running of the company's business. No one individual should have unfettered powers of decision.

3.2.1 Principles supporting division of responsibilities

The **chairman** is responsible for:

(a)   Leadership of the board, ensuring its effectiveness on all aspects of its role and setting its agenda
(b)   Ensuring that the directors receive accurate, timely and clear information
(c)   Ensuring effective communication with shareholders
(d)   Facilitating the effective contribution of non-executive directors in particular
(e)   Ensuring constructive relations between executive and non-executive directors

3.2.2 Provisions supporting division of responsibilities

1   The roles of chairman and chief executive should be exercised by **different individuals**. The division of responsibilities between the chairman and chief executive should be clearly established, set out in writing and agreed by the board.

2   The chairman should on appointment be **independent**.

3   A **chief executive** should not go on to be **chairman** of the **same company**. If exceptionally a board decides that a chief executive should become chairman, the board should consult major shareholders in advance. It should set out its reasons to shareholders at the time of the appointment and in the next annual report.

3.3 Balance and independence of the board

Principle

The board should include a balance of executive and non-executive directors (and in particular independent non-executive directors) such that no individual or small group of individuals can dominate the board's decision making.

3.3.1 Principles supporting a well-balanced board

The board should be **big enough** that the balance of skills and experience is appropriate for the requirements of the business, and that changes to the board's composition can be managed without undue disruption. The board should **not be so large** as to be unwieldy.

There should be a **strong presence** on the board of both executive and non-executive directors, so that power and information are not concentrated in one or two individuals.

Membership of board committees needs to be refreshed and undue reliance should not be placed on particular individuals, such as the committee chairman.

Only the committee **chairman** and **members** are entitled to be present at a meeting of the nomination, audit or remuneration committees, though others may attend at the invitation of the committee.

3.3.2 Provisions supporting a well-balanced board

1   The board should identify in the annual report each non-executive director (excluding the chairman of the board) it considers to be independent. The board should determine whether the director is

independent in character and judgement and whether there are relationships or circumstances which are likely to affect, or could appear to affect, the director's judgement. The board should state its reasons if it determines that a director is independent notwithstanding the existence of relationships or circumstances which may appear relevant.

2   A director **may** be determined as being **not independent** if he/she:

- Has been an employee of the company or group within the last five years;
- Has, or has had within the last three years, a material business relationship with the company either directly, or as a partner, shareholder, director or senior employee of a body that has such a relationship with the company;
- Has received or receives additional remuneration from the company apart from a director's fee, participates in the company's share option or a performance-related pay scheme, or is a member of the company's pension scheme;
- Has close family ties with any of the company's advisers, directors or senior employees;
- Represents a significant shareholder; or
- Has served on the board for more than nine years from the date of their first election.

3   At least 50% of the board excluding the chairman, should comprise of **independent non-executive directors**.

4   The board should appoint one of the independent non-executive directors to be the **senior independent director**. The senior independent director should be available to shareholders if they have unresolved concerns, or where contact with executive directors is inappropriate.

3.4 Appointments to the board

Principle

> There should be a formal, rigorous and transparent procedure for the appointment of new directors to the board.

3.4.1 Principles supporting the procedure for board appointment

Appointments to the board should be made **on merit** and against **objective criteria**. Especially for chairmanship, care should be taken to ensure that appointees have **enough time** available to devote to the job.

The board should satisfy itself that plans are in place for orderly **succession for appointments** to the board and to senior management. The plans should **maintain an appropriate balance of skills and experience** within the company and on the board.

3.4.2 Provisions supporting board appointment procedure: the nomination committee

1   There should be a **nomination committee** which should lead the process for board appointments and make recommendations to the board.

2   Over **50%** of members of the nomination committee should be independent non-executive directors.

3   The board chairman or an independent non-executive director should **chair the committee**. However, the board chairman should not chair the nomination committee when it is dealing with the appointment of a successor to the chairmanship.

4   The nomination committee should make available its **terms of reference**, explaining its role and the authority delegated to it by the board.

5   The nomination committee should evaluate the **balance of skills, knowledge and experience on the board**. Then, in the light of this evaluation, prepare a description of the role and capabilities required for a particular appointment.

6   For the appointment of the **board chairman**. The nomination committee should prepare a job specification, including an assessment of the time commitment expected, recognising the need for availability in the event of crises.

7   A chairman's other **significant commitments** should be disclosed to the board before appointment and included in the annual report. Changes to such commitments should be reported to the board as they arise, and include in the next annual report.

8   No individual should be appointed to a **second** chairmanship of a FTSE 100 company.

9   The **terms and conditions of appointment** of non-executive directors should be made available for inspection at the registered office.

10   The **letter of appointment** for non-executive directors should set out the expected time commitment. Non-executive directors should undertake that they will have **sufficient time** to meet what is expected of them.

11   Non-executive directors should **disclose** their other **significant commitments** to the board before appointment and the board should be informed of subsequent changes.

12   A full time executive should not be allowed to take on **more** than one non-executive directorship in a FTSE 100 company nor the chairmanship of such a company.

13   A separate section of the **annual report** should describe the work of the nomination committee, including the process it has used in relation to board appointments.

14   An explanation should be given if neither an **external search consultancy** nor open **advertising** has been used in the appointment of a chairman or a non-executive director.

3.5 Information for and professional development of the board

Principle

> The board should be supplied in a timely manner with information in a form and of a quality appropriate to enable it to discharge its duties. All directors should receive induction on joining the board and should regularly update and refresh their skills and knowledge.

3.5.1 Principles supporting the well-informed, professional board

The board chairman is responsible for ensuring that the **directors receive accurate, timely and clear information**. Management is obliged to provide such information but directors should seek clarification or amplification where necessary.

The board chairman should ensure that the **directors continually update their skills** and the knowledge and familiarity with the company required to fulfil their role both on the board and on board committees. The company should provide the necessary resources for developing and updating its directors' knowledge and capabilities.

Under the direction of the chairman, the **company secretary's** responsibilities include ensuring good information flows within the board and its committees and between senior management and non-executive directors. They should facilitate induction and assist with professional development as required. The company secretary should also be responsible for advising the board through the chairman on all **governance matters**.

3.5.2 Provisions supporting the well-informed, professional board

1   The chairman should ensure that the new directors receive a **full, formal and tailored induction on joining the board**. As part of this, the company should offer to **major shareholders** the opportunity to **meet a new non-executive director**.

2   The board should ensure that directors have access to **independent professional advice** at the company's expense where they judge it necessary to discharge their responsibilities as directors.

3   **Committees** should be provided with sufficient resources to undertake their duties.

4   All directors should have access to the advice and services of the **company secretary**, who is responsible to the board for ensuring that board procedures are complied with.

5   Both the **appointment and removal of the company secretary** should be a matter for the board as a whole.

3.6 Evaluation of the board's performance

Principle

The board should undertake a formal and rigorous annual evaluation of its own performance and that of its committees and individual directors.

3.6.1 Principles for evaluating the board's performance

Each director should be **individually evaluated** to ensure they continue to contribute effectively and to demonstrate commitment to the role. The chairman should **act on the results of the performance evaluation** by recognising the strengths and addressing the weaknesses of the board. Where appropriate, the chairman should propose that new members be appointed to the board, or should seek the resignation of directors.

3.6.2 Provisions for evaluating board performance

1   The board should state in the **annual report** how performance evaluation of the board, its committees and its individual directors has been conducted.

2   The **non-executive directors**, led by the senior independent director, should be responsible for performance evaluation of the chairman, taking into account the views of executive directors.

3.7 Re-election of directors

Principle

All directors should be submitted for re-election at **regular intervals**, subject to continued satisfactory performance. The board should ensure planned and progressive refreshing of the board.

3.7.1 Provisions for re-election of directors

1   All directors should be subject to election by shareholders at the **first AGM** after their appointment.

2   All directors should be subject to re-election thereafter at intervals of **no more than three years**.

3   The names of directors submitted for election should be accompanied by sufficient **biographical details** and any other relevant information to enable shareholders to take an informed decision on their election.

4   **Non-executive directors** should be appointed for specified terms subject to re-election and to Companies Acts provisions relating to the removal of a director.

5   Accompanying a resolution to elect a non-executive director should be papers from the board setting out **why** they believe an individual should be elected.

6   The chairman should **confirm** to shareholders that, following formal performance evaluation, the individual's performance continues to be effective and to demonstrate commitment to the role.

7   Any term beyond **six years** for a non-executive director should be subject to particularly rigorous review, and should take into account the need for progressive refreshing of the board.

8   Non-executive directors may only serve longer than **nine years** if they are subject to **annual re-election**. Serving more than nine years could be relevant to the determination of a non-executive director's independence.

3.8 Level and make-up of directors' remuneration

Principle

Levels of remuneration should be sufficient to **attract, retain and motivate directors** of the quality required to run the company successfully. A company should avoid paying more than is necessary for this purpose. A significant proportion of executive directors' remuneration should be structured so as to **link rewards to corporate and individual performance**.

3.8.1 Principles supporting the right level and make-up: the remuneration committee

In relation to the level and make-up of directors' remuneration, the **remuneration committee** should judge where to position their company relative to other companies. They must **avoid an upward ratchet of remuneration levels with no corresponding improvement in performance**. They should also be sensitive to pay and employment conditions elsewhere in the entity especially when determining annual salary increases.

3.8.2 Provisions supporting the right level and make-up of remuneration

Remuneration policy:

1   The **performance-related elements** of remuneration should:

(a)   Form a significant proportion of the total remuneration package of executive directors, and

(b)   Be designed to align their interests with those of shareholders, and

(c)   Give these directors keen incentives to perform at the highest levels.

2   **Executive share options** should not usually be offered at a discount.

3   Levels of remuneration for **non-executive directors** should:

(a)   Reflect the time commitment and responsibilities of the role

(b)   Not include share options (as these can undermine independence). This is unless shareholder approval is sought in advance and any shares acquired by exercise of the options are held until at least one year after the non-executive director leaves the board.

4   Where an executive director is released to serve as a non-executive director elsewhere, the **remuneration report** should include a statement of whether the director will retain such earnings and, if so, what the remuneration is.

Service contracts and compensation:

1   The remuneration committee should carefully consider **compensation commitments** for early termination of service contracts. The aim should be to avoid rewarding poor performance. They should take a robust line on reducing compensation to reflect departing directors' obligations to mitigate loss.

2   Notice or contract periods should be set at **one year or less**. If it is necessary to offer longer notice or contract periods to new directors recruited from outside, such periods should reduce to one year or less after the initial period.

3.9 Transparency of remuneration

Principle

> There should be a formal and transparent procedure for developing policy on executive remuneration and for fixing the remuneration packages of individual directors. No director should be involved in deciding his or her own remuneration.

3.9.1 Principles supporting transparency

The **remuneration committee** should:

(a)   Consult the chairman and/or chief executive about their proposals relating to the remuneration of other executive directors

(b)   Be responsible for appointing any consultants in respect of executive director remuneration

Where executive directors or senior management are involved in advising or supporting the remuneration committee, care should be taken to recognise and avoid **conflicts of interest**.

The board chairman should ensure that the company maintains contact as required with its **principal shareholders about remuneration** in the same way as for other matters.

3.9.2 Provisions supporting transparency

1   The board should **establish a remuneration committee** of at least three independent non-executive directors.

2   The board chairman may be a member of, but **not chair**, the committee if he or she was considered independent on appointment as chairman.

3   The remuneration committee should make available its **terms of reference**, explaining its role and the authority delegated to it by the board.

4   Where **remuneration consultants** are appointed, a statement should be made available of whether they have any other connection with the company.

5   The remuneration committee should have delegated responsibility for **setting remuneration for all executive directors and the chairman**.

6   The committee should also recommend and monitor the **level** and **structure** of **remuneration** for senior management. The definition of 'senior management' for this purpose should be determined by the board but should normally include the first layer of management below board level.

7   The board itself or, where required by the Articles, the shareholders should **determine the remuneration of the non-executive directors** within the limits set in the Articles. Where permitted by the Articles, the board may however delegate this responsibility to a committee, which might include the chief executive.

8   **Shareholders** should be invited specifically to approve all new **long-term incentive schemes** and significant changes to existing schemes.

3.10 Financial reporting

Principle

> The board should present a balanced and understandable assessment of the company's position and prospects.

3.10.1 Principle supporting balanced and understandable financial reporting

The board's responsibility to present a balanced and understandable assessment extends to:

(a)   **Interim reports**
(b)   **Other price-sensitive public reports**
(c)   Reports to **regulators**
(d)   The **statutory financial statements**

3.10.2 Provisions supporting good financial reporting

1   The directors should explain in the annual report their **responsibility for preparing the accounts**

2   The **auditors** should explain their reporting responsibilities in the annual report

3   The directors should report that the business is a **going concern**, with supporting assumptions or qualifications as necessary

3.11 Internal control

Principle

> The board should maintain a sound system of internal control to safeguard shareholders' investment and the company's assets.

3.11.1 Provision supporting internal control

The board should, at least annually, conduct a **review of the effectiveness of the company's system of internal controls** and should report to shareholders that they have done so. The review should cover all material controls, including **financial controls** and operational and compliance and risk management systems.

3.12 Auditing

Principle

The board should establish formal and transparent arrangements for considering how they should apply the financial reporting and internal control principles and for maintaining an appropriate relationship with the company's auditors.

3.12.1 Provisions supporting audit

1   The board should establish an **audit committee** of at least **three independent non-executive directors**.

2   At least one member of the audit committee should have **recent and relevant financial experience**.

3   Role and responsibilities of the audit committee:

- To monitor the **integrity of the financial statements** of the company, and any formal announcements relating to the company's financial performance, reviewing significant financial reporting judgements contained in them;

- To review the company's **internal financial controls** and to review the company's internal control and risk management systems;

- To monitor and review the **effectiveness of the company's internal audit function**;

- To make recommendations to the board and thereby to shareholders for their approval in general meeting regarding the **appointment, re-appointment and removal of the external auditor**. This includes the approval of the **remuneration and terms of engagement** of the external auditor;

- To review and monitor the external auditor's **independence and objectivity** and the effectiveness of the audit process, taking into consideration relevant professional and regulatory requirements;

- To develop and implement policy on the engagement of the external auditor to supply **non-audit services**, taking into account relevant ethical guidance; and to report to the board on this.

4   A separate section of the **annual report** should describe the work of the audit committee in discharging its responsibilities.

5   **Whistle-blowing**: the audit committee should review arrangements by which staff of the company may, in confidence, raise concerns about possible issues of financial reporting or other matters. Arrangements should be in place for the proportionate and independent investigation of such matters and for appropriate follow-up action.

6   The audit committee should monitor and review the effectiveness of the **internal audit** activities. Where there is no internal audit function, the audit committee should consider annually whether there is a need for an internal audit function and make a recommendation to the board.

7   The audit committee should have primary responsibility for making a recommendation on the appointment, re-appointment and removal of the **external auditors**. If the board does not accept the audit committee's recommendation, it should include in the annual report, a statement from the audit committee explaining the recommendation and set out reasons why the board has taken a different position.

8   The annual report should explain to shareholders how, if the auditor provides **non-audit services**, auditor objectivity and independence is safeguarded.

3.13 Dialogue with shareholders

Principle

There should be a dialogue with shareholders based on the mutual understanding of objectives. The board as a whole has responsibility for ensuring that a satisfactory dialogue with shareholders takes place.

3.13.1 Principles supporting relations with shareholders

Nothing should override the general requirements of law to treat shareholders **equally** in access to information.

Most shareholder contact is with the chief executive and finance director. However, the board chairman (and the senior independent director) should maintain sufficient contact with major shareholders to **understand their issues and concerns**.

The board should **keep in touch** with shareholder opinion in whatever ways are most practical and efficient.

3.13.2 Provisions supporting relations with shareholders

1   The board chairman should ensure that the **views of shareholders** are communicated to the board as a whole.

2   The chairman should **discuss governance and strategy** with major shareholders.

3   **Non-executive directors** should be offered the opportunity to attend meetings with major shareholders and should expect to attend them if requested by major shareholders.

4   The **senior independent director** should attend sufficient meetings with a range of major shareholders to listen to their views in order to help develop a balanced understanding of the issues and concerns of major shareholders.

5   The board should state in the **annual report** the steps they have taken to ensure that the members of the board, and in particular the non-executive directors, develop an understanding of the views of major shareholders about their company. For example through face-to-face contact, analysts' or brokers' briefing and surveys of shareholder opinion.

3.14 Using the AGM

Principle

> The board should use the AGM to communicate with investors and to encourage their participation.

3.14.1 Provisions supporting the use of the AGM

1   At any general meeting, the company should propose a **separate resolution on each substantially separate issue**. In particular, proposing a resolution at the AGM relating to the **report and accounts**.

2   For each resolution, **proxy appointment forms** should provide shareholders with the option to direct their proxy to vote either for or against the resolution or to withhold their vote.

3   The proxy form and any announcement of the results of a vote should make it clear that a **'vote withheld'** will not be counted in the calculation of the proportion of the votes for and against the resolution.

4   The company should ensure that all **valid proxy appointments** received for general meetings are properly recorded and counted.

5   For each resolution, after a vote has been taken, except where taken on a poll, the company should ensure that the following **information is given at the meeting and on the company website**:

  •   The number of shares in respect to which proxy appointments have been validly made;
  •   The number of votes for the resolution;
  •   The number of votes against the resolution; and
  •   The number of shares in respect of which the vote was directed to be withheld.

6   The chairman should arrange for the **chairmen of the audit, remuneration and nomination committees** to be available to answer questions at the AGM, and for **all directors to attend**.

7   The company should arrange for the Notice of the AGM and related papers to be sent to shareholders at least **20 working days** before the meeting.

3.15 Dialogue with companies by institutional shareholders

Principle

Institutional shareholders should enter into a dialogue with companies based on the mutual understanding of objectives.

When evaluating companies' governance arrangements, particularly those relating to board structure and composition, institutional shareholders should give due weight to all relevant factors drawn to their attention.

3.15.1 Principles supporting dialogue by institutional shareholders

Institutional shareholders should consider carefully explanations given for **departure from this Code** and make reasoned judgements in each case. If they do not accept the company's position they should give an explanation to the company, in writing where appropriate, and be prepared to enter a dialogue. They should avoid a box-ticking approach to assessing a company's corporate governance. They should bear in mind in particular the size and complexity of the company and the nature of the risks and challenges it faces.

3.16 Voting by institutional shareholders

Principle

Institutional shareholders have a responsibility to make considered use of their votes.

3.16.1 Principles supporting voting by institutional shareholders

Institutional shareholders should take steps to **ensure** their **voting intentions** are being translated into practice.

On request, they should make information available to their clients on the **proportion** of **resolutions** on which votes were cast and non-discretionary proxies lodged.

Major shareholders should attend **AGMs** where appropriate and practicable. Companies should facilitate this.

4 Legal regulation of corporate governance

FAST FORWARD

Much of the law we have studied since Chapter 12 has involved to some extent the **regulation** of corporate governance through statute.

Other than aspects of the Companies Act there is currently **no legal regulation** of corporate governance in the UK that is comparable to the combined code. However you have already studied aspects of the Companies Act aimed at tightening up corporate governance. These are summarised below.

4.1 Company law

Some provisions of the Act cover the same or similar ground as the Combined Code.

(a) **Members' agreement** is required for directors' notice periods under service contracts of more than two years. In the Combined Code, any such period longer than one year initially must reduce quickly to one year or less.

(b) A **general meeting** is required to remove an auditor or a director.

(c) At least **21 days** notice must be given to shareholders of a listed company's AGM.

(d) Listed companies can put the results of a poll at a meeting on their **websites**.

In terms of **clarifying relations** between directors, shareholders and auditor, the Companies Act also seeks to support good corporate governance in quoted companies by:

(a) **Ensuring** that a **company's constitution** is contained just in the articles plus company resolutions. There are different model articles available for different types of company so this should help to avoid confusion

(b) Providing that **company directors** must be at least **16** years of age

(c) Providing that companies must have at least **one natural person** as a director

(d) **Codifying directors' duties** to their company

(e) **Revising** and **clarifying rules** on **loans** to directors

(f) Making **directors' service agreements** available to members

(g) **Extending** and **clarifying** the definition of the people to whom a director is deemed to be 'connected'

(h) Clarifying the procedure by which members may bring **actions** against a director or former director for breach of duty

(i) Allowing shareholders with at least **5%** of a company's shares to call for an independent report on a poll vote

(j) Requiring auditors to **disclose fees** paid for non-audit services

(k) Allowing the auditor of a listed company to **report** on resignation

4.2 State regulation of corporate behaviour

FAST FORWARD

The Financial Services Authority (FSA) is the **regulator of the financial services industry, company markets** and **share exchanges** in the UK.

In the UK, state regulation of corporate behaviour is effected through the Financial Services Authority (FSA), which regulates company markets, share exchanges and the financial services industry in the UK.

The FSA is **not a government agency**. It is a private company limited by guarantee, with HM Treasury as the guarantor. It is financed by the financial services industry. The Board of the FSA is appointed by the UK Government Treasury Department.

The FSA:

- Is the **authorising** body for those carrying on regulated activities
- Is the **regulator of exchanges and clearing houses** operating in the UK
- **Approves companies** for listing in the UK
- Is a **rule-making body**
- Undertakes **supervision**
- Has powers of **enforcement**

The FSA has four objectives:

- To **maintain confidence** in the UK financial system
- To **promote public understanding** of the financial system
- To secure an appropriate degree of **protection for consumers** whilst recognising their own responsibilities
- To **reduce the scope for financial crime**

The FSA is the **Listing Authority** in the UK. This means that it supervises the rules which listed companies are required to follow. We are also interested in the role the FSA plays in relation to **company investigations**, particularly in relation to market abuse, insider dealing and money laundering.

4.3 Company investigations

The FSA has wide powers to investigate suspicions of certain offences, such as **money laundering**, **insider dealing** and **market abuse**.

The FSA is authorised to carry out **company investigations** to investigate suspicions of:

- Market abuse
- Misleading statements and practices
- Insider dealing
- Breaches of the Listing Rules
- Suspicions of money laundering

It **shares power** to investigate companies with the Government, which also carries out investigations in relation to the **liquidation of companies**.

Exam focus point

Exam questions often focus on the offences of insider dealing and money laundering which we shall look at in the final chapter of this Study Text, as they are criminal offences. For now, you should bear in mind that the FSA has a significant role to play in policing and punishing those crimes. We shall look in more detail here at the civil offence of market abuse.

4.4 Market abuse

Market abuse in relation to qualifying investments is a crime.

Key term

Market abuse is behaviour which satisfies one or more of the prescribed conditions likely to be regarded as a failure on the part of the person or persons concerned to **observe the standard of behaviour reasonably expected of a person in his position in relation to the market**.

The new offence of **market abuse** under the Financial Services and Markets Act 2000 complements legislation covering insider dealing and market manipulation. The FSA has issued a **Code of Market Conduct,** which applies to any person dealing in certain investments on recognised exchanges and which does not require proof of intent to abuse a market.

The FSA has statutory civil powers to impose unlimited fines for the offence of **market abuse. It also has statutory** powers to require information, and requires anyone to co-operate with investigations into market abuse.

Market abuse could consist of:

(a) **Misuse of information**, for example, knowingly buying shares in a takeover target before a general disclosure of the proposed takeover. This is similar to insider dealing.

(b) **Market distortion**, which is interfering with the normal process of share prices moving up and down in accordance with supply and demand for the shares.

(c) **Creating a false or misleading impression** about supply and demand or prices and values of investments. An example might be posting an inaccurate story on an internet bulletin board.

(d) Recklessly making a statement or forecast that was **misleading, false or deceptive**.

(e) Engaging in a **misleading course of conduct** for the purpose of inducing another person to exercise or refrain from exercising rights in relation to investments.

Criminal offences are punishable by an **unlimited fine** and/or **imprisonment** for up to seven years. Remarks made by the judge when sentencing in *R v Bailey 2005* suggested that directors will be held personally responsible for public announcements in order to ensure the integrity of the market is preserved and the public protected.

4.5 The Sarbanes–Oxley Act 2002

In some jurisdictions, most notably the **US**, the approach taken to corporate governance has been overwhelmingly statutory rather than being based on extra–legal codes of practice. In 2002 the Public Company Accounting Reform and Investor Protection Act, commonly called **Sarbanes-Oxley**, **SOX** or **SarBox**, was passed. It was in response to several major failures of corporate governance and accounting, including Enron, Tyco and WorldCom. These led to a serious loss of public trust in accounting and reporting practices in particular.

The most common transgressions of good corporate governance in the US before Sarbox can be identified as follows:

- **Directors' remuneration** being **grossly disproportionate** to the company's results
- Promotion of **share issues** on the basis of **questionable** or **unproven** business concepts
- **Misuse** of company funds
- **Insider dealing** in company shares, particularly by managers exercising share options that reward short-termism (that is, acting to achieve good results in the short term at the expense of long term success);
- **Misrepresentation** of the true earnings and financial condition of some companies; and
- **Obstructing justice** by concealing activities or destroying evidence.

The people who could be identified as being to blame for these transgressions were:

- **Passive**, **non-independent** boards of directors
- **Chief executives** and **senior managers** with serious conflicts interest between their own and their company's interests
- **Biased** and **non-independent investment analysts** and **fund managers**
- **Non-independent audit firms**; and
- **Regulators** not paying enough attention to the **systemic conflicts** of interest at the core of poor corporate governance

The core problem was that non-performing managers, directors and auditors, acting in a **fiduciary position** as agents, were not being held accountable to the shareholders as principals. Corporate governance should aim to guarantee performance excellence by management and the board of directors when performing their agency duties for shareholders.

The Act established **new** or **enhanced standards** for all US public company boards and senior managers, and for audit firms.

The Act:

- **Established** a new **quasi-public agency**, the Public Company Accounting Oversight Board (PCAOB)
- **Required** that **public companies** evaluate and **disclose** the effectiveness of their internal controls as they relate to financial reporting in the form of an internal control report
- **Required** that **independent auditors** for public companies 'attest' or **agree** to such disclosure
- **Required** that **certain financial information** concerning material changes in the company's financial condition or operations should be disclosed more quickly
- **Required** that **financial reports** should be **personally certified** by chief executive officers (CEOs) and chief financial officers (CFOs) as being free from misrepresentation
- **Banned external auditors** from undertaking certain types of work for audit clients
- **Required** the **company's audit committee** to **pre-certify** all other types of non-audit work to be undertaken by the external audit firm
- **Required** that **companies listed** on stock exchanges should have **fully independent audit committees** overseeing the relationship between the company and its auditor
- **Banned** most **personal loans** to any executive officer or director
- **Accelerated reporting** of dealing by insiders

- **Prohibited deals** by insiders during certain reporting periods
- **Enhanced criminal** and **civil penalties** for violations of the law on share issues
- **Enhanced criminal penalties** for **altering**, **destroying**, **mutilating** or **concealing any document** with the intent of impairing its use in an official proceeding
- **Set longer maximum jail sentences** and **larger fines** for executives who knowingly and willfully misstate financial statements
- **Protected employees** who '**blow the whistle**' on problems in the company, allowing corporate fraud whistleblowers to be compensated for loss of office etc

Chapter Roundup

- Corporate governance is simply a term used for **the way that companies** (corporate) **are managed** (governed).

- There are many different **stakeholders** in most companies.

- The stakeholders most closely involved in corporate governance are the **directors** (the managers of the company) and the **shareholders** (who have some ultimate controls in general meeting).

- Directors must prepare **financial statements** for shareholders annually, and these are independently audited to provide an objective check on the directors.

- At the AGM the shareholders can exercise their **ultimate control**.

- Following high-profile corporate failures, corporate governance codes set out **best practice**.

- Whether their status is down to **voluntary** or **statutory** rules, there are certain aspects of governance, or 'governance structures' which are generally acceptable.

- Many companies have a **unitary board** system, where there is one board to run a company.

- In Germany and some other countries, a supervisory (or dual) board system is used. This means that there is a **management board to run the company** plus a **supervisory board to oversee** the management board.

- In practice, the principles of **independence** and **verification** behind both the **unitary** and the **dual systems** are increasingly growing closer. Both systems face **similar problems** in terms of finding **suitably qualified people** to undertake supervisory roles and to be an **independent** voice in a company.

- Guidance on the composition of a board in the UK is given in the **Combined Code on Corporate Governance**. This sets out a series of principles about how boards should be composed: effective board collectively responsible for the success of the company; balance of non-executive and executive directors; division of responsibility between the chief executive and the chairman.

- Much of the law we have studied since Chapter 12 has involved to some extent the **regulation** of corporate governance through statute.

- The Financial Services Authority (FSA) is the **regulator of the financial services industry**, **company markets** and **share exchanges** in the UK.

- The FSA has wide powers to investigate suspicions of certain offences, such as **money laundering**, **insider dealing** and **market abuse**.

- **Market abuse** in relation to qualifying investments is a crime.

1 Complete the definition.

   The Cadbury report defined .... as 'the system by which companies are directed or controlled'.

2 Which of the following criteria might indicate that a director was not independent?

   • Being an employee of the group in the previous 5 years
   • Being a qualified accountant
   • Having been employed by the company's audit firm 10 years ago
   • Representing a significant shareholder
   • Having served on the board for 6 years

3 Name three criticisms of the unitary board approach.

   (1) ....

   (2) ....

   (3) ....

4 Name three board committees required by the Combined Code.

5 Which one of the following is not an objective of the FSA?

   (a) Maintain confidence in the UK financial system

   (b) Promote public understanding of the financial system

   (c) Take legal action against companies who have not complied with the Combined Code

   (d) Reduce the scope for financial crime

Answers to Quick Quiz

1 **Corporate governance**

2 Being an employee in the last five years, representing a significant shareholder

3 (1) Being both a manager and a supervisor is too awkward a task for non-executives
   (2) The independence criteria is too difficult to meet
   (3) The system does not properly account for representing the needs of employees

4 Nomination, remuneration and audit

5 (c) The FSA cannot take legal action against companies who have not complied with the code as companies are not legally required to follow it.

Now try the questions below from the Exam Question Bank

Number	Level	Marks	Time
Q28	Examination	10	18 mins

23

Fraudulent behaviour

Topic list	Syllabus reference
1 Financial crime	H2(a-d)
2 Insider dealing	H2(a)
3 Money laundering	H2(b)
4 Criminal activity relating to companies	H2(c), H2(d)

Introduction

We introduced the concept of criminal law in Chapter 1. In this chapter, we shall look specifically at some **financial crimes** and the **measures** that have been put into place to combat them.

Insider dealing is a statutory offence. It has proved difficult to convict people of the crime of insider dealing, hence the introduction of the civil wrong of market abuse, discussed in Chapter 22. We shall set out the law on insider dealing and its effectiveness in Section 2.

The issue of **money laundering** is, in particular, a highly topical issue. Money laundering is the process of 'legalising' funds raised through crime. Money laundering crosses national boundaries and it can be difficult to enforce the related laws

Finally we shall look at offences in relation to insolvent companies.

Study guide

(H)	Governance and ethical issues relating to business	Intellectual level
2	Fraudulent behaviour	
(a)	Recognise the nature and legal control over insider dealing	2
(b)	Recognise the nature and legal control over money laundering	2
(c)	Discuss potential criminal activity in the operation, management and winding up of companies	2
(d)	Distinguish between fraudulent and wrongful trading	2

Exam guide

Financial crime is highly examinable, in both types of question. Expect questions requiring you to identify whether or not a crime has been committed, or explain the opportunities that exist for perpetrating such crimes.

1 Financial crime

FAST FORWARD

Crime is **conduct prohibited by the law**. Financial crime can be international in nature, and there is a need for international cooperation to prevent it.

We introduced the concept of **crime** in Chapter 1. Remember, it is **conduct prohibited by the law**.

Law tends to be organised on a **national basis**. However, as we shall see later in this chapter, some crime, particularly money laundering, is perpetrated **across national borders**. Indeed; the international element of the crime contributes to its success.

Particularly with regard to money laundering, international bodies are having to **cooperate** with one another in order to control financial crimes which spreads across national boundaries.

1.1 Example: international financial crime

Money laundering is a crime in Country A but not in Country B. Money laundering can be effected legally in Country B and the proceeds returned to Country A. Hence Country A cannot prosecute for the crime of money laundering, which has not been committed within its national boundaries.

2 Insider dealing

FAST FORWARD

Insider dealing is the statutory offence of **dealing** in securities while in **possession** of **inside information** as an insider, the securities being price affected by the information.

The **Criminal Justice Act 1993** (CJA) contains the rules on **insider dealing**. It was regarded and treated as a crime since a few people are enriched at the expense of the reputation of the stock market and the interests of all involved in it.

2.1 What is insider dealing?

Key term

Insider dealing is dealing in securities while in possession of inside information as an insider, the securities being **price-affected** by the information.

To prove insider dealing, the prosecution must prove that the possessor of inside information (under s 52 CJA):

- **Dealt** in **price-affected securities** on a regulated market, or
- **Encouraged another** to **deal** in them on a regulated market, or
- **Disclosed** the **information** other than in the proper performance of their employment, office or profession

2.1.1 Dealing

Dealing is **acquiring or disposing** of or **agreeing** to **acquire** or **dispose** of relevant securities whether **directly** or **through an agent** or nominee or a person acting according to direction: s 55 CJA.

2.1.2 Encouraging another to deal

An offence is also committed if an individual, having information as an insider, **encourages another person** to deal in price-affected securities in relation to that information. They must **know** or have reasonable cause to believe that **dealing** would **take place**.

It is irrelevant whether:

- The person encouraged realises that the securities are **price-affected** securities
- The **inside information is given** to that person. For example, a simple recommendation to the effect that 'I cannot tell you why but now would be a good time to buy shares in Bloggs plc' would infringe the law
- **Any dealing takes place**, the offence being committed at the time of encouragement

2.2 Securities covered by the Act

Securities include shares, debt securities and warranties: s 54 CJA.

2.3 Inside information

Key term

> **Inside information** is **'price sensitive information'** relating to a **particular issuer** of **securities** that are price-affected and not to securities generally: s 56 CJA.

Inside information must, if made public, be likely to have a **significant effect on price** and it must be **specific or precise**. Specific would, for example, mean information that a takeover bid would be made for a specific company; precise information would be details of how much would be offered for shares.

2.4 Insiders

Under s 57 a person has information as a **primary insider** if it is (*and* they **know** it is) inside information, and if they have it (*and* **know** they have) from an inside source:

- Through being a **director**, **employee** or **shareholder** of an issuer of securities
- Through access because of **employment**, **office** or **profession**

If the direct or indirect source is a person within these two previous categories then the person who has inside information from this source is a **secondary insider**.

2.5 General defences

Under s 53, the individual has a defence regarding dealing and encouraging others to deal if they prove that:

- They did **not expect** there to be a **profit** or avoidance of loss
- They had **reasonable grounds** to **believe** that the information had been **disclosed widely** enough to ensure that those taking part in the dealing would be prejudiced by having the information
- They would have **done** what they did **even** if they did not have the **information**, for example, where securities are sold to pay a pressing debt

Defences to disclosure of information by an individual are that:

- They **did not expect** any person to deal
- Although dealing was expected, **profit** or **avoidance of loss** was **not expected**

2.6 'Made public'

This term is not exhaustively defined by the statute, leaving final determination to the Court. Information **is** made public if:

- It is **published** under the rules of the regulated market, such as the Stock Exchange
- It is in **public records**, for example, notices in the *London Gazette*
- It can **readily be acquired** by those likely to deal
- It is **derived** from **public information**

Information **may** be treated as made public even though:

- It can **only** be **acquired** by **exercising diligence** or expertise (thus helping analysts to avoid liability).
- It is **communicated only** to a **section** of the **public** (thus protecting the 'brokers' lunch' where a company informs only selected City sources of important information).
- It can be **acquired** only by **observation**.
- It is **communicated** only on a **payment of a fee** or is published outside the UK.

2.7 Penalties

Maximum penalties given by the statute are **seven years' imprisonment** and/or an **unlimited fine**. Contracts remain valid and enforceable at civil law.

2.8 Territorial scope

The offender or any professional intermediary must be **in the UK** at the time of the offence or the market must be a UK regulated market.

2.9 Problems with the laws on insider dealing

FAST FORWARD

> The law on insider dealing has had some **limitations**, and new offences, such as market abuse, have been brought in to reduce security related crime.

The courts may have problems deciding whether information is **specific** or **precise**.

The statute states that information shall be treated as relating to an issuer of securities not only when it is **about the company** but also where it may **affect the business prospects** of the company.

The requirement that price-sensitive information has a **significant effect on price** limits the application of the legislation to fundamental matters. These include an impending takeover, or profit or dividend levels which would be out of line with market expectations.

As we discussed in Chapter 22, a new offence of **'market abuse'** was introduced in the UK in 2000. This was partly in response to the perceived ineffectiveness of the insider dealing provisions in the Criminal Justice Act 1993.

3 Money laundering

3.1 What is money laundering?

FAST FORWARD

Money laundering is the attempt to **make money from criminal activity appear legitimate**, by disguising its original source.

Key term

> **Money laundering** is the term given to attempts to make the proceeds of crime appear respectable.
>
> It covers any activity by which the apparent source and ownership of money representing the proceeds of income are changed so that the money appears to have been obtained legitimately.

Money laundering is a **crime** that is **against the interests of the state**, and it is associated with drug and people trafficking in particular, and with organised crime in general.

Money laundering legislation has been influenced on a number of different Acts of Parliament:

- Drug Trafficking Offences Act 1986
- Criminal Justice Act 1993
- Terrorism Act 2000
- Anti-terrorism Crime and Security Act 2001
- Proceeds of Crime Act 2002 (PCA)

3.2 Categories of criminal offence

FAST FORWARD

In the UK, there are various offences relating to **money laundering**, including tipping off a money launderer (or suspected money launderer) and failing to report reasonable suspicions.

There are **three categories of criminal offences** in the Proceeds of Crime Act.

- **Laundering**: acquisition, possession or use of the proceeds of criminal conduct, or assisting another to retain the proceeds of criminal conduct and concealing, disguising, converting, transferring or removing criminal property. This relates to its nature, source, location, disposition, movement or ownership of the property.
- **Failure to report** by an individual: failure to disclose knowledge or suspicion of money laundering (suspicion is more than mere speculation, but falls short of proof or knowledge).
- **Tipping off**: disclosing information to any person if disclosure may prejudice an investigation into, drug trafficking, drug money laundering, terrorist related activities, or laundering the proceeds of criminal conduct

For the purposes of laundering, '**criminal property**' is defined by s 3 CJA as a property which the alleged offender knows (or suspects) constitutes or represents being related to any criminal conduct. This is any conduct that constitutes or would constitute an offence in the UK.

In relation to **laundering**, a person may have a **defence** if they make disclosure to the authorities:

- As soon as possible after the transaction
- Before the transaction takes place

Alternatively, they may have a defence if they can show there was a **reasonable excuse** for not making a disclosure.

In relation to **failure to report**, the person who suspects money laundering must disclose this to a nominated money laundering reporting officer within their organisation, or directly to the National Criminal Intelligence Service (NCIS). This has responsibility in the UK for collecting and disseminating information related to money laundering and related activities. The nominated money laundering reporting officer in an organisation acts as a filter and notifies NISC too.

In relation to **tipping off**, this covers the situation when a person making a disclosure to NCIS also tells the person at the centre of their suspicions about the disclosure. There is a **defence** to the effect that the person did not know that tipping off would prejudice an investigation.

3.3 Penalties

The law sets out the following penalties in relation to money laundering:

(a) 14 years' imprisonment and/or a fine, for knowingly assisting in the **laundering** of criminal funds

(b) 5 years' imprisonment, for failure to report knowledge or the suspicion of money laundering

(c) 5 years' imprisonment for 'tipping off' a suspected launderer. The suspected launderer must not be alerted

Question	Money laundering

Why should a professional adviser not give a warning to a client whom he suspects of money laundering?

Answer

Tipping off a suspected money launderer is an offence. Alerting the suspect would be likely to hamper any subsequent investigation by the authorities.

The money laundering process usually involves three phases:

- **Placement** – this is the initial disposal of the proceeds of the initial illegal activity into apparently legitimate business activity or property

- **Layering** – this involves the transfer of monies from business to business or place to place to conceal the original source

- **Integration** – having been layered, the money has the appearance of legitimate funds

For accountants, the most worrying aspect of the law on money laundering relates to the offence of '**failing to disclose**'. It is relatively straightforward to identify actual 'knowledge' of money laundering, and therefore of the need to disclose it, but the term 'suspicion' of money laundering is not defined. The nearest there is to a definition is that suspicion is more than mere speculation but falls short of proof or knowledge. It is a question of judgement.

3.4 The role of the Financial Services Authority

The **FSA Handbook** and the **Joint Money Laundering Steering Group (JMLSG)** guidance include similar, and therefore parallel but separate, rules and guidance. Investment firms (that is, firms who sell financial services or shares) are required to have:

(a) **Control systems** in place to monitor possible money laundering activities.

(b) A **Money Laundering Reporting Officer (MLRO)** who is responsible for the oversight of the anti-money laundering activities.

(c) **Internal reporting procedures**. Staff must be able to identify suspicious transactions, understand reporting procedures, and be able to notify the MLRO of any person who they suspect of engaging in money laundering.

(d) **Adequate records** such as:

(i) A copy of the evidence of identity obtained

(ii) A record of where a copy of the identity evidence can be obtained

(iii) Procedures for internal and external reporting

(iv) Evidence of an applicant's identity must be retained for five years from the end of the firm's relationship with the client, or

(v)   Money laundering training given to all staff who handle transactions (or who manage others who are responsible for handling transactions) that may involve money laundering

Although investment firms may be particularly at risk of being involved with clients who are seeking to launder money, **methods used** for laundering such dirty money **can be extremely complex**. They may involve **trusts, companies** (both offshore and onshore) and could involve the use of relatively complex bank instruments.

Therefore **all companies**, their **managers** and their **advisers need to be aware** of the issue of money laundering and not fall foul of the regulations.

There is a **legal requirement** for organisations to take the following actions.

- To set up procedures and establish accountabilities for senior individuals to take action to prevent money laundering
- To educate staff and employees about the potential problems of money laundering
- To obtain satisfactory evidence of identity where a transaction is for more than £10,000
- To report suspicious circumstances (according to the established procedures)
- Not to alert persons who are or might be investigated for money laundering
- To keep records of all transactions for five years

Exam focus point

You must be clear of how this guidance seeks to prevent or minimise money laundering.

4 Criminal activity relating to companies

We have already seen a number of potential crimes in relation to the operation and management of companies, and the way in which these can be investigated.

With regard to the **operation and management of companies**, a company as a legal person may be prosecuted for many different types of crime. However, this is nearly always in conjunction with the directors and/or managers of the company. Companies have been prosecuted for manslaughter (unsuccessfully), fraud, and breaches of numerous laws for which fines are stated as being punishment, such as health and safety laws.

Prosecutions are often brought against directors of **insolvent** companies for **fraudulent** trading and **wrongful trading**.

4.1 Criminal offences in relation to winding up

FAST FORWARD

> Criminal offences in relation to **winding up** include: making a declaration of solvency without reasonable grounds; fraudulent trading; wrongful trading.

The law seeks to **protect creditors** who may be disadvantaged by the company being liquidated. **Directors** can be found guilty of various criminal offences if they try to **deceive** creditors, and, in some cases, even if they do not attempt to deceive creditors, but the effect is the same as if they had.

4.2 Declaration of solvency

As discussed in Chapter 21, a winding up can only be a members' voluntary winding up if the company is solvent. If the company is not solvent, the creditors are far more involved in the winding up process. In order to carry out a members' voluntary winding up, the directors have to file a **declaration of solvency**.

It is a **criminal offence** punishable by fine or imprisonment for a director to make a **declaration of solvency without** having **reasonable grounds** for it. If the company proves to be insolvent, they will have to justify their previous decision, or be punished.

4.3 Fraudulent trading

This offence occurs where the business of a company in liquidation has been carried on with **intent to defraud creditors** or for any fraudulent purpose. Courts may declare that **any persons** who were knowingly parties to carrying on the business in this fashion shall be liable for the debts of the company as the court may decide: s 213 Insolvency Act 1986. This is a civil penalty.

Various rules have been established to determine **what is fraudulent trading**:

(a) Only persons who **take the decision** to carry on the company's business in this way or play some active part are liable.

(b) **'Carrying on business'** can include a single transaction and also the mere payment of debts as distinct from making trading contracts.

If the liquidator considers that there has been fraudulent trading they should apply to the court for an order that those responsible are liable to make good to the company all or some specified part of the **company's debts**.

The liquidator should also report the facts to the Crown Prosecution Service and Director of Public Prosecutions so that **criminal proceedings** may be instituted under the Companies Act. This criminal offence may arise with or without liquidation proceedings, and can give rise to a prison term of up to seven years and an unlimited fine.

As in civil cases, the criminal offence of fraudulent trading relates not only to defrauding creditors, but also to carrying on a business for the purpose of any kind of fraud: *R v Kemp 1988.*

4.4 Wrongful trading

The problem which faced the creditors of an insolvent company before the introduction of **'wrongful trading'** was that it was exceptionally difficult to prove the necessary fraud. Therefore a further civil liability for 'wrongful trading' was introduced, which means that the director will have to make such contribution to the company's assets as the court sees fit.

Directors will be liable if the liquidator proves the following.

(a) The director(s) of the insolvent company **knew**, or **should have known**, that there was **no reasonable prospect** that the **company** could **have avoided going into insolvent liquidation**. This means that directors cannot claim they lacked knowledge if their lack of knowledge was a result of failing to comply with Companies Act requirements, for example preparation of accounts: *Re Produce Marketing Consortium 1989* (see below).

(b) The director(s) did not take **sufficient steps** to minimise the potential loss to the creditors.

Directors will be deemed to know that the company could not avoid insolvent liquidation if that would have been the conclusion of a **reasonably diligent person** with the **general knowledge**, **skill and experience** that might reasonably be expected of a person carrying out that particular director's duties. If the director has greater than usual skill then he will be judged with reference to his own capacity.

4.5 Examples: offences in relation to winding up

The standard expected of a listed company director would be **higher** than for the director of a small owner-managed private company.

> *Halls v David and Another 1989*
>
> *The facts:* The directors sought to obtain relief from liability for wrongful trading by the application of s 727 Companies Act 1985. This stated that in proceedings for negligence, default, breach of duty or breach of trust against a director, if it appears that he has acted honestly and reasonably the court may relieve him wholly or partly from liability on such terms as it sees fit.
>
> *Decision:* S 727 is not available to excuse a director from liability under s 214.

> *Re Produce Marketing Consortium Ltd 1989*
>
> *The facts:* Two months after the case above, the same liquidator sought an order against the same directors this time, that they should contribute to the company assets (which were in the hands of the liquidator) since they had been found liable for wrongful trading.
>
> *Decision:* The directors were jointly and severally liable for the sum of £75,000 plus interest, along with the costs of the case. The judge stated that the fact that wrongful trading was not based on fraud was not a reason for giving a nominal or low figure of contribution. The figure should, however, be assessed in the light of all the circumstances of the case.

This case was significant for creditors, since the assets available for distribution in a winding up will (potentially) be much increased by a **large directors' contribution**. It serves as a warning to directors to take professional advice sooner rather than later. The prospect of making a personal contribution may prove much more expensive than winding-up at the appropriate stage.

Chapter Roundup

- Crime is **conduct prohibited by the law**. Financial crime can be international in nature, and there is a need for international cooperation to prevent it.

- Insider dealing is the statutory offence of **dealing** in securities while in **possession** of **inside information** as an insider, the securities being price affected by the information.

- The law on insider dealing has had some **limitations**, and new offences, such as market abuse, have been brought in to reduce security related crime.

- Money laundering is the attempts to **make money from criminal activity appear legitimate** by disguising its original source.

- In the UK, there are various offences relating to **money laundering**, including tipping off a money launderer (or suspected money launderer) and failing to report reasonable suspicions.

- **Criminal offences** in relation to **winding up** include: making a declaration of solvency without reasonable grounds; fraudulent trading; wrongful trading.

Quick Quiz

1   Insider dealing is an offence

     True   ☐

     False   ☐

2   Fill in the blanks

     Inside information is '....... ....' relating to a .... of **securities** that
     are price-affected and not to securities generally. It must, if made public, be likely to have a **significant
     effect on** .... and it must be **specific or precise**.

3   Define money laundering.

4   Which of the following is not a UK offence relating to money laundering?

     A   Concealing the proceeds of criminal activity
     B   Tipping off
     C   Dealing in price affected securities
     D   Failing to report suspicion of money laundering

5   What is placement?

Answers to Quick Quiz

1   True. Insider dealing is a criminal activity.

2   **Inside information** is **'price sensitive information'** relating to a **particular issuer** of **securities** that are
     price-affected and not to securities generally. It must, if made public, be likely to have a **significant effect
     on price** and it must be **specific or precise**.

3   **Money laundering** is the term given to attempts to make the proceeds of crime appear respectable.

     It covers any activity by which the apparent source and ownership of money representing the proceeds of
     income are changed so that the money appears to have been obtained legitimately.

4   C. This could be insider dealing, if the person dealing was an insider and was using inside information.

5   Placement is the disposal of the initial proceeds of the illegal activity.

Now try the questions below from the Exam Question Bank

Number	Level	Marks	Time
Q29	Examination	10	18 mins

Exam question and answer bank

1 County court and high court
18 mins

Explain the importance of:

(a)   The county court (4 marks)
(b)   The High Court (4 marks)

in the system of civil justice.

(c)   Briefly explain where appeals from the decisions of the county court and the High Court are heard.

(2 marks)

(Total = 10 marks)

2 Binding precedent
18 mins

Explain the doctrine of binding precedent in English law paying particular regard to:

(a)   The hierarchy of the courts (5 marks)
(b)   The relative advantage and disadvantages of the doctrine (5 marks)

(Total = 10 marks)

3 Human Rights Act
18 mins

Describe five impacts that the Human Rights Act 1998 has had on the rest of English Law.

(10 marks)

4 Contract basics
18 mins

Explain the difference between essential elements of a contract and matters which affect the validity of a contract.

(10 marks)

5 Offer
18 mins

Explain in relation to the law of contract:

(a)   The rules relating to acceptance of an offer (5 marks)
(b)   The rules relating to the revocation of an offer (5 marks)

(Total = 10 marks)

6 Presumptions of intention
18 mins

Explain the presumptions relating to intention to create legal relations with respect to:

(a)   Domestic and social agreements (5 marks)
(b)   Business agreements (5 marks)

(Total = 10 marks)

7 Privity of contract
18 mins

In relation to the contract explain:

(a)   The doctrine of privity (3 marks)
(b)   How the doctrine can be avoided at common law (4 marks)
(c)   How the doctrine is avoided under statute (3 marks)

(Total = 10 marks)

8 Express and implied

18 mins

In relation to the law of contract:

(a) Distinguish between express and implied terms; **(4 marks)**
(b) Explain the circumstances under which terms may be implied in contracts. **(6 marks)**

(Total = 10 marks)

9 Unfair contract terms

18 mins

Outline the main provisions of the Unfair Contract Terms Act 1977 and the Unfair Terms in Consumer Contract Regulations 1999. **(10 marks)**

10 Breach

18 mins

Explain the general meaning and effect of breach of contract, paying particular attention to anticipatory breach.

(10 marks)

11 Remedies for breach

18 mins

Describe in outline the remedies which may be available to the injured party in relation to breaches of contract.

(10 marks)

12 Negligence

18 mins

Whizbang Ltd is a professional firework display organiser with an impeccable safety record. On 5th November 20X0 it put on a display in Loutsville. After Whizbang had cleared up and gone, Garry and Larry find a number of 'Mighty Thunderbolt' rockets near to where the fireworks were launched that had not exploded. They decide to light one of the rockets and throw it at each other for 'a laugh'. The firework explodes causing serious burns to each of them.

Advise Whizbang Ltd.

(10 marks)

13 Professional advice

18 mins

Sofa Stores plc sell a wide range of chairs and sofas through its national network of shops. The board of directors decided to expand its operations to include carpets and floor tiles as well. This would be achieved by taking over a popular national company called Carpet Warehouse plc. After much research it valued the target and was ready to make an offer to buy it.

A substantial part of the valuation was based on the profitability of the company. The accounts stated that it made a profit in the last financial year of £100m.

The finance director of Sofa Stores arranged a meeting with the senior partner of Carpet Warehouse's auditors (Smythe and West LLP) to confirm the accounts were correct.

During the meeting, the senior partner of the auditors advised the finance director that he 'absolutely stood by the accounts as a robust and accurate representation of the financial position of Carpet Warehouse plc at the balance sheet date.'

Relying on the advice given, the finance director authorised the takeover. In the weeks following the takeover it became clear that Carpet Warehouse was operating at a substantial loss rather than a healthy profit and that the valuation made on the basis of the accounts was wildly inaccurate.

Can Sofa Stores recover any damages from Smythe and West LLP?

(10 marks)

14 Employers' duties
18 mins

What terms may be included in a contract of employment? Where might they be found?

(10 marks)

15 Redundancy and dismissal
18 mins

Brian is the manager of a distribution warehouse which supplies a number of Do-It-Yourself stores. Following the introduction of a new computerised stock record system, Brian is dismissed, because he is unable to adapt to the new working practices. Brian has worked for the company for fifteen years.

As a result of the re-organisation John is also dismissed because of his involvement in trade union activities. He has worked for the company for nine months.

Brian is seeking compensation for redundancy and in addition, both he and John intend to make a claim for unfair dismissal.

You are required to advise Brian and John of their respective legal positions.

(10 marks)

16 Creating an agency relationship
18 mins

Explain how an agency relationship can be established in the following ways:

(a)	By agreement	(2 marks)
(b)	By ratification	(2 marks)
(c)	By estoppel	(3 marks)
(d)	By necessity	(3 marks)

(Total = 10 marks)

17 Unlimited and limited partnerships
18 mins

(a) What is meant by 'apparent authority' in the context of partnership law? (5 marks)

(b) What are the main requirements of a limited liability partnership with regard to formation and publicity of information? (5 marks)

(Total = 10 marks)

18 Companies
18 mins

In relation to companies explain the following:

(a)	A public limited company	(3 marks)
(b)	Parent and subsidiary companies	(4 marks)
(c)	A multinational company	(3 marks)

(Total = 10 marks)

19 Incorporation and promoters
18 mins

(a) Explain what is meant by the following in company law:

(i)	A promoter	(3 marks)
(ii)	A pre-incorporation contract	(3 marks)

(b) Describe the liability of a promoter on a pre-incorporation contract. (4 marks)

(Total = 10 marks)

20 National Hair Brushes

18 mins

National Hair Brushes plc was incorporated in June 20X6.

Required

(a)   The company wishes to trade under the business name 'Wave Oh'. State the statutory requirements with which the company must comply.   **(5 marks)**

(b)   The directors have received a letter from another company, Lancashire Hair Brushes plc, stating that it was incorporated in 20X5, that its business is being adversely affected by the use of the new company name and demanding that National Hair Brushes plc changes the company name.

Advise National Hair Brushes plc.   **(5 marks)**

(Total = 10 marks)

21 Articles

18 mins

Explain the content and effect of a company's articles of association.   **(10 marks)**

22 Shares

18 mins

(a)   What is a company's share capital?   **(5 marks)**

(b)   Explain the meaning of the following:

    (i)   Issued capital   **(2 marks)**

    (ii)   Paid up capital   **(3 marks)**

(Total = 10 marks)

23 Debentures and charges

18 mins

In relation to companies' loan capital explain the following terms.

(a)   Debenture   **(3 marks)**

(b)   Fixed charge   **(3 marks)**

(c)   Floating charge   **(4 marks)**

(Total = 10 marks)

24 Issuing shares

18 mins

Explain the meaning of the following:

(a)   The issue of shares at a premium   **(5 marks)**

(b)   The prohibition on the issue of shares at a discount   **(5 marks)**

(Total = 10 marks)

25 Statutory duties

18 mins

Briefly explain any FIVE of the statutory duties owed by directors to their companies.   **(10 marks)**

26 Hydrangea

18 mins

The directors of Hydrangea plc, a company selling garden furniture, wishes to call an AGM at which the accounts will be approved and all the directors re-elected. It also wishes to change the name of the company to Motormowers plc.

Required

(a)   The directors seek your advice on the statutory requirements which apply to the calling of the meeting, the notice of the meeting and to ensure the resolutions gain legal effect when passed.

(5 marks)

(b)   Provide advice to the directors on how the votes of members and proxies should be taken and counted at the meeting.

(5 marks)

(Total = 10 marks)

27 Liquidation

18 mins

Explain the meaning of compulsory and voluntary liquidation and the main differences between them.

(10 marks)

28 Boards

18 mins

In the context of company law, explain:

(a)   Non-executive director   **(2 marks)**
(b)   Executive director   **(2 marks)**
(c)   Single board   **(3 marks)**
(d)   Supervisory board   **(3 marks)**

(Total = 10 marks)

29 Financial Services Authority

18 mins

Explain the role of the Financial Services Authority as a regulator of company markets in the UK, paying particular attention to its role with regard to market abuse and money laundering.   **(10 marks)**

1 County court and high court

Top tips. Do not be tempted to start writing about criminal law issues. Be clear about the court structure – the diagram in the Study Text should be in your memory, showing the routes of appeal.

(a) The **county court** is a court of original jurisdiction. It hears only civil cases, but deals with **virtually every type of civil matter** arising within the geographical area which it serves. In some types of case, its jurisdiction is concurrent with that of the High Court. It is involved in hearing the following, subject to limits applied in some categories.

  (i)   Contract and tort claims
  (ii)   Equitable matters concerning trusts, mortgages and partnership dissolution
  (iii) Disputes concerning land
  (iv)   Undefended matrimonial cases
  (v)   Probate matters
  (vi)   Miscellaneous matters conferred by various statutes, for example the Consumer Credit Act 1974
  (vii) Some bankruptcy, company winding-up and admiralty cases

(b) The **High Court** also deals with civil cases at first instance. It is divided into **three divisions**. The **Queen's Bench Division** deals with common law matters, such as contract and tort. It also includes two specialist courts, dealing with Admiralty and Commercial matters. **The Chancery Division** of the High Court deals with equity matters such as trusts, bankruptcy and taxation, and also has a special Companies Court. The **Family Division** of the High Court deals with matrimonial and similar family cases. The Family Division also has a limited appellate function in that it hears some appeals on domestic matters from the magistrates' court.

Cases are allocated either to the **small claims track** or the **fast track** or the **multi-track**, taking into account the financial value and complexity of the claim. Generally speaking, county courts hear small claims and fast track cases and the High Court hears multi-track cases.

Under the small claims track, cases are heard where the claim is for less than £5,000 (or £1,000 in the case of personal injury claims, claims for possession of land, housing disrepair claims and harassment claims). If the claim is for more than the stated amount, the parties may still elect to use the small claims track, subject to the **court's approval**. The small claims track is intended to permit litigants to conduct their case in person if they so wish as the procedure is less formal, cheaper and quicker than court proceedings. The arbitrator is usually the district judge or may be appointed by the parties.

Cases under £15,000 may be allocated to the 'fast track'. This is a strictly **limited procedure**, designed to enable cases to be brought to trial within a short but reasonable timescale. Costs are fixed and hearings are designed to last no longer than one day.

Finally, the multi-track approach is intended to provide a **flexible regime** for the handling of claims over £15,000 in value. These are the cases that tend to be more complex. Soon after allocation of the case to the multi-track, a **'case management conference'** will be held to encourage the parties to settle the dispute or to consider the merits of alternative dispute resolution. The trial judge sets a budget and a final timescale for the trial.

(c) From a decision of a county court there is a right of appeal to the **Civil Division of the Court of Appeal**. In bankruptcy cases an appeal goes to the Chancery Division of the High Court.

Appeals from the High Court in civil cases may also be made to the Court of Appeal (Civil Division) or alternatively (and unusually) to the House of Lords, under what is known as the **leapfrog procedure**. For the leapfrog procedure to be followed, all parties and the House of Lords must give their consent to it and the case must involve a point of law of general public importance. Also, the point of law must already be the subject of an existing Court of Appeal decision.

The Civil Division of the Court of Appeal is presided over by the Master of the Rolls. Normally, three judges sit together, although in important cases five may sit.

2 Binding precedent

(a)   The doctrine of binding precedent, or *stare decisis*, is essential to the English legal system. It provides that in determining any case, where the facts of the case are materially the same as in a previous case heard by a superior (or sometimes equal) court, then the court will be bound by any proposition of law which formed part of the *ratio decidendi* of that previous case. The purpose of the doctrine is to provide coherency, consistency and, therefore, predictability and fairness in the development of case law.

Only a proposition of law, as opposed to a statement of fact, will be binding. The *ratio decidendi* of a case has been defined as 'any rule of law, express or implied, treated by a judge as a necessary step in reaching his conclusion, having regard to the line of reasoning adopted by him, or a necessary part of his direction to the jury' (Cross). The *ratio decidendi* is often difficult to identify and should be contrasted with *obiter dicta* which might be propositions of law which do not form part of the basis for the decision or statements based on hypothetical facts rather than the actual facts before the court. *Obiter dicta* are of persuasive authority only and do not bind later courts.

The hierarchy of the courts is as follows.

Decisions of the **Magistrates' Courts** and **County Courts** do not constitute precedent and are therefore not binding on any court, but each of these courts is bound by decisions of the High Court, Court of Appeal and House of Lords.

The **Crown Court** is bound likewise by the superior courts and its decisions are of persuasive authority only.

A decision of the **High Court** (an individual judge) binds all lower courts, but does not bind another High Court judge. It is however of persuasive authority and tends to be followed in practice. A decision of a **Divisional Court of the High Court** binds any other divisional court as well as a judge sitting alone. A Divisional Court decision usually binds another divisional Court, although in rare circumstances it may have regard to the exceptions available to the Court of Appeal arising from the *Bristol Aeroplane* case (see below).

The **Court of Appeal's** decisions are binding on all English courts (except the House of Lords). The Court is normally bound by its own previous majority and unanimous decisions, by those of its predecessors and by those of the House of Lords. In *Young v Bristol Aeroplane Co 1944*, it was established that it is not bound by its own previous decisions where:

(i)   Two of its previous decisions are in **conflict** with each other;

(ii)   The previous decision conflicts with (ie has been **overruled** by) a subsequent House of Lords judgment; or

(iii)   The previous decision was made *per incuriam*, through **lack of care**, for example failure to observe some relevant statute or precedent.

The Judicial Committee of the **House of Lords** stands at the apex of the English judicial system. Its decisions are binding on all other English courts. The House of Lords generally regards itself as bound by its own earlier decisions but, it reserves the right to depart from its own precedents in exceptional cases, although this discretion is rarely exercised.

Decisions of the **European Court of Justice** are binding on all English courts including the House of Lords in so far as they have a bearing on the interpretation of Community treaties or the validity and interpretation of secondary community legislation.

Since the implementation of the **Human Rights Act 1998**, it should also be noted that the House of Lords is bound by the European Court of Human Rights in respect of human rights issues.

(b) There are a number of widely accepted advantages to the doctrine of binding precedent.

    (i) **Certainty**: the doctrine helps to ensure certainty, fairness and predictability of decisions. The need for costly and time-consuming litigation can be avoided where the facts of a case are so materially similar to those of a previous case that the outcome can be foretold. The doctrine also gives guidance to judges and leads to consistency in decisions from different judges in different courts and in different parts of the country.

    (ii) **Clarity**: since only propositions of law forming part of the ratio decidendi of a case constitute binding precedent, it should be the case that the doctrine gives rise to a healthy source of statements of legal principle that can helpfully and clearly be applied to new cases generally. This leads to a saving of time for all concerned, in that cases do not need to be put before the courts and argued afresh.

    (iii) **Flexibility**: the doctrine allows the law to grow and be developed in accordance with changing needs and circumstances of society and allows a much more flexible judge-made law than Parliament-enacted legislation.

    (iv) **Practicality**: Another advantage of the doctrine of judicial precedent sometimes put forward is that it has its roots in tried and tested cases and not in theory, as is often the case with new legislation. As a result, there should perhaps be less uncertainty and misunderstanding in its application.

A number of disadvantages can also be identified.

    (i) It can be argued that with certainty comes **rigidity, inflexibility** and undesirable decisions being reached because judges are obliged to apply earlier decisions (where they are unable to distinguish them on the facts). This makes the law more complicated especially where judges are clearly at pains to avoid being bound by a precedent which would cause such a result.

    (ii) There may also be a **lack of clarity**. Although possibly not strictly a 'disadvantage' of the doctrine, the criticism is sometimes made that these propositions of law are often not clear enough and there may appear to be conflicting propositions in the same judgment or discrepancies between propositions reached in more than one case.

    (iii) There can also be **uncertainty**, because there is only a finite number of precedents available and so it is often not possible to predict exactly how a court may decide a particular case.

    (iv) It may also be argued that the doctrine is **unconstitutional**. It is sometimes said that the flexibility given to unelected judges is too great as it effectively allows them to make law not just to apply law.

    (v) **Complexity**. The disadvantage of the level of detail often contained in judgments is that the bulk of material makes subsequent reading, digesting and application of judges' decisions unnecessarily difficult and complicated. The distinguishing of cases can also become more tenuous the more detail is included.

3 Human Rights Act

> **Top tips.** This question is not exam standard. However it summarises all the things you need to know about the HRA98 and is a useful consolidation exercise.
>
> The question explains eight points although you were only required to explain five.

The Human Rights Act 1998 enacts the rights set out in the European Convention on Human Rights into English law. The impact it has on English law is that **UK courts** are now **required to interpret UK law in a way that is compatible with the Convention**, as far as it is possible to do so. In practice, this has the following effects:

- The courts must interpret English law in a way that is compatible with the Convention so far as it is possible to do so. Where there are different interpretations and one is not compatible with the Convention, the judge must follow the interpretation that is compatible.

- They must take into account judgements made by the European Court of Human Rights even though these judgements are not binding in UK courts.

- If a court feels that a provision of existing legislation is incompatible with the Convention, it must make a declaration of incompatibility.

- Any law declared incompatible in this way is still valid in domestic law until it is amended.

- The legislator may make adjustments to the legislation to remove the incompatibility using a fast-track procedure is required.

- Individuals and companies may now bring a case claiming infringement of human rights to the UK courts. Thereafter an appeal may be made to the European Court of Human Rights.

- When presenting new legislation to Parliament, the person proposing the legislation must make a statement of compatibility with the Convention.

- If the provisions of the bill are not compatible with the Convention, the person proposing them must state so, they must also state that the government nevertheless wants to proceed with the legislation.

4 Contract basics

> **Top tips.** Again, this question is not exam standard, but it is absolutely vital that you grasp the basics of contract, so it is useful for you to work through this question. Use the answer in your revision.

In order to be legally binding, a contract must contain three essential elements. The three essential elements are:

- Agreement (offer + acceptance)
- Intention to create legal relations
- Consideration

Without these three essential elements a contract is no more than an agreement, and does not have any legal weight or recourse.

There are also factors which will impact on the validity of a contract. The distinction between these factors and those above is that without essential elements, there is no contract (no legally binding agreement). Without the presence of validity factors, there is a contract, but it may be fundamentally flawed, and various results arise.

Examples of validity factors include **capacity** and **form**. A company is restrained in its acts by its constitution. Certain contracts may be outside the scope of its capacity and hence void. Similarly, some contracts must be made in a certain form.

If these factors prove invalidity, a contract which exists (as it has the three essential elements above) may be declared void, voidable or unenforceable depending on the invalidating factor.

5 Offer

(a) **Valid acceptance** of a valid offer is one of the essentials of a contract, the others being an intention to create legal relations and consideration.

The acceptance must be an **unqualified agreement to the terms of the offer**. If it in fact introduces new terms then it is a counter offer (which might then be accepted by the original offeror) and not an acceptance.

Thus in *Hyde v Wrench 1840*, where an offer was made to sell land for £1000 and the plaintiff made a counter offer of £950 but later sought to accept the original offer, it was held that the claimant's counter offer had terminated the original offer.

A **response** to an offer which is actually a request for further information will not constitute acceptance but it is **not** a counter offer, and acceptance made 'subject to contract' will not amount to a valid acceptance until the proposed formal contract has been signed.

The acceptance may be by **express words** or be **inferred from conduct**: *Brogden v Metropolitan Rly Co 1877*. In a unilateral contract (as in *Carlill v Carbolic Smoke Ball Co 1893*), performance of the act required by the offer or advertisement constitutes acceptance. There must be some act on the part of the offeree, however, as mere passive inaction is not capable of constituting acceptance: *Felthouse v Bindley 1862*. Acceptance of an offer may only be made by a person authorised to do so, usually the offeree or his authorised agent.

Generally speaking, acceptance must be communicated to the offeror before it can be effective, unless the offeror expressly waives the need for communication (as in Carlill's case). The offeror may stipulate the sole means of communication in which case only compliance with his or her terms will suffice.

If the offeror specifies a means of communication but does not make it absolutely compulsory, then acceptance by another means which is equally expeditious and does not disadvantage the offeror in any way will be sufficient: *Yates Building Co v R J Pulleyn and Sons (York) 1975*.

Communication of acceptance by post is subject to the postal rule established in *Adams v Lindsell 1818*. This provides that where the use of the post is in the contemplation of both parties and the acceptance is correctly addressed and stamped and is actually put in the post, then acceptance will be valid and effective once posted and it is irrelevant whether the offeror actually receives the letter. There is no need for the offer specifically to state that acceptance must be communicated by post – whether this was in the contemplation of the parties may be deduced from the circumstances, for example if the offer was itself made by post: *Household Fire and Carriage Accident Insurance Co v Grant 1879*.

Clearly if it is evident that the parties did not intend the postal rule to apply – for example where the offer requires 'notice in writing'– then the rule will be excluded: *Holwell Securities v Hughes 1974* (where it was held that the stipulation for 'notice in writing' meant that notice of acceptance actually had to be received by the offeror).

(b) The offeror may **'revoke'** (or cancel) the offer at any time prior to acceptance: *Payne v Cave 1789* unless by a separate option agreement, for which consideration must have been given, he has agreed to keep the offer open for a certain period of time: *Routledge v Grant 1828*. Once accepted, an offer cannot be revoked.

Revocation may be made by an **express statement** to that effect or may be **implied from an act** of the offeror indicating that the offer is no longer in force (for example sale of the goods to a third party). Whatever form it takes, it is essential that the revocation is communicated to the offeree in order to be effective. Revocation of an offer may be communicated by the offeror or by any third party who is a sufficiently reliable informant: *Dickinson v Dodds 1876*.

While a postal acceptance of an offer is usually **effective** from the **time of posting**, a postal **revocation** of an offer **does not take effect until received** by the offeree (ie communicated to the offeree). Thus, where a letter of revocation of an offer crosses in the post with a letter of acceptance, a legally binding contract will have been formed from the time the letter of acceptance was posted: *Byrne v van Tienhoven 1880*.

Where an offer is intended to be accepted by conduct (a **unilateral contract),** it has been held that the offer cannot be revoked once the offeree has begun to perform the necessary act required to accept the contract

6 Presumptions of intention

> **Top tips**. It is not enough to state that certain arrangements do or do not create legal relations – you must use the law to explain **why** they would or would not.

(a)   **Domestic and social agreements**

Domestic agreements are **generally presumed to be informal** rather than contractual, unless the facts indicate otherwise. At one time, it was firmly considered that in an agreement made in a domestic context there was no implied intention to create legal relations if none had been expressed. Thus an agreement by a husband to pay an allowance to his wife during his absence abroad was not legally binding (*Balfour v Balfour*).

The presumption that no legal relations are intended is, however, rebuttable and the **courts may decide that there was an intention to create legal relations in an agreement between husband and wife**. This is particularly the case if they are no longer living together and/or if there is other **evidence that legal relations were intended**, such as the agreement being formally drawn up and signed (*Merritt v Merritt*).

Where the agreement relates to **property matters**, it is perhaps more likely that the courts will infer an intention to create legal relations.

In *Jones v Padavatton*, a mother promised her daughter a monthly allowance if the daughter would return to England to read for the Bar. The daughter did so and the mother refused to pay the allowance. It was held that there was no intention to create legal relations and that the agreement was not therefore legally binding.

In other relationships, for example those involving relatives or friends, the courts appear to be more readily disposed to assume that the parties did in fact intend that a financial agreement should be binding.

This may apply if there is a **'mutuality in the arrangements'** amounting to a joint enterprise, for example where persons jointly enter a competition (*Simpkins v Pays*). In this case, a woman, her granddaughter and a paying lodger took part in a weekly competition in a newspaper, which they entered in the grandmother's name. One week they won £750 and the lodger was denied a third share. It was held that there was a mutuality of agreement and that this was not a 'friendly adventure' but a contract.

(b)   **Business agreements**

In commercial agreements, the **courts will normally infer that there is an intention to create legal relations** unless there is evidence to the contrary (*Rose and Frank v Crompton*). In *Edwards v Skyways* an agreement entered into to make an 'ex-gratia' payment as part of a larger negotiation was held to be legally binding.

The issue of whether legal relations were intended may sometimes arise when a **supplier of goods has published an advertisement** which may be an offer to sell the goods or to give some guarantee in respect of them. This was the case in *Carlill v Carbolic Smoke Ball Co*. In this case the manufacturer argued (unsuccessfully) that his offer to pay a sum of money to any user of his medicine whom the medicine did not cure was a mere 'puff' not intended to create a legally binding agreement.

The court decided against him because his advertisement stated that as proof of the seriousness of his assurance he had deposited money in a bank account to meet claims. This fact **implied** that his advert was **intended to be legally binding** and it overrode any deduction about the general effect of an advertisement.

Some commercial agreements may be described by the parties as **'binding in honour only'**. This amounts to an express denial of intention to create legal relations and is effective to rebut the presumption (*Jones v Vernon Pools*). **'Letters of comfort'** given to creditors of subsidiary companies are presumed to be statements of present intentions only and not legally binding (*Kleinwort Benson Ltd v Malaysia Mining Corpn Bhd*).

A lock-out agreement which is unsupported by consideration will be presumed not to carry the necessary intention to create legal relations. As mentioned above, in *Rose and Frank v Crompton*, a statement that the arrangement was not subject to legal jurisdiction was held to be effective.

7 Privity of contract

> **Top tips**. This answer is far more extensive than what you would be required to produce in the exam.
>
> Use the law you have studied and turn it around to come up with methods of avoiding this doctrine.

(a) The doctrine of privity of contract provides that only a **party to the contract** has enforceable rights and obligations under it and a person who is not party to the contract cannot enforce it, even if the promises are given for his benefit.

In the leading case in this area, *Dunlop v Selfridge 1915*, Dunlop supplied tyres to a distributor, for resale, and the distributor sold them to Selfridge. The contract between Selfridge and the distributor provided for payments to Dunlop if Selfridge sold the tyres at less than a fixed price. Although Selfridge failed to observe this clause and sold the tyres at a lower price, Dunlop was unable to enforce the promise. It was held that this was part of the contract between Selfridge and the distributor, to which Dunlop was not a party.

There are some exceptions to the general rule of privity of contract, both at common law and under statute, where a third party may be allowed to enforce a contract:

(b) **Common law**

(i) Where the beneficiary may sue in some other **capacity**: In *Beswick v Beswick 1968* a widow sued for specific performance in her capacity as her husband's administratrix (rather than simply as his widow) to enforce a contract between her husband and the successor to his business. The contract provided for payment of an annuity to the widow. In her capacity as administratrix, she was able to enforce the contract for her own benefit as third party to the contract. In her personal capacity as recipient, she had no right of action.

(ii) Where there is a **collateral contract**: In *Shanklin Pier v Detel Products Ltd*, the claimant entered into a contract to have his pier repainted. The painters used a particular paint produced by the defendant as required by the claimant. The paint was unsatisfactory. The defendant fought an action by the claimant on the basis that it had only entered into a contract of supply with the painters and since the claimant was not a party to that contract he could not enforce it. The court held that there was a collateral contract between the claimant and the defendant by which the defendant guaranteed the suitability of the paint in return for the claimant requiring the painters to use it.

(iii) Where a party validly **assigns the rights** contained in a contract (other than rights of action for unliquidated damages or rights so personal that they are unassignable) to a third party: A party may not assign the burden of his contractual obligations without the other party's consent.

(iv) Where **breach of contract results in loss or damage to a third party which was clearly foreseeable**: Thus in *Linden Gardens Trust Ltd v Lenesta Sludge Disposals Ltd 1994*, a contract for works was entered into with the likelihood that the property would subsequently be transferred to a third party. Although no formal assignment was made, the House of Lords held that the original promisee should be able to claim full damages on behalf of the third party for breach of contract. The commercial nature of the contract and the circumstances which made the subsequent transfer so likely were relevant factors.

(v) Where **equity** provides that an **implied trust** has been created: Thus in *Gregory and Parker v Williams 1817*, Parker owed money to Gregory and Williams and agreed to transfer his property to Williams if Williams paid Parker's debt to Gregory. When the property was transferred, Williams refused to pay Gregory who was clearly not a party to the contract between Parker and Williams. Nonetheless, the court held that Parker could be regarded as a trustee for Gregory under an implied trust and so Gregory could bring an action jointly with Parker.

(vi) Where there is an **agency** relationship: If an agent enters into a contract with a third party apparently on his own behalf but in fact on behalf of an undisclosed principal, the agent may sue the third party (since he is treated as the other party to the contract) until such time as the principal intervenes and enforces the contract on his own behalf. Where the principal is disclosed, the contract is treated as one between the principal (and thus enforceable by the principal) and third party even though made by the agent.

(vii) Where there is a **restrictive covenant** that attaches to the land so that successors in title are bound by covenants to which they were not originally covenanters *(Tulk v Moxhay 1848)*.

(c) **Statutory exceptions**

Some statutory exceptions to the doctrine exist, for example a road accident victim can claim from the other party's insurers (RTA 1972) and the Married Woman's Property Act 1882 allows a husband or wife to enforce life insurance taken out by the other for his or her benefit.

The principal statutory exception is contained in the *Contracts (Rights of Third Parties) Act 1999* which sets out the circumstances in which a third party can enforce a contract in the event of breach, or have it varied or rescinded. These are either (a) where the contract expressly so provides or (b) where the term confers a benefit on the third party (unless it appears that the contracting parties did not intend him to have the right to enforce it). The third party must be identified in the contract by name, class or description but need not be in existence when the contract is made. The Act does not confer third party rights in relation to employment contracts nor does it affect the operation of s.14CA 1985.

8 Express and implied

> **Top tips.** The key to the difference between express and implied terms is the court's approach to them. Don't dwell too much on implied terms in part (a) as you can discuss them at length in part (b).

(a) As a general principle, the parties to a contract may include in their contract whatever terms they choose. The agreement reached on the terms must be **complete** in order to be legally binding and those terms must be sufficiently **clear and precise** *(Scammell v Ouston)*. However, it is always possible for the parties to leave an essential term to be settled by specified means outside the contract, for example by agreeing to sell at open market value on the day of delivery or to invite an arbitrator to determine a fair price *(Hillas & Co Ltd v Arcos Ltd)*. If, however, the parties defer an essential term for later negotiating (rather than specifying a means for its ascertainment), there is no binding agreement.

An **express term** may be defined as any term which has been included by the parties. It may be written or unwritten and the court will ascertain as a question of fact whether any oral statement constitutes a term of the contract or simply a representation. However, if a contract exists and contains all necessary terms to make it an effective contract, generally speaking oral evidence will not be admitted in order to add to, vary or contradict any of the written terms.

An **implied term** is one which is deemed to form part of a contract even though not expressly stated by the parties, whether orally or in writing. Some terms are implied by the courts as necessary to give effect to the parties' presumed intentions or by statute or in accordance with relevant trade practices. Implied terms can normally be excluded or varied by the parties save where this is prevented by relevant statutory provisions.

(b)   The usual reason for a court to imply a term in a contract is in order to give **business efficacy** to that contract. In such cases the term which is implied will be one which, it appears to the court, the parties inadvertently omitted or which is so obvious that it goes without saying and it can be assumed that the parties simply took it for granted that such a term would apply. The courts will be **keen to prevent the failure of an otherwise sound contract** and to implement the manifested intention of the parties (*The Moorcock*).

The test, commonly referred to as 'the bystander test' was formulated in *Shirlaw v Southern Foundries:* 'Prima facie that which in any contract is left to be implied and need not be expressed is something so obvious that it goes without saying; so that, if while the parties were making their bargain an officious bystander were to suggest some express provision for it in their agreement they would testily suppress him with a common 'Oh, of course' '.

The court may imply terms which it considers to be required implicitly by the nature of the contract itself. In *Liverpool City Council v Irwin*, the defendants were tenants of a maisonette in a tower block owned by the claimants with no formal tenancy agreement. The defendants withheld rent, alleging that the claimants had breached implied terms because (*inter alia*) the lifts did not work and the stairs were unlit. The court concluded that since tenants could only occupy the building with access to stairs and/or lifts, therefore terms needed to be implied on these matters, including an implied obligation on the landlord's part to keep these parts reasonably safe.

The courts have also established a number of **implied terms into employment contracts** concerning employers' and employees' duties.

(i)   Terms will be implied by statute where that is the expressed intention of the legislation, for example under The Sale of Goods Act 1979, terms are implied as to the vendor's **title** and the **description** and **quality** of the goods in a contract for the sale of goods. In some cases, the statute provides that the implied terms cannot be overridden (there are several instances of this in SGA 1979, but in others, express provisions to the contrary will prevail).

(ii)   The parties may be considered to have entered into a contract subject to a **custom or practice of their trade**. In *Hutton v Warren*, the defendant landlord gave the claimant, a tenant farmer, notice to quit the farm. He insisted that the tenant should continue to farm the land during the period of notice. The tenant asked for 'a fair allowance' for seeds and labour from which he received no benefit (as he left before harvest time). It was held that by custom he was bound to farm the land until the end of the tenancy, but he was also entitled to a fair allowance for seeds and labour. However, any express term overrides a term which might be implied by custom (*Les Affreteurs v Walford*).

9 Unfair contract terms

The **Unfair Contract Terms Act 1977** seeks to clarify the law and supplement case law on the validity of exclusion clauses by making it clear that in some situations an exclusion clause will not be enforceable, notwithstanding the wording of the clause itself.

The Act seeks to strike a balance between:

- The principle that parties should have complete freedom to contract on whatever terms they wish, and
- The need to protect the public from unfair exclusion clauses.

However it does not seek primarily to limit the use of exclusion clauses between businesses trading together who have equal bargaining power, rather it seeks to protect the consumer who is dealing with a company.

There is a clear distinction between business contracts and consumer contracts. A **business contract** arises when two businesses are entering a contract together, for example buying goods for use in a business. The law assumes that they can look after themselves in the making of a contract, and they have equal bargaining power. In some cases, exclusion clauses in business contracts are valid if they are reasonable. A **consumer contract** arises when a **private buyer deals with a person in business**. A consumer contract does not include the situation when a private buyer and a private seller contract together, so the legislation does not cover, for example, an individual buying from someone else at a car boot sale.

Death and personal injury

A person acting in the course of business cannot exclude or restrict liability for death or personal injury resulting from negligence. For example if a supermarket has a sign on its premises stating that it accepts no responsibility for any injury to customers however caused, that clause will be totally ineffective. A company injured on the premises due to the negligence of a member of the supermarket's staff will still be able to sue the supermarket for damages.

Sale and supply of goods

No contract, whether consumer or non consumer, for the sale or hire purchase of goods can exclude the implied condition that the seller has a right to sell the goods.

A consumer contract for the sale or hire purchase of goods cannot exclude or restrict liability for breach of the conditions relating to:

- Description
- Satisfactory quality
- Fitness for purpose and
- Sale by sample

that are implied by the Sale of Goods Act 1979. In the case of a non-consumer contract, such exclusions are subject to a reasonableness test.

Reasonableness test

The term must be fair and reasonable having regard to all the circumstances which were, or which ought to have been, known to the parties when the contract was made. The burden of proof lies with the person who is seeking to rely on the clause. In judging what is reasonable the courts will consider factors such as:

- The relative bargaining strengths of the parties
- Whether any inducement such as a reduced price was offered to the customer to persuade him to accept the existence of the exclusion clause

- Whether the customer knew or ought to have known of the existence and extent of the exclusion clause
- Whether the goods were made to a special order of the customer.

The **Unfair Terms in Consumer Contracts Regulations 1999** implemented an EC directive on unfair contract terms, but UCTA 1977 still applies.

There are now three 'layers' of law:

- The common law, which applies to all contracts regardless of whether or not one party is a consumer
- UCTA 1977, which applies to all contracts (business or consumer) but which has specific provisions for consumer contracts
- The Unfair Terms in Consumer Contracts Regulations, which apply only to consumer contracts and to terms that have not been individually negotiated.

According to the Regulations, an unfair term is any term that causes a significant imbalance in the parties' rights and obligations under the contract, to the detriment of the consumer.

Certain terms in consumer contracts are rendered unfair by the Regulations:

- Excluding or limiting liability of the seller when the consumer is injured or dies resulting from an act or omission of the seller
- Excluding or limiting liability where there is partial or incomplete performance of a contract by the seller
- Making a contract binding on the consumer where the seller can still avoid performance

    Where a consumer is bound by a contract containing an unfair term, he can go to court to ask the court to ask that the unfair term should be declared not to be binding, or he can complain to the Director General of Fair Trading. Additionally, under the terms of the Regulations it is possible for the offending clause to be removed from the contract altogether.

10 Breach

> **Top tips.** This question asks you to define breach of contract and explain the results of it. It also asks you to cover anticipatory breach – so make sure you do!

A party is said to be in breach of contract where he fails to perform his contractual obligations precisely and where there is no lawful excuse for non-performance.

In the event of a breach of contract, the party not in breach may, in certain circumstances, treat the contract as discharged and, in all cases, may sue for damages.

Anticipatory breach

Breach of contract normally becomes apparent at or following the time for performance under the contract. Anticipatory breach, on the other hand, **occurs before the due time of performance** and may be express or implied.

Thus, for example, anticipatory breach occurs where one party declares that he will not perform the contract when the appointed time arrives (*Hochster v de la Tour*). It also occurs when a party renders himself unable to perform the contract at the appointed time, for instance by selling specific contract goods to a third party before the date of delivery under the contract.

Actions of the injured party

In the event of anticipatory breach, the injured party **may treat an anticipatory breach as if the breach had already occurred** and sue for breach of contract from that date without having to wait until the actual date of performance under the contract.

The injured party **may allow the contract to continue and not treat it as discharged**. However, the party in anticipatory breach may subsequently change his mind and perform his part of the contract after all.

If the injured party permits the contract to continue and incurs expense by preparing to perform it, he **may recover the agreed price for his services** (*White & Carter (Councils) Ltd v McGregor*). Thus **anticipatory breach does not of itself bring the contract to an end** but simply **gives the innocent party the choice of affirmation or rejection** and the normal duty to mitigate losses does not apply.

11 Remedies for breach

> **Top tips.** Focus your attention on damages as the main remedy, and the principles relating to it, such as remoteness and measure of damages.

Damages

Damages are a **common law** remedy intended to restore the wronged party to the position he would have been in if the contract had been performed but not to put him in a better or more profitable position. This is sometimes referred to as protecting the **expectation interest** of the claimant.

The claimant's expectation loss may be defined as the loss of what the claimant would have received had the contract been properly performed. A claimant may alternatively seek to have his **reliance interest** protected; this refers to the position he would have been in had he not relied on the contract. Because they compensate for wasted expenditure, damages for reliance loss cannot be awarded if they would put the claimant in a better position than he would attain under protection of his expectation interest.

Measurement of financial loss may be made with reference to the **market price** rule. Thus if a buyer refuses to take delivery of goods which he has contracted to buy, and the seller sues for loss of profit on the transaction, the existence of a market in which there is an excess of supply over demand will lead to a successful claim (as in *Thompson Ltd v Robinson (Gunmaker) Ltd 1955*), whereas if there is an excess of demand over supply, only nominal damages will be payable (*Charter v Sullivan 1957*). Damages will be awarded only in respect of **reasonably foreseeable** loss, not damage which is too **remote**: *Hadley v Baxendale 1854).*

The amount of damages payable is usually quantified as a **financial loss**, based on the **actual loss** suffered, although some types of **non financial loss** are recoverable, for example personal injuries or distress caused by a holiday failing to match the brochure's promises: *Jarvis v Swan Tours 1973.*

In some cases the cost of putting the claimant in the position he would have been in had the contract been performed may be extremely large relative to the actual loss suffered. In such cases the court **may** restrict the amount of damages.

For example, in the case of *Ruxley Electronics and Construction Ltd v Forsyth 1995*, contractors built a swimming pool which was shallower than the contractually specified depth. The householder claimed damages based on the cost of digging up the pool and constructing a new one. The court held that such a course of action was out of all proportion to the benefit of such rectification and instead awarded a lesser sum as compensation for the loss of a pleasurable amenity.

The claimant must take reasonable steps to **mitigate his loss** or he may not receive his full losses: *Payzu v Saunders 1919.* This means that he must take reasonable steps to put himself in as good a position as if the contract had been performed. For example, where goods are not delivered the buyer must take steps to buy the same goods from elsewhere as cheaply as possible. He does not have to take discreditable or risky measures to mitigate his loss: *Pilkington v Wood 1953.*

Liquidated damages

The parties to a contract may seek to avoid complicated calculations of loss and disputes as to damages by providing a formula for the calculation of such damages in the contract itself, for example a daily rate of payment in the event of late completion or late delivery of goods. This is called **liquidated damages**. This must be contrasted with a **penalty clause** in a contract. Here the clause operates to impose a penalty on the person in breach, with no attempt to link the payment to the other party's losses.

The distinction is important. A liquidated damages clause will be upheld by the court in the event of breach. If, however, the arrangement is not a genuine attempt to anticipate the appropriate level of damages it will not be enforceable (*Ford Motor Co (England) Ltd v Armstrong 1915*) and certainly any term which amounts to a penalty clause will be **void**. In determining whether the clause in question is a penalty clause or a liquidated damages provision the courts will look to see if the cause represents a genuine pre-estimate of loss: *Dunlop Pneumatic Tyre Co Ltd v New Garage & Motor Co Ltd 1915*. If so, the clause will be upheld, even if the actual loss is greater or smaller.

Action for the price

If the breach of contract is one party's failure to pay the contractually agreed sum, the other party should bring a personal **action for the price** against the party in breach provided property in the goods has passed to him and (generally speaking) provided that any sums due after an anticipatory breach will only be recoverable where he affirms the contract.

12 Negligence

> **Top tips.** When answering scenario questions you should use the following method.
>
> 1. Identify the issue
> 2. State the law
> 3. Apply the law
> 4. Conclude your answer

Whizbang Ltd may be liable for damages to Larry and Garry if they were **negligent** when clearing up after the display that they organised.

To succeed in their claim against Whizbang, Garry and Larry will have to prove that:

(a) Whizbang Ltd owed them a **duty of care** to not cause them injury
(b) Whizbang Ltd **breached** that duty of care
(c) As a **natural consequence** of the breach they suffered injury

Duty of care

The following three-stage test for a duty of care evolved from the case of *Caparo Industries plc v Dickman (1990)*.

- Was the harm reasonably foreseeable?
- Was there sufficient proximity between the parties?
- Given the circumstances, is it fair, just and reasonable to impose a duty?

It is likely that a court would find that the harm is reasonably foreseeable. Whizbang appears not to have cleared up competently. It follows that if someone finds the fireworks they may light them and cause themselves injury.

There is sufficient proximity between Whizbang Ltd and Garry and Larry since they had found one of the fireworks that it left behind.

Given the circumstances it could be argued that Whizbang owed a duty of care to clear up thoroughly after the display and that it is reasonable to impose a duty on it. Had Whizbang cleared up correctly, the injuries would not have been caused.

Breach of duty

Where there is a high risk of injury, the defendant must meet a higher duty of care than it otherwise would do. The nature of fireworks means a high risk of injury exists if they fall into the wrong hands. The cost of clearing up the display site is minimal and it is common practice for such organised events to arrange a thorough clean up operation.

Therefore it is likely that Whizbang has breached its duty of care.

Causality

The 'but for' test is used to determine causality. If Whizbang had cleared up the rockets then the injuries could not have occurred. However Whizbang can claim that the claimant's actions were not reasonable in the circumstances, intervening in the chain of events and breaking the chain of causality. This view is likely to be supported by a court – had the two not lit the firework and played with it the injuries would not have occurred.

Defence

Whizbang will have the defence of volenti non fit injuria should the court not support the view that the pair intervened in the chain of events. They knew lighting a firework and playing with it was dangerous and by their actions voluntarily accepted the risk. This is similar to the case of *ICI v Shatwell (1965)* where it was held that two employees consented willingly to a reckless act by disobeying safety instructions.

13 Professional advice

> **Top tips**. Scenario questions may be based on facts very similar to real life cases and this is a good example of that. Even if you cannot remember the case name you will probably recall the decision. Use this decision and the reasoning behind it to answer the question in hand – this is a very good reason to read as many cases as you can.
>
> You will also notice the layout of this answer is similar to the previous negligence question in this bank. This is because the same method of tackling the question applies; it is just the facts and case law that differ.

Sofa Stores could recover damages from Smythe and West on the basis of negligent advice if it can prove:

(a)   Smythe and West owed them a duty of care
(b)   Smythe and West breached that duty of care
(c)   As a natural consequence of the breach they suffered damage

Duty of care

In the case of *Caparo Industries plc v Dickman (1990)* it was decided that auditors owe a duty of care to the shareholders of a company in respect of their audit work. This duty does not extend to the world at large or to shareholders increasing their stakes in the company.

This means that Sofa Stores is not owed any duty in respect of its reliance on the accounts for making its investment decision. However, the company could argue that a 'special relationship' had been established since Smythe and West provided information in the knowledge that it was contemplating an investment and would rely on the information provided by the senior partner when deciding on whether or not to proceed with it.

Similar facts occurred in *ADT Ltd v BDO Binder Hamlyn (1995)*. In this case, similar comments were made by an audit partner in respect of a proposed takeover. The court decided that the auditors assumed responsibility for the comments made and held that a duty was owed.

It is therefore likely that Sofa Stores is owed a duty of care by Smythe and West.

Breach of duty

Where auditors provide information that is to be used in important business transactions, takeovers, a higher standard of care is required; *Morgan Crucible Co plc v Hill Samuel Bank Ltd and others (1990)*. On the facts of the case it is likely that Smythe and West will be found to have breached this duty as they did not carry out any extra work to support the advice given by the senior partner.

Causality

It is clear that the negligent advice caused the loss to Sofa Stores plc – had they been advised that the figures were inaccurate then it is unlikely that the takeover would have gone ahead.

Defences

Volenti non fit injuria does not apply in this case and the actions of Sofa Stores seem reasonable in the circumstances. Therefore Smythe and West LLP would not have a defence to a claim against them.

Conclusion

On the facts of the case and that of *ADT Ltd v BDO Binder Hamlyn*, it is likely that Sofa Stores could recover damages from Smythe and West LLP for the loss they suffered.

14 Employer's duties

> **Top tips.** This question is a useful run through the main issues relating to an employment contract.

Terms

The terms to be included will be found in a number of sources.

Express terms need not be set out in writing but within eight weeks of an employee commencing employment (presuming he works more than 8 hours a week), his employer must give him certain written particulars of his employment covering such things as salary, hours of work, sick pay, holidays, notice and so on: s 1 Employment Rights Act 1996. Terms outlining the disciplinary and grievance procedure must also be notified. This will not be necessary if, as is usual, the written particulars refer the employee to some other written notice of the terms, usually included in an employee handbook, wall notices and other documents.

An employee is also entitled periodically to receive a pay statement itemising gross pay and deductions.

Many terms are inserted through **collective agreements** made between employer and union or employee representatives. They are not legally binding, as the individual employee is not a party to the agreement, but in fact are observed by both parties to the contract and thus become part of the individual employment contract. Terms may also be implied by reference to an employer's customary practice with his workforce. Examples are wage-rates and working hours.

Other terms are inserted **by operation of law**. Case law has led to certain terms being implied into contracts such as the employee's duty to carry out his work in good faith (*Boston Deep Sea Fishing & Ice Co v Ansell 1888)* and the employer's duty to provide work to a person specifically employed to do that work: *Collier v Sunday Referee Publishing Co 1940*.

A more important source is the extensive **legislation** on employment which imposes a number of requirements on the parties as to the terms of employment. An employee has rights to engage in union duties and activities (ss 168-170 TULRCA 1992), and he will be protected from discrimination on the grounds of race or sex (Equal Pay Act 1970, Sex Discrimination Acts 1975 and 1986, Race Relations Act 1976). The 1996 Act gives important rights as to dismissal and redundancy and to minimum periods of notice. Statute also allows time off from main duties to find work if an employee is about to be made redundant.

The employer has a duty to provide a safe system of working, to select proper staff and to provide adequate materials. These common law duties are supplemented by the extensive statutory requirements of the Health and Safety at Work Act 1974 and the Occupiers' Liability Acts.

Duties

The **implied duties** owed by an employer to his employee will be governed both by common law and statute, subject to any express agreement between the parties to the contrary, assuming that such agreement is not contrary either to law or public policy.

The common law implies several terms into the contract of employment, all of which are fundamental to the relationship. First, the employer has a duty to take reasonable care for the **safety** of the worker. Thus, he must provide competent staff, safe premises and equipment and a safe system of work. This term is also governed by statute and the employer must comply with those regulations too.

In the unlikely circumstances of there being no agreement as to remuneration, the rate of **remuneration must be reasonable**. However, statute largely governs the method and rate of payment.

In certain circumstances, the common law will imply a duty to **provide work**. Employees protected include those paid on a piecework or commission basis and those whose earning power and reputation is founded on active occupation; such workers would include actors and journalists: *Collier v Sunday Referee Publishing Co Ltd 1940*. Further, if an employee is appointed to a particular post, there will be an implied duty not to remove the employee from that post or to abolish it.

The employee is also entitled to **reasonable management**, so that arbitrary and inconsiderate action may constitute a breach of contract.

Where no specific period of notice has been agreed, the employer has an implied common law duty to give **reasonable notice** in the event of a dismissal. Whether the period of notice given is reasonable will depend on the particular circumstances of the employment. This term is also governed by statute which provides a minimum period of notice which cannot be varied by agreement.

If an employee properly incurs **expenses** in the performance of his duties, the employer has a common law duty to **reimburse** him. The employee must also be indemnified against liability for any unlawful act, provided that he has no knowledge that the act is unlawful.

There are many terms implied by **statute** into the employer/employee relationship. It would be impractical to attempt to deal with more than a selection of these terms.

The most fundamental include the **anti-discriminatory provisions**. These relate to trade union membership and activities, gender and race. They also apply to equal pay for men and women working in comparable posts. The provisions are generally designed to regulate the advertisement of posts and the selection for appointments, promotions and dismissal, although some situations must of necessity be excluded.

For example, in the case of selection for appointment, the requirement of decency may necessitate single-sex workers, or there may be a genuine occupational qualification such as the necessity that an actress play the part of Joan of Arc.

The employer must in certain circumstances allow his employee **time off work**. This would include time to attend for ante-natal and other maternity care and to perform duties for local government or as a magistrate. In some cases the employee will be paid for the time spent away from work.

Finally, there are statutory provisions regulating the **termination of employment**; that is, redundancy and unfair dismissal. These provisions are too complex to be discussed in the context of this question, but, basically, they protect the worker in circumstances where the employment is terminated through no fault of his own.

15 Redundancy and dismissal

Top tips. Your statutory references should be mainly to the Employment Rights Act 1996. The compensation payable is subject to a maximum which is in addition to the basic award.

Brian

Brian has been dismissed because he has been unable to adapt to new works practices, not by reason of redundancy. In any event it is not redundancy where an employer alters his methods of work so that the same work has to be done by different means which are beyond the capability of an employee: *North Riding Garages v Butterwick 1967*. He has been employed by the company for 15 years. He proposes to make a claim for unfair dismissal.

Unfair dismissal is a statutory concept contained in the Employment Rights Act 1996. An action may be brought by an employee who satisfies the statutory criteria. Firstly he must have been continuously employed for at least one year either full time or part time. Secondly, the employee must have been dismissed, either by the employer bringing the contract to an end (with or without notice) or where a fixed term contract ends and is not renewed or where there is a constructive dismissal. Finally the dismissal must have been unfair. The employee does not have to prove this; it is for the employer to show that it was not unfair by giving a good reason. Even if he does, the tribunal may still decide that the dismissal was unfair.

Unfair dismissal may arise if the employer does not act reasonably, by following correct procedures, by taking all circumstances into account and by doing what a reasonable employer would have done. Some reasons for dismissal are automatically unfair eg dismissal for trade union membership or because of pregnancy.

To defeat a claim for unfair dismissal the employer must show his main or sole reason for the dismissal which must be either one of those listed in the 1996 Act as being automatically fair (eg redundancy, employee's conduct or legal restrictions) or must be some other substantial reason which justifies dismissal (eg a refusal to accept changed work practices agreed by a majority of the workforce).

Brian has been dismissed for being incapable of performing his job with the new working practices. Such alleged incapability will be judged with reference to the requirement of the contract, the work standards achieved by employees generally and by the employee in question. Even if the employer proves an acceptable reason for dismissal, he must also show (and the test applied is an objective one) that he acted reasonably in dismissing the employee.

He must have applied the correct disciplinary procedure (for example by giving warnings in the case of all but the most serious misconduct, or consulting the appropriate employee representatives when considering redundancies). He must have taken account of all the relevant circumstances. This means that he must take previous conduct into account before dismissing for misconduct, or must offer help to an employee who has difficulties with his work before dismissing on grounds of incapacity.

Evidence of an employer's reasonable conduct in this regard would be consultation with the employee to determine the areas of difficulty, allowing a reasonable time for improvement, providing training if necessary and considering all alternatives to dismissal.

It is clear in this case that whatever the extent of Brian's incapability, the employer has not acted reasonably in simply dismissing him. His dismissal is therefore unfair and Brian's claim should succeed. He must apply to the employment tribunal within 3 months of his dismissal.

Once unfair dismissal is established, an employment tribunal may first consider reinstatement (ie a return to the same job without any break in the continuity of employment) or re-engagement (which is a different but comparable job with the same employer). Practical considerations and all other relevant factors, including the employee's wishes will be taken into account. Compensation is the most usual award. This consists of a basic award, calculated on age, length of service (up to 20 years) and weekly wage. There may also be a compensatory award for additional losses calculated on ordinary principles of breach of contract (up to a limit of £57,500) which should represent the amount which the tribunal considers to be just and equitable in all the circumstances: s 123.

He does not have a claim for redundancy (see *North Riding Garages* case referred to above).

John

John has been dismissed because of his involvement in trade union (TU) activities and has worked for the company for 9 months. He intends to make a claim for unfair dismissal.

Under s 152 TULRCA 92 a dismissal is automatically unfair if it is on account of an employee's membership (actual or proposed) of an independent TU or his taking part at an appropriate time (outside work hours or within those hours at an agreed time) in the activities of such a TU or refusal to be a member of a TU. Under s 154, where dismissal is for TU membership, the condition of continuous service does not apply and John has a valid claim.

16 Creating an agency relationship

> **Top tips.** Creating an agency is a highly examinable topic both as a question on its own and as part of a question on directors. This question is split into four parts, which helps you to focus your answer and to allocate your time. As you will see in our answer, we have defined agency so as not to repeat ourselves in answering the parts of the question.

Agency is a relationship that exists between two parties (the principal and the agent) in which the function of the agent is to bring the principal into contractual relations with one or more third parties.

(a) **Agreement**

Agreement can be established by straightforward agreement between the agent and the principal. Usually the principal expressly appoints the agent verbally or in writing, the later being preferred since the exact nature and scope of the relationship can the be set down. Some kinds of agent must be appointed in writing, such as when a person is given power of attorney over someone else's affairs (this must be in the form of a deed). It is also possible for a principal to appoint an agency by implied agreement. In this case agency is implied to have been established from the relationship between the parties or from their conduct. For example, it is possible to imply an agency relationship between an employer and an employee, if, as part of the employment relationship between them, the employee makes contracts with third parties on the employer's behalf.

(b) **Ratification**

An agency relationship may be established retrospectively by the principal ratifying a 'contract' which was formed by the 'agent' on behalf of the 'principal' before the agency relationship had actually been established. In order for a principal to ratify such a contract, the principal must have existed and had legal capacity at the time the contract was formed; the entire contract must be ratified within a reasonable time and ratification must be communicated to the third party. On ratification the position is that the agency relationship was established *before* the contract was formed. It must have been clear to the third party that the agent was not acting on their own behalf, it is possible for an unnamed principal to ratify a contract, but not for an undisclosed principal to do so.

(c) **Estoppel**

Agency may be created without the express or even implied agreement of the principal when it arises from the principle of estoppel or 'holding out'. This arises when a principal holds out to third parties that a person is their agent even if the principal and the 'agent', have not as such agreed to form such a relationship. It must be the principal, not the 'agent' who does the holding out, and the third party must have relied on the facts as held out; if this is so then the principal is 'estopped' from denying that the 'agent' is indeed their agent.

(d) **By necessity**

Agency by necessity comes into being occasionally when there is an emergency, the person who owns goods cannot be contacted and so another person acting in good faith, has to take action in regard to that person's goods. The former becomes the principal by necessity, and the latter becomes an agent by necessity. An example is a ship's captain who sells perishable goods that the ship is carrying before they spoil for the best price they can get.

17 Unlimited and limited partnerships

> **Top tips.** This is a straightforward factual question and is nicely broken down so that you should be able to gain good marks on each part. Notice that part (b) is asking specifically about limited liability partnerships, so you should restrict your answer to consideration of those.

(a) Partners in a firm are regarded as having both **actual** and **apparent authority** to bind the firm. Their actual authority is the authority given to them by the partnership agreement to carry out certain acts.

Their apparent authority is defined by the **Partnership Act 1890**. This states that every partner is an agent of the firm and the other partners for the purpose of the business of the partnership. The partner's actions in the normal course of business, of a sort that the firm would normally be expected to do, bind the firm and the other partners, so that they too are liable to the third party. However, if the partner does not have the authority to make the contract, and the **third party knows that to be the case or does not know or believe him to be a partner**, then the firm will not be bound.

For example, X is a partner in a firm that runs a garage buying and selling second hand cars, but the partnership agreement states that the firm is not to trade in new cars. If X enters a contract for the purchase of a new car from a third party who is not aware of the prohibition in the partnership agreement, then the firm as a whole would be bound by that contract, as X had apparent authority to enter into it.

The purpose of the law is the **protection of third parties**, and the nature of the authority often depends on the perception of the third party involved. If the third party genuinely believes that the partner has authority, the firm is likely to be bound by the partner's actions.

(b) A **limited liability partnership (LLP)** formed under the Limited Liability Partnership Act 2000 is a corporate body with separate legal personality from its members, but it retains some of the features of a traditional partnership.

In order to be incorporated, the subscribers must file details with the Registrar and pay a £95 fee:

(i) The name of the LLP
(ii) The location of its registered office (ie England and Wales, Wales or Scotland)
(iii) The address of the registered office
(iv) The names and addresses of all the members of the LLP
(v) Which members are to be designated members, who take responsibility for the publicity requirements of the LLP.

The designated members of a LLP are required to:

(i) File notices with the Registrar, for example when a member leaves
(ii) Sign and file accounts
(iii) Appoint auditors if appropriate

18 Companies

> **Top tips.** This question is extremely straightforward, and if you are well-prepared, you should be able to score very well on it indeed. Remember to attempt each part of the question to give yourself every opportunity of scoring highly.

(a) **Public limited company**

A public limited company is a company (an entity so registered under the Companies Act) that states in its constitution that it is a public company and has complied with the registration procedures for such a company.

Special registration procedures

As well as stating in the constitution submitted to the Companies Registrar that the company is public, a company registering as a public limited company must obtain a special trading certificate to allow it to trade.

Distinguished from a private company

A company which does not meet the criteria to be a public company is by default a private company. The key difference between them is that public companies are entitled to offer their shares to the public. Public companies can (although they do not have to be) therefore be listed on stock exchanges, whereas private companies may not.

(b) **A parent company**

A parent company is a company which **controls** another company (the subsidiary) by virtue of one of:

- Holding a majority of voting rights in the other company
- Being a member of the other company able to appoint/remove directors
- Holding the right to exercise a dominant influence over the other company
- Controlling the voting rights in the other company
- Being a parent company of a company that fulfils one of the above

The parent company and the subsidiary company form a simple **group of companies**. Groups of companies can be much larger that two companies, as a company may control a large number of other companies (each of which is therefore a subsidiary) and subsidiary companies may also be parent companies. As can be seen in the last bullet point above, when a subsidiary company is also a parent company, its parent company is also a parent company of the subsidiary's subsidiary. This is illustrated in the following diagram.

P1 – Parent (of S1, and by virtue of S1's relationship with S2, of S2)

S1 – Subsidiary (which is also a parent of S2)

S2 – Subsidiary

(c) **Multinational company**

A multinational company is one which produces and markets its products in more than one country. Such companies may also be listed on several different national stock exchanges, although it is not the multiple listing which renders a company multinational, but its actual operations.

The vast majority of companies in the world simply operate in one country, even if their products may be exported, but some huge multinational companies such as Microsoft or Coca Cola operate in many different countries and are genuinely global.

19 Incorporation and promoters

> **Top tips.** The question is very specific about the information required for each part. You should follow a similar approach if you are asked to write generally about pre-incorporation contracts. Remember that pre-incorporation contracts cannot be ratified when a company is incorporated; evidence of a new contract is required.

(a) (i)   **Definition**

A company is usually formed by a **promoter**, who is 'one who undertakes to form a company with reference to a given project and to set it going and who takes the necessary steps to accomplish that purpose'. It is a promoter who enters into pre-incorporation contracts.

Pre-incorporation expenses

A promoter cannot enter into a contract to be paid for expenses incurred before incorporation, such as drafting legal documents, because the company does not possess legal capacity prior to being incorporated. However, he can generally arrange that the first directors, of whom he may be one, should reimburse him or pay the bills.

(ii)   **Definition**

A **pre-incorporation contract** is a contract made in a company's name before it is formed. Companies are not bound by such contracts as they do not exist when the contracts are made.

Company cannot ratify

It follows that a company can never ratify a pre-incorporation contract made on its behalf. Since it did not exist when the pre-incorporation contract was made, it cannot be made a party to it.

Need for novation

Once the company is incorporated there must be **novation** for a pre-incorporation contract to be enforced. This means that a new contract is made with the same subject matter, or the terms of the contract modified to the extent that it constitutes a new offer.

(b) **Liability of promoter**

Although a company is not liable on a pre-incorporation contract the promoter may nevertheless incur personal liability in statute.

S 51(1)

S 51(1) of the Companies Act contains the statutory provisions relating to pre-incorporation contracts. It states that where a person contracts in the name of, or as agent for, a company before its incorporation, that person will be personally liable unless there is agreement to the contrary.

20 National Hair Brushes

MEMORANDUM

To: Board of Directors, National Hair Brushes plc
From: Adviser
Date: 30 June 20X7
Subject: Formation matters

(a) In order to carry on its business under the name 'Wave Oh', National Hair Brushes plc must comply with certain requirements as follows.

   (i) It must **state** its **registered name, number** and **address** legibly on all business letters (including emails), invoices, receipts, written orders for goods and services and written demands for payment of debts.

   (ii) It must **display** its **registered name** and address in a prominent position in any **business premises** to which its customers or suppliers have access.

   (iii) It must **give notice** of its **registered name** and address to **anyone who does business** with the company and who requests that information.

   (iv) The **address** must be one at which **service of a document** relating to the business will be **legally effective** and must be within Great Britain.

(b) **Passing-off action**

Lancashire Hair Brushes plc may seek to bring a **'passing-off action'**, a common law action which applies when one company believes that another's conduct (here the use of a company name) is causing **confusion** in the minds of the public over the goods which each company sells. Lancashire Hair Brushes plc would apply to the court for an injunction to prevent National Hair Brushes plc from using its name.

However, in order to be successful, Lancashire Hair Brushes plc will need to satisfy the court, that:

   (i) **Confusion** has arisen because of National Hair Brushes use of its registered name.

   (ii) It lays claim to **something exclusive** and distinctive and not something in general use. The courts are unlikely to rule that the name is exclusive and distinctive here.

Appeal to the Company Names Adjudicator

Alternatively Lancashire Hair Brushes plc might object to the Company Names Adjudicator that the name National Hair Brushes is too like its own name and is causing confusion, thus appealing for him to exercise his power under the Companies Act to compel a change of name. In these circumstances, the adjudicator would review the case and decide whether or not the name should be changed, if so the adjudicator may decide upon the name. If the case goes against National Hair Brushes, it can appeal to the court which may reverse the adjudicator's decision or affirm it. The court has the power to determine a new name.

21 Articles

> **Top tips.** It is essential that you have a good understanding of the articles of association, since reference to them is needed when considering many aspects of company law. Ensure you can explain how the articles constitute a binding contract, and do not confuse the articles with the memorandum.

Content of articles

A company's articles of association form the basis of its constitution along with its resolutions and agreements. It lays down rules governing its **internal management** and the rights of its shareholders and directors.

The principal areas covered will be the issue and transfer of shares, members' rights and the conduct of general meetings, the appointment, dismissal, powers, responsibilities and liabilities of company directors, dividends, class meetings, communication with members and documents and records.

Where a company does submit its own articles on incorporation, these must be **signed** by the **subscribers** to the memorandum of association. Companies which do not submit articles on registration will be allocated default, or model, articles relevant to the type of company registered.

Legal effect of articles

S 33 states that the constitution of a company (and therefore its articles) **bind the company and its members** to the same extent as if they had been signed and sealed by each member and each member had covenanted to observe all their provisions. Thus the articles are treated as a binding contract between the company and its members and as a binding contract between the shareholders.

Thus the company's articles were enforceable by the company against one of its shareholders in *Hickman v Kent or Romney Marsh Sheepbreeders Association 1915*. The rule applies only where the shareholders' rights affected are their rights as members and not in any personal capacity or capacity as director: *Eley v Positive Government Security Life Assurance Co 1876*.

The case of *Rayfield v Hands 1958* illustrates the existence of a contract between company members under s 33. In this case the articles required that the directors should purchase the shares of any member wishing to transfer his shares and also that the directors should also be shareholders. When the directors claimed that their liability was not as members and that the article was not enforceable by members, it was held that the article created an enforceable contract between the claimant members and directors as members of the company.

The articles do **not constitute a contract with any third party** by virtue of s 33: *Eley v Positive Government Security Life Assurance Co 1876*. However, where a contract between a company and a third party fails to address an issue which is covered in the company's articles, the relevant provisions may be taken to supply a missing contract term: *Re New British Iron Co, ex p Beckwith 1898*.

If legislation enables a company to do something provided its articles contain appropriate authority, the company, in the absence of such authority, will need to **alter** its **articles** first of all before doing the thing permitted. The alteration must be *bona fide* for the benefit of the company as a whole, meaning the individual hypothetical member. Alterations cannot be made if their effect is to place the articles in conflict with the general law or statute. The courts will look with suspicion upon changes that give some members the power to expel others (*Dafen Tinplate Co Ltd v Llanelly Steel Co (1907) Ltd*), unless the benefit to the company is clear (for example expulsion of a member who is competing with the company: *Sidebottom v Kershaw Leese & Co Ltd 1920*). The fact that a contract with a third party may be broken by a change in the articles does not invalidate that change, however damages may be payable: *Southern Foundries v Shirlaw 1942*.

In some cases, provisions of a statute may prohibit a company from doing something notwithstanding anything to the contrary in its articles of association.

A company may alter any of its articles (usually) by the passing of a **special resolution** to that effect. However s 22 permits companies to 'entrench' provisions into their articles. This means specific provisions may only be removed or amended if certain conditions (which are more restrictive than a special resolution) are met.

22 Shares

(a)   **Share capital**

A share is 'the **interest of a shareholder in the company measured by a sum of money**, for the purpose of a liability in the first place, and of interest in the second, but also consisting of a series of mutual covenants entered into by all the shareholders *inter se'*.

A share must be **paid for** and it gives a proportionate entitlement to **dividends**, **votes** and any **return of capital**. It also constitutes a form of bargain **between the shareholders**, underlying such principles as majority control and minority protection.

A share is a form of **personal property** carrying rights and obligations, which is **transferable** in accordance with the company's articles on transferability of shares. Shares in a public company are freely transferable provided the appropriate procedures are followed.

The **nominal value** of the share usually fixes the amount of the shareholder's liability, ie how much he can be required to contribute to the company's assets. The shareholder's right to share in the company is the right to receive a **dividend** in the company's profits and not a share of the company's **capital assets**.

(b)   **Types of share capital**

(i)   **Issued share capital**

This is the nominal value of all shares which have been **allotted to members and issued as share certificates**. Where part of its share capital has not been issued, this part is called the unissued share capital. A public company must have at least £50,000 issued share capital.

The issued share capital is the measure of the substance of a company.

(ii)   **Paid up share capital**

This is the proportion of the nominal value of the issued capital actually **paid**. An allottee of shares must pay the **nominal value** of those shares plus any **premium due** on them.

Once the amount due has been paid, the shares are **'fully paid'**. However, it is possible for part of the payment (or all of the payment in the case of private companies only and very rarely) to be **deferred** to a future date (either fixed or on demand from the directors for example) or to be payable in **instalments**. In such cases the shares are referred to as **'partly paid'**. In the event of the shares being transferred, the unpaid capital passes with the shares as a debt payable by the holder at the time when payment becomes due.

In the case of public companies, at the time of allotment the company must receive payment for at least **one quarter of the nominal value of the shares and the whole of any premium**. Thus partly paid shares of a public company (except those issued under an employees' share scheme) must always be at least one quarter paid up.

23 Debentures and charges

(a)   There is no statutory definition of 'debenture' (though s 738 Companies Act 2006 states that a debenture includes debenture stock, bonds and any other securities of a company, whether or not constituting a charge on the assets of the company).

In essence, a **debenture** is a document which states the terms on which a company has borrowed money (creating or acknowledging the debt).

A debenture is often **secured** (by also creating a fixed or floating charge over some or all of the company's assets) but may be unsecured, in which case it is likely to be called an unsecured loan note to distinguish it from a secured debenture.

A debenture usually takes the form of a printed legal document, setting out the **terms** of the loan and providing for the payment of **interest** to the debenture holder (regardless of profits). It might be a single debenture or one of a series ranking **pari passu** (for example, where the directors or members provide different loan amounts at different times but all loans are intended to rank equally). It might be one which governs the issue of debenture stock subscribed to by a large number of lenders (typically the public at large).

(b)   A **fixed charge** attaches to a specific asset as soon as the charge is created. If the company fails to honour its commitment to pay interest or repay the amount borrowed or goes into liquidation, the asset will be passed to the chargeholder, or sold to realise the debt, and the proceeds of the sale will go to the fixed chargeholder in preference to preferential creditors and floating charges. The company cannot dispose of the asset without the consent of the chargeholder.

The fact that a document is called a fixed charge will not be conclusive where in fact the company is still permitted to deal with the charge without reference to the chargee: *R in Right of British Columbia v Federal Business Development Bank 1988.*

Examples of fixed charges are legal mortgages of shares or land, or charges over other property.

(c)   A **floating charge** is:

(i)   A charge on a **class of assets** of a company, present and future

(ii)   Which class is in the ordinary course of the company's business **changing** from time to time, and

(iii)   Until the holders enforce the charge the company may **carry on business** and **deal** with the asset charged: *Re Yorkshire Woolcombers Association Ltd 1903.*

A floating charge can apply to fixed assets and current assets. It does not attach to any assets until crystallisation (when it becomes a fixed charge).

24 Issuing shares

> **Top tips.** You need to spend a similar amount of time on both parts of this question as they are for similar marks. Remember the golden rule when it comes to issuing shares (never at a discount to nominal value) and state it clearly.

(a)   A company may issue shares for a price **in excess of the nominal value** of those shares. The excess is called the **'share premium'** and must be credited to a share premium account.

It is not necessary for the articles of association to include a **power** to issue shares at a premium since it is **implied**. Where the shares are issued for a non-cash consideration in excess of the shares' nominal value, the excess should still be credited to the share premium account, since the statutory rule applies to issues of shares 'at a premium whether for cash or otherwise'.

The general rule is that reduction of the share premium account is subject to the same restrictions as reduction of share capital.

(i)   **No part** of the account can be distributed as **dividend**.

(ii)   The account can be used to pay up fully paid shares under **a bonus issue** since this operation simply converts one form of fixed capital into another.

(iii)   It can also be used to pay **issue expenses** and **commission** in respect of a **new share issue**.

The share premium account is included in the **'undistributable reserves'** when determining whether a **dividend** can lawfully be declared by a public company (which can only make a distribution if its net assets are not less than the aggregate of its called up share capital and undistributable reserves).

(b) **Every share has a nominal value and cannot be allotted at a discount to that value**. A company must obtain in money or money's worth consideration of a value at least equal to the nominal value of the shares allotted plus the whole of any premium. If shares are allotted at a discount, the allottee (and subsequent ones) is liable to pay the full nominal value together with interest at the appropriate rate.

The issue of shares at a price which is less than the market value (but equal to or more than the nominal value) of existing shares does not contravene the provision.

In the case of **private companies only**, shares may be allotted for inadequate consideration by the acceptance of **goods or services** at an over-value. A blatant and unjustified overvaluation will not, however, be upheld. **Non-cash consideration must be independently valued in the case of public companies**.

25 Statutory duties

Top tips. Limit your answer to a sentence or two on each duty as you need to explain five duties.

The Company's Act 2006 introduced seven statutory duties that directors must meet.

(a) **Duty to act within powers (s 171)**

This duty requires directors not to exceed the powers given to them by the company. In particular they must only exercise powers for the purpose for which they were conferred.

(b) **Duty to promote the success of the company (s 172)**

The principle of 'enlightened shareholder value' requires directors to act in a way which is most likely to promote the success of the company for the benefit of the members as a whole.

(c) **Duty to exercise independent judgement (s 173)**

Directors must exercise independent judgement. They must not delegate their powers or be swayed by the influence of others.

(d) **Duty to exercise reasonable skill, care and diligence (s 174)**

Directors have a duty to exercise the same standard of care, skill and diligence that would reasonably be expected of a reasonably diligent person with;

(i) The general knowledge, skill and experience which may be reasonably expected of a person in their position and

(ii) The general knowledge, skill and experience they actually have.

(e) **Duty to avoid conflicts of interest (s 175)**

The Act suggests a number of circumstances where a director's personal interests may conflict with the company's interests. Directors have a duty to avoid such circumstances.

(f) **Duty not to accept benefits from third parties (s 176)**

This duty prevents directors from accepting benefits from parties outside the company (usually bribes). It supports the duty under s 175 by preventing a potential conflict of interest.

(g) **Duty to declare an interest in proposed transaction or arrangement (s 177)**

Directors must declare the nature and extent of any proposed arrangement or transaction they may be involved in with the company either personally or through a third party. Disclosure may be given by written or general notice or a board meeting, but must be made to the directors, as disclosure to the members is not sufficient to discharge the duty.

Note only an explanation of five of the duties was required in the question.

26 Hydrangea

> **Top tips.** The marks in this question would have been weighted towards giving details of what the **notice** of the meeting should contain; as the directors are unsure about the requirements, it is quite possible that the notice would not contain sufficient details if you just told them that they had to give notice.
>
> To pass (a), you would also have had to identify correctly the **types of resolution** required; special for a change of name, ordinary for routine business.
>
> In (b) your answer should have stated that votes are normally taken on a show of hands. Because holding a poll depends on certain conditions being fulfilled, you needed to describe what these conditions were.

(a)   **Calling of the meeting**

All the business can be handled by an AGM so no other general meeting is required.

Notice of the meeting

Notice of the AGM must be sent to every **member** of the company who is entitled to attend and vote at the meeting. It should also be sent to the directors and auditors. The notice should:

(1)   Give adequate information concerning the **date, time and place** of the meeting

(2)   Specify it is an **AGM**

(3)   Describe the proposed **special resolution** as such

(4)   Give sufficient **details** of the **proposed business** at the meeting to enable recipients of the notice to understand what it is proposed to be done at the meeting

Length of notice

The length of notice required for AGMs is 21 clear days notice.

Approving the accounts and re-electing directors

These resolutions are deemed ordinary business and should be passed by an ordinary resolution of the company, which is carried by a simple majority (over 50%) of votes cast.

Changing the company's name

Authority to change the name of a company requires a special resolution of the company, which means a 75% majority of votes cast is needed to pass it.

(b)   **Voting rights of members**

The **rights** of members **to vote** and the **number of votes** to which they are entitled will be **determined by** the company's **articles**.

Show of hands

Voting is normally done by a **show of hands** by each member present in person. Each has **one vote**.

The chairman's declaration of the result on a show of hands (in the absence of it being fraudulent or manifestly wrong) will be conclusive. **Voting** by **show of hands** will **not be effective**, however, where a poll is properly demanded.

Polls

There is a statutory right to a poll wherever a special resolution is proposed. Voting on a poll may be demanded by at least **five members** or by **members representing at least one tenth of the voting rights** or by members holding **at least one tenth of the paid-up capital** conferring voting rights. (A company's articles cannot make these criteria more onerous from the shareholders' point of view.)

Where voting is on a poll, every member present may cast the **full number** of votes to which they are entitled. This is normally one per share held.

Voting rights of proxies

Every member entitled to **attend** and **vote** at a meeting may instead appoint at least one proxy to attend and vote for him. The proxy need not be a member.

Notice of the meeting must contain a statement which explains each member's **right to appoint** a non-member proxy. **Proxies may vote on a poll** since they have the same right to demand a poll as the member whom they represent. Most companies issue **two-way proxy cards** on which the member instructs his proxy to vote either for or against each resolution.

27 Liquidation

> **Top tips.** Topics such as insolvency are highly detailed and it is easy to waste time writing too much. Keep your answers focussed on the question in hand and avoid getting bogged down in detail. Remember there are only ten marks on offer!

When a company cannot meet its **financial liabilities** it is likely to enter a process of liquidation. This process sees the company's **assets** realised and arrangements made to settle its **liabilities** where possible. Liquidation can be compulsory or voluntary.

Compulsory liquidation

Under this method, the company is forced into liquidation by one or more of its creditors.

Under s122 of the Insolvency Act 1986 creditors may apply to the court for the compulsory liquidation of a customer for seven reasons. The two most important reasons are:

- The company **cannot** pay its debts
- It is **just and equitable** to wind up the company (members may also apply)

Voluntary liquidation

Voluntary liquidation is a decision taken by the members to wind up the company. There are two methods that can be used.

- **Members' voluntary winding up** – where the company is solvent but the members decide to close the business down.
- **Creditors' voluntary winding up** – where the company is insolvent and the members decide to wind the company up in conjunction with the creditors.

Differences between compulsory and voluntary liquidation

Timing

A compulsory winding up commences (once granted by the court) on the day the court is presented with the petition. Voluntary liquidation commences on the day the resolution to wind up the company is passed.

Liquidator

The official receiver administers a compulsory winding up, the members and creditors chose and appoint a liquidator under the voluntary process. Unlike the official receiver, this liquidator is not an officer of the court.

Legal action

Unlike compulsory liquidation, under the voluntary process the company receives no automatic stay of legal proceedings. However the liquidator can apply to the court for any order that it would grant under compulsory liquidation.

Employment

Employees are not automatically dismissed under voluntary liquidation. In circumstances of compulsory or 'insolvent' liquidation, employment contracts are effectively repudiated as the company can no longer pay its staff.

28 Boards

> **Top tips.** Do not be tempted to write too much for each part. Keep your answer focussed and do not waste time with waffle.

(a) **Non-executive director**

A non-executive director is a fully appointed director of the company who does not have executive powers ie does not have a functional role in the company's management. Non-executive directors' primary duty is to attend meetings of the board, at which they are expected to play an objective, questioning role.

(b) **Executive director**

An executive director is a **director who performs a specific role in a company** under a service contract which requires a regular, possibly daily involvement in management.

Such directors are often employees of the company, and if they have **specific management duties**, they are often given a relevant title, for example, finance director or sales director.

The contrasting type of director, often found in listed, public companies where they are a requirement of the Combined Code, are non-executive directors, who simply serve on the board of directors.

(c) **Single board**

A single, sometimes known as unitary, board is the typical board structure in the UK and the US and many other countries. It is **where the company is managed by a single board of directors**.

Such a board may simply comprise executive directors, but may also include non-executive directors, particularly in listed, public companies, where a combination of executive and non-executive directors is encouraged by the corporate governance code.

The single board has collective responsibility to manage the company and has power delegated to it as a collective body.

(d) **Supervisory board**

The supervisory board is the superior board in a system used in several countries, where there is a **dual-board system** comprising a **management board** and a **supervisory board**.

The supervisory board consists of members elected by the shareholders and the employees and it has an advisory role in relation to the business. It also carries out certain duties, such as electing members of the management board and receiving reports from the management board on company business.

29 Financial Services Authority

> **Top tips.** This question is not broken down into parts, so it is important that you read it very carefully and answer all the relevant parts of the question. It requires you to explain the role of the FSA in respect of company markets. This will involve an explanation of what the FSA is. It then asks you to pay particular attention to market abuse and money laundering. Both of these concepts will also require definition as you explain what the FSA does in respect of them. To score highly you need to write a complete, well-balanced answer, and not fall into the trap of writing about anything not required by the question, for example, other roles that the FSA has.

Financial Services Authority (FSA)

The Financial Services Authority is the regulator of the financial services industry and company markets and share exchanges in the UK. In this answer, we shall concentrate on its role with regard to companies. It is not a government agency, but has links to the government. It is a private limited company of which the UK government's treasury department is the guarantor. It is financed by the financial services industry.

Companies

Specifically in relation to companies, the FSA approves companies for listing in the UK, supervises companies and has powers of enforcement with relation to companies. Two of its aims are to secure an appropriate degree of protection for consumers in the market and to reduce the scope for financial crime (for example, market abuse and money laundering, both of which we consider below in more detail below).

The FSA is authorised to carry out investigations of companies when the following matters are suspected:

- Market abuse
- Misleading statements and practices
- Insider dealing
- Breaches of the Listing Rules of the Stock Exchange
- Money laundering

The power to make such investigations is shared with the Government's Department of Trade and Industry.

Market abuse

Market abuse is behaviour by one person or in concert which occurs in the UK in relation to qualifying investments traded on a designated market, which satisfies one of the prescribed conditions and which is likely to be regarded by a regular user of the market, who is aware of the behaviour, as a **failure** on the part of the person or persons concerned to observe the **standard of behaviour** reasonably expected of a person in his position in relation to the market: Financial Services and Markets Act 2000. It is improper conduct that undermines UK financial markets or damages the interests of ordinary market participants.

Market abuse could consist of **misuse of information**, **market distortion**, creating a **false or misleading impression**, recklessly making a statement, promise or forecast that was **misleading**, **false** or **deceptive**, or inducing **another person** to exercise or to refrain from exercising rights in relation to investments.

The description of market abuse above shows that it is quite a judgemental exercise determining whether a party has committed the offence. The FSA has a key role in making that determination. It achieves this by:

- Issuing a **Code of Market Conduct**, to set a standard of behaviour that is deemed acceptable
- Making investigations as discussed above

The FSA has statutory powers to impose unlimited fines for the offence of market abuse.

Money laundering

Money laundering is the term given to attempts to make the proceeds of crime appear respectable. It covers any activity by which the apparent source and ownership of money representing the proceeds of income are changed so that the money appears to have been obtained legitimately.

As discussed above, the FSA also has powers to conduct investigations into such activity. Money laundering is a criminal offence, so the FSA will work jointly with the National Criminal Information Service and the police in respect of this crime.

List of cases and index

Review Form & Free Prize Draw – Paper F4 Corporate and Business Law (ENG) (6/08)

All original review forms from the entire BPP range, completed with genuine comments, will be entered into one of two draws on 31 July 2008 and 31 January 2009. The names on the first four forms picked out on each occasion will be sent a cheque for £50.

Name: _____   **Address:** _____

_____

_____

How have you used this Text?
(Tick one box only)

☐ Home study (book only)

☐ On a course: college _____

☐ With 'correspondence' package

☐ Other _____

Why did you decide to purchase this Text? *(Tick one box only)*

☐ Have used BPP Texts in the past

☐ Recommendation by friend/colleague

☐ Recommendation by a lecturer at college

☐ Saw information on BPP website

☐ Saw advertising

☐ Other _____

During the past six months do you recall seeing/receiving any of the following?
(Tick as many boxes as are relevant)

☐ Our advertisement in *Financial Management*

☐ Our advertisement in *Pass*

☐ Our advertisement in *PQ*

☐ Our brochure with a letter through the post

☐ Our website www.bpp.com

Which (if any) aspects of our advertising do you find useful?
(Tick as many boxes as are relevant)

☐ Prices and publication dates of new editions

☐ Information on Text content

☐ Facility to order books off-the-page

☐ None of the above

Which BPP products have you used?

Text	☑	Success CD	☐	Learn Online	☐
Kit	☐	i-Learn	☐	Home Study Package	☐
Passcard	☐	i-Pass	☐	Home Study PLUS	☐
MCQ cards	☐				

Your ratings, comments and suggestions would be appreciated on the following areas.

	Very useful	Useful	Not useful
Introductory section (Key study steps, personal study)	☐	☐	☐
Chapter introductions	☐	☐	☐
Key terms	☐	☐	☐
Quality of explanations	☐	☐	☐
Case studies and other examples	☐	☐	☐
Assessment focus points	☐	☐	☐
Questions and answers in each chapter	☐	☐	☐
Fast forwards and chapter roundups	☐	☐	☐
Quick quizzes	☐	☐	☐
Question Bank	☐	☐	☐
Answer Bank	☐	☐	☐
Index	☐	☐	☐

Overall opinion of this Study Text   Excellent ☐   Good ☐   Adequate ☐   Poor ☐

Do you intend to continue using BPP products?   Yes ☐   No ☐

On the reverse of this page are noted particular areas of the text about which we would welcome your feedback.

The BPP author of this edition can be e-mailed at: stephenosborne @bpp.com

Please return this form to: Lesley Buick, ACCA Publishing Manager, BPP Learning Media Ltd, FREEPOST, London, W12 8BR

Review Form & Free Prize Draw (continued)

TELL US WHAT YOU THINK

Because the following specific areas of the text contain new material and cover highly examinable topics etc, your comments on their usefulness are particularly welcome.

Please note any further comments and suggestions/errors below

Free Prize Draw Rules

1   Closing date for 31 July 2008 draw is 30 June 2008. Closing date for 31 January 2009 draw is 31 December 2008.

2   Restricted to entries with UK and Eire addresses only. BPP employees, their families and business associates are excluded.

3   No purchase necessary. Entry forms are available upon request from BPP Learning Media Ltd. No more than one entry per title, per person. Draw restricted to persons aged 16 and over.

4   Winners will be notified by post and receive their cheques not later than 6 weeks after the relevant draw date.

5   The decision of the promoter in all matters is final and binding. No correspondence will be entered into.